Also by William H. Gass

FICTION

Omensetter's Luck
In the Heart of the Heart of the Country
Willie Masters' Lonesome Wife
The Tunnel
Cartesian Sonata

NONFICTION

Fiction and the Figures of Life
On Being Blue
The World Within the Word
The Habitations of the Word
Finding a Form
Reading Rilke
Tests of Time

A Temple of Texts

A
TEMPLE
OF TEXTS

Essays

William H. Gass

ALFRED A. KNOPF
NEW YORK
2006

Grateful acknowledgment is made to the following for permission to reprint previously published material.

Alfred A. Knopf: Excerpt from "The Snow Man" from *Harmonium* by Wallace Stevens. Reprinted by courtesy of Alfred A. Knopf, a division of Random House, Inc.

Pollinger Limited: Excerpt from "Stand Up" from *Pansies* by D. H. Lawrence. Reprinted by permission of Pollinger Limited and the proprietor.

Scribner and AP Watt Ltd: Excerpt from "Under Ben Bulben" from *The Collected Works of W. B. Yeats, Volume 1: The Poems, Revised* edited by Richard J. Finneran. Copyright © 1940 by Georgie Yeats. Copyright renewed © 1968 by Bertha Georgie Yeats, Michael Butler Yeats, and Anne Yeats. Reprinted by permission of Scribner, an imprint of Simon & Schuster Adult Publishing Group and AP Watt Ltd on behalf of Michael B. Yeats.

Library of Congress Cataloging-in-Publication Data

Gass, William H., [date]
    A temple of texts : essays / William H. Gass.—1st ed.
        p. cm.
    ISBN 0-307-26286-3 (alk. paper)
        1. Gass, William H., [date]—Authorship. 2. Gass, William H., [date]—Books and reading. 3. Literature—History and criticism. 4. Books and reading—United States. 5. Authorship. I. Title.
PS3557.A845T46 2006
808—dc22   2005045140

FOR MARY
my architect

CONTENTS

Acknowledgments   ix

To a Young Friend Charged with Possession of the Classics   3
Influence   12
A Temple of Texts : Fifty Literary Pillars   29

The Blessed Company   *The Book of Prefaces*   61
Erasmus   *The Praise of Folly*   72
Anonymous   *A Thousand and One Nights*   87
François Rabelais   *Gargantua and Pantagruel*   96
Robert Burton   *The Anatomy of Melancholy*   114
Gertrude Stein   *Three Lives*   124
Flann O'Brien   *At Swim-Two-Birds*   141
Ernesto Sábato   *On Heroes and Tombs*   152

A Defense of the Book   162

William Gaddis   And His Goddamn Books   178
Elias Canetti   *The Tongue Set Free*   206
John Hawkes   *Humors of Blood & Skin*   220
Robert Coover   *The Public Burning*   231
Gabriel García Márquez   *Chronicle of a Death Foretold*   242
Stanley Elkin   Open on the Sabbath   246

Contents

The Sentence Seeks Its Form   272

Rainer Maria Rilke   *Auguste Rodin*   288
Rainer Maria Rilke   Rilke and the Requiem   316

Sacred Texts   358
Spectacles   375
Evil   397

ACKNOWLEDGMENTS

Earlier versions of these essays have appeared, often with different titles as well as different texts, in the following: "A Temple of Texts: Fifty Literary Pillars," Special Collections, Olin Library, Washington University, Winter 1991; "Flattery and Whining," a review of *The Book of Prefaces, London Review of Books* 22, no. 29 (2000); "Afterword" to *The Praise of Folly,* by Erasmus, 2d ed. (New Haven: Yale University Press, 2003); *"The Arabian Nights: A Book at Bedtime," London Review of Books* 16, no. 1 (1994); "La Vie Treshorrificque," a review of François Rabelais's *Gargantua and Pantagruel, Harper's Magazine,* October 2004; "Introduction" to *The Anatomy of Melancholy,* by Robert Burton (New York: New York Review of Books Press, 2001); "Also Known As," an introduction to *At Swim-Two-Birds,* by Flann O'Brien (Normal, Illinois: Dalkey Archive Press, 1998); "A Case of Sincerity and Obsession," a review of Ernesto Sábato's *On Heroes and Tombs, The New Republic,* September 23, 1981; "Preface" to *The Recognitions,* by William Gaddis (New York: Penguin Classics, 1993); "The Road to the True Book," a review of Elias Canetti's autobiography, *The New Republic,* November 1982; "Introduction" to *Humors of Blood & Skin,* by John Hawkes (New York: New Directions, 1984); "Introduction" to *The Public Burning,* by Robert Coover (New York: Grove Press, 1998); "More Deaths Than One," a review of *Chronicle of a Death Foretold,* by Gabriel García Márquez, *New York,* April 1983; "Foreword" to *The Franchiser,* by Stanley Elkin (Boston: David Godine, 1980); "The Infinite's Jest," a review of *The Living End,* by Stanley Elkin, *Harper's Magazine,*

Acknowledgments

May 2004; "Rilke and the Requiem," *The Georgia Review,* Winter 2004; "Sacred Texts," an introduction to *The Writer and Religion* (Carbondale: Southern Illinois University Press, 2000); "Evil," *Harper's Magazine,* January 2004; "A Defense of the Book," *Harper's Magazine,* November 1999.

"Three Lives" was delivered as a lecture, "The Melodies of Melanctha," at the New York Public Library in 2002, and "Spectacles" was a lecture given at the German International University in Bruchsal in 2003.

A Temple of Texts

TO A YOUNG FRIEND
CHARGED WITH POSSESSION
OF THE CLASSICS

I'm here to tell you—speaking through the glass, between the bars, by slow post, in the babelous halls of the Academy—what you would like to hear: why, in doing what you've done, you've done the right thing.

They say you have been reading, even studying, the classics. You have been doing this at a time when not only are the classics regarded by many as one cause of our wretched world's unjust condition but at a time when the very word *classic* has become suspect, and is used most neutrally now to qualify old cars in good condition or to single out products stuck in an agreeable rut while the world furiously alters around them, such as Classic Saran Wrap or Classic Coke, although *original* is more frequently preferred, along with *old-fashioned,* to describe the Colonel's original recipe, or dad's best girl before she became his ball and chain.

When coined in the reign of Servius Tullius during the sixth century B.C., it meant the group, among citizens, to be called upon first; that is, during a time of war, the strongest, boldest, bravest, most fit to fight; while, when the state faced choices of difficulty and moment, the wisest, most temperate, and fair; so that then, when it was used of writers, it referred to those of the first rank, and also, by an obvious step, to their works. Therefore it should now designate, with regard to the education of a citizenry still concerned with their community, the books that have most completely represented and embodied its culture, as well as those that will best instruct, enlarge, and ennoble the mind, discipline the passions, and encourage a useful and respectful approach to experience.

A classic in its field is a work with which one should begin if one expects to master its subject; something that is therefore seminal, not only begetting more books that take it as their topic but also one that contains the discipline's founding principles, or serves as the starting point for its exploration, as Jefferson City, Missouri, once did for wagons entering our uncharted West. Even if you are in determined opposition to some traditional position, it is with the classic text you must begin the fight, though if the fight is to be fair, you must accept the risk, implicit in the inequality of the contest, of defeat, and of a turn to your heart, and of a change to your mind.

Literary classics break new ground, instigate change, or establish fresh standards of value, enlarging the scope of the canon, discovering new qualities of excellence, and confirming the importance of range, depth, mastery, and perfection in any artistic activity. It is instructive to observe that those who have carefully cultivated such a field of endeavor are not after yield per acre, but excellence per inch.

Oddly enough, people have always distrusted the classics, but it is now publicly acceptable to take pride in such distrust. We all dislike intimidation, so we worry about being overwhelmed by these tomes above which halos hover as over the graves of the recently sainted, because we wrongly believe they are fields full of esoteric knowledge worse than nettles, of specialized jargon, seductive rhetoric, and swarms of stinging data, and that the purpose of all this unpleasantness is to show us up, put us in our place, make fun of our lack of understanding; but the good books are notable for their paucity of information—a classic is as careful about what it picks up as about what it puts down; it introduces new concepts because fresh ideas are needed; and only if the most ordinary things are exotic is it guilty of a preoccupation with the out-of-the-way, since the ordinary, the everyday, is their most concentrated concern: What could be more familiar than a child rolling for fun down a grassy slope—that is, when seen by Galileo, a body descending an inclined plane? What could be more commonplace than Bertrand Russell's penny, lying naked on an examining table, awaiting the epistemologist's report on the problems of its perception? What could be less distinguished a subject for Maynard Keynes's ruminations on the source of its value than such a modest coin? Why should the question—What good is that?—alarm us, or why, in an age when most of the world worships money but calls its chosen God Father instead of Chairman, Lord instead of Coach, Most High instead of Star, should we shy from the same questions Plato asked, and not ask them about our business, about our love affairs, about our lip-served gods, about democracy?

Classics are by popular accord quite old and therefore out of date; while by the resentful they are representative only of the errors of their age, their lines sewn always on the bias, their authors willing tools of power and unjust privilege. Odd, then, that the good books were usually poisons in their time, when those biased pages were burned, those compliant authors jailed, and their ideas deemed diseases of the worst kind—corruptions of the spirit—to be fought with propaganda first, followed by prison, fire and firing squad, the gallows and the stake, all at the behest of the powers in place— majesties, Popes, czars, sultans, CEOs, and CIAs—the writers' names made to stand for Machiavellian casts of character, Marxian acts of mischief, Humean disbelief, and not for the clear-eyed hard-boiled arguments, exposures, revelations, condemnations, and realities their works contained.

The good books are the fruit of the tree of knowledge all right, and the devil is always offering us another fellow's damned opinion, which, were we to sample it, might cause the scales to fall from our eyes, so to see suddenly that king and queen, God and all the angels, are naked, shivering, and in sore need of shoes. That is why just one good book, however greatly good, when used to bludgeon every other, turns evil; why we should be omnivorous: try kale, try squid, try rodent on a spit, try water even though there's wine, try fasting even, try—good heavens!—rice with beans. The good books are cookbooks and good readers read them, try them, stain their pages, adjust ingredients, pencil in evaluations, warn and recommend their recipes to friends.

I think it is usually wise to approach a contemporary work with skepticism; it is the new work's task to establish its authority, to persuade you to believe in its essential worth whatever strange or commonplace thing it may say or do. With a classic, the situation is otherwise. Arnold Bennett once wrote a little book he called *Literary Taste,* a work of such immense good sense, it surprised me, for I did not expect it from a devoted follower of Zola's naturalism, an Edwardian down to his steam yacht. It is a book of admirably blunt assurance. He informs his readers, and there were many, that *"your taste has to pass before the bar of the classics.* That is the point. If you differ with a classic, it is you who are wrong, and not the book." Bennett is talking about taste—the perception of excellence—not about truth. Regarding the truth, you are earnestly entreated to differ. Appreciation is Bennett's subject and reading's desired result. If you do not admire the writings of Thomas Hobbes, it is not Hobbes whose ghost now has to feel uneasy. Of course, adjustments must always be made. It may be that in a state of nature, since it is a state of war, the life of man is solitary, poor, nasty, brutish, and short, but in our present state of mediocrity, it is cowardly, shallow, tedious, banal, and uselessly drawn out.

The good books provide us with the most varied of intellectual diets, and not liking broccoli or squid or beets or brains or kidneys or kohlrabi is not permitted the cultivated palate, nor is a disdain for Pascal, which I confess I have, nor a dislike for Saint Paul, despite his disagreeable ideas, nor a failure to appreciate the sublime vision of Plotinus and to shiver at his ecstatic yet melancholy summation of the highest spiritual life of man—with its unbearable lightness of being—as "detachment from all things here below, scorn of all earthly pleasures, and flight of the alone to the alone." The healthy mind goes everywhere, one day visiting Saint Francis, another accepting tea from Céline's bitter pot—ask for two sugars, please—

and hiking many a hard mile through Immanuel Kant or the poetry of Paul Celan—a pair who will provide a better workout than the local gym—before taking a hard-earned vacation in the warm and luscious fictions of Colette. You will live longer and better by consuming deliciously chewy fats and reading Proust than by treadmilling to a Walkman tune and claiming to be educated because you peruse the *Wall Street Journal* and have recently skimmed something by Tom Wolfe.

Nothing too much but everything a little bit—this describes the classic diet. One needs a bit of Wittgenstein to balance all that Hegel, a dash of Chekhov to counter Dostoyevsky, and some Sterne to maintain one's sanity after a series of unscheduled encounters with Sir Walter Scott. It is a blessed variety, like that of a blooming garden: so many ways to grow, to be fruitful, to captivate, to soothe, and to be beautiful.

Emerson understood well the importance of keeping company with greatness, for you cannot improve your chess game by playing against those whom you can speedily put to rout; only when you take on opponents who can give you a sound thrashing will you learn how to win with grace. Yet, what is the goodness that makes the good books good? That confers this greatness on the great ones? Whence comes the character of "the classic" that gives it that cachet?

They glow because their authors are such fine, upstanding people from the best families, graduates of the most expensive schools, and representative of the nobler classes. When I was your age, we would have said to that suggestion: in a pig's ear. Do you see a halo hanging over Heidegger's head? Their authors are murderers, thieves, traitors, mountebanks, misogynists, harlots, womanizers, idlers, recluses, sots, sadists, liars, snobs, lowlifes resentful of any success, vicious gossips, gamblers, addicts, ass-lickers, parvenues, whose pretenses to nobility were (and are) notorious: for instance, the clown whose father was a highland peasant named Balssa, lately come to town, and who renamed himself Balzac after an ancient noble family, and finally put a "de" before it, as if he were parking a Rolls in front of a tenement in the belief it might cause the johns to flush—a house, when Henry James paid a visit to Tours to take in the birthplace, he found to have been recently built but already a ruin, a row house that could at least have had the dignity, he said, to be "detached"—yes, a cheap pretender, this Balzac, who would go on to create a world more orderly than God's, almost as complete, and from beginning to end in better words, commencing with the fact that they were French. How about alleging that they glow because the good books uphold the finest ethical examples, support the highest values, display the most desirable attitudes? The way *The Inferno* is a testimonial to forgiveness? Or the *Iliad* a paean to pacifism? And by such edifying examples of revenge or the pleasure of killing an enemy, morally improving their readers, agenbiting their inwits, bestirring them to love their neighbors a bit better than themselves. Well, up a donkey's rear to that, too. One of the many lessons our great teachers, the Nazis, taught us is that no occupation, no level of society, of wealth or education, no profession, no religious belief, no amount of talent, intelligence, or aesthetic refinement can protect you from fascism's virus, not to mention a dozen others. It is not a contradiction for the Chaucer scholar to beat his wife, especially if she resembles the Wife of Bath.

Okay. So the glow of the good books is the glow of truth: That's why we read them, why we treasure a play like *Hamlet* or a poem like *Faust* or a treatise like Aristotle's *Physics*. Oh sure. There's another bit of nonsense to blow out your nose. The human world has always been one of violent disagreement. This disagreement may have its source in the simple determination of who shall get what, but it expresses itself in a quarrel of customs, disputes among doctrines, in bigotry, calumny, profanation, in tribal, religious, and racial hatreds. Moreover, this divisive plurality of opinion is not just between one man and another or one segment of society or political party or sect and another, but between one era and another, one civilization and another, one way of life and—not another, but—*all the others.*

Just as we find formerly forged links between languages that are now apparently different, and can group them into families, some quarrelsome, some benign, we can also collect cultural opinions and practices into cliques or classes or covens; but these similarities will not save us from their contradictions, any more than folks in families stop shouting, needling, or knifing one another the moment they recognize their connections. No line is cut, no blood is spilled, more readily, more frequently, with more ardor, than the bloodline. Saturn swallowed his children because he could do it; other fathers must resort to more ordinary methods of domination and revilement. Mothers kill their children oftener than strangers do, and a brother begins to hate his brother before that brother's born.

The opposing sides of a contradiction may both be false, we know, but only one of them can possibly be true, and this simple certainty ensures that most claims, among the Wars of the Words, are without truthful merit; that when ways of life brag of their correctness, they make such boasts against the chances; and how shall we choose between the Aztecs and the Romans, the Zoroastrians and the Hindus, or among one of seven saviors, or select from the myriad descriptions of the world, which no more resemble it than our fat aunt's hat, the one we want to wear? No, the good books don't sing harmony. They cannot be good because of that.

But in them, comprising them—as the atom the molecule, the molecule the compound—there are more sentences than people alive in this world, sentences that exhibit a range of savors surpassing your spice rack. Anyone who looks with care into the good books shall find in them fine sentences of every length, on every imaginable subject, expressing the entire range of thoughts and feelings possible, in styles both as unified and various as the colors of the spectrum; and sentences that take such notice of the world that the world seems visible in their pages, palpable, too, so a reader might fear to touch those paragraphs concerned with conflagrations or disease or chicanery lest they be victimized, infected, or burned; yet such sentences as make the taste of sweet earth and fresh air— things that seem ordinarily without an odor or at all attractive to the tongue—as desirable as wine to sip or lip to kiss or bloom to smell; for instance this observation from a poem of Elizabeth Bishop's: "Greenish-white dogwood infiltrated the wood, each petal

burned, apparently, by a cigarette butt"—well, she's right; go look—
or this simile for style, composed by Marianne Moore: "It is as
though the equidistant three tiny arcs of seeds in a banana had been
conjoined by Palestrina"—peel the fruit, make the cut, scan the
score, hear the harpsichord transform these seeds into music (you
can eat the banana later); yet also, as you read these innumerable
compositions, to find there lines that take such flight from the world
that the sight of it is wholly lost, and, as Plato and Plotinus urge, that
reach a height where only the features of the spirit, of mind and its
dreams, the pure formations of an algebraic absolute, can be made
out; for the *o*'s in the phrase "good books" are like owl's eyes, watch-
ful and piercing and wise.

And many of these sentences the reader will wish to commit to
memory in order to carry them about like a favorite tune, to hum and
to encourage and guide them through bad moments, boring conversations, or bouts of insomnia. Let me cite an example from one book
good as any, Frances Bacon's *Advancement of Learning,* at the point
where he tells us that "learning endueth mens mindes with a true
sence of the frailtie of their persons, the casualtie of their fortunes,
and the dignitie of their soule and vocation." Thinking produces its
own endorphins, and encountering a fine thought is as thrilling as
the sight of the bluebird, partly because both have been threatened
with extinction.

It is not their nouns and verbs alone that make the good books
good, then; it is their adjectives and adverbs, their prepositions—
their qualities and their relations.

Charles Sanders Peirce said, "My book is meant for people *who
want to find out;* and people who want philosophy ladled out to
them can go elsewhere. There are philosophical soup shops at every
corner. . . ."

Respect for experience, rigor in reasoning, passion in the service
of selfless ideals, every one of the human urges allowed to represent
itself without apology or hypocritical disguise, the architectural
impulse, too, constructing cathedrals, even countries, out of concepts, and making spaces for the imagination to soar through, high

but hawk-eyed, hungry but discriminating: These qualities, rather than simply opinions and prejudices, fill the good books; but mixed with these perfections, not always easily identified, are all our failures, too, each weakness like a model on display, dressed in our most attractive, come-hither silks; here is the severe, the ugly, the sordid, the cruel, rendered by a Goya or a Grünewald, who bravely puts paint where no paint should go, who dares to depict the nightmares that shadow our sunlamp lives.

They will not do us any good—the good books—no—if by good we mean good looks, good times, good shoes; yet they still offer us salvation, for salvation does not wait for the next life, which is anyhow a vain and incautious delusion, but is to be had, if at all, only here—in this one. It is we who must do them honor by searching for our truth there, by taking their heart as our heart, by refusing to let our mind flag so that we close their covers forever, and spend our future forgetting them, denying the mind's best moments. They extend the hand; we must grip it. Spinach never made Popeye strong sitting in the can. And the finest cookbook ever compiled put not one pot upon the stove or dish upon the table. Here, in the library that has rendered you suspect, you have made their acquaintance— some of the good books. So now that you've been nabbed for it, you must become their lover, their friend, their loyal ally. But that is what the rest of your life is for. Go now, break jail, and get about it.

INFLUENCE

What does Dr. Johnson's *Dictionary* say? That the stars are said to influence the order of nature and the affairs of men; that when God withdraws His attention, annihilation follows; yet his *Dictionary* also states that a wise man has a greater grip on his own well-being than the stars can claim direction; that the effect of religion is so benign, it ought to be supported (one good deed deserves another); that inconstancy in the pursuit of our goals has a bad influence on their realization; that some consequences stain but others are easily removed; and that the truth ought to have more clout than it has. The entry does not mention advertisers, PR flacks, product endorsers, spin doctors, ghostwriters, salespersons, or other professional manipulators of opinion. In cruder, blunter times like Dr. Johnson's, public executions were designed to deter evildoers from further crime. Now, with our advanced media skills and gulling savvy, we perform these public tasks with more sophistication and similarly vagrant results.

Of course, Dr. Johnson's *Dictionary* does not actually say these things; it gives us instances of the concept's usage; it relies on quotes that stress the importance of various influences on behavior, but lessening, if I may say so, the influence of *influence* as it goes along, ending with a wish rather than, as with the constellations, a prognostication. Influence ends up weaker than a compulsion or an itch. It claims responsibility for some part of what has been effected, but only as a challenge and incentive to the will. If I push a paperhanger from a ladder, I do not influence his fall, but cause it; however, if I lodge in his psyche a prior fear of falling, for instance, I have possibly predisposed his limbs; or if I have encouraged him to climb with his pastes and papers while carrying an angry dog or a kitchen cabinet, I have had a hand.

Does Dr. Johnson's choice of authorities—Milton thrice, Rodgers twice, Prior, Sydney, Hooker, Tillotson, Addison, Atterbury also twice, Newton, each as eminent as a peak—make them influences concerning the proper use of *influence* or is it the doctor's selection or Sam Johnson's clout that does that?

Dictionaries are supposed to influence usage. Usage is what dictionaries record. "This is what we have meant," they say; "continue in the same vein so that communication will be accurate, reliable, and fluent." Then the next dictionary will record that fidelity, and issue the same command, which will complete the cycle. Among users, however, there are many who are incompetent, inventive, or disobedient. The French Academy tries to drive strays back into the herd. English has no comparable guardian and its speakers lack every discipline. Soon meanings have multiplied or slid or mushed, and niceties—delicate distinctions—lost along the way. In this haphazard fashion, *influence* has come to mean a kind of causality that operates only through the agency of a consciousness. Where this puts the stars, I'm not sure. Because of smog or city glare, we often don't even know the stars are there.

The niceties must be observed. That means distinctions are required when considering *influence* as much as we might employ for any other word. Suppose my father is an angry, disappointed man. Suppose I dislike him and vow not to imitate him in anything. Yet I find that I, too, am an angry, disappointed man. His influence has been counterproductive because the opposite of my father's behavior was aimed at, although the target was poorly struck. However, it is inadvertent, since he certainly did not intend to pass on his resentments, and they express no intention of mine, either. But he was also an accomplished public speaker—banquets and such—and I did hope to follow his lead in that regard. He ruled his classroom with an iron hand, and conveyed his scrupulosity of design to his students, some of whom showed similar qualities in their work, while others bore no evidence of it. In short, influences are positive or negative, advertent or accidental, direct or devious, general or targeted, unidirectional or reciprocal, effective or futile, actual or merely believed.

Influences are also due or appropriate and undue or improper. As the president's adviser, if I speak the truth and report the facts, then those facts—the truth—may influence his subsequent decision, not I; but if I rhetorize and wrangle, insinuate and connive, intimidate or flatter, no matter the soundness of my suggestions otherwise, I shall have led my leader by the nose, though I was not elected to that office; and I remain responsible if I have allowed him to choose among alternatives already carefully narrowed to my purpose. All such influence is undue. If the president knows that his old crony is a truthful man—moreover, that he usually has a good command of the facts—and so follows his lead instead of the direction the data have indicated, he has made his pal's influence inappropriate, and himself a stooge. Though if heeding another's advice leads to success, being your own man and following your own nose is usually deemed an unaffordable luxury.

Most influence is whispered in an ear, not delivered like a push, though we do admit that liquor puts drivers under its spell, and that we've had to widen the crime of DWD to DUI in order to include drugs of other kinds. Driving under the influence of hubris is not yet a yellow-sheet offense.

No evil can befall a good man, Socrates said, because evil efforts achieve evil effects only when they leave their victims morally worse than they were, and for evil to do that to a good man would mean he had frailties so far unrecognized, and his character was not as stout as had been rumored. Iago plays upon Othello in a similar fashion: Once the weak key is found and repeatedly struck, the murderous

chord finally sounds. Neither Plato nor Aristotle wa_
applaud those whose virtue was chiefly measured by the _
their triumph over temptation; they thought it safer if your c
accountant, business manager were oblivious to beguilements._

An intelligence without integrity (a condition so often found _
people of public life) is likely to succumb to the blandishments of
ideology; otherwise, the mind's inherent skepticism will guarantee
its safety from superstition and other forms of sugary conjecture.
Socrates knew nothing really awful could happen to him if he kept
his mind free of unwarranted opinions. True strength, throughout its
spectrum, shows itself through unflustered gentleness and forbearance, since only such strength has nothing to fear. The con man suc-
ceeds by exploiting the greed of his marks and is often reluctantly
admired because wit is on his side, as well as discipline. His cyni-
cism is just good sense and his nose for moral weakness is like the
dowser's wand for water. Similarly, when ill-formed or palpably false
ideas make their way through the multitude, it is because the comforts they bring are so ardently desired.

If you enjoy the opinions you possess, if they give you a glow, be
suspicious. They may be possessing you. An opinion should be
treated like a guest who is likely to stay too late and drink all the
whiskey.

Plato treated poetic inspiration as a case of such irrational infec-
tion: The gods bypass sober skill to make the pen prophetic so
that the resulting poem, recited by a rhapsode similarly tranced,
becomes an incitement to the mob. Or an unconscious wish, sneaky
as an odor, enters the author's awareness disguised as its opposite,
and arranges the stage for a *coup d'éclat*. Thus the magnetic coil is
closed: muse to poet, poet to page, page to performer, and performer
to audience, whose applause pleases the muse, encourages the poet,
and grants his forbidden desire: to rule.

This pattern repeats itself precisely with religious texts: God to
prophet, prophet to his books of revelation, those to the mullahs,
pastors, and the priests, priests and pastors to their congregations.

Indeed, the spread of illness was influence's ancient occupation:

It was either the source of a seizure induced by a divinity or a sickness of the system later called influenza, and because of its mysterious onset, a malady consigned to alignments of the heavenly bodies, an origin suggested by one of Dr. Johnson's definitions. I have long suspected certain concepts of causing mental aberrations in those who entertained them ("substance," "essence," "soul," or "angel," "salvation," "spirit," "sin," "transmigration," "grace," "phlogiston," "zeitgeist," and "wavicle" come to mind), and it seems to me superstitions operate on the sly, like poets and musicians, placing in our innocent ears a poisonous distillment, so that we wake to find ourselves a ghost in armor on a battlement—perhaps on an ill-fated crusade—or a victim of the stars and a casualty of the flow of macrocosmic fluid into sublunary things in somewhat the same way Greek and Latin are presently seeping into my Anglo-Saxon. I am informed that nowadays astrologers are no longer so naïve and simpleminded as to credit the constellations with all these abilities by themselves, when influences also stream from the zodiac, from planets and their angular relationships, from nodes, as well as from countless other cosmic phenomena. It's a big world. There are sun flares. There are comets. Quarks. Strings. Holes. And viruses unidentified. Growing immune. Gathering strength.

Nowadays, instead of the stars, in place of the Fates, in lieu of the family curse, or the theory of the humors, we can cite genetic dispositions, and blame our irascibility on grandpa as automatically as we see in him our unruly red hair.

Wills (probably another unnecessary concept) . . . wills aren't really strong or weak; it is the characters that they express and serve that are. Consequently, young people, who are often thought willful but whose natures are not yet fully formed, are most easily driven from fad to fad like sheep by dogs; or it is old people, whose minds move as unsteadily as their bodies do, who are likely to suffer the theft of their nest eggs by cuckoos, cowbirds, and other con artists. The flimflam man finds allies in the willies, the fuddles, the general neediness of his marks, and he speaks to them like a friend about their present illness, their meager widows' portions, their imminent demise, or to youths of their acned chins, tepid dates, and dwindling desirability, to each and everyone of loneliness and laggardly self-esteem. Meanwhile, the socially defined good people—parents, an older brother, the parish priest, a teacher, the coach (we assume)—are working the right side of the street, leading by precept and example, threat and plea, toward success, licensed fornication, and financial security. We might expect, then, that literary influences, when they occur, would follow a similarly forking path of edification, seduction, and disillusionment.

Sometimes great books have deleterious consequences for other writers, creating footsteps that can't be walked in, shade the sun can't penetrate, expectations that have no grounds. Gabriel García Márquez's *One Hundred Years of Solitude* crushed the hopes of scores of young Colombian writers, and the spread of magic realism was not exactly beneficent, since it takes a magician to work magic and because rabbits don't hide in just anybody's hat. Movements of most kinds flow downhill.

Bad companions, a rum crowd, pinko friends are thought to have a great deal of influence, but there is no group or figure to match, for "all aboard" magnetism, the "role model"—that "Do as I do, be as I be" advertisement for the good life. Pied Pipers are an admitted draw, but they play a different tune. Role models are to be imitated—their lifestyle aped from cereal to shoe. Pied Pipers are only to be followed. Out of town. Toward the front. And everyone's disaster. No one asks the rats to huff a fife, just to stay in line, keep up, and step smartly.

Writers and scholars do not have role models, nor do they heed pipers; they have mentors. A mentor is a teacher who becomes a mentor by exceeding his authority and meddling with the student's life. Writing students want mentors because their instructors are believed to have friends (that is to say, influence) in important publishing firms or are intimate with editors of important magazines. So they do their best to write as will please these persons; to flatter them by appearing to be under their wide benevolent wing (such students are said to be "teachable"); moreover, they seek out counsel from their wiser, more accomplished elders, not only on the course of careers but also on matters of the heart and the problems of life, payment for which sometimes includes the offer of sexual favors. Among the things that swell in such circumstances is the mentor's pride at his apprentices' achievements. Reflected glows are as good as sunlamps. To be attractive, especially if a girl or a gay person, often outstrips the need for talent, and frequently makes it unnecessary. Good looks, a little talent, and a slavish wish to please make an irresistible combination.

European students are particularly eager to capture a powerful sponsor. The hierarchical system from which they have come is feudal still, even if not quite so tyrannical as in Hegel's day, when Hegel was Germany's philosopher in chief. One needs a protector, as Rabelais and Erasmus did, someone with influence at the Vatican or at court. One needs an agent's eye, an editor's ear—an "in." Why? The answer comes ready-made: because every editorial office is a speakeasy, a restaurant overbooked before it was built, a disco that admits only celebrities. Myth or truth, the belief of beginners is that it's whom you know, while those who already have powerful patrons are convinced that their skill got them into the loop and their charm passed them round like snacks at a party.

Influence is one thing when it has a definable goal, a definite result—to sign the poultry-protection bill, to build the new bridge, to vote for Bob the Blackmailer, to care for the city's bank deposits, to blurb a book—and another when it wants to alter a state of mind, a way of life, a manner of writing. And taking the latter's measure is more difficult than obtaining the inseams of an octopus. Both might be easier to understand if looked at from the place where influence has come to rest—with the banker, the bidder, the buyer, the bribed—in the student, the reader, the well beloved—at the turn of the last page, a week after exposure or the first interest payment or a month in jail, upon returning to the text, leaving the book on the plane.

For instance, St. Louis's two best-selling novelists have been Winston Churchill and Patience Worth, one an actual author with the same name as the British prime minister, himself a composer of thundering prose, the other the Ouija board alter ego of someone we might call a "neighbor lady." Both had print runs longer than the Olympic torch's and enjoyed more luminous results. Our Churchill ruled the American literary scene during the early years of the twentieth century. He published seventeen books of drama, fiction, and poetry during the twenty years of his reign, his ten novels each enjoying worldwide sales of half a million in fifty-four editions. Surely that should amount to influence in boxed lots. There was, however, no effect that history noticed, except the other Winston's annoyance at the occasional confusion of their persons.

Patience Worth was invented on July 8, 1913, when she appeared as a spirit who directed the planchette on Pearl Curran's Ouija board to spell out the four million words that were reverently copied down and subsequently gathered into seven substantial books, along with thousands of poems, numerous short stories, aphorisms and epigrams, and sheaves of conversations Patience enjoyed with guests who came by the hundreds to call on her at Pearl's residence, ironically located on the same long street in St. Louis where the T. S. Eliot family lived and where Tennessee Williams would later stay like a restless captive for a while until his family moved their unhappiness into another neighborhood.

Yet for all her popularity—despite the Ouija board sales she stimulated, or the copycats who claimed Mark Twain was gracing their board with a new novel, even the affinity of the spirit world for soggy souls and weak minds—neither Patience Worth nor her amanuensis, Pearl Curran, are remembered in St. Louis today, let alone within the wider audience she once reached, now that the generations who read her have passed into their own mythology.

Counting copies is not a reliable method, then. Merit, as we may imagine it, will not succeed, for we would not want to include *Mein Kampf* among the sacred books, though its influence resembles theirs, while *Gone With the Wind,* a mediocrity, has not only sold as widely as Winston Churchill did but has hung on, thanks to the cinema and Southern chauvinism, with more determination than most. Many movies that have circled the globe like some satellite have nevertheless left nothing more substantial than a vapor trail behind them. However, Latin American writers have testified to the impact thirties and forties films in particular had on them—we must specify—when they were young.

It is easy to hear Rudyard Kipling in Robert Service, although both were balladeers who liked to frequent severe frontiers, or a cinch to catch Faulkner's cadences in early Styron. We can feel the Salinger effect in the increased production of books with similar adolescent attractions, as is common in such cases.

> Salinger has become such a notable literary figure that he actu-
> ally appears as a character in W. P. Kinsella's *Shoeless Joe,* the
> novel on which the picture *Field of Dreams* was based, but his
> importance can best be measured in the way *Catcher* has influ-
> enced books that have been written after it. *Last Summer* by
> Evan Hunter, *The Bell Jar* by Sylvia Plath, *The Last Picture
> Show* by Larry McMurtry, *The Basketball Diaries* by Jim Car-
> roll, *A Separate Peace* by John Knowles, *Birdy* by William
> Wharton, *Less Than Zero* by Bret Easton Ellis, *Bright Lights,
> Big City* by Jay McInerny, *Girl, Interrupted* by Susanna
> Kaysen—these are just a few books written in the tradition of
> *The Catcher in the Rye.* (Paul Alexander. *Salinger: A Biography.* Los
> Angeles: Renaissance Books, 1999, pp. xiii–xiv.)

Those literary scholars who are economists at heart like to count citations in order to lay claim to a readership for the books listed on their CVs. To live on as a footnote is to achieve important academic authority, for many a journal article walks on ibid. and op. cit. feet. Instead of this decorous tiptoe, a book may strike a single blow and disappear like a mysterious assailant, leaving injury and altered lives behind it.

Critics lamenting that poetry no longer makes a difference do not have in mind the difference made by Wilkes's obscene parodies of Alexander Pope's Essay on Man. Arguably, however, these are the most influential poems in English or American literature. They made more happen. (Regina Janes. "The Salacious Sorrows of Scholarship," in *Salmagundi*, no. 143, Summer 2004, p. 222.)

"They made more happen." Pope himself could carve a couplet on the brow of some unfortunate opponent that no cosmetic might hide, an *A* for ass or *D* for dolt, in lines that licked their lips before they pursed them. Of course, Pope meant to requite his enemies, but he also intended to cleanse the literary scene of the Welsteds, Curlls, Lintots, Ducketts, Herveys who are always with us, though they die before the day is done, because another batch swarms out to pester the next sun.

Pope makes known what spurs him into song by mentioning his servant (John), his wife, or friends and enemies, local contretemps, in his verse—"Shut, shut the door, good John! fatigu'd I said, / Tye up the knocker, say I'm sick, I'm dead"—or by simply announcing that a poem is an imitation of Rochester, Waller, or Cowley, or by telling us, with the sweet smile of a child, that he is imitating Spenser when he writes about an alley, stinking with stinky things, more in the manner of Hogarth than his alleged high-minded model: "How can ye, mothers, vex your children so? / Some play, some eat, some cack against the wall, / And as they crouchen low, for bread and butter call." But we always have to bear in mind that these excuses for compliment or complaint are of Pope's choosing, not his pals' or opponents', so that calling them "influences" might be a stretch.

If Dickens improved conditions in orphanages and workhouses, or Steinbeck the lives of migrant workers . . . well, these are results to be admired and celebrated; and if *Mein Kampf* or the *Protocols of the Elders of Zion* did the dirty work often attributed to them . . . well, these are influences worse than influenza and their quirky spread can be followed through the writings and speeches that have welcomed them and gloried in the symptoms.

The Tweedledumbing that goes on about the effects of porn on lonely people or of snuff films on murder rates and flog flicks on leather futures; or rape and rob movies that do or do not encourage rob and rape; cigarette and liquor ads and their appeal to parched throats and teens yearning for sophistication: This pitiless bickering does not encourage confidence, especially when the inability of the truth to penetrate the convictions of voters or other fans of fidelity to party, God, and country is a given.

Comparative studies also can be promising, provided points of comparison are made specific enough. There is always the possibility (to which in gloomy moods I cling) that Dickens's orphanages were about to be improved anyway, or that the similarities of style between types like Kipling and Service have often been due to common natures and shared circumstances rather than to any literary contagion. According to Regina Weinreich, five kinds of correspondence between Thomas Wolfe and Jack Kerouac can be discerned: their common love for sensory catalogs and Whitman-like emotional overloads; their love of the land and the townscape; their nostalgic tone; their pell-mell method of composition; and their narcissistic subject matter—mememoreme. (*Kerouac's Spontaneous Poetics*. New York: Thunder's Mouth Press, 2001, p. 19.) It is significant, however, that these characteristics are all external and exhibit preferences for subject matter or cite similar working habits.

There are influences as huge as oceans—that of the Italian Renaissance on nineteenth-century England or that of ancient Greece on Germany—so that one hardly knows where to begin, or if it would be wise to begin at all. And then there are those that interest me—so minor in their manifestations, so quiet, so internal to the self, they hardly seem blips on any screen. Yet I remember actually sucking in my breath upon reading the opening line of Pound's "Sestina: Altaforte," "Damn it all! all this our South stinks peace," or, in another time, with similar astonishment, Hardy's "If it's ever spring again, / Spring again, / I shall go where went I when / Down the moor-cock splashed, and hen . . ." while recognizing, despite the distance between the two occasions, in the bump in Hardy's syntax, a relation to the strangeness of Pound's bump that was of fundamental importance. The match, I think, was this: The sum of my reading experience had deposited in me a number of convictions that I could not up to then express, and these lines exemplified one of them. I might still find it difficult to state what that certainty was, but whatever it was, "I shall go where went I when / Down the moor-cock splashed, and hen" had it. The line stumbled to a stop at "when," looked over its cliff, and watched the next line begin "Down." Hardy's "where went I when" was the finest assemblage of four words I could then imagine, and I repeated them, I'd be later told, like a mantra. An old poeticism had been rejuvenated, leading to a law confirmed, if not a lesson learned. And how had Hardy gotten away with rhyming "again," "when," "hen," and "then," or with dangling "hen" from its line like something plucked? Afterward, I ran to Gerard Manley Hopkins like a lover.

But what is a gasp? An ooph of surprise? A moment of wonder? A reaction so strong that its source should be a real influence? That is, alter in some important way one's inherent nature, one's determined outlook, or a style that's been raised from a child?

The moments most marked as influential by their owners are often epiphanies that were waiting to happen. Elias Canetti gives us a splendid account of one such, and with his help we can identify the preparatory stages. In Vienna, when Canetti was twenty-two, he witnessed the burning of the Palace of Justice by a crowd protesting a verdict of not guilty that had just been given two alleged murderers. When those fighting the flames were prevented from reaching the site by the mob, the police opened their own fire, and in the shooting and its subsequent panic, ninety people were killed and many more injured. This event so marked Canetti that he spent much of his adult life trying to understand it. His initial attempt resulted in the novel *Die Blendung* (literally, "The Blinding," but translated into English as either *Auto-da-Fé* or *The Tower of Babel*); and his final effort in the study *Crowds and Power*. The second precondition was the completion of *Die Blendung* at the age of twenty-six, which left Canetti empty, exhausted, and remorseful. He felt almost morally responsible for the burning of books that comprises the climax of the work. The torching of the library by the novel's protagonist, the sinologist, Peter Kien, was, after all, composed by Canetti, and in that odd way, the author was responsible for a truly dastardly deed. Moreover, after at first naming the character Kant, he called him Kien, meaning "kindling," so what was possible for that person but ignition? The burden Canetti felt was also the consequence of his complete immersion in the work, his subsequent exhaustion, and postpartum gloom, which made him feel useless and empty. Even reading, the customary way writers rescue themselves from disagreeable states of soul, was denied him. "I had lost my right to books," he says in the final volume of his autobiography, *The Play of the Eyes,* "because I had sacrificed them for the sake of my novel." His favorite books repel him. He lets fall Stendhal, Gogol strikes him as silly, and finally he leaves his shelves untouched. The emptiness that had filled him now poured out in every direction, as if he were leaking sterility, since he had burned the contents of these books when he had burned their fictional exemplars in *Auto-da-Fé.*

Then one night, in a state of mind that could not have been more desolate, I found salvation in something unknown, which had long been on my shelf but which I have never touched. It was a tall volume of Büchner bound in yellow linen and printed in large letters, placed in such a way that it could not be overlooked, beside four volumes of Kleist in the same edition, every letter of which was familiar to me. It will sound incredible when I say that I had never read Büchner, yet that is the truth. Of course, I knew of his importance, and I believe I also knew that he would someday mean a great deal to me. Two years may have gone by since I had caught sight of the Büchner volume at the Vienna bookshop in Bognergasse, taken it home and placed it next to Kleist. (*The Play of the Eyes,* trans. Ralph Manheim. New York: Farrar, Straus & Giroux, 1986, p. 7.)

Accidentally, but who knows by what unconscious prompting, with a memory for the body of the book as well as its mind, the twenty-six-year-old Canetti chooses the linen-covered volume of a writer who died of typhus at twenty-three, and allows his fingers to open it to a section from *Woyzeck (Wozzeck)*. "It was as if I had been struck by lightning." He reads the scene, soon the entire play, again and again. Then, still in a most agitated state, he takes the early-morning train to see his girlfriend, in a sense to blame her for not recommending Büchner to him before this. To make it up to Canetti, she suggests he read a tale about a madman called Lenz—in actual fact, a poet friend of Goethe. "My novel that I'd been so proud of crumbled into dust and ashes."

Into dust and ashes. As dusty books burn down to bookish ashes. A parliament building on fire, a library consumed: They have occurred more than once in the world; but Canetti's own conflagration has an internal reality that exceeds them. Canetti's sinologist also burns on the pyre of his books, but his author has put him there and lit the match. Mind broken, Kien travels from the dust he was made of to the ashes he ends in, from first words to their erasure. Büchner is alleged to have said, on his deathbed (for the speaking of last words, beds are inevitable): "We are death, dust, ashes, how should we complain."

Kien's crumbling mind precedes his devastation. Canetti is fascinated by states of consciousness, especially ones that range far beyond the boundaries of the normal: the peculiar character of the crowd, which always seems to have a will of its own; the agonies and insights of schizophrenia; the derangements of society that so riled Büchner. Although he could not have foreseen the sort of idiocracy that America has become, aristocracies everywhere were giving way and the masses were on the move. Canetti admires in Woyzeck the way its characters condemn themselves—thoughts attacked by their own actions, actions at odds with their intentions—and contrasts this with the denunciations Karl Kraus (perhaps Canetti's first hero) regularly administered to Viennese society—complaints that came not from the miscreants themselves, who stood at the edge of disaster, banal as babies, as unaware as rocks, until Kraus drove them before him with the lash of his language and hurled them into the abyss. Büchner's people always offer evidence of their tortured interiors by their own painful behavior. These observations are important, but they do not, I think, entirely account for Canetti's sudden recovery of spirit. Büchner's scenes were cinematic and flowed in and out of one another, yet it was impossible to be certain what their correct order was, or even if there was one, and the play feels unfinished yet somehow all there, like so many of our human relations. It was how Büchner did it that transfixed Canetti—in dramas that did not narrate in the customary way, in a novella that refused to render madness as a mere aberration—and he almost immediately turned to the theater to write his play *The Wedding*, then read it to Hermann Broch, while Broch, utterly silent, appeared to be holding his breath.

I've had my own brief "Wow!" in Büchner's youthful pages. Büchner begins his first work, a pamphlet made of polemic rather than paper, with this sentence—which persuaded me of everything: "The life of the rich is one long Sunday." After which, he writes more, but unnecessarily. Canetti, too, liked sentences that had the hardness of stones, particularly those that shamed their creator by revealing a weakness in the writer otherwise invisible to him, such as, I suspect, one true of many: *"Er hat sich an den Einteilunger seines Lieblingsphilosophen erhängt,"* which Broch de Rothermann translates thus: "He has hanged himself from the categories of his favorite philosopher." (*The Agony of Flies,* New York: Farrar, Straus & Giroux, 1994, p. 59.)

Büchner, Kraus, Broch, Musil, Mann, Canetti: what a line of march! After reading the manuscript of *Die Blendung,* Broch says, "You're terrifying. Do you want to terrify people?" "Yes," Canetti answers. "Everything around us is terrifying. There is no longer a common language. No one understands anyone else. I believe no one *wants* to understand." (*The Agony of Flies,* p. 36.) The substance of this remark will remain with him like a scar. In the notebook published in 1994, his last year of life, Canetti quotes Goethe: "The human race uses thought only as an evasive tactic." (*Notes from Hampstead.* New York: Farrar, Straus & Giroux, 1998, p. 69.)

Die Blendung—"The Blinding"—appeared to appreciation and praise in 1935. In 1938, Hitler annexed Austria. The Austrians applauded the Nazis' military parades. In November of that year, Canetti and his new wife fled Vienna for Paris.

These remarks about Canetti were not a digression. Literary influence of more than momentary significance is the result of a context of conditions that permit one author to be particularly sensitive to another; in Canetti's case, some of these were previous events, like the burning of the Vienna Palace of Justice, the psychological tensions in his own history and the consequential dislike of Freud, the literary climate that featured Karl Kraus's attacks on the Austrian monarchy and its bourgeois toadies, as well as the reinforcing example of writers like Broch, Mann, and Musil, who combined novelistic skill with intellectual reach, erudition, and demanding ethical ideals. Works like *Woyzek* could then set going the dynamics of his mind, and rally his own strengths, set a salutary example that was at once a technique and an ideal.

I began to mull over the nature of literary influence (*mull* is not a word indicating any kind of progress) when I was considering opening this book with a pamphlet that the International Writers' Center and the Washington University Library published to celebrate the center's birth in 1990. We arranged an exhibit of books and manuscript materials to accompany a list of fifty works that I was prepared to say had influenced my own work. Our aim was modest: merely to get our endeavor noticed on a busy campus. I dashed my minicatalog off in a few days as books called out their authors' names to me, and I could have gone on I don't know how much further. To my dismay, this list was immediately taken to be a roll call of "best books," an activity I have no sympathy for, and certainly did not apply in this case, because not all great achievements are influential, or at least not on everybody. So Proust was not there, or Dante or Goethe or Sophocles, either. Awe often effaces every other effect.

Reading over this catalog, I realized that some of my responses had been immediate, some delayed, while most had depended upon an array of circumstances: a few literary, others personal or bused in from other arts; moreover, many had been the consequence of dislike and opposition, instead of admiration and emulation. Developing his own views about "power" and government, Canetti was forced to fight his way by Hobbes and Nietzsche, for instance, and his own wildly oedipal relationship with his mother forced him to resist Freud. Nor would he have allowed the least suggestion of naïveté to yield a simple "Gee gosh" before Grünewald's Isenheim Altarpiece, or Büchner's *Lenz*, whereas I'd had many such dumbfoundings, which just left me dazed for days, as thoughtless as a spinning top until, tired and turvied, I came to rest. And I certainly found myself far more open to certain texts during times that were politically particularly onerous, such as were McCarthy's filthy fifties, the vicious years of Vietnam, or our present time, when so many of our good citizens go to church in the comfort of their arrogance, their ignorant antique orthodoxies, and with smug fanaticism push the nation and the world toward catastrophe. Everything around us is terrifying, as Canetti wrote. And an influence.

FIFTY LITERARY PILLARS

Plato's *Timaeus*

I have been teaching Plato for fifty years. I know I have sometimes bored my students, but Plato has never bored me. His dialogues are among the world's most magical texts. I remember how the *Republic* set fire to my head, and among the other dialogues it is difficult to choose a favorite, but I should say, now, that the *Timaeus* strikes me as his strangest, and perhaps his most profound—at once most mystical and mysterious, hardheaded and mathematical. Beneath the surface of this "likely story" of how the universe was formed, Plato's conception of our world, as the qualitative expression of quantitative law, runs like a river.

Aristotle's *Nichomachean Ethics*

Following my first encounter with Plato, it was hard for me to imagine an equal mind, yet Aristotle showed up shortly after to astonish me. He is, in so many ways, his teacher's opposite: secular and scientific—not soaring—as ripe with common sense as an orchard, and an unrivaled intellectual inventor. Edison's bulbs burn out, but Aristotle's creation of the treatise form, his discovery of the syllogism, his establishment of scientific method remain incandescent. Aristotle's occasional path to a false conclusion is more scenic and exhilarating than a hike in the mountains. Finally, though, it is the commonplace nobility of the *Ethics* that wins me. There is scarcely a badly reasoned or backward line in this book. Plato can sometimes be sourly scary, but Aristotle is solid, forthright, sunny. He may even be right.

Thucydides' *History of the Peloponnesian War*

Here is history seen, endured, and created at the same time. He made many a Greek great by giving them his own thoughts, his own words, by lending them the extraordinary sheen of his mind; and it is there they are reflected like shadows cast by the ghosts of their real selves, for the war need never have taken place. It takes place now, and repeatedly, in this great cool prose, in these half-fictive events passing through an ideal disillusionary mind. Hobbes's mind, Machiavelli's mind, Thucydides' mind, are minds that allow little room for romance, and they became the romantic, unrealized, model for mine. If you will believe only that which you know to be true, you will trouble yourself very little with belief.

Thomas Hobbes's *Leviathan, or the Matter, Form, and Power of a Commonwealth*

Hobbes translated—magnificently—Thucydides' *History of the Peloponnesian War*. Moreover, he learned from that work how to look at the world. The first two books of the *Leviathan* are usually the only ones read, but I was equally impressed with the latter half. The book sets the biggest and best intellectual trap I know. In the first part, Hobbes argues that if you are a materialist, and do not believe in any life but this one, you must embrace an absolute sovereignty in order to establish and preserve peace. In the second half, he argues that if you are a Christian, and believe in a life everlasting, then a proper reading of Scripture will convince you to embrace an absolute sovereignty in order to achieve peace and properly obey God. The prose is unequaled in English philosophy.

Immanuel Kant's *Critique of Pure Reason*

It is, of course, a commonplace to admire this book, although it is one panel of a mighty triptych. The *Critique*'s thorny style, its difficult terminology, its original and complex thought drove me crazy when I first tried to cope with it. I wanted to blame Kant for my weakness of intellect, my inadequate background, my flabby character, my toddler's mind-set, and at college I actually threw my copy through a closed schoolroom window. (I attended school at a time when you could commit such childish things if you paid promptly for the labor and the glass. Beer bottles were often pitched out dorm windows. My breakage had to be a cut above.) The three *Critiques*, among many large things, do an important small one: they render the difference between the sort of thought and writing which is inherently and necessarily hard and the kind, like Heidegger's, which forms a soft metaphysical fog around even the easiest and most evident idea.

Ludwig Wittgenstein's *Tractatus Logico-Philosophicus*

A lightning bolt. Philosophy was not dead after all. Philosophical ambitions were not extinguished. Philosophical beauty had not fled prose. I remember that we approached this text (as we did Bertrand Russell's and Alfred North Whitehead's *Principia Mathematica*) with all the reverence due a sacred, arcane work. From the resonant and dark opening lines, *"Die Welt ist Alles, was der Fall ist,"* to its stunning conclusion, we are in the presence of logic delivered as music. How flat the translations are: How unmelodious, unmystical, unmysterious is "The world is everything that is the case." Who would want to consider seriously such a flat-earth remark? Well, a great many, apparently. Wittgenstein's project was akin to Spinoza's (who wrote his own Tractatus), and, as Spinoza's does, it puts us in the presence of the philosophical sublime. The fact that the *Tractatus's* fundamental assumptions may be quite wrong seems almost beside the point.

Gaston Bachelard's *Poetics of Space*

La favorita. This is writing which gives me a warm feeling, like sunny sand between the toes, or like one of Bachelard's own hearth fires. Bachelard was trained as a positivist; and as an historian of science, he specialized in the alchemists. He wrote an interesting book on relativity, and in *The Philosophy of No,* he laid down a speculative history of the development of intellectual thought which is certainly in the spirit (even if it wildly surpasses it) of Auguste Comte. His interest in the persistent errors which scientists make (alchemists in particular) led him to write, in a psychoanalytic mood, his wonderful books on the four elements. *The Poetics of Space* is his first venture into phenomenology, and what an adventure it is. A famous lecturer, Bachelard was also a very gifted reader, and by "gifted," I mean he knew what a gift a great book is, and responded to each present with witty and intelligent passion. *The Poetics of Space* has the ability to reorganize one's attitude toward reality in an enormously enhancing way.

Samuel Taylor Coleridge's *Biographia Literaria*

I am not the only reader who considers the *Biographia* the greatest work of literary criticism ever—even if Coleridge plagiarizes from the German idealists. I was lucky enough to study it under the gentle and wise guidance of Professor M. H. Abrams. The seminar was built on one directive: We would not only read the *Biographia* but would (by sharing and parceling out the labor) read every book it quotes from, mentions, or alludes to. The result was, in miniature, a university education. In researching my papers for the course, I also learned never to rely on secondary sources, but to trust only primary ones—a teaching that leads directly to this ideal: Write so as to become primary.

Paul Valéry's *Eupalinos, ou l'architecte*

The *Eupalinos* is a dialogue, but it is my favorite essay, and, in the William McCausland Stewart translation, it seems to me to be one of the supreme works of English prose. Valéry had a breathtaking mind, and the quality of his thought was like the quality of his poetry, where nuance was a thing in itself. Culture is a matter of considered and consistent choice, and high culture is concerned with estimations of quality. No writer I know, writing on any subject, demonstrates such a perfect power of discrimination. Here, writing on architecture, Valéry imitates a Platonic dialogue, and without in any way aping the master, he certainly rivals him. Thucydides, writing about the plague in Athens and the revolution in Corcyra, can make your hair stand on end. Valéry, writing about the mysteries of making *anything,* can cause you to lose your breath, or your hair, too, if it has already risen.

Sir Thomas Malory's *Le Morte d'Arthur*

What a debt I think I owe this transcendental fable! Although I had passed out of third grade, I was still a lazy, bored, slow, and inaccurate reader. I disliked school, did sums with all the enthusiasm I would later summon up to clean latrines, and lied a lot to entertain myself. Then at some point in fourth grade, while still floundering in school, I found myself inside some doubtless cleaned-up and dumbed-down version of Malory. Even youthanized, it was faithful enough. And I was lost. The ordinary world was ordinary in a way it had never been before—ordinary to the googolplex power. I knew now what was real, and I would never forget it. I began to eat books like a alien worm. From three a week, I rose to one a day. The page was peace. The page was purity. And, as I would begin to realize, some pages were perfection.

Sir Thomas Browne's *Hydriotaphia: Urne Buriall, or a Discourse of the Sepulchrall Urnes lately found in Norfolk*

The full list, the final role of honor, would include all the great Elizabethan and Jacobean prose writers: Traherne, Milton, Donne, Hobbes, Taylor, Burton, the translators of the King James Bible, and, of course, Browne, or "Sir Style," as I call him. I would later find them all splendidly discussed in a single chapter of George Saintsbury's *A History of English Prose Rhythm,* the chapter he called "The Triumph of the Ornate Style." Of course, there are great plain styles. Of course, positivists, puritans, democrats, levelers, Luddites, utilitarians, pragmatists, and pushy progressives have something to say for themselves. There are indeed several musicians after Handel and Bach. And there are other mountains beyond Nanga Parbat. But. But the great outburst of English poetry in Shakespeare, in Jonson, in Marlowe, and so on, was paralleled by an equally great outburst of prose, a prose, moreover, not yet astoop to fictional entertainments, but interested, as Montaigne was, in the drama and the dance of ideas. And they had one great obsession: death, for death came early in those days. First light was so often final glimmer. Sir Style is a skeptic; Sir Style is a stroller; Sir Style takes his time; Sir Style broods, no hen more overworked than he; Sir Style makes literary periods as normal folk make water; Sir Style ascends the language as if it were a staircase of nouns; Sir Style would do a whole lot better than this.

Laurence Sterne's *Tristram Shandy*

I think all my choices are obvious. Only what is left out of the temple is not justifiable. (Why weren't you influenced by Proust? Well, that was probably a good thing.) We always speak of Sterne as ahead of his time, but what was it about Sterne that made him permanently avant-garde? His honesty about artifice? "Leave we then the breeches in the taylor's hands . . ." Henry James once said, in his snobbiest manner, "I see all round Flaubert." That's what Sterne did. Fiction had scarcely gotten started, and, already, Sterne saw all round it—as well as through. For example, this: "A cow broke in (tomorrow morning) to my Uncle Toby's fortifications. . . ."

Virginia Woolf's Diaries

Pepys, everybody knows about. The lover of diaries, however, is familiar with them all, from André Gide's famous work to Emanuel Carnevali's more obscure entries. Actually, Gide kept a journal, while Cesare Pavese kept a diary, and the difference between a notebook of the sort Henry James tended, which was his workshop, the record of activities that makes up the diary, and the kind of "thought-clock" the journal resembles is an interesting one. Loneliness is the diary keeper's lover. It is not narcissism that takes them to their desk every day. And who "keeps" whom, after all? The diary is demanding; it imposes its routine; it must be "chored" the way one must milk a cow; and it alters your attitude toward life, which is lived, finally, only in order that it may make its way to the private page. It is a pity Virginia's could not have held her head above water a while longer.

Ford Madox Ford's *Parade's End* (the Tietjens tetralogy)

Ford is, for me, a much-maligned, misunderstood, and heroic figure, the author of at least three great works, the *Fifth Queen* trilogy, the masterful epistemological novel *The Good Soldier,* and his Tietjens books. He was a wonderful memoirist, too, a great editor, and a true friend of literature, "a man mad," as he said, "about writing." About fifteen years ago [now nearer thirty], talking to a group of literature students at the University of Leeds, I asked them their opinion of Ford, and fewer than a handful had ever heard of him. No wonder the empire fell into decay. Largely through the efforts of Sondra Stang, Ford's reputation has grown since then, but he is still not accorded the position he deserves. *Some Do Not,* the first volume of the four, was written in 1924, the year of my birth. I still think it is the most beautiful love story in our language. It is a modern love story, with this astonishing difference: Everything is treated with profound irony except the love itself.

William Shakespeare's *Antony and Cleopatra*

There are many famous works, and a few famous writers, who are not among my fifty. It is not just some reasonable limit that has kept them off. My list is supposed to represent works which, I feel, have changed me as a writer in some important way, and while making such a list may be an act of egotism, it does not possess the arrogance of a roll call of Great Books. That is not to suggest that I do not believe in great books, for I believe in very little else—some music, some paintings, a few buildings, perhaps. Great books are great for innumerable reasons, but one of them surely is that they will remain faithful to the values they are made of. And it happens that if an author is too obviously great, the reader can never have the delirious excitement of discovering him or hearing his special note strike, because it has been broadcast in bits and pieces over a whole life. This is so often true concerning Shakespeare. Our society disarms genius. Beethoven is played to death, van Gogh tacked to closet doors, Burns's songs sung by drunks, sublime lines mouthed by movie stars. This play by the Bard, whom immortality has murdered, his texts chewed by actors dressed in business suits, his corpse cut to pieces by directors and the remains dragged by popularity through the street, rose for me in a manner more vibrant than life. The language is yet a cut above the most high, the imagery so flamboyant sometimes as to establish a new style. I became properly fatuous in his presence. I said: "Boy, you sure can write."

Ben Jonson's *The Alchemist*

A man after my own heart. He is capable of the simplest lyrical stroke, as bold and direct as a line by Matisse, but he can be complex in a manner that could cast Nabokov in the shade. Like

Rabelais and Joyce, he is a master excrementalist. *The Alchemist* (and the belly is the best one) is no stroll through the park. It is an arduous, even odious, climb. Shakespeare may have been smarter, but he did not know as much. Nowadays, knowing a lot is often thought to be a part of the equipment of a bore, a handicap to the personality, an office impediment. Jonson also makes marvelous lists, and I love lists. His are not as supreme, perhaps, as Rabelais's, but they are quite calorific. The true alchemists do not change lead into gold; they change the world into words.

James Joyce's *Ulysses*

When I was in high school, I tried to smuggle a copy of this once-banned and still "dirty" book past the resolutely puritanical eyes of my hometown librarian. No luck. I'd have placed a curse upon her ovaries had I known where ovaries were. But everything works out for the best, as Dr. Pangloss says. I was then too young for *Ulysses*. When I did read it, I was not struck dumb, as I should have been. Rather, I was flung into a fit of imitation. Like Dante, like Milton, like Proust, like Faulkner, like García Márquez, Joyce is too towering to imitate. It would be years before I could escape his grasp, and I still avoid *Ulysses* when I am working. The only words that dare follow "Stately, plump Buck Mulligan . . ." are Joyce's.

James Joyce's *Finnegans Wake*

. . . Yet no song the sirens sang is as beguiling as the song Anna Livia Plurabelle sings while she rubs her wash clean on a rock by the Liffey. We literary snobs once dressed in *FW* as if it were the latest and most expensive and most extreme of fashion. Like *Tristram Shandy*, it is permanent member of the avant-garde, and immune to popularization. Graduate students will be forced to corrupt it, of course, and its music will fall into footnotes.

Joyce was recorded reading portions of this work, and his performance is unforgettable and wholly convincing. Passages linger in the memory. The conclusion of the *Wake* is among the most poignant I know, and the idea that it is a cold labor of anal obsessiveness is all-the-way-round wrong. *FW* is the high-water mark of Modernism, and not to have been fundamentally influenced by it as a writer is not to have lived in your time. Not to live in your time is a serious moral flaw. Although not to object to our time is an equal lapse in values and perception.

Flann O'Brien's *At Swim-Two-Birds*

My only problem with Brian O'Nolan (two of whose pseudonyms are Flann O'Brien and Myles na Gopaleen) is that he seemed too satisfied to be Irish to be sane. You ought to live in your time, I thought, but try never to be what you have been. Like Joyce and Beckett, O'Brien was an accomplished linguist; like them, too, a darkly comic writer, and a master of pastiche. A cult is all, so far, that he has been able to gather to him, which is too bad, for O'Brien is also an innovator in language. *At Swim-Two-Birds* (the name of an inn, a pub, a puddle of texts) was published in 1939, the year *FW* appeared, and World War II broke out, which makes that date ideal as Modernism's triumph and its knell. If you are caught in O'Brien's web of words, you will not be sucked dry and left a hull, but incredibly enriched, filled to the bloat point, ready to pop. There aren't many funnier books. He was also a fine journalist and not a total drunk. He read contemporary literature in five languages, wrote regularly in two, and if he is uneven, he is uneven as a roller coaster is, and not rough as a rough road.

Beckett's *How It Is* and "Ping"

His name is the same as a saint's. He represents perfectly one supreme pole of the art of writing, along with Rilke, Valéry, and Flaubert. His dedication was so total, it regularly threatened his existence. Most of us compromise. That is how one gets on in life, avoids labor disputes, saves a marriage, ducks a war. Even principles get dirtied and we have to wash them periodically like clothes. Beckett is a minimalist because he is as devoted to his ideals as a Shaker and thinks most things frivolous, or decorative, or vain. And he is no doubt right. He writes equally well in two languages: Nitty and Gritty. He is a minimalist because he compresses, and puts everything in by leaving most of it out. Joyce wished to rescue the world by getting it into his book; Beckett wishes to save our souls by purging us—impossibly—of matter. Only Borges has had a comparable influence. I have only known one other man who bore the brunt and brilliance of his art in his person, who literally "stood for" what he stood for in the best sense, and that was Ludwig Wittgenstein, the only other saint in my modest religion.

The library at Washington University has a wonderful Beckett collection. There you may actually observe (in a manuscript like "Ping" in English, "Bing" in French) the hand of the master at work—with a mind that's mathematical, musical, always skeptical, Cartesian—crossing out, writing in, encircling, fretting in the margins. When I first held "Ping" in my hands, my hands shook, not because of a reverence for relics, but because the pages were pure epiphany.

José Lezama Lima's *Paradiso*

The translation by Gregory Rabassa reads wonderfully, but we know that the jungle has been cleared, the nighttime lit, the tangles, at least some of them, straightened. If *How It Is* is one polar cap of my little literary world, *Paradiso* lies at the other: both forbidding, both formidable, both wholly formed, though so differently achieved. Beckett was as spare in person as his work. Lezama Lima was large, and wore (I believe) a wide white hat, and held forth in cafés, and put his loving fat hands on young men and blessed them with his attention. The Latin American literary boom has heard the firing of many cannons, but none sounds more loudly in my ears than *Paradiso*. Surely, with Carlos Fuentes's *Terra Nostra*, Julio Cortázar's *Hopscotch*, Gabriel García Márquez's *One Hundred Years of Solitude*, and Cabrera Infante's *Three Trapped Tigers,* it forms a fresh Andes. I shall now make a bad joke: If Sir Style is the king of the Baroque, here is the queen. Long may they live and break wind, as Pantagruel would say.

Julio Cortázar's *Hopscotch*

Of the astonishing Latin American writers, I am including only a few in my fifty, simply because only these few jarred as much my writing hand. But the work of Fuentes, Paz, Neruda, Carpentier, Vallejo, Rulfo, Puig, Donoso, Cabrera Infante, Sarduy, Sábato, García Márquez, Vargas Llosa, and so on, should not be in any sense skimped or neglected. These writers now own the novel. We others, who try our hand at it from time to time, we merely rent. And *Hopscotch* is one reason for the preeminence of the Spanish language in contemporary literature. Rich, inventive, sprawling, intelligent . . . I halt on this word, not one I should assign as a special quality to many writers. Joyce, for instance, picks up ideas the way a jackdaw steals buttons off of hanging wash—because they are bright—and he carries them back to his nest, another shiny trophy. But he does not know the inside of any of them. He knows the brutalities of theology, the beauty of its pageantry, the fearfulness of its fanaticism, but not its internal intellectual power. But so many of the great Latins do. They are smart. Many have been diplomats. They are smooth. They have seen their countries ravaged by carpetbaggers and impoverished by homegrown dictators. They are really pissed off.

Jorge Luis Borges's *Labyrinths*

Another amazing mind. Here is the consciousness of a devoted, playful, skeptical intelligence, a man made civilized by the library, as if to prove it can be done. At what a deliciously ironic remove does he observe (through words) the world. What this blind seer sees is just how little we see if fully sighted; how little there is to understand in all we think we know. But Borges is not a man for despair; that, too, is vanity. Nor is there anything new under the sun, not even a new view: that the sun is a hotheaded youth drag-racing the moon to his doom; that it is a hot rock; that it is an idea in God's mind; that it is a bundle of burning perceptions; that it is; that it is not. Borges is a fine poet, too, but he revolutionized our conception of both the story and the essay by blending and bewildering them. He will not be forgiven or forgotten for that.

Thomas Mann's *The Magic Mountain*

Lifetimes don't last long enough for us to have more than two or three vocational revelations. Perhaps I was fifteen when I first read "Disorder and Early Sorrow," but I still remember part of my emotion. I desperately wanted to be "like Mann." It was not just that I wanted to write as powerfully or as profoundly, or even that I wanted to have his art or his mind. I remember trying to understand my desire for that likeness, and it was only later that I decided what my feeling really was: I wanted to be like that story—to have that measured depth, that subtlety, that sense—yes—of its own importance, and even to be its problems, endure its theme. And later I would devour everything he wrote, especially *Death in Venice. Dr. Faustus* is an equally admirable novel, I think; but *The Magic Mountain* is a work I have read more often than any other novel, and one I studied carefully when young, and began to see as a complex textual world. I loved the fact that I could read its brief passages of schoolboy French. At St. Louis's yearly Book Fair (the region's most important cultural event), I found a few years back a nice copy of *Joseph in Egypt*. On the flyleaf, in Mann's hand, was a thank-you note to his St. Louis hostess. The book cost me a buck.

Franz Kafka's *A Country Doctor and Other Stories*

Kafka was for me a perfect example of "getting to the party late." By the time I arrived, I had heard of Kafka for several decades; I had read his imitators, and his critics. I had played with his angst as if it were a football. I did not expect to be impressed (something had held me from him), though impressed I was—mightily. But he would not be "an influence." Then, in the middle of Kafka—a Kafka I had begun to teach—I found *A Country Doctor*, a mysterious and extraordinary prose lyric, a Kafka in a Kafka. And suddenly, all of Kafka grew more luminous and impenetrable at the same time. Kafka is my next writing project. If I can get to him. [I never did.] I don't play with his angst anymore—the game is no longer a game. He is a great letter writer, a great diarist, too.

Herman Broch's *The Sleepwalkers*

Broch may be the most neglected writer on my list, next to Flann O'Brien (over whom he would tower). I think of Elias Canetti's *Auto-da-Fé,* as well, or Robert Musil's *The Man Without Qualities,* but Canetti is a Nobel laureate now, and Musil is well known, though only from infrequent sightings, like a family ghost. An equally neglected work is Broch's own *Death of Virgil*. Certainly, his books have been translated into many languages, and he has been given the flattery of polite applause. Exiled to the United States, he won awards and received grants. Yet he has been neglected by being insufficiently singled out, his excellence hidden in the hubbub ordinariness predictably receives. *The Sleepwalkers* begins as a psychological narrative, passes through a center made of the "real" world's descriptive surface, and ends as a philosophical lyric. Each phase is masterfully done, but it is the direction of the change that is most significant. If we were to think of the traditional novel as a pane of glass, then *The Sleepwalkers* is a thrown stone, and *The Death of Virgil* its shattered window. We can no longer see out because there is nothing to see through. Like Mann, he is a "philosophical novelist." Unlike Aldous Huxley, George Orwell, or Anatole France, he is not a novelist of ideas.

Italo Svevo's *Confessions of Zeno* (or *Zeno's Conscience* in William Weaver's marvelous recent translation)

How different German and Italian ironies are. Svevo takes the world seriously by refusing to do so; his touch with everything is light. Mann takes the world seriously in order to make something serious out of what, after all, is rather an absurd affair. His lightest touch leaves a bruise, but not one a bully's blow leaves, one the doctor's inoculation causes. My colleague Naomi Lebowitz has written wonderfully of Svevo, who called himself, on the late occasion of his fame, as she reports, a *"bambino di 64 anni."* But when he met Joyce, he was a businessman named Ettore Schmitz, and as Ettore Schmitz he lent the impoverished Irishman money. However, when Joyce recommended *Zeno* to Ford Madox Ford and T. S. Eliot (among others of influence), he was the Svevo we know and the author also of an earlier work we didn't know, called *Senilità*—itself quite beautiful. Svevo did not take himself seriously as a literary personage, or romanticize about himself as a pursuer of the great arts. He was in the glassware business. He wrote, sufficiently, not solely, for himself. Svevo is on this list, however, because he opened up Italian literature for me. It was a world to which I had been almost totally oblivious. Dante had been my final stop. And once I had entered the country through Trieste, where one day D'Annunzio would hang his banner, I would make my way slowly and stay in many regions: in Pavese, for example, in Montale, Pratolini, Vittorini, and later in Emilio Gadda's Rome, in the Turin of Primo Levi, in the dreamlands of Italo Calvino.

Gustave Flaubert's Letters

Here I learned—and learned—and learned. My letters. I did not learn how to write. You learn that by writing. After you have read much. I learned what and how to think about writing. I learned what literary ideals were and why they were important. I became only a third-grade fanatic, but every advancement helped. I also got to understand something of my own anger by studying Flaubert's rage. I must say I trust hatred more than love. It is frequently constructive, despite the propaganda to the contrary; it is less frequently practiced by hypocrites; it is more clearly understood; it is painfully purchased and therefore often earned; and its objects sometimes even deserve their hoped-for fate. If you love the good, you have to hate evil. I cannot imagine a love so puerile and thin and weak-kneed it cannot rage. But hate killed Flaubert, I think, and it didn't do Céline many favors. If I had any advice to give a young writer (and I haven't), I would suggest an enraptured reading of these letters. One ought not to feel about women as Flaubert did—he could be coarse and brutal—but he will teach you how to treat a page. Maybe I go too far if I say that every *mot* is *juste,* but certainly every other one is.

Gustave Flaubert's *Bouvard and Pécuchet*

I had read and admired everything else by the master but this late text. I had swallowed the stories, been overwhelmed by *Bovary* and *Education,* admired even Flaubert's oriental excesses. But I had not gotten to the great "put-down." This book is not for the faintly minded. It is a devastation, a blowup as total as the bomb, of our European pretensions to knowledge. B and P are silent film comics, almost. They Laurel and Hardy their way through wisdom, and leave it a wreck. Their sincere admiration for any subject is equivalent to the announcement of its disgrace. I had thought these things already, thought them all, but I had never found them quite so well expressed. So this work changed me through its confirmation of my prejudices. It made certain that to this set of attitudes, I should remain not only wed but faithful.

Stendhal's *The Red and the Black*

Boston, 1943. I am about to go down to the submarine base to test out for the school there. I have come into possession of the Liveright

Black and Gold edition. (What a wonderful series. I loved them all. There was Jules Romain's *The Body's Rapture,* a kooky, overwrought book, I know now, but it was sex, and it was French. There was Remy de Gourmont's *The Natural Philosophy of Love,* more sex, more French. There was Balzac's *The Physiology of Marriage,* more sex, more French. There was Stendhal's own *On Love,* ditto. There was *The Collected Works of Pierre Loüys,* double dots, double ditto. There was Alexandre Dumas's *The Journal of Madame Giovanni,* which was simply French, a disappointment. And *The Red and the Black,* like checker squares.) Anyway, I am lining up New London in my train table's sights, and scanning the novel I have bought because of the series it is in, thinking that I'm not going to like climbing a rope through all that water, and thinking that the first chapter, a description of a small town, is commonplace, ho-hum, and will I be put in a pressure chamber at sub school like a canned tomato? When suddenly, I am suckered into Stendhal, and no longer read words (against all the rules of right reading I will later give myself), but barrel along like my own train, a runaway, holding my breath oftener and oftener, aware only of a insistently increasing tension, and it is not because I am underwater; it is because I am inside the magic of this narrative master. *The Charterhouse of Parma* would do exactly the same thing to me, except that I didn't let a sub school come between us, but covered its lengthy length as nearly in one sitting as might be managed, snacking at the edge of it as though it were on a TV tray. That sort of gluttonous read is rare, and never happens to me now, when I read, because I read to write or teach or otherwise to talk, and not because I am a reading madman about to lose his soul to the seductions of a sentence.

Colette's *Break of Day*

Books to go to bed with; books better than most breasts; books that feel like silk sheets someone has spilled crumbs on, for they are not so totally smooth as not to scratch. *Adoration* is the right word if spoken with the right accent. Colette was a heroine, too, who threw off the bribing bangles of her captors, dared to kiss other girls in public, or to appear nude (but so motionless, the tableau might not be living). Works in which the juice runs through your closing teeth. And wise, or, maybe, shrewd. Observant not as a god is, but as an adolescent looking on love, and later like a whore looking on lovelessness and age. Semiautobiographical the way one is semidressed. Never breathless as a schoolgirl, though, or like this prose, disjointed, but long and slow and generous and fine as the line of the leg. *Regarde,* she commanded. And in *Chéri,* she looked at age as it comes to those whose means of life depend on their physical attractions, or, at least, on the promises of the body. *Break of Day* is the classic menopause book. Resilient and resigned, yet rich in resolution, *Break of Day* does not translate *La Naissance du Jour* very well, when what is meant is something like the dawning of the end. American students, I have discovered to my sorrow, do not take kindly to Colette. Is it because, though they exercise their bodies, they never exercise their senses? Or because, though they know a bit about sex, they prefer not to know about sensuality?

John Donne's Poems and Sermons

"Batter my heart," he did. I grew up during the Age of Donne, the era of the New Criticism, when the metaphysical poets were brought, by T. S. Eliot and William Empson, to center stage, where they stood in front of Wordsworth and Shelley and wore outlandish conceits. It was Marvell and Donne, mainly, who set the standard. Crashaw had his thumb on the scale. I learned how admirable oxymorons were, and how to perform catachresis. We hunted ambiguities feverishly, as if they were bedbugs in the blankets. Gotcha. For all their excesses, the New Critics were generally sound about the reading of poetry, and their techniques are still standard. "The circle of bright hair about the bone," we would whisper in one another's ear while dancing, which was probably an improvement on humming along with the band, though no less absurd. Having drunk the poetry, I found the prose. And what prose! He raised rhetoric like a club of war. I must quote. How shall we be when we are angels? "The knowledge which I have by Nature, shall have no Clouds; here it hath: that which I have by Grace, shall have no reluctation, no resistance; here it hath: That which I have by Revelation, shall have no suspition, no jealousie; here it hath: sometimes it is hard to distinguish between a respiration from God, and a suggestion from the Devil. There our curiosity shall have this noble satisfaction, we shall know how the Angels know, by knowing as they know." You have to admire the punctuation. He was another Sir Style, of course, and another deeply doubting believer. Or deeply believing doubter. It depended on the poetic subject. The poet's real loyalty is to the rhyme and to the repetition of that "hath."

Friedrich Hölderlin's Hymns

I like Hölderlin best when his critics say he is mad. Whenever an artist bursts through the limits, he is said to be astigmatic, immoderate, deaf, arthritic, depressed, drunk, insane, syphilitic. Literature has many wonderful poets, each as mad as Blake. However, there are a few poets whose poetry outmodes poetry itself, the way very late Beethoven seems to transcend music and seek another realm. Mallarmé is a prime example. One might include Paul Celan. As if whatever had been done before was no longer enough, as if every old depth had dried up and shown itself shallow, as if every use of language had worn its edge round; the poet at first flutes on his instrument, until finally he finds a way to play backward through it, or upside down, or without using any breath, or simply by thinking through the tube, sounding the sense somewhere. The hymns and the late poems of Hölderlin, like the elegies of Rilke and the last lays of Yeats, are no longer poems. They have eluded her grasp and that of every category. Hölderlin once said this about the death of his wife: that she had borne his children, who were Popes and sultans, and that then *"Närret isch se worde, närret, närret, närret!"* ("She went mad, she did, mad, mad, mad!") Near his own end, Hölderlin wrote the poem that passes poetry like an errant bus may run through all its stops. It is the one that begins, in Richard Sieburth's English:

> In lovely blue the steeple blossoms
> With its metal roof. Around which
> Drift swallow cries, around which
> Lies most loving blue. . . .

And as I read on, I, who am not a believer, said, my single sincere time, with wonder and devotion, "My God . . ."

Stéphane Mallarmé's *Un Coup de dés*

Hölderlin had tried to live through a revolution, and felt that in poetry, too, there should be a similar upheaval. Mallarmé made quietness cover his life like a cloth—teaching in a high school, inviting a few friends in of an evening, talking and talking, quietly, in a prose pointed at poetry. In that quiet, gray, low-key, laid-back, nothing life, except for the language devoted to his love of language, he hatched a revolution that has yet to come round to its beginning. A piece of paper, where it became a page, became pure space, a space over which a divinity brooded as though it were the primeval waste. And words were not to be words. When were words in poems ever words? And a book, a book was not to be a book. Open one. Perhaps that opening exposes a great snowfield where a word, now a single dead bird, lay in the snow and sang nothing . . . sang it. I always thought it very exciting to know that there were men who looked on language and its page like that, who lived in a withinness wider than any without, who quietly blew up the Customary (Nietzsche said his books were bombs), so quietly, customers purchased the ruins to furnish their flats. Of course, it is a corrective to remember who came to take tea on Tuesdays at the schoolmaster's: nearly every important literary figure in Paris, or anyone significant who was passing through. Among the Mardistes, talk was animated and wide open.

Manet watched from a wall. Space was made in the dining room for the crowd. The cat, Lilith, sat on the sideboard. Everyone rolled their own. Odilon Redon prepared himself to collaborate on *Un Coup*. Now and then, a flirt would call. Some evenings (at the god-awful hour of 10:00 p.m.) the Pauls Verlaine and Valéry would seat themselves among young men thoroughly cowed and quieter than the furniture.

Ezra Pound's *Personae*

The power of these poems has paled. Pound was the number-one teach in the old days, and T. S. Eliot was number two. Pound told us to "make it new." He cajoled editors to print avant-garde work. He fought for the right and the good and the ideals of art. Maybe I wore Ez out. I certainly wore out Eliot. Some of one's gods grow dim, and perhaps it's because the eyes begin to weaken, or possibly it is because the idols themselves have wearied of their own tainted divinity. It is still beautiful stuff, but I am conscious now of how much pastiche is present, how deep the posturing goes. Perhaps the chaos of the *Cantos,* a work I would once have fought for like a hunting territory, cannot be saved by commentary. Anyway, when I met these poems, they were fresh, their author was brash, and I was young, and still unread.

William Butler Yeats's *The Tower*

Wouldn't we all like to grow old full of lust and rage as Yeats did? Wouldn't we all like to have a late phase that would unlace the stays, and unwrap everything, and lay it bare for our wise, ripe, appreciative, and lascivious gaze? *The Tower* is not a volume of the late poems. Those I admire even more than the masterpieces here, but this is the book that did its worst and best with me. Poetry has been a beleaguered castle on a cliff for a long time, and my castle had four towers: Yeats, Valéry, Rilke, and Wallace Stevens. Their period produced some of the greatest lyric poetry our European culture has ever seen—perhaps its last gasp. These poets understood that poetry was a calling—and to consciousness a complete one. Yeats wanted to be a seer, and if, as it happened, there was nothing to see, he would invent it, not simply for himself but for everybody else, too. He sets Byzantium down in Sligo. Yeats invested his language with an original richness, as if every word were a suitcase he would open, rummage around in, and carefully repack, slipping a few extras in among the socks. I read him in one gulp—the *Complete Poems*—from end to end, and then in small bites, and finally in ruminative chews. *The Tower* became a tree, and rooted itself in me. Yeats grew old disgracefully. It is the only way to go.

Wallace Stevens's *Harmonium*

I have always believed that genius and originality should be evident almost at once and delivered like a punch—in a paragraph, a stanza, even an image. One should not have to eat the whole roast to determine it once was a cow. That's why I always liked Ford Madox Ford's "page ninety-nine test." (Wyndham Lewis also laid claim to this method.) Open the book to page ninety-nine and read, and the quality of the whole will be revealed to you. (Of course, if you do that to *Harmonium,* you will read from "Anecdote of the Prince of Peacocks," lines stamped with the poet's individuality, but not, I think, genius. Nevertheless, overleaf, you will encounter a poem entitled "A High-Toned Old Christian Woman," and all doubts will be dispelled. Although some individuality is lost, since it might—almost—have been written by Edith Sitwell—"Such tink and tank and tunk-a-tunk-tunk.") With Stevens, you will not be kept long in suspense, if you've begun at page one, as one ought. Shortly you will sense that something extraordinary is happening to the language. By page five, you are reading of "golden quirks and Paphian caricatures," and by page sixteen, you come face-to-face with the first masterpiece, "The Snow Man," which quietly begins "One must have a mind of winter," a line that does true justice to *m* and *n,* and then concludes, so characteristically:

For the listener, who listens in the snow,
And, nothing himself, beholds
Nothing that is not there and the nothing that is.

Listening, our breath taken, we behold it. Later, in that same first work, we shall encounter "Sunday Morning," perhaps the pinnacle of the metapoetical—do I dare to say?

Henry James's *The Golden Bowl*

Here is the late phase, and what the late phase can do. James was born in a late phase and grew phasier all his life, like a jungle vine. By the time he was truly old, he was beyond time, and need not have marked his birthdays. *The Golden Bowl,* the critics said, was James indulging himself, James parodying James. Critics are a dim lot. It was James being James right enough. I could have listed half a dozen of his novels (from *The Portrait of a Lady* through *The Spoils of Poynton* to *The Wings of the Dove* and *The Ambassadors*) or half a dozen of his tales, and called upon his travel work as well, so that to place only the great *Bowl* here is a bit perverse. I do so because what affected me most about Henry James lay not in some single work itself, but in his style—that wondrously supple, witty, sensuous, sensitive, circumloquatious style—and the *Bowl* is that style brought to its final and most refulgent state. Like Valéry in the realm of the mind, James was a nuancer, and believed in the art of qualification, the art of making finer and finer distinctions (an art that some have said is the special province of philosophy). And Henry James formed the phrase—the slogan—the motto—which I would carve on my coat of arms if I had one: "Try to be someone," he said, "on whom nothing is lost."

He is also supposed to have said, at the moment of his death, "So here it is at last, the distinguished thing." What he actually said, of course, was, "So here it is at last, the extinguishing thing." People will embroider.

Henry James's Notebooks

The workshop of Henry James was the third major classroom of my writer's education. Flaubert's letters were the first course, Gertrude Stein's lectures and stories made up the curriculum of the second, and James's notebooks would constitute the third. What a workshop it was. Transmutations were made there an alchemist might envy. I could see how James's fascination with gossip and social trivia was transformed into his burning moral concerns, and how these, in their turn, were refined in a manner of writing so scrupulous, so delicate, so reflective it became an indictment of the very material it had risen from, as if the odor of the roast were to blame the pig for being pork. Like Proust, James knew how to read and how to write the language of society. Like Proust, too, what he wrote was devastating. To look in this book is like looking into the master's head, into that majestic dome, in order to watch the cogs. Only these cogs don't simply go click.

William Faulkner's *The Sound and the Fury*

American literature, it is often said, has two poles: the conscience-haunted and puritanically repressed novel of "bad" manners, represented by Nathaniel Hawthorne and culminating in James, and the wild and woolly frontier baroque, pioneered by Herman Melville (whose whale ought also to be here), that triumphed in the historical hungers and, far from manifest, destinies we find in Faulkner. His name ought properly to stand here in front of a fistful of titles: *Light in August, As I Lay Dying, The Hamlet,* and so on. *The Sound and the Fury* is a little too Europeanly experimental to be ideal Faulkner. Still, it was just this bridgelike quality to which I initially responded. If he wrote in the world of Joyce, he had to be all right. However, Faulkner wrote in another world as well, in the world of the old-fashioned (as well as the newfangled) epic, and his work has that sort of sweep: It is multitudinously peopled, as foreordained as film, as rhetorical as the circuit rider or the tent-pole reformer.

Faulkner's career illustrates another thought for the dark: You can take yourself seriously about only one thing at a time. When Faulkner began to take himself seriously as a thinker, his work as an artist precipitously declined.

Katherine Anne Porter's *Pale Horse, Pale Rider*

What James called "the beautiful and blessed novella" often comes in triads, possibly because a novella is roughly a third of a novel in length, so that it takes three to make a book. There is Flaubert's *Three Tales*, for instance, Stein's *Three Lives*, and Porter's *Pale Horse*. We could compose our own such trios for Chekhov, James, Joyce, Conrad, Faulkner, Colette, too, as well as a number of others. And we would hear no finer music made than here. From her first tale to her last, she was in complete command of her manner—a prose straightforward and shining as a prairie road, yet gently undulating, too. But above all, for me, it was the sharpness of her eye that caught mine, and the quiet reach of her feeling. If *Noon Wine* shook you, *Pale Horse* swooped you, and its lyricism put me to bed with a fever. Its song is matched in our fiction by what? Conrad Aiken's "Silent Snow, Secret Snow" perhaps? Or J. F. Powers's "Lions, Harts, Leaping Does"? A tough lady. She did me the honor of liking my early work. I had the manuscript of my first novel, *Omensetter's Luck*, stolen from me, and the same thief purloined an essay of mine on Katherine Anne, which he changed scarcely at all, and published under his name (Edward Greenfield Schwartz) in the *Southwest Quarterly Review*. He also swiped someone else's essay on Nathanael West. Alas, with her name, I still associate this professional plagiarizer.

Gertrude Stein's *Three Lives*

The circumstances of the blow are so often fortuitous. I read Tolstoy or Proust and say, "Of course." Greatness as advertised, like the beauty of the Alhambra or the Amalfi coast. Cervantes, certainly, no surprise. And have a helping of Dante or Boccaccio. (I tried to seduce a young lady once through the present of the *Decameron,* but that doesn't come under the principle of this collection.) There are texts, and there are times, and sometimes both are right and ring together like Easter changes. (I remember, at Wells Cathedral, the shock of such bells, whose vibrations made me sound.) I didn't read Stein until my first year in graduate school, and I was ready. No prose ever hit me harder. This was the work of the woman they called "the Mother Goose of Montparnasse"? How could you read the central story, "Melanctha," and not take everything she did seriously? I read with an excitement that made me nearly ill, and having finished the book at 1:00 a.m. (having never contemplated reading it in the first place, having been lured, suckered, seduced), I immediately began reading it again from the beginning, singing to myself, and moaning, too, because this tension had caused my stomach to hurt quite fiercely. My head also ached. I was sort of sore-eyed. Was this how it felt to have a revelation? Her prose did produce in me some of the same exhilaration that, say, the description of the Great Frost does, in Virginia Woolf's *Orlando,* and some of the terrible tension I have when, in John Hawkes's *The Lime Twig,* Margaret is beaten with the wet rolled-up newspaper; but in addition it produced discovery, amazement, anger (at having been told yet more lies about values by critics and colleagues and teachers). And so at the end, I was sick, and though hanging over the mouth of the john (where my fears were not confirmed), I knew I had found the woman my work would marry. And I would, in effect, always carry three great faces in my wallet: Virginia Woolf's, Colette's, and Gertrude Stein's. If you ask, like a cinema soldier in a movie foxhole, I will take them out and show them to you.

William Gaddis's *The Recognitions*

It sometimes happens in a writing life that you get lucky, and I have been lucky often. I think that perhaps *JR* is the greater book, but it hardly matters. *The Recognitions* was a thunderclap. It was a dull decade, the fifties, but here was a real sound. [I must have been thinking of American literature too exclusively when I wrote this, because no decade could be dull that saw both William Gaddis and Malcolm Lowry appear with major works. *Under the Volcano* should have been an entry among this fifty. Imagine it as the roof. It took me three starts to get into it; my resistance to it is now inexplicable, though I suspect I knew what I was in for. I have never read a book more personally harrowing. It is also a rare thing in modern litera-ture: a real tragedy, with a no-account protagonist to boot. The Con-sul is one of the most completely realized characters in all of fiction. However, enough of this effort to make up for a shocking omission.] Okay, it was a dull decade. *The Recognitions* made a real sound. And the sixties would be the novel's best ten years. But here was Mr. Cranky to accompany Sir Style. Here was a man even madder about the general state of things than I was. Here was a man whose busi-ness was seeing through—seeing through bodies, minds, dreams, ideals—Superman was Mr. Magoo by comparison. And here was a man who immediately reminded me of another hero (they can't all be present), the Viennese culture critic, Karl Kraus, because this man collected mankind's shit, too, and knew where to throw it, and knew where to aim the fan. Then, as affairs would fall out, I had the good fortune to be on the jury that awarded *JR* the National Book Award, and got a little recognition for an author who, till then, had been the idol of a clique. In time, as it also turned out, I met William Gaddis and became his friend. Thus my third rule was realized: In this business, to have the respect of those whom you respect is the only genuine reward. And that reward is quite enough.

John Hawkes's *The Lime Twig*

This novel humbled me in a number of ways. I was reading manu-scripts for a magazine called *Accent,* and had in front of my prose-bleary eyes a piece called "A Horse in a London Flat." And I was in a doze. More dreariness. More pretension. When will it all end? How shall I phrase my polite rejection? Something, I don't remember what it was now, but something ten pages along woke me up, as if I had nearly fallen asleep and toppled from my chair. Perhaps it was the startle of an image or the rasp of a line. I went back to the beginning, and soon realized that I had let my eyes slide over paragraphs of astonishing prose without responding to them or recognizing their quality. That was my first humiliation. I then carried the manuscript to my fellow editors, as if I were bringing the original "good news," only to learn that they were perfectly familiar with the work of John Hawkes and admired it extravagantly. Hadn't I read *The Cannibal*, or *The Goose on the Grave*? Where had I been! What a dummy! (Though my humiliation would have been worse if I had written that rejection.)

A number of years had to erode my embarrassment before I could confess that I had not spotted him at once (as I initially pretended). What a dummy indeed. *The Lime Twig* is a beautiful and brutal book, and when it comes to the engravement of the sentence, no one now writing can match him.

Rainer Maria Rilke's
The Notebooks of Malte Laurids Brigge

There have been books that have struck me like lightning and left me riven, permanently scarred, perhaps burned-out but picturesque; and there have been those that created complete countries with their citizens, their cows, their climate, where I could choose to live for long periods while enduring, defying, enjoying their scenery and seasons; but there have been one or two I came to love with a profounder and more enduring passion, not just because, somehow, they seemed to speak to the most intimate "me" I knew but also because they embodied what I held to be humanly highest, and were therefore made of words which revealed a powerful desire moving with the rhythmic grace of Blake's Tyger; an awareness that was pitilessly unsentimental, yet receptive as sponge; feelings that were free and undeformed and unashamed; thought that looked at all its conclusions and didn't blink; as well as an imagination that could dance on the heads of all those angels dancing on that pin. I thought that the *Notebooks* were full of writing that met that tall order. Of the books I have loved (and there are so many, many more than I could have collected here), from the electrifying alliterations of *Piers Plowman* ("Cold care and cumbrance has come to us all") to the sea-girt singing of Derek Walcott's *Omeros,* there has been none that I would have wished more fervently to have written than this intensely personal poem in prose, this profound meditation on seeing and reading—on reading what one has seen, on seeing what one has read.

Rainer Maria Rilke's *Duino Elegies*

I became a Rilke junkie. I cannot let many days pass without having a fix. The relationship cannot be rationally explained, and I no longer feel the need to. I am not a reader who reads to learn about an author, and I rarely pursue the writer into his or her privacy on account of that person's public utterance; but in Rilke's case, I did: I collected and read every word I could find, whether on or by him, and that is a whole lot of lard. He is the only writer I ever tried seriously to translate, despite his difficulty, and my foreign-language handicaps, for the truth is, I am really a monoglot. Well, I would buy Rilke's kiddie car at auction if it ever came to the block. Who, if I cried, the *Elegies* shout, would hear me among the orders of angels? But I felt I had cried long ago and often, only to be heard now by these poems. They gave me my innermost thoughts, and then they gave those thoughts an expression I could never have imagined possible for them. Furthermore, the poet who thought and wrote these things, for all his shortcomings, actually endeavored to be worthy of his work—and that effort made him, in my eyes, the most romantic of romantics. My passion for this poet was, I thought, a private one, yet I taught his work for thirty years, and even wrote a book, all the while treating his presence in my life as something I kept in a drawer. Strange. These poems also have a remarkable compositional history, and many are the result of the most exemplary inspirational storm our weather-keeping records record.

Rainer Maria Rilke's *Sonnets to Orpheus*

Written in an unheralded and unparalleled burst at the same time that he was furnished the conclusion of the *Elegies,* these poems are also truly awesome, as my daughters, I'm afraid, would say. It is probably embarrassingly clear by now that works of art are my objects of worship, and that some of these objects are idols at best—rich, wondrous, and made of gold—yet only idols; while others are secondary saints and demons, whose malicious intent is largely playful; while still others are rather sacred, like hunks of the true cross or biblical texts, and a few are dizzying revelations. Orpheus is the singing god, whose severed head continued its tune as, in addition to its other modes of dying, it drowned.

And even if one of them suddenly held me against his heart (doesn't the "First Elegy" say?), I would fade in the grip of their completer existence. It is one of Rilke's doctrines, expressed most directly in his poem "The Torso of an Archaic Apollo," that works of art are often more real than we are because they embody human consciousness completely fulfilled, and at a higher pitch of excellence than we, in our skinny, overweight, immature, burned-out souls and bodies, do. Rilke's poems very often seem to me to have been written by someone superhuman.*

I. 1

There rose a tree. O pure uprising!
O Orpheus sings! O tall tree in the ear!
And hushed all things. Yet even in the silence
a new beginning, beckoning, new bent appeared.

---

*All quotations from Rilke's poetry are from William H. Gass. *Reading Rilke.* New York: Alfred A. Knopf, 2000.

Creatures of silence thronged from the clear
released trees, out of their lairs and nests,
and their quiet was not the consequence
of any cunning, any fear,

but was because of listening. Growl, shriek, roar,
shrank to the size of their hearts. And where there'd been
ramshackles to shelter such sounds before—

just dens designed from their darkest desires,
with doorways whose doorposts trembled—
you built a temple in the precincts of their hearing.

Rainer Maria Rilke's Letters

We say that in some letters we see their authors come forth
and reveal themselves, often quite plainly and directly, as D. H.
Lawrence and Lord Byron do in their delicious correspondence;
sometimes inadvertently, as Proust does, with his toadying and his
flattery, which is as insincere as Pascal's wager; or deviously, on tiptoe, as Henry James often does. I think in Rilke's letters we see
someone creating a persona, not hiding or revealing one. He (the
person) wishes he had the sentiments, the style, the skills, the
virtues, which he (the poet) exemplifies and champions in his work.
Eventually, we can see what began as pretense becomes truth; the
person and the poet coalesce. We tend to think of Rilke as a poet
who also wrote an odd, experimental novel; but Rilke's prose is not
confined to one or a few public prose pieces. He wrote thousands of
letters. In these letters, he made his best friends, had his best
thoughts, made his best love. He is present in his letters, when in his
person he is often waving farewell as he says hello. And his letters,
like his poems, were sent to their recipients in his own calligraphi-
cally ornate and careful hand. One has the sense, reading Rilke, that
he is making even the ink.

Postscript

I originally compiled a much longer list, and pared it for the exhibition, mentioned earlier. After I had made my choices and pell-melled my notes about them, I realized that one book was missing which ought—absolutely—to have been present: Freud's *The Interpretation of Dreams,* a work, among all of his others, that made a convert of me for more than twenty years. This masterpiece I just—well, I just forgot. Let it stand for the Nothing that is not here, and the Nothing that is.

THE BOOK OF PREFACES

The editor of this *Book of Prefaces,* Alasdair Gray, has opened it with what he calls an "Advertisement" and followed that with an essay entitled "On What Led to English Literature." Since he deliberately does not distinguish between the various sorts of front matter a volume may contain, they both might be characterized as prefaces. I encountered this laxity with some dismay, although I understand it. The editor did not wish to inhibit his choice of materials by drawing lines none of his examples would obey anyway, or slow his process of selection with quibbles. Nevertheless, to protest sloppy common usage, as well as some traditional waywardness, I think the necessary distinctions should be made.

A *prologue* imparts information that is necessary for the reader to have before beginning a book or watching a performance. The narrative aria that opens *Tristan und Isolde* tells us the story up to the point of the curtain's going up. The prologue to the *Canterbury Tales* describes the occasion for the tale it will frame and introduces the pilgrimage's cast of characters. Prologues are true openings and therefore more essential to the main text than other bits like those souvenir shops on the walk to Saint Michel that may entice readers to dally on their way. For instance, if the main text is in verse, the prologue will feel obliged to follow suit. The prologue should never be by anyone other than the author, though the prologue may be delivered by a prologuer as in *Henry V,* or by a character in the book, play, or opera, as in *Pagliacci,* or by the author under another name.

Carried away by prologomania, Chaucer writes one for his knight, the knight's squire, his prioress, his friar, his monk, his lawyer, his clerk, his merchant, his carpenter, his cook, and so on, including, thank heaven, his good wife from Bath, whose virtue most immediately is that she enables the poet to rhyme "deef" and "Ypres" within the first four lines—and internally to boot. Happily, all of them are included in *The Book of Prefaces*—as well as the stirring prologue to *Piers Plowman.* This is poetry that proves powerful verse needn't be politically puny and pusillanimous just because it alliterates, meanwhile also demonstrating how the deserved vilification of a politician in one period will fit others in other times equally well, corrupt and incompetent governance being drearily the same for every age. Enjoy the lines in which rats consider belling the cat, for instance. An updated English accompanies the original text to facilitate the pleasure.

A *prolegomenon* is a simplified version of a more complicated text or theory; it is therefore something like an introductory course. It covers the main points, leaving out only subtleties and details. The prolegomenon can therefore substitute for the text if you are in a hurry, or can, in some cases, serve as the only text, because, for a prolegomenon, it is the ideas that count. A prolegomenon suggests an intimacy with the thoughts which concern it that only their author might be expected to possess. Immanuel Kant's *Prolegomenon to Any Future Metaphysics* is an example—maybe the only one.

A *preface* explains the meaning, nature, history, or importance of the text, preparing the reader to engage it in a resourceful rather than a dilatory manner, as Granville Barker's *Prefaces to Shakespeare* do. A preface should mean business, but it is not a reduction of its text to bite size. Usually, the works of dead authors get prefaces written by scholars. Imagine the hyena explaining to the jackal the finer qualities of what it is about to eat.

Each of the addenda that concern us here could conceivably be published independently of its home text. This happens, particularly, to prolegomena. They are then said (by me) to be untethered. That is why some of the selections in *The Book of Prefaces* seem sufficient and complete in themselves and others feel fragmentary and rather lost. The selections are frequently abridged, sometimes leaving out both banks.

Occasionally, the forematter is so forceful, so trenchant, so outrageous that it outcrescendos the piece to follow, and subsequently only the overture is played, say it's by von Suppé or Rossini, leaving the opera that occasioned it in wholesome oblivion. A literary example is Theophile Gautier's preface to *Mademoiselle de Maupin*, though it ignores all my splendid distinctions twixt foreword, intro, and preface, as if I hadn't made them yet. This extended polemic has very little to do with the novel itself. It was, in fact, written to lengthen the total text so that it might be issued in two volumes, and would have been better called a fusillade. His attack on the utilitarian character of the bourgeoisie came to be regarded, after May 1834, as Modernism's opening—well, fusillade. Synge's preface to *The Playboy of the Western World* has known a fame equal to the play. Wordsworth's Preface to the *Lyrical Ballads* approaches it.

Although every one of these pieces of prior matter is made of language, only prefaces and forewords must announce an oncoming text. Persons can be introduced, prologues can precede plays, prolegomena run in front of theories. However, a foreword requires a written or printed work it can be the "fore" of. I can say, "Let me preface my remarks . . ." but I cannot permit myself to foreword them. It has been said that the golfer's cry of "Fore!" heralds the ball the way the "Fore!" of a text warns of the word.

An *introduction* should get the reader interested in the subject of the book by briefly describing it, praising its author, and providing a fascinating curriculum vitae without necessarily explaining or parsing the work. The introduction is an extended blurb, a barker's spiel, and hence it is like an old-fashioned advertisement, and may concern itself primarily with the personal history of the author. It permits reminiscence and gossip. Both preface and introduction can apologize for the public's past neglect of the work. The author may write his own blurb, but this is definitely bad form. He will pretend to be introducing his book to the reader, which is a little like introducing his dog. Ideally, it should be by another writer of fame, if not distinction, because an introduction is an endorsement. Introductions are usually a lot of baloney. And there are far too many of them.

If some mushhead were still of the opinion that these aforementioned terms were interchangeable, especially in the mushhead's world, consider this: I may introduce a speaker to an audience, or two people to each other, but I cannot prolegomenon or preface them. I can introduce you to roast quail or to miniature golf, to the prime minister or the Rotary Club, but I cannot even foreword mail.

An introduction presupposes ignorance. When Albert J. Guerard introduced John Hawkes's novel *The Cannibal,* in 1948, he could properly feel both Hawkes and his novel were unknown to most readers. But this is what Guerard begins by saying: "Many introductions exist to persuade the reluctant reader that the classic text under consideration is deservedly a classic, with hidden meanings and beauties." Guerard had been teaching too long and assumed rows of ignorant students were sitting in front of him. You can't call a new novel a classic, however fine you think it is, without puffing a sail loose. An introduction is an introduction, not a nomination. "This is Helen Hoho; she teaches at Heehaw" is quite enough. Not: "This is Helen Hoho, and despite what you have heard, she isn't bad in bed, is rather good with pilaf, and can darn cotton socks like crazy." Indiscreet praise is still slander.

Martin Samson says, endeavoring to "introduce" *The Ambassadors,* "The main purpose of an introduction, as usually written, seems to be the statement of a critical opinion of the literary work concerned. Possibly the best place for such an opinion would be not as prologue but as epilogue, to be read when the book was finished and when one's own tentative judgment had been formed." His loose use of "prologue" should leap out at us by now. In an introduction, some innocuous praise is permitted: "This is Helen Hoho; she is a wonderful teacher, too bad she's been stuck at Heehaw for thirty years."

An *epilogue,* now that it's come up, like its older brother, is a part of the text. It may satisfy the reader's curiosity about the fate of the characters, or contain some acid account of the likely course of its tale, but remarks about the resistance of publishers to genius or the blindness of reviewers to subtlety and wit, as well as pleas for pity on the part of the author for his undeserved plight, should be reserved for an *afterword.*

A *foreword* should be written by the author, at the time of publication, explaining perhaps why the piece was written, anticipating difficulties, alerting the reader to its special qualities, removing current misconceptions, apologizing in advance for defects it may be perceived—vengefully—to possess.

Sometimes a foreword is added to later editions in order to attack previous reviewers, and defend the text from their criticisms (which the author, if shrewd, will never spell out), or to brag in a modest manner about why a new edition seemed necessary, and point to corrections and additions whose prior absence, as useful or required as they may seem now, did not prevent the book from being a big hit.

Perhaps this is the place to warn the reader that the tome he might be holding, titled *Oceans of the World,* also includes seas because the difference between oceans and seas, let alone bays and gulfs, was to the author of *Oceans* never clear or never considered.

Forewords are so often self-serving that I tend to skip them, hoping to hold on to some regard for the writer at least until after the first pallid pages of his book have slipped away into the "nevermore to be remembered." Their premature celebrations of genius are usually a proclivity of men, but a few are so wise and so just their recommendations should be piously followed. Such is the case with King Alfred's greeting to his bishops on the occasion of sending them his translation of Pope Gregory's *Pastoral Care.* "Think how we would be punished in this world, if we neither loved learning ourselves or let other men love it: that we had the name of Christian only, and few of the virtues." He remembers how the Greeks translated every text into their own language, and he encourages this practice in his bishops, so that what is locked in Latin, and so kept from the people, will be set free in their understanding. A great good king indeed.

Early on, information we would now think properly put on the acknowledgments page was consigned to a foreword, as is the case here with the Venerable Bede, who is careful to inform his patron, King Ceolwulf, concerning the sources of the stories he is about to relate, so he may have the comfort of saying, Don't blame me; it's what I've been told: "Of things known about the faith of Christ in Northumbria up to the present day, I do not use the authority of one person, but the words of many truthful witnesses, who knew and remembered the events. . . ."

Addresses are of three kinds. The first (often a poem) is by the author to his or her issue: "Go dumb born book . . ." et cetera, and explores the conceit, frequently invoked, that the book has been whelped the way mammals are, and is sent forth, now, like an orphan, to make its way. The second (often a poem) is directed to the author's patron (or hoped-for patron) (some highborn lowbrow nobleman normally), as Robert Herrick's is posted to the Prince of Wales, and packed with obsequious lies: "Well may my Book come forth like Publique Day, When such a Light as You are leads the way"; the third (often a poem) is from the author to the reader, pretending to be a personal letter from one to the other, and often slyly performing some of a foreword's business.

Caedmon considers his patron to be God. Naturally, he addresses Him, but he does so publicly, letting the rest of us overhear. The regularity in which this is done (in addresses to the Deity) suggests that there is a real concern God may be turning a deaf ear, if He has any ear at all, so someone else had better be listening, if only for the record.

An *author's note* or just a *note* usually serves as a foreshortened preface, though sometimes it combines that with the task of an acknowledgments page. A note had better be a note—that is, a paragraph or two, max—and contain information—several facts per sentence—that may be "tucked away."

Any one of these otherwise-innocent textual members may be misused, for instance, when E. E. Cummings bestows a *dedication* upon all the publishers who have rejected his work.

The above-listed elements may not be explicitly named "Preface" or "Foreword." You have published, in the sixties, a book for which you supplied a preface; now you are reissuing it with additional material called, perhaps, "A View from the Seventies." Whatever it is labeled, if it takes account of the preface to the first edition (as it should), then it is a metapreface. With "metas," all bets are off.

In times past, it was customary to load a book with more of these burdens than is the habit now. Normally, we save introductions for reissues. A fancy edition of *The Way of All Flesh* may contain a frontal essay by Theodore Dreiser, while a cheap "just for study" copy will be hawked by a professor from the Virginia Polytechnic Institute. My treasured copy of Robert Burton's *The Anatomy of Melancholy* has a Preface by F. D. and P. J.-S. and an introduction whose part 1 is by P. J.-S. and whose part 2, briefer, is by F. D., which suggests these initials know the difference. This is followed by Burton's poem, "The Argument of the Frontispiece," next by the frontispiece itself (and another poem, longer, which is an address by the author's pseudonym, Democritus Junior, to his book: "Go forth, my book, into the open day . . ." This done, space is made for still another set of verses titled "The Author's Abstract of Melancholy," with its famous refrain, "Naught so sweet as Melancholy," when, hard upon, I shall encounter an introduction, "Democritus Junior to the Reader," of ninety-three pages. Have we got to grandmother's house yet? No. We now turn a leaf headed "To the Mischievously Idle Reader," written in both prose and verse, and subsequently find the four-page synopsis of the *Anatomy*'s "First Partition," laid out like a densely plowed field.

The Book of Prefaces is got up to resemble a book of bygone days, with much accompanying material in both red and black ink: endpapers with drawings resembling a mural, a decorative title page that finds icons for every English-speaking nation these prefaces have been drawn from, an equally elaborate copyright notice and dedication, unexpectedly a sheet containing the pen-and-ink portraits of every soul who has been remotely connected to the project, and who would permit Alasdair Gray to draw them, including its first and last typists and the project's only sponsor. The margins are crowded with columns in two shades of red ink, called "glosses," and these actually exceed biographical aims to become—well, glosses. A nice touch is an errata card, also doubly inked and in matching type, which can serve as a bookmark, although a purple ribbon leaks out of the book's bottom edge.

Font sizes change like evil purposes; more images (of those who have volunteered glosses and were paid in portraits) clog the rear, where there's a postscript and an index, as well. Dates in very large type fix each entry in its time and control their order, so that were a reader to read this collection straight through (no one expects it, and for dipping into or sipping from this volume, hotels and bathrooms are the venues suggested), they might experience the rich course of English prose from nowhere to now, and also profit from the enterprise by observing changes in the manners and morals of our authors, in their plights and perilous status, from hence to thence.

Alasdair Gray cuts this historical sweep into steps or eras of his own (suffering our customary doubts)—English Remade, c. 1330 to c. 1395; A Great Flowering—Hakluyt to Coke; The Establishment, Dryden to Burns, et cetera, and between them he adds valuable explanatory material. These intersticed essays have, I regret to say, no name. They exist, all the same.

There are supposed to be some Irish authors (harps are pictured), but none of them are very Irish, except Synge. I looked for Yeats and Flann O'Brien but didn't find them. That they didn't write prefaces is scarcely an excuse. Anyway, Synge is almost enough, as he concludes his preface to *The Playboy of the Western World* with these fine lines: "In Ireland, for a few years more, we have a popular imagination that is fiery, and magnificent, and tender; so that those of us who wish to write start with a chance that is not given to writers in places where the springtime of the local life has been forgotten, and the harvest is a memory only, and the straw has been turned into bricks." "In Ireland, for a few years more, we have . . .": What an anguished twist of syntax is this, worthy of a condemned man, and how lovely the phrase "where the springtime of the local life has been forgotten," whose lilt is the last pure lilt in my memory bank, if any lilt is left.

Each section is upfronted by an *epigram* as if engraved upon a calling card of flamboyant design, and some of these are quite likable, as well as brief and paradoxical, as required by the OED. According to Ivor Cutler, "Lord Finook sometimes had to boil his cottages—to get the cottagers out." The divisions of the book that these epigrams grace are more than purely descriptive. One is headed "How Class War Dulled English Literature." Alasdair Gray has provided us with a brief opinionated history of England to accompany his chronologically arranged prefaces. Unopinionated histories are uninteresting.

Most of the examples from earlier times are encrusted with Christianity, but gradually the disagreeable Coverdale is supplanted by gents such as Arthur Golding, who writes a verse forward to his translation of Ovid's *Metamorphoses*. Even so (it is 1565), he is constrained to begin by apologizing: "I would not wish the simple sort offended for too bee, When in this booke the heathen names of feynèd Godds they see." After which we move ahead smartly through Ascham, Holinshed, and North to Hakluyt, Marlowe, and Spenser, where we encounter a true *invocation*. Moral instruction is still uppermost in the minds of our authors, even when they are themselves the sad example, as in the case of Robert Greene, who also warns Marlowe of actors like Shakespeare, whom he believes is a scene thief.

Moral instruction continues to direct matters even when these authors are disavowing it. One hears, almost for the first time, in Marlowe's prologue to *Tamburlaine*, words whose sense says, Reader, it's up to you: "View but his picture in this tragicke glasse, And then applaud his fortunes as you please." Robert Greene, in his preface to *Greenes Groats-worth of Witte*, repents of his life, and warns his fellows, Marlowe in particular, of that upstart crow and thief of baubles, a certain Shake-scene, an ape of excellence. One of the marginal glosses helpfully reminds us that Shake-scene borrowed (and did not return) the plot of *The Winter's Tale* from one of Greene's romances, though Greene was well dead when he did it. Equally often, history was Shake-scene's muse—the muse of Purloinment—but his prologues pretend to call on higher powers: "O for a Muse of Fire, that would ascend The brightest Heaven of Invention . . ."

Aside from flattering their patrons, covering their asses, explaining why they were compelled into publication, diffidently praising their performance, and making promises for their art that not even a muse of fire could quite put a torch to (all sensible moves, I should add, amusing, even edifying, to observe, and certainly not mentioned for censure), the preface is most often the place for a preemptive strike. Occasionally, the writer, anticipating only too accurately a negative response, hands his critics their weapons, as Wordsworth does, moreover with a condescension as massive as a landslide:

> Readers of superior judgment may disapprove of the style in which many of these pieces are executed. It must be expected that many lines and phrases will not exactly suit their taste. It will perhaps appear to them, that wishing to avoid the prevalent fault of the day, the author has sometimes descended too low, and that many of his expressions are too familiar, and not of sufficient dignity. It is apprehended, that the more conversant the reader is with our elder writers, and with those in modern times who have been the most successful in painting manners and passions, the fewer complaints of this kind will he have to make.

In the preface to his *Dictionary*, Dr. Johnson whines (another persistent feature of the genre)—"It is the fate of those who toil at the lower employments of life, to be rather driven by the fear of evil, than attracted by the prospect of good; to be exposed to censure, without hope of praise; to be disgraced by miscarriage, or punished for neglect, where success would have been without applause, and diligence without reward"—a whine, yes, but how perfectly composed. As the reader reads these prefaces, ticked across a clock of ages, he can be expected to exclaim, Another lame excuse, still further transparent self-flattery, one more bitter complaint, abject apology, resentful pose, inadequate defense, insufficient explanation; yet gladly add, on account of the pure delight to the eye they are, But when has lameness or insufficiency—so common, so ordinary; when has flattery—oft offered, oft bought—been so acceptably employed, so agreeably offered, or so well and comfortably expressed?

Erasmus

AN AFTERWORD TO
THE PRAISE OF FOLLY

There is the fool who is foolish from the weaknesses of a mad mind; who honestly knows not what he does, and is ignorant of consequences. There is God's fool, who is foolish because he is indifferent to material concerns, and pursues virtue in a world that has no real regard for righteousness and seldom rewards it. There are fools who feel fortunate to have been made misery's muse; and fools who sincerely believe with the preacher that all is vanity, that nothing is new, yet that everything passes like a fart from a fat meal—gone and good riddance; nevertheless, these fools manage to remain vain, attending their tailor despite the flightiness of fashion, furnishing their flat, purchasing old masters, investing in oil lamps and rubber-soled shoes. There is the fool who has made God's work his business out of presumption, greed, and a passion for power. There is the befooled fool, who lives in a landscape of myth and legend, false promises, and payments to be made now for rewards to be received beyond the grave. There is the fool of meaningless feats: the fool who has written more zeros than anyone alive; who has leaped out of unbuttoned pants; who construes one couplet per academic year, and has carried commas over distances of forty miles. There is the fool of diet, of drink, of dalliance, dice, high jinks, and derring-do; the fool who accepts like Hugo's Hunchback the humiliation of a king's crown and pretends to rule, during the besotted hours of a single day, a rabble who dance like tops and swap their venereal diseases. And there is the fool who plays the fool to save his wisdom from calumny and himself from the gibbet, since if a fool be mad, what he does and says can be excused as merely madness and the devil's inspiration, while if he be a jester and mad only for the moment, still his madness may amuse as his madness is paid to do, so he is protected from complaint and reprisal by becoming a witless hireling; yet because his witlessness has wit, he's attended to, and his riddles turned as a spitted bird is turned till done on all sides. There is no end to fools and foolishness, since each of us can seem a fool to a fool, fool others, be fooled, and fool ourselves; for were we not bamboozled about who we are and how we live and nature's ways, we would have to become—in self-defense and for survival in the face of pitiless truth—one of those fools we, a moment ago, began with: namely, fools who are foolish from a mind gone mad and, like the philosopher Democritus, laugh with a laughter that appreciates the absurd, sees its point, and deftly dodges its damage.

Erasmus, and Thomas More, the man he most admired, were cold-climate humanists: they knew of snow and sleet and frozen fog, chimney smoke and fur; there was no sunny seaside life to be had where they lived, and when pagan thought swept back into Europe, it tended to divide its influence, the Greeks conquering the south, even where Rome once ruled, while Roman ideals plodded off north, where stoic duty would be appreciated, and where the new learning could be pursued in familiar monkish surroundings.

Nothing much is known about Erasmus's unfortunate parents, an ignorance that Charles Reade found to be an advantage, for there were few facts to hinder him when he wrote a novel of thwarted young love purportedly about them, called *The Cloister and the Hearth.* They were, in any case, Dutch, and consequently bore a name—Gerardszoon—quite unlike the Latin one the youthful Erasmus gave himself, adding a bit of hometown distinction: Desiderius Erasmus Rotterdamus, the latter then a village whose precincts had been recently saved from the sea. As his birthplace grew into a town, so did the plot of the family romance, embellished by Erasmus's rivals during his days of fame. His father—it was eventually said—fell in love with a young woman, Margaret, who permitted the expression of his passion with the usual unfortunate results, especially since neither of their families appears to have approved the proposed marriage, let alone their liaison. Gerard was at this delicate moment called away to Rome for causes that remain unknown, and there, although intending to return to rescue Margaret's reputation and save the name of their child, he was delayed for reasons presumably pressing and certainly obscure. Meanwhile, villainous relatives sent him false word of Margaret's death. In the grip of grief, he became a priest, although, I imagine, not before singing an aria so moving it brought a curtain down to conceal his pitiable form.

Upon Gerard's return, he discovered the boy born, Margaret alive, and himself bound by other vows. These vows did not prevent the lovers from living together until the plague made its rather regular return. Unfortunately for the reliability of this tale, Erasmus had an older brother, throwing its timing off. One might conjecture that this elder brother was Margaret's by a previous suitor, which would account for family objections to Gerard's plans. He was certainly as slow and ill-starred as Erasmus was quick and, by fortune, favored. Or maybe he was the child born while Gerard was dawdling about in Rome, and Erasmus was the product of their later and steadier relationship, but this is not an hypothesis a novelist would find appealing.

Although Erasmus does seem to have been illegitimate, his parents formed a firm and caring family that provided for him and his early education. The lay society where his father sent him to school was called the Brethren of the Common Life. It emphasized the teachings of Jesus and recommended a biblically directed though relatively undoctrinal Christian existence. The Brethren had schools throughout the Netherlands and northern Germany, and were known for their emphasis on the inward and purely spiritual qualities of Christianity, but this renown did not guarantee that a particular school might not be more worried about discipline and a compliant demeanor than any actual moral development, and from Erasmus's later accounts, he little liked their repressive strictures or protective ignorance.

Though some of his schoolmates became notable, the lot was like most lots, frugal with curiosity, keenness, and ambition; so the youth must have been a daunting handful, committing Horace and Terence to memory, as J. A. Froude reports, devouring every book that he was permitted to open, excelling at debate, writing essays, odes, and heroic poems, as well as dispatching imprudent letters to his superiors in a Latin so excellent that, in place of praise, only their penmanship could be faulted—which it most predictably was.

Although Erasmus was a bastard and as such was technically barred from any basic service within the Church, at fourteen, after the plague bore his parents off, his guardians, who apparently frittered away his meager patrimony, decided to give Erasmus over to the care of a gang of religious recruiters called the Collationary Fathers. According to Froude, they "made their living by netting proselytes for the regular orders. Their business was to catch in some way superior lads, threaten them, frighten them, beat them, crush their spirits, tame them, as the process was called, and break them in for the cloister." (*Life and Letters of Erasmus.* New York: Charles Scribner's, 1895, pp. 7–8.) As Erasmus's many letters show, his memory was not for words alone. He forgot no imbecility, no injustice or obstruction, no slight or humiliation, no browbeating, bullyragging, or flogging.

So, in due course, Erasmus was placed in a monastery, where his priestly life, equally illegitimate, would begin, though it was already too late for its teachings to alter his early sympathy for simple Christian virtue, or his passion for books, or his tendency to challenge his superiors, whom he perhaps was too ready to think lazy, inept, or foolish. During Erasmus's entire life, he spoke well of a modesty, a humility, a forbearance he could never have found flourishing in himself.

The monastery, like so many, was long on discipline, middling about academic regimen, and short on learning. Erasmus found no pleasure in his fellow monks' pleasures; he avoided his brothers, as brothers are inclined to do; his aloofness was interpreted as disdain; his rations were cut, except for Friday's inevitable salt cod, whose flavorless flesh and harsh smell he could scarcely stomach, so consequently his delicate constitution suffered; he slept poorly; his books were removed from his cell and the library closed to him—it was apparently better to be habitually drunk than persistently studious. Erasmus detested each of the monastery's rules and every routine. He resolved to live his life outside all walls and beyond the hearing of orders.

As for fish, Erasmus waited until 1526 to publish his funny and scurrilous dialogue between a fishmonger and a butcher: *Concerning the Eating of Fish*. The butcher alleges that a dispensation is coming from the College of Cardinals, permitting people to eat what they wish, which means the fishmonger will soon be out of business. But the monger is as delighted as the butcher, for when meat was forbidden, it was desired; now that it is allowed, flesh will lose its allure, and thus more fish will be scaled than before. This is only an opening exchange, of course, in a dialogue of some length, which became, along with *In Praise of Folly*, another center of dispute. Its blunt speech and boisterous tone remind us that François Rabelais was a contemporary.

Importunate people frequently discover that their disagreeable pushiness profits them, and Erasmus was able to obtain a position as secretary to the bishop of Combray, a post that bore him away from one service into that of another; for which he was grateful, but not sufficiently to remove discontent, so that shortly the bishop was relieved to advance Erasmus's education by allowing him to proceed to Paris, where his poems had preceded his trunks, thus permitting him to revolve in witty but indolent circles.

Paris, then as now, was generous with its pleasures—amusements which Folly would later be ready to recommend—but it was also prepared to ruin his stomach with sorry fish, surround him with friendly companions who couldn't care less about anything at all, so that, once more, he would see how purely formal devotions and unkempt dissolution had replaced study and discovery. Desperately in need of money, if he were to live on his own, he wrote finely phrased but begging letters and did hack work when he could obtain it. Finally, a friend found him a job as a tutor to the son of a landed Zeeland lady. The fruitless journey there involved such a remarkable incident, as Hendrik Willem van Loon reports, that I must repeat it here, though I encourage a prudent disbelief as the safest attitude for the reader.

Erasmus and a companion needed to travel north, during what was a dreadful winter, to an island, Noord-Beveland, which a sizable leak in the land had created, but they were driven to a halt by the worst sleet storm (it was said) in a hundred years. Although the water was frozen, they could not see or stand, and had no sleigh, so they sat on their bottoms with their backs to the wind and let it blow them across the ice to the other side. On account of the lady's most recent romance, the disapproval of her relatives, and a lack of cash, the job disappeared into the winter where the scenery dwelled, making their bottom-borne voyage vain.

Alas, Folly seems to have authored this fiction. Erasmus went north for other reasons, and relates van Loon's anecdote in vivid yet less mythmaking prose:

> Juno, who hates poets, called in Æolus to help her, and Æolus beat down upon us with hail, and snow, and rain, and wind, and fog—now one—now all together. After the storm came a frost; snow and water froze into lumps and sheets of ice. The road became rough. The mud hardened into ridges. The trees were coated with ice. Some were split, others lost their branches from the weight of the water which had frozen upon them. We rode forward as we could, our horses crunching through the crust at every step, and cutting their fetlocks as if

with glass. Your friend Erasmus sate bewildered on a steed as astonished as himself. I cursed my folly for entrusting my life and my learning to a dumb beast. Just when the castle came in sight we found ourselves on a frozen slope. The wind had risen again and was blowing furiously. I got off and slid down the hill, guiding myself with a piked staff which acted as rudder.

(First version: *The Praise of Folly*, introduced and illustrated by Hendrik Willem van Loon. New York: Classics Club, 1942, p. 53; second version: Froude, quoting a letter of Erasmus, pp. 28–29.)

"Erasmus of Rotterdam" was losing its meaning. "Far from Rotterdam" would be more appropriate. Classical scholars were rare and in demand. Erasmus became peripatetic and thus more European by the year, and when he finally settled down, it was to be in Switzerland. By 1499, he was in London, and would soon visit Oxford and Cambridge, as well. There he met Thomas More, even younger than he; John Colet, precisely his age; a passionate humanist, William Grocyn, who introduced the teaching of Greek to Oxford; and Thomas Linacre, scholar and medico, later physician to Henry VIII. These new friends reinforced Erasmus's desire to learn Greek, and in three years—he was so energized—Erasmus was translating and editing Greek texts, from whose pages he picked ripe and relevant quotes for a compilation of aphorisms, to which he tacked his own, mostly amused, reflections. After citing the passage in Scripture that says that priests are obliged to devour the sins of their flocks, Erasmus remarks that these sins appeared to be so severe that only fine wine enabled the holy fathers to digest them. Since his pockets were, as usual, out of pence, he published these gems under the title, *Adagia*. The book was immensely popular, causing him to enlarge the collection through many editions; consequently when *The Praise of Folly* made Erasmus famous, it did so only by adding soup to a full bowl.

Erasmus returned to England many times to visit his friends and refuel his engine. Because their relationship was one of face-to-face conversation and wine-smoothed dispute, they were able to take the measure of one another, and the influence of a personality was often greater than that of any written work. Because his visits were repeated and often lengthy, each of these men, as well as many others in France, Germany, Italy, and Switzerland, became lifelong friends and stimulating associates.

Erasmus wanted the Church to allow the study of pagan authors because he often found them wise and in every way as virtuous as the accepted saints. Horace and Cicero, among them, praised the kind of character and recommended sorts of action that any Christian might admire and seek to emulate. Young Erasmus's first effort, *The Book Against the Barbarians,* argued for a harmony between classical and Christian virtues. There were many others—Boccaccio and Chaucer had already made fun of the nobility and the holy servants of the Church—who shared his desire to widen the scope of the mind so that reason might determine one's worldly views, duty dominate the social sense, and Jesus command the affections. In the spirit of the Old Testament prophets, these critics felt the Church was too devoted to ritual and rigmarole, to hollow argument and token service, to the secular profits of its sacred calling, and should practice what it ought to preach: a little gentle forbearance and liberality, some generosity and acceptance. To be honest and trustworthy, one did not need to consult the schoolmen ("Why is it not enough to hate sin?" he asks); the truth did not require a doctrine drawn up in its defense before it could be uttered; learning did not ask ignorance to keep scholarly subjects safely circumscribed; yet as Erasmus writes—again, in one of his letters:

> It may happen, it often does happen, that an abbot is a fool or a drunkard. He issues an order to the brotherhood in the name of holy obedience. And what will such an order be? An order to observe chastity? An order to be sober? An order to tell no lies? Not one of these things. It will be that a brother is not to learn Greek; he is not to seek to instruct himself. He may be a sot.

> He may go with prostitutes. He may be full of hatred and mal-
> ice. He may never look inside the scriptures. No matter. He
> has not broken any oath. He is an excellent member of the
> community. While if he disobeys such a command as this from
> an insolent superior there is stake or dungeon for him instantly.
> (Froude, p. 68.)

Keep the hours, tally your attendance at Mass, tell your beads, fon-
dle the relics, bruise your knees, but do not imitate Christ. When, in
1503, Erasmus published *Handbook of a Christian Soldier,* that was
his complaint.

Erasmus tells us that the title *Encomium Moriæ* was a pun on
Thomas More's name, and that the idea of the work came from con-
versations they had together. In a sense, then, it is also "A Praise of
More," and, in the spirit of George Santayana's sonnet, which begins
"It is not wisdom to be only wise, / And on the inward vision close
the eyes, / But it is wisdom to believe the heart," we can understand
Folly to be wiser than it was sometimes wise to be.

For who but Folly can recognize the many follies that exist, let
alone know how to praise them? Because that is what Folly does: it
sees that what is commonly called folly is folly only in ways hidden
from view and rarely discerned, and what is called churchly and
scholarly and righteous and sensible is seldom so, but more likely a
further form of foolishness. Those who pretend to represent the best
may be among the worst, while those who are said to revel in vice
may be promoting life.

The response to Erasmus's books was enthusiastic from the first.
The Church was widely felt to be tyrannical, self-serving, and corrupt, as I've said, and the dissatisfactions that Luther would exploit
were ready to welcome the work of More and Erasmus as they
already had that of Thomas à Kempis. Yet it was Erasmus's translation of the New Testament's Greek, and his correction of Saint
Jerome's Latin version, that earned him such esteem that a scholar
might boast he had received a letter from Erasmus and gain respect
by virtue of its signature.

Formidable bastions like those the scholastics had erected to protect themselves may appear to fall suddenly (the Soviets lose their Union seemingly overnight), but many small enemies have been at work undermining the walls for a long time, not just one large army at the gates armed with shouts, showy uniforms, and flags. Nation-states were forming and towns were growing by guilds and leagues. Voyages of discovery, both geographical and scientific, had lengthened every distance, even to the stars. Athens and Rome were being rebuilt by the imagination and occupied by the mind. Erasmus—immensely civilized and cosmopolitan—was just the man for this enterprising and industrious wider world.

In his letters, Erasmus often referred to himself in the third person, especially when adopting an ironic mode, so that one message might begin: "Your Erasmus gets on well . . ." This is precisely the strategy chosen for *The Praise of Folly*. Folly's tone is also present in the correspondence, letters that got handed round like leaflets.

> . . . the English girls are divinely pretty. Soft, pleasant, gentle, and charming to the Muses. They have one custom which cannot be too much admired. When you go anywhere on a visit the girls all kiss you. They kiss you when you arrive. They kiss you when you go away; and they kiss you again when you return. Go where you will, it is all kisses; and, my dear Faustus, if you had once tasted how soft and fragrant those lips are, you would wish to spend your life here. (Froude, p. 45.)

Erasmus always spoke and wrote his mind, so it seems right that the first folly should be frankness: Say whatever comes into your head, without circumspection and revision. When we edit ourselves, we seek to persuade by means of flourishes that conceal the naked truth the way calligraphy may obscure the letter it celebrates; or we worry about whether what we say shall be well received, and so soften our thoughts, or turn them to show a nicer side. It is folly to speak as an innocent child does, as an idiot savant can, or as a follower of Christ should.

Folly claims Plutus and Neotes—wealth and youth—as parents;

nowadays we would say moneybags and a gold digger, perfectly paired. They called their child Moria, as if they knew that, ages after, Sir Thomas More's name would complete the pun, just as this exemplary man would laugh as Democritus had done at the diligent foolhardiness of his fellows. More, like Folly himself, was doubtless born smiling. He died with a grin on his severed head, we must imagine, because he is reputed to have asked his executioner to spare his beard, since his beard at least had committed no crime. Serious levity is permitted the Christian, for did not Jesus rename Simon, his disciple, in Aramaic, Cephas, or "rock," which in the Greek gospels is translated as Peter (*petra,* also "rock") so he might then say, "Upon this rock I shall build my church"?

Suckled by two pairs of breasts, Drunkenness and Stupidity, and surrounded by her handmaidens, Self-love, Flattery, Forgetfulness, Laziness, Pleasure, Delirium, and Luxury—the seven indolent sins—Folly is raised royally: a nutty, rich, sybaritic, ass-kissing, daydreaming narcissist, supremely suited for service at court, in business, or a papal entourage. So she would soon know what went on in self-serving society as well as in the selfish self.

The presence of Folly's second folly is made obvious by her boast: that among the gods, Folly is the one who brings good things to man—existence itself, as if that were a good—for if lustful pleasure did not drive men to risk their dignity, their fortunes, and their lives in heedless fornication, wombs would starve, and the race would become endangered, dwindle away; there'd be no souls to save or faggots to furnish the fires of hell that, with nothing to consume but themselves, would end utterly ash.

To argue the least obvious, to plead the absurd, to fly in the face of received opinion—that is Folly's office—but she is to do so by employing a strategy worthy of her, a strategy that depends, as the con artist does, on the greedy desires of men. She recommends sin, and her listeners laugh because they are supposed to be, like Calvin Coolidge, against it; but her discourse discloses the truth: If we are enjoying anything, it is probably deemed wicked and should be denied us, and if we seek release from our pain, we ought to be blamed for our intent and punished for its success; meanwhile, priests, Popes, cardinals, kings, bishops, princes, monks, nuns, abbots, ministers of state, courtiers, friars, theologians (in short, our leaders and their lackeys) relish their depravity and everything forbidden—no otherwise than we in what we want, only otherwise in what we and they receive.

To act as if existence were to be prized, guarded, extended, ennobled even, is to commit the folly of follies. In 1500, life was hard: its beginnings hazardous, its maintenance laborious, its span brief, its conclusion miserable. Erasmus, whose conditions were more comfortable than most, writes to a friend:

I am not so greatly attached to life; having entered upon my fifty-first year, I judge I have lived long enough; and on the other hand, I see in this life nothing so excellent or agreeable that a man might wish for it, on whom the Christian creed has conferred the hope of a much happier life, in store for those who have attached themselves closely to piety. Nevertheless, at present, I could almost wish to be rejuvenated for a few years, for this only reason that I believe I see a golden age dawning in the near future. (Quoted by J. Huizinga. *The Waning of the Middle Ages.* New York: Doubleday Anchor, 1954, p. 32.)

If monks clung to the writings of the Church as they might logs in an open ocean, and even skeptics like Erasmus saw the promise of land in a drowned leaf, poets exhibited no such sanguinity. Eustache Deschamps, for example, made the following moan:

> Time of mourning and temptation,
> Era of anger, envy, consternation,
> Time of torpor and damnation,
> An age defined by declination,
> Time of terror, error, horror,
> Period of falsehood, pride, and strife,
> Time without honor or honest judgment,
> World full of sorrow that shortens life.

Gold is not a good color for an era anyway. Money, for instance, is our motto, and it has tarnished us. But, for Erasmus, gold it would be.

> Learning is springing up all round out of the soil; languages, physics, mathematics, each department thriving. Even theology is showing signs of improvement. Theology, so far, has been cultivated only by avowed enemies of knowledge. The pretence has been to protect the minds of the laity from disturbance. All looks brighter now. (Froude, p. 186.)

Golden ages are baubles that bewitch. Nowadays, Folly would be quick to point out that this or that church's promises of paradise are merely encouragements to the miserable to endure with docility their slavery and suffering in this life out of their hope for a future one—a salvation whose failure to appear never disappoints. The more immediate progress that Erasmus foresaw was not to happen, either. Sectarian conflict made such hopes wholly vain and deepened the darkness of his declining days. In less than a year, resentments that had lain fallow burst forth like eager weeds, because the earth was being turned. Clergy everywhere had suffered his lash for a long time; now the monks of Louvain found the courage to attack him; this pulpit—and then that—followed suit, and was the place for an angry sermon. His supporters were no help, returning shout for shout and answering every invective with a curse.

Erasmus hoped to harmonize classical and Christian ways; that proved impossible. He wished to reform the Church from within by filling it with Christianity once again; instead, it leaked like a sieve. He was accused of attacking an ancient institution without offering anything rejuvenating in return; however, he would not replace the dogmas he despised with others equally awful. So in the face of Luther's challenge, and the promise of reforms Erasmus had often urged, the humanist appeared to temporize, to attack the priesthood while enjoying the protection of the Pope; when, in fact, for a man whose contempt was cold and scorn rational, between two fanaticisms, there was nothing to choose. In fact, there were madmen everywhere, and no one they would amuse.

> [April 10, 1532] The factions here will leave no one alone. Where the Evangelicals are in power they do as they please, and the rest must submit; we are already Lutherans, Zwinglians, and Anabaptists; the next thing will be we shall turn Turks. [August 20, 1531] Never was so wild an age as ours; one would think six hundred Furies had broken loose from hell. Laity and clergy are mad together. . . . I do not know what the Pope intends. As burning heretics at the stake has failed, the priests now wish to try the sword. It is not for me to say if they are right. The Turks perhaps will not leave them leisure for the experiment. The better way would be to restore the Gospel as a rule of life, and then choose a hundred and fifty learned men from all parts of Christendom to settle the points in dispute. Opinions on special subjects need not be made Articles of Faith. (Froude, pp. 396–397.)

Murder, Erasmus knew, solved nothing. It only made murderers. Reason could only look on in despair, another human faculty to be abused—along with the ability to laugh.

Time has destroyed many things, including the clock's face: Countries have changed their names, their occupants even; cities have risen, only to be ground into dust; seas have dried up, islands sunk, glaciers melted, mountains exploded; wealth, regal power, influence has been dissipated—inheritance frittered, credit used up, goodwill wasted; customs have changed—clothes, cosmetics, manners, diet (what is safe to eat, what is forbidden)—turned like collars, altered like cuffs; standards of beauty are, like heroes on horseback, extolled, then toppled from their mounts, or screwed like a whore in a cheap house; methods and means of war are embraced or abandoned; the way plagues rage—even what the epidemics are—shift as the winds do their force and direction; beliefs have been dissed, disposed of, replaced, species exterminated, languages lost, words forsaken or respelled, for who reads Chaucer easily now without a bit of practice, even the Franklin's tempting menus . . .

> Without bake mete was never his hous,
> Of fissh and flessh, and that so plenteuous
> It snewed in his hous of mete and drynke.
> Of alle deyntees that men koude thynke . . .

so that we often cannot recognize the past when we first encounter it: Who is a béguine? How long is a paternoster? What are gillies? Yet there remain constants: the greed of our guts, the desires of our loins, the hopes of our hearts, our fears, our anxious eyes, our need of love; because people have always cherished memories of evil done to their ancestors; they have gotten drunk, stolen kisses, picked pockets, eaten too much, murdered their enemies, whose grandfathers are said to have murdered theirs, lied to authorities, believed bunk, betrayed their gods, their kings, their countries, their spouses, beaten their children, seduced the maids, backbit and tattled, slandered and perjured and maligned. Be reminded that even in Erasmus's day games and sporting affairs were often forbidden because of the violence they provoked—men were murdered for cheating at chess; and though we now sometimes play bingo at the behest of the Church, the casino is as common as the cold, and the state runs the numbers racket for the sake of the public schools. Over time, only what has been enjoined has changed, not its practice, for we beat up our umpires and upbraid our opponents as we have in all the so-called golden ages; consequently, Folly may preach to us today as it spoke to yesterday's fools and dupes and victims, in the same terms, in the same tones, to complain of our life's bitter business and all the blood shed in wars between snarling dogmas—vicious and unrestrainable—when what is wanted is a bit of simple decency, an honest show of kindness, and a soft foot for the common road.

A THOUSAND AND ONE NIGHTS

We all know about Aladdin, Sinbad, Ali Baba, the rook's egg, the thieves' cave. There's a rule that requires us to begin our lives as children. We will have seen or heard and thereby passed a night or two, in some pop or papped-up version, even if we have never leafed the picture book or read Burton's luxuriant prose. Splendid stories eminently suitable for children—that's the line. Yet these tales were originally told not by a campfire, in some mom's soothing voice, or listened to in the lap of dearest daddy, but—instead of the once-customary cigarette—enjoyed during the calm following copulation, after lengthy and enervating lovemaking: the man a murderer of his mistresses, the woman a willing but oft-tupped victim, while a third, the belabored lady's sister, naps beneath the bouncing bed, where she's been staying out of love's way until tale time comes and she can clear her throat to request a bit of postcoital edification and escape.

Sex doesn't save the women the king beds. Their cries of pleasure, faked or real, only remind him of the faithlessness of the female, and the shame that is their game. Fictions, instead, do the trick. They do the trick because they charm, but charm because they never really end—or rather, because the climax of each tale, prolonged sometimes over many nights, occurs only within the words, and affects their always-eager auditors in quite another way than physical release. Tale time is dream time, although everyone's awake. Replete, the king sinks into story instead of sleep. It is the dream alone that defers the dream spinner's death—on one thousand and one occasions.

How shall we say it came into being—this strange, perhaps magical, text? The way small creeks and streams combine to create a river? As alleys in an ancient Arab town stumble and twist into a market square? In order, later, to present for the pleasure of Jorge Luis Borges the offspring of a labyrinth? Or as if many days, over and done with and torn from the calendar, had nevertheless survived their own passing to come together and shape another life—a night life, this time? And who knows when or how this new union may dissolve as Destiny decides?

At least as early as the middle of the ninth century, a cycle entitled *The Book of the Tale of the Thousand Nights* was apparently put together and written down in Arabic. In its nearly thousand-and-one-year journey to our time, these Arabian contes drew additions, endured omissions, submitted to revisions, suffered expurgations, were betrayed by translations, fussed over by annotations, and stuffed into editions aimed at special interests, while experiencing normal negligence and the customary incompetence of sellers, scribes, scholars, and consumers: the tattering, dispersal, and destruction of copies, the corruption of the text, the misunderstanding of its meaning, the exploitation of its exotic scenes and settings, as well as the decline of its importance into what, so ironic for the *Nights,* we call bedtime stories.

Robert Irwin's companion to *The Arabian Nights* will describe how these humble and mainly entertaining street stories grew into an enormously influential masterpiece. He will talk about the way the themes in these stories manifest themselves; he will point out their motifs and explain the uses, often odd, to which they have been put; he will describe the vicissitudes these adventures underwent, and the unlikelihood of their accumulation; he will admire their earthy details, their shrewd understanding, the splendid craft of their contriving; he will walk the same streets the stories do and enjoy the sights; he will learnedly, yet without pomposity, discuss the ambivalence of these tales regarding homosexuals, the character and status of the women in them, the mostly futile attempts to evade what Destiny has writ; and he will comment fairly on the *Nights'* love of the ordinary, their attraction to the miraculous, their occasional cruelty, their matter-of-fact but bawdy interests; he will explain the relation of these frequently fantastic tales to the routines of every day, to the fated outcomes of actions, to the relentless harshness or unmerited good luck of one's lot. (In Arabic, he will point out, sometimes the sentence never stops.) Every dimension of his scholarship is impressive, but most admirable of all is the easy and eloquent manner of its presentation. So I suggest that you think of this book as a true and unstealthy companion, such as Dunyazade, Scheherazade's sister, was; and keep it conveniently by, though not beneath, your bed, where you can follow the pleasure of the *Nights* themselves (in Husain Haddawy's readily available and fine contemporary translation), along with another from Robert Irwin's chapter on lowlife, or the one on marvels—whatever properly complements the story you've just concluded.

The origins of storytelling are all oral, of course. Some stories are reverently believed and retained in the tribal memory through repeated voice, thereby placing the community in the handhold of its history. But belief by itself is a state of mind easily feigned, a gift as temporary as attention, offered and withdrawn like a smile, so that storytellers plying their trade in the bazaar are both believed and doubted at the same time. They sometimes instruct, satirize, and warn; they sometimes tie their tales to precise times, exact facts; but, more often, their words create a world of might and maybe, both magical and matter-of-fact, far off and nearby, wondrous and banal. They are paid by the ears they please. They learn to entertain. Kings may have their jesters and their troubadours, while ordinary folk get small relief from work and worry, chained to their daily chores; but there are always layabouts, idlers who fill the bars, who hang out in the markets, and whose heads are empty enough to let in the sounds of another life.

All sorts listen, of course—these stories have a broad appeal—but listening and looking, writing and reading, have always required leisure, whether laziness provided it, or inherited money, or sheer luck. Madame Bovary read too many romances. Villon hung out with a bad lot. The theater is filled with pimps and whores. And the widely running tale takes time to tell, time off to listen to, rest to revel in, and a meditative mind to relish. Proust is several summer vacations long. And *A Thousand and One Nights* will not pass in a wink, though in some of the stories events may move so fast or be so compressed, life will seem that swift.

The storyteller has to have a head full of history, narratives and characterizations, epithets and verbal formulas, moral lessons and other upshots. Though no retelling will be word for word and there are many ways to pluck a plot, the essentials have got to be there, the proper effect achieved. The Jewish physician's tale has to stay the Jewish physician's tale. Moreover, recital is a slow sit in the seats compared to the rapidity of reading, especially now, when we tend to look at language rather than listen to it; so the rhapsode or the tale spinner, like the Ancient Mariner, will want to keep one hand on our lapel. He will certainly not ignore the response of his audience, but learn what pleases, what bores, what reinforces active prejudices, what brings down the house or sets the table on a roar. But just as surely, he will suit his own fancy, too, and allow his inventions to have their moment in his hour.

He'll pick up an anecdote in one town, a colorful phrase in another; from a talkative traveler hear a bit of business too good to be left out of his repertoire. And his stories, like the analyst's fifty-minute hour, will tend to round themselves off at a point near his listeners' patience, perhaps at a moment of anxious expectation, so that the audience will return on the morrow for another of poor Pauline's perils, and her hoped-for rescue from the clutches of the villain by Hairbreath Harry.

And in the process, stories will pass from one language to another. Action, agent, outcome, lesson best survive such movements, for fancy verbalization is just dress and fashion. It can be added at whim, divested with a wink. The tales will consequently be like large handsome houses with surprisingly cramped interiors (a complaint about the *Nights* that has been frequently voiced); but I like to think that the readers who listen to Scheherazade, as if they wore the ears of the king, will invent a motive and create a character for this young lady who has willingly placed her life in jeopardy; who allows herself to be fondled while in fear of death; and who boldly figures to ward off the fate of so many others by telling tales until dawn interrupts and the sun is suspended, as the king's interest is, till darkness stimulates desire again (the rhythm is one of love/breath), and the stories can be begun again.

King Shahriyar has persuaded himself (not without evidence) that the women he wives will betray him during the first half instant of opportunity, and, as he knows, with anyone handy, too—kitchen boys, black slaves—no one is secure, for the king himself, his royalty unknown, has made a cuckold of a demon while the demon slept like still grass through the transports of his accomplished wife's newest adultery. In order to avoid being deceived a second time, King Shahriyar decides to marry for one night only, devouring, like an ogre, an apple a day, and in this fashion prevent his betrayal and shame, and keep his peace of mind. The community soon begins to feel the drain. The king's desire has become a plague. So the beautiful, well-read, and wise Scheherazade offers to risk her life—risk it, but not surrender it, because she has a plan.

The frame for these tales is concerned with one thing: the restoration of the king's trust. Scheherazade will bear her husband three children before his "fatwa" is lifted, so that she will have been pregnant during at least 710 of their 1,000 nights of love—and, presumably, recovering from childbirth for many of the rest. But these are details that have no bearing on the content or continuity of her accounts; nor is the state of her father's—the vizier's—health of any concern, although he must execute his daughter Scheherazade if her strategy fails; nor is the king's habit of falling asleep on state occasions, neglecting the country's business, worth a moment's mention; nor the fact that while the string of these stories protects them like an amulet, the virginal daughters of the kingdom have been regularly spirited away to stay with relatives in London, Berlin, New York, and Paris, so that by tale's end Scheherazade's sister, Dunyazade (nightly asnooze beneath the bed, don't forget), is the only comely maiden remaining in the entire realm.

Realism in *The Arabian Nights* is reserved for other things: food, for instance, such as the pomegranate-seed dish (preserved in almonds and sweet julep and flavored with cardamom and rosewater), which plays such an important role in the witty and altogether wonderful "Story of the Two Viziers." Here, whether there is too little sugar or not enough pepper in the food is crucial. Nor are the little rituals of dining neglected.

> They ate together, and Badr al-Din kept putting morsels, now in 'Ajib's mouth, now in the eunuch's, until they were satisfied. They rose up, and Badr al-Din poured water on their hands and, loosening a towel from his waist, gave it to them to wipe their hands with, and sprinkled them with rosewater from a casting bottle. Then he ran out of the shop and rushed back with an earthenware pitcher containing a sweet drink, flavored with rosewater and cooled with snow. (Husain Haddawy's translation.)

Perhaps the flattest chapter in Robert Irwin's otherwise perfectly flavored book is the one called "Formal Readings." This is not through any fault of his, but because the efforts of scholars, critics, and folklorists to classify and anatomize the *Nights* seem for the most part quite beside the point, and their remarks on repetition (so central to the structure of these tales as a whole, as well as to their various parts) are relatively tame and predictable.

I won't retell the "Story of the Two Viziers," though I feel temptation take me by the pen and pull me to its paper. It should be sufficient to say that a cook's shop has been vandalized, the cook thrashed, and then carted about in a locked chest, apparently because he has not put enough pepper in one dish. Here's how one portion of the cook's lament sounds in Husain Haddawy's splendid version.

Badr al-Din said, "Because the pomegranate dish lacked pepper, you have beaten me, smashed my dishes, and ruined my shop, all because the pomegranate dish lacked pepper! Isn't it enough, O Muslims, that you have tied me and locked me up in this chest, day and night, fed me only one meal a day, and inflicted on me all kinds of torture, because the pomegranate dish lacked pepper? Isn't it enough, O Muslims, to have shackled my feet that you should now make a crosslike figure to nail me on, because I have cooked a pomegranate dish that lacked pepper?" Then Badr al-Din pondered in bewilderment and asked, "All right, suppose I did cook the dish without pepper, what should my punishment be?" The vizier replied, "To be crucified." Badr al-Din said, "Alas, are you going to crucify me because the pomegranate dish lacked pepper?" and he appealed for help, wept, and said, "None has been crushed as I have been, and none has suffered what I have suffered. I have been beaten and tortured, my shop has been ruined and plundered, and I am going to be crucified, all because I cooked a pomegranate dish that lacked pepper! May God curse the pomegranate dish and its very existence!" and as his tears flowed, he concluded, "I wish that I had died before this calamity."

The almost fugal return of the missing pepper to the prose—the phrase beginning a sentence for the pleasure of ending it—perfectly mimics poor Badr al-Din's bewilderment, his futile exasperated outrage, and elevates the absurdity of his crime, as well as his threatened punishment, to operatic heights—well, at least those of Gilbert and Sullivan.

This frame tale, to distinguish it from its imitators (*The Decameron, The Heptameron, The Pentameron, The Canterbury Tales*, Borges, Barth, Calvino), might better be called a "chain tail," because its framing devices do not merely box its stories in, imbed them, as logicians so appropriately say; they link them by beginning a new one while the old one is being told, and continuing it into still a third, as if to staple or stitch (as the ancient rhapsodes were said to do) these narratives together. The frame appears in the very number, now famous, which names them: **I** o o **I** . . . one thousand nights and a night—that is, for a very long time, and then some.

The frame-tale format seems to spring naturally from the way gossip comes and goes, as well as the way we interrupt ourselves, start several hares at once: Fred told me that Mae said Irene was sleeping with that guy Ralph described as a Don Juan. (Don Juan's conquests came to 1,003, the odd number always suggesting that additions might be made at any moment.) Do we want to learn more about Ralph before we return to Irene and her guy? He's a hunk, I hear, who was a lifeguard in Santa Monica once.

Certainly, Scheherazade admits to no originality. "I heard, O happy King," she says; or "It is related, O King, that Ja'far said to the caliph . . ." She has been an auditor, herself, as her sister and the king are (as we are, sitting on Dunyazade's stool), and now they can transmit the gift she gives them to others, without losing the least feature of the story. For each tale ends in an ear, only to begin life on the tongue again. Moreover, it is the pull of the possible dénouement that gives us the patience to take pleasure in the many delays which lovemaking imposes on the way to its climax; for lovers can be in many places at once, lips and thighs and fingers touching (the parenthetical is an unexpected caress); there is a rhythm to it, as well as a pattern of uncovering and discovering, of encountering developments so surprising, so tender, so alluring, the lovers nearly break into song (or, anyway, into poetry, as the tales often do in their post-mod way); nor can we avoid the resemblance between the king's two intentions (which amount to taking a maiden's head), and what goes on in Scheherazade's bed (since it is truly her bed now), or with what happens when our companion, Robert Irwin's enticing book, tells us how . . .

But morning overtook this reviewer, and he lapsed into silence.

La Vie Trèshorrificque

GARGANTUA AND PANTAGRUEL

So what does our ancient author say is the shape of Socrates' nose? A nose of such importance, always well into other people's business, might be imagined to be sharp as a knife, pointed like a whittled stick, nostriled in the style of the truffle pig so as to capture the least whiff of opinionated puffery and to disinhale when the odor proves to be misleading—in truth, a *nez pointu,* the term our esteemed authority uses for the description of his mentor and his muse; however, Andrew Brown, the most recent translator (2003) of Rabelais's masterpiece, *Gargantua and Pantagruel,* knows that Socrates is never represented thus, but was given pop eyes and a snub nose whenever his visage was set in stone, so he silently corrects the text and blunts the knife: ". . . with his snub nose, his eyes like a bull's, and the face of a madman." Besides, John Cowper Powys, who Englished his favorite selections in 1948, set the precedent in nose snubbing. One wonders how many such corrections Brown has made, tacit as a Trappist.

Rabelais writes for the convivial, and consequently for those who must have poisoned their livers and contracted the pox, because syph was the New World's swap with Europe in their exchange of epidemics; it was the sixteenth century's AIDS, heedless pleasure's penance; and, although the clap can now turn on lights, alcohol has never changed its ways. Thus he welcomes us to his feast on what might be Inflation Sunday during Hypocrites' Holiday in the year of the Warmonger, 2004, or maybe 1532—it's much the same, since swilling, swiving, corruption and conniving, fanaticism, bigotry, and bloodshed haven't changed, and the sports bars are still full of opinion.

For a work that is rumored to be loose as a noodle, *Gargantua* moves immediately to make significant allusions. The first is to Plato's *Symposium* and the speech of Alcibiades in praise of his mentor, Socrates, whom he compares to an apothecary's box that is adorned with improbable figures, from harpies and satyrs to flying goats and saddled ducks, each image designed to provoke mirth, yet a box whose interior is as precious as a casket of the Magi, full of . . . well, among our several renderers, there is some difference. Thomas Urquhart, the earliest and most esteemed translator (1653), offers "balm, ambergreese, amomon, musk, civet, with several kinds of precious stones, and other things of great price," and our aforesaid Andrew Brown follows suit, overall more obedient to the text, while Penguin Classic's J. M. Cohen replaces "precious stones" with "mineral essences," perhaps an improvement; however, Jacques LeClercq (whose version [1936] spoke so persuasively to me when I was a tad because it was the translation in the Modern Library, the first library I knew) is expansive and explanatory, with "balsam of Mecca, ambergris from the sperm whale, amomum from the cardmon, musk from the deer and civet from the civet's arsehole—not to mention various sorts of precious stones, used for medical purposes, and other invaluable possessions."

Rabelais does that to you. He fills you with wind. You outgrow several sizes. Words multiply in your mind immediately, the way ants invade a larder, soon more plentiful than the grounds that were spilled on the kitchen counter while making morning coffee. In *Gargantua*'s day, they were revered, despised, traded, banned, liberated, loved. At the wine-soaked tables of the inns, one exchanged views, lies, brags and other tales; in the markets, bargaining went on in a dialect as local and delicious as their greens; in the doss-houses,

grunts were gratefully given and received; at church, the air was
Latinated and, like the light, stained its priestly columns, brightened
its aisles or occluded niches, and lengthened even the grief in kneel-
ing figures. Most of all, there were old animosities and new views,
among them the sight of the Greek language, to which aspiring
humanists paid a visit as though the script were sea-girt Greece
itself—books that the Church confiscated and held incommunicado
to prevent the spread of error among the learned. A few of these
fresh readers of Greek were those who felt they had been given two
new languages: their earthy everyday tongue (in this case, French,
often seen for the first time in printed books) as well as the works of
the great pagan philosophers and the New Testament itself, where
creation began with the *logos* just as it seemed to be beginning for
them; and even though the world was everywhere widening to reveal
fresh continents to be discovered and despoiled, heathen souls to be
sought out and saved, nevertheless ordinary life was the richest land
so far claimed for any kingdom, because along with common things
came their common names, and with the names came common
knowledge: *mud puddle, haymow, oxen, minnow, lettuce, fart, smirk,
seaport, wink.*

(François Rabelais paid homage to three tongues when he
Latinized his French name to inscribe it in his books, and followed
that with an accompanying phrase in Greek—"François Rabelais'
Book and His Friends"—assigning ownership to himself in Latin
and borrower's rights to his close associates in Greek, a generosity
necessary to the spread of knowledge when books were rare, and,
since they were so rare, a generosity indeed. The elaborateness of
his signature was matched by the general shape of his hand, which
affected the scrolls and parasitic letters of the legal profession his
father practiced, and was symbolic of a writing style, some thought,
that fastened afterthoughts to every final flourish.)

Books were rare and books were revered. The opened cover was
compared to the opened eye, to a chest of treasure, a doorway to the
divine, the cork in a bottle; however, books bore error on through

time as well as truth, opinion, hypothesis, and conjecture, and they could fuddle the mind as well as wine. Mistakes, fakes, and false-hoods, in an opportune place, can become history, as the many mis-translations camped out on sacred tomes attest. Alcibiades did not compare Socrates to an apothecary's box, but to those "Silenus-figures that sit in the statuaries' shops . . . when the two halves are disjoined, they are seen to possess statues of gods within" (215a6–b4, Stanley Rosen's version, *Plato's Symposium*, 2d ed. New Haven: Yale University Press, 1987, p. 297). The actual reference is no less suit-able to Rabelais's purposes than the mistaken one, yet about it the translators gather, honor-bound to preserve and repeat it.

And if we broke free of words to inspect the philosopher in per-son, as if that were possible, we would still have a book bag for a head, eyes colored by custom, commonplace, and superstition. He would not "look" wise, as if we knew what wisdom wore to appear stupid—furrowed brow or quizzical smile, bald because his head steamed. ". . . you would not have given the peel of an onion for him," Urquhart says; you'd not have offered "an onion skin," declares LeClercq; not "the top of an onion," Powys puts it; nary "a shred of an onion for him," Cohen has it; or "you wouldn't have given the shred of an onion skin," in Brown's opinion, accepting most that has come before but declining the tuffet; while Rabelais, if we want to bother with the source, wrote, ". . . *n'en eussiez donne un coupeau d'oignon*," not realizing that *coupeau* would become obsolete and that his metaphor would therefore be lost: ". . . you would not give the hilltop of an onion for him."

This is a minor matter indeed, but it is interesting to note that Powys (*Rabelais*. London: Bodley Head, 1948), who creeps closest to his quarry, has complained of Samuel Putnam, whose translation he praises and many favor, for ruthlessly updating the text, thus making it more readable for his generation while depriving Rabelais's own time its age and voice. I might add: and some of his art.

Who cares whether Grandgousier, or Great Gullet, was a rollicking blade and a superlative toper, as one translator describes him; or—

since there is no reference to anyone's gullet in the passage I'm looking at—was just a good fellow in his time, and notable jester, according to another; or, as Andrew Brown describes him for us, was
instead "a real barrel of laughs"? Brown also advises us to "check
out" texts and "knock back" drinks, as we are wont now to do. He
makes us feel comfortable in the Renaissance, as if it were putting
on its show in our living room. Certainly, Brown's version is more
zippy and even more accurate than many. Picky points perhaps. But
imagine these modest disagreements multiplied through five volumes and 100,000 times.

In his lively introduction to *Pantagruel*, Andrew Brown points
out, apropos the same contrast between Socrates the Silenus and
Socrates the Sage that opens the work, that interpretation, in
Rabelais's day, was a dangerous undertaking, as much for what you
might be thought to be learning as for what you actually did; but
because he is translating a later version of the text, one that Rabelais
judged to be more prudent to publish than the original, there are
bits, offensive to Church authorities, omitted.

Jean Plattard (*The Life of François Rabelais*. London: Cass & Co.,
1930, p. 4) thinks that Rabelais was born around 1494 on his father's
farm, two gunshots from the Abbey of Seuilly, and a league from
Chinon, the town where he grew beneath his father's wing until he
began his studies to become a Franciscan monk. By the time he
pens *Pantagruel* (of which *Gargantua* is a prequel), he is familiar
with at least four professions and one art: the law from his father, the
priesthood and medicine from their practice, the new learning from
ancient sages, and poetry through his epistolary exchanges in verse
with the poet Jean Bouchet. What a stock of technical terms, argument forms, and higher powers Rabelais could employ, parody, and
appeal to; what grammatical categories, rhetorical schemes, *rimes
équivoques* and *batelées* (lines ambiguous and overloaded as a boat);
what changes rung from words like those from bells might he muster:
sixty-four verbs in the imperfect tense, necessary to roll a barrel out
of town in a cluster of shove and sound, *"le tournoit, viroit, brouilloit,*

garbouilloit, hersoit, versoit, renversoit . . ." and so on . . . *"nattoit, grattoit, flattoit . . ."* as, in English, we might group "crash, clash, mash, smash, slash, bash, trash, gnash . . ." to depict the passage of our armored vehicles through a village. (Donald Frame. *François Rabelais.* New York: Harcourt Brace, 1977, pp. 140–41.)

Later in his life, in his role as a physician, Rabelais often traveled to Lyons or Rome as a part of Cardinal Jean du Bellay's retinue, but as a young priest he did his rounds in the region of his birth, *la molle et douce* Touraine, and in the regal town of Chinon itself, once capital to a shrunken France (1528–1529), known to tourists now for one of Joan of Arc's early exploits. Scholars have frequently remarked Rabelais's intensive knowledge of the region: its cloth, its donkeys, its windmills, the height of its hemp, its "sweet, easy, warm, wet and well-soaked soil," and how well he rendered them all—towns, towers, lanterns, rivers, walls—in properly apportioned paragraphs. "Dressed in his Benedictine's habit, he mixed with the people more than any writer of his time. He knew the art of loosening the tongues of the cattle-drover in the field, the artisan in his workshop, the merchant in the inn. He can, on occasion, make use of their dialect, their familiar metaphors, their customary swearwords," Plattard writes (pp. 38–39). *Gargantua* and *Pantagruel* are so drenched, like the soil, in locales that Albert Jay Nock devoted a chatty travelogue to these places (*A Journey into Rabelais' France.* New York: Grosset & Dunlap, 1934).

The heroes of the New Learning—beginning with Guillaume Budé, Thomas More, Desiderius Erasmus, his self-designated student, Rabelais, and flowering in the great Baroque outbursts of Michel de Montaigne, Robert Burton, and, later, Sir Thomas Browne—were devoted multilingual quoters; however, in them, as often as not, the citations were offered as examples of ignorance and superstition on the part of their authors and held up as warnings to the unwary: What oft's been thought is now so little thought of.

To quote pagan authors is more than fun—it suggests that there are other authorities than have been favored by the scholastics—and to write about them in the vulgate is to invite readers to look on pages that the Church has resolutely kept from popular perusal, as if, on their own, such readers would be prone to misconstrue—taking a path that led straight to the stake. Moreover, it had been a habit through many centuries to consult books rather than inspect afresh what the books were presumed to be about; to cite authorities, to quote the fathers of the Church, to pit one scholar's paragraphs against another's; thus to debate each issue inside the precincts of the word, and this lawyerlike practice was hard to break. For instance—ah yes, an instance!—a scholar whose work Rabelais read in his youth (a man pridefully disputatious, whose skull will grind its teeth at going nameless here) had written a brief essay on marital proprieties, the illiberal views of which had elicited a sturdy defense of women's rights from—worse yet!—his closest friend. This required a rebuttal, duly given in a second edition, where he beat his opponent about the brow and brain by citing, in confirmation of his position, "authorities as numerous as they were varied. [He] quoted pell-mell philosophers and poets, historians and orators, Livy and Cicero, Plato and Petrarch, Ezechiel and Propertius. The work became thus considerably enlarged. From the 27 pages which composed the original edition it had grown to 276," as—the whistle of my own citation can be heard—Jean Plattard reports (p. 28).

Socrates' presence is pointed in other ways than that of his nose, since, at least as early as Abelard's *Dialectica* (1118), the Greek philosopher was a figure of fun for the schoolmen. Abelard does a jocose dance about the proposition—"if Socrates is asinine, some man is asinine"—though, as his biographer M. T. Clanchy reports, he later softened his moral disapproval (*Abelard: A Medieval Life*. Oxford: Blackwell, 1997, p. 275). Clanchy remarks that "logicians had traditionally and unthinkingly treated Socrates disrespectfully because they were not concerned with historical realities nor with people's feelings."

If Alcibiades can serve up Socrates as a sample of the wise fool, and Rabelais's reader can then remember how the renowned Erasmus has praised folly while wondering who the truly foolish are, then perhaps I may make my own reminder of how frequently it was felt that wild, unseemly, flatulated words would surely issue from a similarly grotesque and corpulent person. Gargantua, our hero here, is as fulminatious as his flesh is flabby, and only after decency has been drilled into him can he deliver an admirable speech in a restrained and balanced Ciceronian style. Shakespeare's Falstaff and Molière's Tartuffe are outstanding examples, as is the lesser-known character, Vanderhulk, of Thomas Nashe's *The Unfortunate Traveller,* a grotesque whose existence I was made aware of by Wayne Rebhorn in *The Emperor of Men's Minds* (another citation within a citation, worth doubled points). This fellow "had a sulphurous, big, swollen, large face like a Saracen, eyes like two Kentish oysters, a mouth that opened as wide every time he spake as one of those old knit trap doors, a beard as though it had been made of a bird's nest plucked in pieces which consisteth of straw, hair, and dirt mixed together (480)" (Rebhorn, p. 220). One must remark, by the way, that Rabelais would never mess up his line with real redundancy the way Nashe did—"big, swollen, large" indeed. No, Rabelais's redundancies redound. But what is a "knit trap door"? Is it a concealing rug? A confederate of the tea cozy? Or a round sphincter-type opening that closes behind a netted fish? To meet new words is to encounter new wonders.

Nor should we be deceived, as we read—by coarseness, indulgence, logorrhea—to suppose there is nothing but mooning going on in *Gargantua* or *Pantagruel,* naught but cocking a snook at authority, and other boyish pranks, or simply exuberance fizzing from bottle end and fundament like an organized spritzelation of shaken soda. The point of the opening reference to Socrates' appearance and the reality of his payoff remains unaffected: This book will appear wooly and rough, its course haphazard, but its sense is consistent, unified, pure yet iridescent, as though silk had swallowed water, and it has been set down more in weeping than in writing, more in despair than glee, more when sober than when drunk; and though drunkenness is a frequent occupation of its actors, we should fear not an actual stagger, because stage cups are always full of tea. Our author is besotted, but by words; he is intoxicated with learning, with his own strength; walls are a-tumblin' down, those of castle and cathedral, city and convent, college and library.

At the close of Plato's banquet, at daybreak, when all the evening's revelers and rhetoricians have passed out, Socrates rises from among the sleepers and goes to spend the balance of the day in his customary manner, for the philosopher feels no fuddle, and reason does not weary of its work; nor will it here, because the philosopher's distant student has also wakened early, left the priestly functions toward which his studious nature had initially inclined him, and begun his service as a physician, consequently as a scholar of Hippocrates and Galen, among the Greeks the more empirically inclined. Now to Rabelais's dislike of traditional schoolmen is added a disdain for the traditional physician. "These fellows get their experience by killing folks (as Pliny once complained); and they are a source of greater danger, even, than any that comes from disease itself." (Quoted by Samuel Putnam. *François Rabelais: Man of the Renaissance.* New York: Cape & Smith, 1929, p. 269.)

Princes and their petty yet ruinous wars; indolent, hypocritical monks and their parasitical lives; the theologians of the Sorbonne, who misuse reason and disgrace intelligence; the venerators of holy relics and pious pilgrims; purveyors of popular superstitions of every stripe—these are the objects of our author's scorn, as it should be our concern to steer clear of them today, though they may call their sects, professions, and their parties by newer noble-sounding names.

Rabelais's anger at those who are tethered to their texts is evidence of his own released mind, but it is partly paradoxical, since he is as bookish as they. He, however, is eating fresh fruit from old trees instead of winter's barreled apples, and we can turn to him as he returned to Plato and Socrates. *Gargantua* and *Pantagruel,* so far in the past, as comets come, can arrive like a new age to surprise our eyes. These works seem written for today; they are as relevant, and possibly as futile. Between the brackets insert your favorite bêtes noires. "[These scholars and medics] can well enough see the light-boat of lies battered and leaking in every part; yet they insist upon retaining, by force and by violence, those works to which they have been accustomed from their youth up. If one endeavours to snatch these away from them, they feel that he is, at the same time, snatching away their very souls." (Putnam, p. 269.) Did the humanists not feel similarly violated when the Church arrested their Greek books? And burned pages, set fire to their authors, and lit their readers, too, as Brown notes. After Rabelais edits a new edition of Hippocrates, he has a Latin couplet placed upon its title page, which reads: "Here is the overflowing font of healing lore. Drink here, unless the stagnant water of a ditch tastes better to you." (Putnam, p. 271.)

Scholars have noticed the metaphoric connection of science with salubrious imbibing in Rabelais, though it must be remembered that reading a book of symptoms is not the same as taking a pulse. "Drink" is what Gargantua cries as he's being born, instead of the customary "waa waa"; the third and fourth books are given over in large part to a search for the Divine Bottle, as if it were the Holy Grail; and in the fifth part, whose authenticity is disputed, the oracle of the *Divine Bouteille* delivers wisdom's secret, which is—no surprise from the lips of a bottle—Drink! Moreover, Pantagruel makes a pre-Rabelasian appearance in a medieval mystery play, where his role is that of an impish devil who gathers salt from the seashore to shake down the throats of snoring drunkards.

His salary at the Great Hospital of Lyons did not achieve jingle, and, deprived of the Church's free room and board or the indulgences of some courtly master, Rabelais must have often slept without covers or companion, eaten tack, and drunk from a dry glass. So straitened circumstances probably alerted him to the possibility of a windfall of his own when a small book, the illegitimate offspring of the Arthurian legends, anonymously transcribed from the oral tradition, sold more copies in two months than Bibles in nine years (Plattard, p. 120). It retold the story of how Merlin, the magician, created a family of giants, sort of medieval superheroes, out of the bones of two male whales, a sprinkle of clippings from Queen Genièvre's nails, plus a soupçon of blood from one of Sir Lancelot's wounds, to help out King Arthur through his many tribulations. In his study of Rabelais, Donald Frame tells us (p. 12), that the loving pair, Grant-Gosier (or the Great Gullet that LeClercq has insisted on inserting into his translation wherever possible) and Galemelle (who, as Gargamelle, bears Gargantua for eleven months in Rabelais's version before dumping him with a thump into a nest of citations that prove why lengthy gestations are necessary for masterpieces) . . . well, the two make their way between grasping parentheses, bearing their brute of a boy on the back of a city-size mare, "through France to join Arthur; but the parents [who suffer a fever like a wound along the way] die at Mont-Saint-Michel for lack of a purgative. Merlin transports Gargantua to Arthur on a cloud; fighting for Arthur, Gargantua conquers the Gos and Magos, the Dutch and the Irish, and a twelve-cubit giant in single combat. Finally, after two hundred years, he is translated to fairyland. . . ." On the other hand, Paul Eldridge (*François Rabelais: The Great Storyteller*. Cranbury, N.J.: A. S. Barnes, 1971) claims that the parents died because of the purgative, not for want of one, and boasts that Gargantua forced all of the prisoners he'd taken (as if they were sweets, I suppose) into his hollow tooth in lieu of a filling (Eldridge, p. 70). But I have heard (from Plattard, p. 121) that he also stuffed the cuffs of his sleeves, his game bag, and the toes of his hose with his victims. Tales of yore should yield such variations; the more there are, the merrier they make us. Always consult many authorities; they will infect you with suspicion—a desirable service. (All over France still, Eldridge says, there are menhirs and dolmens named Gargantua's Chair or Gargantua's Spoon, Finger, Shoe, Pissing Rock, Tomb. It gives pleasure to know these things.)

This anonymous author happily supplied the details necessary to tall tales, and we are familiar with them in the form of the Paul Bunyan legend, or many of the stories that floated with the boatmen down the Mississippi, or those that boasted of trappers who, bare-handed, fought bear and cougar in a frontier forest. How big, how strong, how hungry was the lumberjack, the boatman, the hunter? ". . . Gargantua lunched off two shipfuls of fresh herrings and three casks of salted mackerel; . . . he dined on three hundred cattle and two hundred sheep; . . . he carried off the bells of Notre-Dame de Paris to hang them on his mare's neck; . . . his peals of laughter were heard seven and a half leagues away . . ." Not a decibel less, not a yard more. (". . . this specious exactitude is another feature of popular comedy." [Plattard, p. 122.])

So Rabelais's monsters must outdo the outdoers . . . and they do. Their habits of hyperbole do not exclude their author, who swears in *Pantagruel*'s prologue: "may I be carried off by a hundred thousand basketfuls of fine devils, body and soul, innards and entrails, if I lie by so much as a single word in the whole story . . . ," a protestation exceeded only by the punishments to be inflicted upon readers who do not obediently believe. Like the pamphlet that preceded it, *Pantagruel* is packed with gross-out japes and overscale jokes, with mythological deeds that mock the social and religious figments that one must pretend to believe out of fear of just those pains Rabelais promises his own disbelievers—"sulphur, flames and the bottomless pit."

By turning everything topsy-turvy, it mimics the meanings and rituals of medieval carnivals and festivals, too, a fundamental aspect of Rabelais's human comedy famously described by Mikhail Bakhtin (*Rabelais and His World*. Cambridge, Mass.: MIT Press, 1968). The school of Russian formalists with which Bakhtin was associated had made considerable advances in the study of folktales and legends, particularly in terms of their narrative forms; so Rabelais's reliance on the life and laughter of common people made ideal material for the Russian critic's cast of mind. *Gargantua* and *Pantagruel* belonged to the culture of popular carnival humor, of which there were, he felt, three basic manifestations: ritual spectacles, such as carnival pageants, fools' day celebrations, and marketplace entertainments;

written as well as oral parodies in both Latin and their local dialects; and various sorts of slanging matches, cursing patterns, catch-phrases, and what we call "trash talk" now.

So the giants are giants because they began their lives outside of Rabelais's world as giants. Rabelais acknowledges this in his pro-logue to *Pantagruel*. However, they remain giants; they flourish as giants for further reasons, many of them naming and enumerative, and because a giant was a good visual symbol for a group, a class, an order, a faith, an army, a nation. Our author was painfully aware of the rapacity of kings, counts, cardinals and bishops, whose entourages ate like the armies that periodically swept over the countryside, gobbling up everything that couldn't be hidden from them. His imagery anticipates Hobbes's invention of that artificial body, the "corporate giant."

In 1651, when Thomas Hobbes published his great work on our need to relinquish rights to form an absolute sovereignty and escape the chaos of a state of nature, he fronted his text with an engraving that depicted the figure of a king whose body was made of many men—a corporate Leviathan—just as his treatise advised; and to ensure his own safety, during the difficult times of civil war in which he wrote, Hobbes gave the ruler Oliver Cromwell's face, while upon the Lord Protector's head he placed the crown of a Catholic, Charles II—a duplicity Rabelais would have understood, since, like so many others in his time, he published under a pseudonym at first (Alcofribas Nasier, a transparent anagram of his own name), and the books he wrote were regularly proscribed.

The little story of the medlars that appears on the first pages of *Pantagruel* furnishes a good context for the understanding of the pre-ternatural swellings that afflict this text and all its occupants. When Cain kills Abel, the earth becomes soaked in the blood of the victim and bears in consequence an abundance of fruit. The normally com-pact leathery crab apples that the medlar tree produces were in the subsequent season so large that three of them sufficed for a bushel. The text has scarcely taken a step, yet it has managed to traduce two biblical tales, pun on God's injunction to "be fruitful," and redo Eden's celebrated seduction as a menacing farce—which, come to think of it, it is. The side effects of medlar gorging were not all benevolent, nor should we have expected them to be, if we remember the blood of injustice that stimulated their growth. "All of them [who ate the apples] suffered from a really horrible swelling on their bodies, but not all of them had it in the same place." (B 7.) Some grew bellies so big, they were called "Almighties" to mock the manner in which the Apostles' Creed refers to God, but they were good people "and from this race sprang St Paunch, and Pancake Day" (which is Brown's translation of its calendar name, Shrove Tuesday, and true to its spirit). Some became hunchbacks; soon there were those who had phalluses so long, they wrapped them around their waists like belts; still others had to bear bollocks the size of the medlars responsible, and so on into a parody of the generational lists of Genesis. This augmentation is best achieved grammatically by dispensing with the general term and replacing it with an organized mob of particulars or requiring a noun to do the work of an adjective or a verb, as in this passage that drew Albert Jay Nock's admiration.

There was then in the abbey [of Seuilly] a claustral monk called Friar John of the Funnels, young, gallant, frisk, lusty, nimble, quick, active, bold, adventurous, resolute, tall, lean, wide-mouthed, long-nosed, a rare mumbler of matins, unbridler of masses and runner-over of vigils; and to conclude summarily in a word, a right monk, if ever there were any, since the monking world monked a monkery. (Nock, p. 68.)

Whether, as the schoolmen had debated, there were real universals, which had being apart from that of their particulars, or only specific material things enjoyed existence, Rabelais knew that Man the Mighty was like a giant individual, and since he was a creature principally engaged in eating, excreting, killing, and begetting—one that used its brain to obtain cash and buy comfort, a friend of whoever might be of service, always seeking personal security, pleasant company, and a tapped keg, and forever in need of enemies to justify its own excesses—we might expect it to lay waste much wherever it was, if only by snoring, thus breaking windows, or by poisoning crops before they could be eaten through breaking wind from its last debauch. This special giant, Pantagruel, was already known to all as a provoker of thirst, a harbinger of drought and cracked earth, and in Rabelais's terms, he creates desire as well, needs that swell like cheeks about an infected tooth.

But Rabelais is not long content with giants, and soon introduces a Ulysses of his own—Panurge—a cunning riddler, a sly boots, a devious trickster yet a loyal friend, whom Pantagruel meets upon the road in a wretchedly disheveled condition and whom he questions before deciding to offer assistance. In a brilliant bravura passage that could have been stolen from Joyce's *Ulysses,* Panurge replies first in German, then in Gibberish, Italian, Scots, Basque, Lanternlandish, Dutch, Spanish ("I am tired of talking so much"), Danish, Ancient Greek, Utopian, Latin, and finally, of course, in his native tongue, the French of Touraine. Impressed—as who wouldn't be?—Pantagruel orders Panurge to be properly fed, after which the polyglot sleeps till dinnertime the next day, when he comes to table "in a hop, skip, and a jump." (Chapter 9.) Which is American for *quickly.*

I remember a similar kind of academic contest. In Germany, a number of writers had passages from their books recited to them in a language they were unlikely to understand (in this case, it was Romanian). We were asked to identify the authors of each passage. Would we even recognize our own? I remember it well because I won. The secret was in the rhetorical rhythms that the translations retained. There is plenty of rhetorical rhythm in Rabelais, and it conveys a zest and energy, a boyish nose-thumbing glee, that is not equaled, to my ear, by any other writer. But it is not always used to make jokes, for there is much here that is serious on its face as well as strongly meant in its heart. Nor does the fun Rabelais has with higher education, the law, or the Church mean that he has embraced ignorance, lawlessness, and disbelief; it is, rather, that, then as now, the stupid, the greedy, the hypocritical, the disloyal or tyrannical serve virtue as badly as they profit vice. Our lawyer jokes should not suggest we wish to dispense with legal services—just shysters; and neither should Erasmus's anticlericalism nor Rabelais's invectives against priests lead us to think they are not utterly devout. The fact is (and it is a sad one) that the age was a lot freer in its permissible range of blasphemy and verbal indecencies than ours is now, though making the wrong enemies then could lose you more than a sect's bloc of bigot votes.

Pantagruel went through two editions with a swiftness that hurried *Gargantua* into existence, a work less dependent upon its predecessors, more inclined to realism than to whimsies about the wearers of the larger sizes or events exceeding the miraculous, and more likely to set its scenes in locales familiar to the reader than in lands far away and never-never. Meanwhile, like a ragman, Rabelais has been collecting his material much as we might imagine Brueghel doing: insults, for instance, children's games, bum wipes, countries that were being conquered during the cake bakers' war. This war, like the disagreements between Tweedledum and Tweedledee in *Alice,* is over a trifling refusal of a bunch of griddlecake bakers to sell a portion of their wares to some shepherds who were passing a few otherwise idle and sheepish hours in preventing starlings from eating the grapes then ripening on the farmers' vines. The shepherds offered the going price, which was apparently less on the road than the bakers expected to collect once they were in town. They fire off a volley of insults in reply: In Rabelais, twenty-eight of them, and in Cohen the same, but from Brown fly only twenty-six, while LeClercq's twenty-seven are more sporadically delivered, and Urquhart overwhelms his victims with forty-two fancy revilements that fall as if a storm of hailstones came in attractively different shapes and sizes.

This rudeness leads to a quarrel that starts a fight, which results in injuries that must be requited, and so from a contretemps set steaming by pride and stirred by greed, ignorance, fear, and suspicion—a nothing upon which are soon erected reasons like artillery positions—a battle—as always, fought with lies and lost

lives—begins what will prosper as a war: a war that forbearance cannot forestall or calm, a war that consumes a list—aforecited—of
conquered countries, but also the spoils of an invading army;
indeed, that list is the pillagers' verbal equivalent. "They made off
with oxen, cows, bulls, calves, heifers, ewes, sheep, nanny-goats and
billy-goats; hens, capons, chickens, goslings, ganders and geese;
pigs, sows and piglets; they knocked down walnuts, harvested vines,
carried off vinestocks, and shook down all the fruit from the trees."
(Brown, *Gargantua,* p. 71.) That, the King of the Offended Bakers
said, "would teach them to eat cake."

But what taskmasters habitually forget is how to teach others
their lessons without having to learn any themselves.

In the course of this contest, Grandgousier (the king of the country attacked and the father of Gargantua) takes a notable prisoner,
called Swashbuckler out of respect for Errol Flynn. After questioning this prisoner in order to learn what his enemy intended by the
invasion, and discovering that Picrochole (for that was the warlord's
name) means to conquer the entire country, Grandgousier (demonstrating his wisdom as well as his relevance to our times, as I am sure
was his intention) releases Swashbuckler with the following observation about his opponent:

> "It would have been better if he had stayed at home, governing
> it like a king—rather than insolently invading mine, pillaging it
> like an enemy. If he had governed his land he would have
> extended it, but by pillaging mine he will be destroyed. Be off
> with you, in the name of God. Follow the Good; point out to
> your king the errors of his that you are aware of, and never give
> him advice for the sake of your own personal profit, for if the
> commonwealth is lost, so is the individual and his property. As
> for your ransom, I give it all to you, and desire that your
> weapons and your horse be returned to you. This is how things
> ought to be between neighbours and old friends. . . ."

Swashbuckler does not depart without gifts. Nor did Rabelais's
readers, who laughed, heartily, most of them, as if they had gotten

the gist, and digested its moral; yet they obeyed kings and cardinals, princes and priests nevertheless, where they believed their interests lay, or where their fears were focused; and so confusion and catastrophe continue, in plenty and in colorful variety, to this day. I notice that there are apples in our shops so huge, it takes only three of them to heap a bushel. Our ferociously fertile earth is that soaked, our fruit that malevolent.

THE ANATOMY OF MELANCHOLY

During the early seventeenth century, men everywhere in Europe were beginning to realize that the institutions that had seemed to offer them hope and keep them from care were actually making them fearful of their fate, and encouraging them to trade their lives for lies. The world was now wider than anyone had previously imagined—ships had sailed it round; the heavens were on quite another course than had been sworn to; social organizations were being drastically revised and power was slipping from Popes to princes, from the universal Church to the secular state; former methods of deciding things were now utterly up in the air; rude and vigorous vernaculars were driving back Latin everywhere (Dante, Descartes, and Hobbes would ennoble several vulgar tongues by their employment); people were lifting their heads from canonical books to look boldly around, and what they saw first were errors, plentiful as leaves. Delight and despair took turns managing their moods.

The past is never lightly thrown off, though it often seems doffed like a hat with a flourish or carelessly tossed like a cape into a corner; it is only a cap that's been removed, only an old coat there in its puddle. Young men were watching the new day dawn with old minds, and traditional intentions. Robert Burton boldly chastises the clergy for their ceremonious pomp, hypocritical zeal, and scandalous lapses, but it is the pomp, the zeal, the lapses he is after, and he is careful to keep his new faith clear of the old Church's ritual forms and corporate grip. Sir Thomas Browne was rewarded for his royalist loyalties with a knighthood, and his most popular book about vulgar errors, the *Pseudodoxia Epidemica,* omitted a number of crucial ones, while he keeps helpfully at hand the "unspeakable mysteries" of the Scriptures; Descartes aimed to set his religion back on sound foundations, even if he did make its bones dance, and rightly feared Bruno's burning at the stake; Burton's skepticism, like Montaigne's, and Descartes's later, is persistent but programmatic, an epistemological strategy, not a deep state of mind; Thomas Hobbes, playing both sides of the English Civil War to perfection, would place Cromwell's face on the giant whose image would serve to front his *Leviathan* (a body politic literally made of a crowd of bodies squeezed into the outline of a sovereign), while on that Protestant head he impressed a Catholic crown; Bacon, More, and Montaigne all sought ways to release science to follow every scent Nature might emit so long as it never treed Divinity.

Of all the habits that were hard to break, being bookish was perhaps the most difficult. Now, in addition to the Scriptures, there would be all the classical authors you had the opportunity to cite— the honor of the first quote in Burton's address to the reader goes to Seneca—thereby showing generosity in the "loan" of the resources of your library and by your readiness to "spread the word," just as you also took good care to gather books and manuscripts, diligently copying passages from the volumes that had to pass through, rather than remain in, your hands. Guided by a genius, the pages of a commonplace book could be transformed into an original and continuously argued text, as Ben Jonson did with *Discoveries*—a form that Burton's *Anatomy* sometimes resembles though never mimics.

These new authorities, who often elbow Matthew, Mark, Luke, and John to one side, supply evidence of two kinds: first, of the breadth of the author's learning, and second, of the rightness of his opinions, because the facts that matter are still those mostly found in books, not those picked like posies out of a meadow or distilled in an alembic; moreover, the words themselves are magical; you cannot have too many of them; they are like spices brought back from countries so far away, they're even out of sight of seas; words that roll, Poloniusly, into the reader's ken in lists that subside, only to resume in no time at all with words even more exotic, redolent, or chewy; for instance, the names and kinds of terrestrial devils that lurk about to pester us: lares, lemurs, genii, satyrs, fauns, fairies, wood nymphs, trolls, and foliots, those visitors to forlorn houses, about whom you may not be familiar, who make "strange noises in the night, howl sometimes pitifully, and then laugh again, cause great flame and sudden lights, fling stones, rattle chains," and if you wake to find your beard shaved and your chin smooth, they will be the impish cause. (*Anatomy*, part 1, section 2, member 1, subsection 2).

To ridicule superstition or succumb to it, embrace the new learning or belabor it, celebrate change or condemn it, relate every tale or tell none; or, more characteristically, to quote, testify, enlarge upon every subject with such serious thoroughness that there could be no response but laughter: In Robert Burton, these impulses blew like winds; no one was ever more an arena for the contest between what was pagan and what was pious, what seemed demonstrable to science and mathematics or what seemed sensible upon textual scrutiny and harmonious with settled doctrine, than this nonconformist clergyman, this quiet monkish man who would pursue secular studies behind the walls of a famous college, a skeptic whose credulity was a welcome you could count on, a pessimist and melancholic whose great celebrational comedy will last as many years as its thousand pages.

Robert Burton may have momentarily put aside his pen on December 5, 1620, to declare his work done; however, since sales were solid and four fresh editions needed, he let his baby grow from gigantic to gargantuan. We have ourselves continued to manufacture material for his *Melancholy*, and were Burton as immortal as his book, he could keep the *Anatomy* routinely up-to-date with the distraughts, foul humors, and tragedies that trouble us today and will beset us tomorrow. What the present reader may find strange is Burton's eager allowance of hearsay and observation, myth and science, superstition and common sense, to help him in his hunt for causes, and provide more than cosmetic in the makeup of his explanations: not merely citing heredity, disease, dotage, and personal loss as sources of melancholy, while displaying a skepticism as ardent as his faith, but blaming God, evil angels as well as devils, a bad balance among the four humors, the discoveries of chiromancy and physiognomy, indurate dishes and sharp sauces, unsuitable parents, odors of the earth, even the stars themselves.

What may strike one as quaint and unfashionable at one time may be the latest wisdom to another. When I was first engaged to Robert Burton's book (my copy's flyleaf says December 1944), the mother's womb was sturdier and more insulated than it is believed to be now, so, when I read that if the mother "be over-dull, heavy, angry, peevish, discontented, and melancholy, not only at the time of conception, but even all the while she carries the child in her womb . . . her son will be so likewise affected" (part 1, section 2, member 1, subsection 6), I thought the risks overstated, for wasn't the moat of amniotic fluid about the baby nearly unswimmable?—what else was it there for?—but I would not think so now—now everything, including noise, gets through and, unless it is the music of Mozart, wreaks havoc.

Unlike Erasmus's famous work, this is no praise of folly; it is, however, a parade of them: every day in Burton's year is Saint Patrick's, bands brag in the streets, beer is the only proffered drink, and the beer is green. Moreover, the parade has a settled order of march; the word *anatomy* signifying its dissected analytical layout, its deployment of commentary descending through partitions, sections, members, into subsections, and adding to those body parts appendices, poetic addresses, a daunting synopsis, and a preface nearly the length of an ordinary book. The analytical outline should not daunt. Burton pays as much attention to his own schematisms as he pays to the syntax of his sentences. Imposing indeed are his inter-connections, but it is rather as if a net had been flung down on top of fish that continue to roil and flop freely about beneath it.

Nor is there much that's melancholy, in our present sense of the word, about the *Anatomy;* and the principal reason for this is that the illnesses Burton discusses and the causes and cures he proposes, have not, in the main, been drawn from bedsides, battlefields, or courts, but from books and reports, descriptions and disquisitions; for it is easy, even agreeable, while enjoying the safety of the page, to face without qualms a situation and its solution as they are set down in some chronicle or almanac, harsh or bizarre as they may combine to be, when in life what it is being reported may encourage harrow-ing practices and produce deplorable pains, such as drilling a hole in a patient's skull to release noxious vapors that have gathered there, or, latterly, prevailing on leeches to bleed a body already badly in need of its blood.

What is not secondhand are Burton's pages on the melancholies of the scholar, the vices of princes, and the deficiencies of the Catholic Church. He has both read and lived these—through an impending civil war, contending clergies, the machinations of a par-liament seeking new powers, and royals protecting traditional privi-leges. Yet when one's nose is in a book, it is as alive and alert as if it were treeing a possum or anticipating the serving of soup—more so, because it is bent over concepts; it is breathing forms; it is becoming acquainted with minds. For Burton, learning is the disease that will cure his other ailments, the way consolidating your debts will bring due only one—still crushing—lump-sum payment.

But Thomas Hobbes, who had Burton and Browne and Mon-taigne in view, was of a different, and, as usual, impressively put, opinion:

> From whence it happens, that they which trust to books, do as they that cast up many little summs into a greater, without con-sidering whether those little summes were rightly cast up or not; and at last finding the errour visible, and not mistrusting

their first grounds, know not which way to cleere themselves; but spend time in fluttering over their bookes; as birds that entring by the chimney, and finding themselves inclosed in a chamber, flutter at the false light of a glasse window, for want of wit to consider which way they came in. (*Leviathan*, part 1, chapter 4, pp. 17–18.)

If he could have had his way, Burton would have preferred to be a poet and playwright, and he did write a comedy in Latin verse, which his students performed in the Great Hall of Oxford's Christ Church in 1617. We have several samples of his occasionally charming doggerel in front of us, one with the well-known refrain: *None so sweet*—so sad, so sour, so harsh, so damned—*as melancholy*. He would also have preferred to write in Latin, but publishers were increasingly reluctant to constrict their sales to the rich and learned; what, after all, was the vernacular to Dante, Descartes, and Hobbes but a paddle to place across the rumps of the schoolmen and punish their inhibiting pedantries? The languages of Italian, French, and English were those of increasingly secular states and their mercantile interests. Robert Burton would also seek a popular public, but under a protective nom de plume, in the shelter of a life whose movements rose and fell as calmly as a cork amid the tumults of the times.

If Burton had wanted us to know who the author of the *Anatomy* was, he should not have chosen a pseudonym behind which to hide (as he himself says); yet if he had not wanted us to know who he was (as he claims) he should not have chosen a name like Democritus behind which to pretend to conceal himself, for that name plainly points toward a position on the nature of things that is material, quantitative, and scientific; moreover, one that soon would have, in the strengthening temper of the time, two great spokesmen— Thomas Hobbes and René Descartes—to represent the rational spirits of Galileo and Copernicus, in whom the Renaissance was realized. But it is the life and character of Democritus (taken from authorities as unreliable as ancient) that our coy author wishes to suggest bear a semblance to his own, and that his epithet, "the Laughing Philosopher," is one Burton also deserves: the sage's quiet, solitary regularities, his ardent devotion to his studies, the elevation that philosophy confers upon his occupations, such as Burton's ministry allowed, and with an interest in mathematics they could share, the enjoyment of rueful laughter, as well as a fondness for the rhetoric of skepticism—the same with men like Montaigne, Lipsius, and Muret, who left their busy lives to dwell in sheltered cells, where their amusement at human behavior would disturb not even the sobriety of birds.

As Democritus Junior, Burton is free to parade folly after folly past Democritus Senior's amused yet scornful eye. The operative phrase is "what would he have said" were he to have thought X, felt Y, seen Z; although the indictment that follows the question has been drawn up by Burton alone. Concerning wars, for instance (the ellipses signify omitted quotations):

> What would he have said to see, hear, and read so many bloody battles, so many thousand slain at once, such streams of blood able to turn mills: because of one man's mad offense, or to make sport for princes, without any just cause . . . whilst statesmen themselves in the mean time are secure at home, pampered with all delights & pleasures, take their ease, and follow their lusts, not considering what intolerable misery poor soldiers endure, their often wounds, hunger, thirst, &c., the lamentable cares, torments, calamities & oppressions, that accompany such proceedings . . . (*Anatomy*, pp. 55–56.)

The book was so popular, it went into six editions during Burton's lifetime, and its gratified author was eager to doff his anonymity after the first. It should have been popular. Although it gave expression to the pains of the people (always a kind of comfort), his *Anatomy* recounted so many sorts of follies that most of them had to have been performed or believed by others rather than ourselves; we could then happily send a hearty guffaw around the common table like a pitcher of ale, and drink to the dunces who had so deluded themselves as to think thus, do such. When the mind enters a mad-house, Burton shows, however sane it was when it went in, and how-ever hard it struggles to remain sane while there, it can only make the ambient madness more monstrous, more absurd, more bizarrely laughable by its efforts to be rational.

For a contemporary Robert Burton whom we might imagine sit-ting down now with tireless zeal and companionable sorrow to record our melancholy lot, there'd be no lack of data either, and the sections he'd have planned for his book would fill up faster than a thimble. What about bad diets as a cause of nervous illness? Both Burtons would have room for that. Or foul air? They could jointly bewail it. Or immoderate exercise? Or a love of gambling? Nothing unfamiliar there, nor with the desperations of imprisonment or the glooms that follow prolonged study, or the despairs impoverishment brings on. What of the consequences, both devious and direct, of festering discontents, of local resentments and historic hatreds, concerning which we have always had an apparently inexhaustible supply? Or the dangerous delusions brought on by self-love and vainglory in an era of shameless self-promotion like our own? Surely our obsession with sex and what Burton calls its "artificial allure-ments" would shock our scholar, while the space in the plan of his book set aside for the miasmas of religion would find sects jostling one another for booths from which to sell their latest absurdities and repeatedly boast of their unique merits and cry aloud their bewares.

Burton himself will pretend to be a plain speaker, and plainly enough he does speak, if one considers the time, and the artificiality of his predecessors; but when he says that his book is "writ with as small deliberation as I do ordinarily speak, without all affectation of big words, fustian phrases, jingling terms, tropes, strong lines, that like Acestes' arrows caught fire as they flew, strains of wit, brave heats, elogies, hyperbolical exornations, elegancies, etc., which many so much affect" (p. 31), what are we now to think? "Strong lines" refers to a preference orators had, in that time, for balance, gnomic terseness, and an elevation of thought and diction that could seem, when it failed, to yield the artificial, riddling, and bombastic;

nevertheless, Burton's looseness can only be called "exuberance" now, a form of celebration, and indicative of a nominalism that feels that if every person huddling under an umbrella is not named, they shall have no protection.

One can only listen. Robert the Ranter rails. It is delicious.

To see [we are still in this rhetorical mode of address, so it is Democritus Senior who is the imagined observer] a man turn himself into all shapes like a Chameleon, or as Proteus . . . to act twenty parts and persons at once for his advantage, to temporize and vary like Mercury the planet, good with good, bad with bad; having a several face, garb, and character for every one he meets; of all religions, humours, inclinations; to fawn like a spaniel . . . rage like a lion, bark like a cur, fight like a dragon, sting like a serpent, as meek as a lamb, and yet again grin like a tiger, weep like a crocodile, insult over some, and yet other domineer over him, here command, there crouch, tyrannize in one place, be baffled in another, a wise man at home, a fool abroad to make others merry. (*Anatomy,* pp. 65–66.)

The sentence indeed does unravel, but into a flouncy tuffet, not into a maze or a strew. Meaning, motion, and emotion are superbly fused. It achieves the tone of a tirade that, in the midst of its fury, smiles at itself—recognizes itself as a recital of fearful changeability and confident clichés. I am also tempted to admire (for it may be merely a textual error, of which in the *Anatomy* there are so many) the odd and awkward phrase "and yet other domineer over him" as a creative misprint for "let." In its anger, its energy, its rhythm, its terminological greed, its sermoniacal excoriations, this prose is a seedbed for the high semisacred styles of Browne's *Urne Buriall,* Donne's *Sermons,* and Taylor's *Holy Dying.*

Be prepared to proceed slowly and you will soon go swiftly enough. Read a member a day; it will chase gloom away. The late section on religious melancholy has been particularly admired. I also have a special fondness for Burton's pages on museums and libraries. But above all, it is the width of the world that can be seen from one college window that amazes me; what a love of all life can be felt by one who has lived it sitting in a chair; and Robert Burton's unashamed display of his lust for the word—his desire to name each thing, and find a song in which each thing can be sung—is a passion that we might emulate to our assuredly better health.

THE MELODIES OF MELANCTHA

Gertrude Stein's reputation among middle-of-the-road readers rests on *Three Lives.* Otherwise, there is the good gossip of the autobiographies and the soporific experimentation of *Tender Buttons, The Making of Americans,* and *A Long Gay Book,* and if the first of these doesn't appear to be worth a second look, the second isn't worth a first. Though Gertrude Stein's reputation has grown rather steadily through recent decades, it is a reputation in constant peril. One kick takes the stool out from under the otherwise-unattractive weight of the lady. Nor would her downfall spoil anyone's afternoon.

Elizabeth Hardwick's recent essay on Gertrude Stein finds the critic compelled to take Stein seriously, forced to be respectful; but discomfort and complaint lead off, and appear and reappear as the account continues. Miss Stein, it is remarked, is a pitiless companion. She is cheerful, which sounds okay, and has lots of confidence, which is nice in moderation, but the adverb "unflagging" takes these gifts away, and in a bit "amazing" and "outlandish" will come along in case anything agreeable is left. Stein's style is full of "insomniac rhythms and melodious drummings." She "likes to tell you what you know and to tell it again and sometimes to let up for a bit only to tell you once more." In short, she writes like rain.

Hardwick quotes others against "this peculiar American princess," as if she needed more guns, a tactic she never uses on anyone else; but T. S. Eliot (whom we know now to be a cheap shirt stuffed with expensive straw) is allowed to say that Stein's writing "has a kinship with the saxophone." This is the kind of cleverly mean comment that one likes, having thought of it, to keep around for its appropriate and most malicious moment of application. Professor Max Black (with whom I studied meanness, among other things) had a one-line review ready for its victim a long time before Irwin Edman's book, *A Philosopher's Holiday*, sailed by to receive it: "Professor Edman is the kind of tourist who sticks gum on the Parthenon."

Eliot was actually a good deal more definite, as Hardwick observes: Stein's work "is not improving, it is not amusing, it is not interesting, it is not good for one's mind." This is a sentence, may I say, that apes its enemy. But it is Gertrude Stein's clearly unwarranted confidence that is most annoying to Elizabeth Hardwick. "In her life, confidence and its not-too-gradual ascent into egotism combined with a certain laziness and insolence." I don't find a lot of confidence in *Q.E.D.*, for instance, or in Gertrude's lengthy dependence on her brother; but there is confidence and confidence, I suppose; for a cripple, even the thought of walking may be absurdly optimistic. For Stein, however, I think *bravado* might be a better word.

Written between the spring of 1905 and that of 1906, silence was all the three stories received from good brother Leo. Gertrude wrote to Mabel Weeks, "I am afraid I can never write the great American novel. I don't know how to sell on a margin or do anything with shorts or longs, so I have to content myself with niggers and servant girls and the foreign population generally." She concluded her complaint, rather unconfidently to my ear, "I am very sad Mamie." "I am all unhappy in this writing, nervous and driving and unhappy in it," she says in another letter. Stein is as blue as Melanctha. "I am really almost despairing, I have really in me a very very melancholy feeling . . ." It is true, nonetheless, that for most of her life, Gertrude Stein does seem to be (in Hardwick's wonderful phrase) "as sturdy as a turnip."

Although every positive note in Elizabeth Hardwick's essay seems played on Eliot's saxophone, she cannot deny the quality and the literary position of *Three Lives*. It is, admittedly, "in every way a work of resonating originality." However, the same sentence continues, "even if no aspect of its striking manner will persist in the eccentric shape of the works that follow." This is the kick that aims to overturn the stool. *Three Lives* is simply too uncharacteristic to count. What is uncharacteristic about it? That it is really quite amazingly good, I guess.

Mr. F. H. Hitchcock, the director of the vanity press that eventually printed the fifteen hundred copies of *Three Lives*, wrote Stein, when the book was at last ready late in 1909, "that I think you have written a very peculiar book and it will be a hard thing to make people take it seriously." To make people take it . . . Yes. Now, however, it is the rest of her serious work that remains under a cloud of doubt. We are familiar, even at this early hour of our dismally dawning century, with such reversals of reputation as *Three Lives* has undergone, since the dense-headedness of even those with pretensions to the literary are a cultural constant.

Mr. Hitchcock did give the author one good piece of advice, which led her to change the title from *Three Histories*, deemed too formal, to *Three Lives*, but the Elizabethan subtitle, "Each One As She May" was retained for "Melanctha." Every one of this additional title's words, as well as those of a similar kind, would receive Stein's lifelong love. *Q.E.D.*, the first version of "Melanctha," even opens with a scene quoted from *As You Like It*.

Melanctha sits by her sick mother's bed; she attends a friend's lying-in and that poor baby's burial after its brief uncared-for life; she listens to the talk of another woman, not her mother, learning the ways of the world from a tough drunk; she is frequently seen in the company of men, one of whom she comes to love, until their affections are worried between them like two cats with one rat; then suddenly she gets sick, and, quick as a paragraph passes, dies of consumption on a pauper's pallet.

Melanctha and her lover, Jess Campbell, live their lives at different speeds: She is quick, certain, and impulsive, while he is slow, ruminative, unsure. For Melanctha, Cupid's arrow is in flight, but Jeff is no more convinced than Zeno that the arrow has flown even a foot from its bow.

Although I had certainly heard the usual things about Gertrude Stein, and had encountered samples that made me think she might indeed be the fake that others had advertised, I did not read *Three Lives* until I was in graduate school at Cornell in—perhaps—1948. I remember the room, the chair, the failing light in which I began the book, going straight through from Anna to Lena and then rereading "Melanctha" immediately after; reading right on through the night, in an actual sweat of wonder and revelation I would experience with this work and no other. My stomach held the text in its coils as if I had swallowed the pages. I am sure I would have taken it as an omen had I known that *Three Lives* had been published on my birthday, July 30. I never slept. First I paced as well as I could, for my room was very small, and then I went out in the foggy early morning to walk, carrying the library's copy with one finger squeezed between its pages and at the lines I'd return to again and again—to listen, verify, reassure—a paragraph I've commented on in another essay, and whose words are Rose Johnson's:

> I don't see Melanctha why you should talk like you would kill yourself just because you're blue. I'd never kill myself Melanctha just 'cause I was blue. I'd maybe kill somebody else Melanctha 'cause I was blue, but I'd never kill myself. If I ever killed myself Melanctha it'd be by accident, and if I ever killed myself by accident Melanctha, I'd be awful sorry.

In my stunned, sickish, and sleepless state, I didn't notice right away that Rose Johnson, when she is speaking about Melanctha's melancholy, says "just because you're blue" (in iambs), but when she is speaking about her own unlikely suicide, she says "just 'cause I was blue" (in spondees). "Because" and " 'cause," " 'cause" and "because." I felt a lot like Jeff Campbell, too. I felt slow and confused. Because: Why hadn't I known long before reading Stein—

was I such a dunce?—that the art was in the music—it was Joyce's music, it was James's music, it was Faulkner's music; without the music, words fell to earth in prosy pieces; without the music, there was only comprehension, and comprehension may have been analysis, may have been interpretation, may have been philosophy, but it wasn't art; art was the mind carried to conclusions ahead of any understanding by the music—the order, release, and sounding of the meaning. Not just because of a little alliteration, the pitter-patter of metrical feet, a repetition like a chant, or rhyme concealed the way Poe's letter was—in plain view—but because of complex conceptual relations made audible.

Suppose Stein had written this story about Jane Harden. "I don't see Jane why you should talk like you would kill yourself just because you're blue. I'd never kill myself Jane just 'cause I was blue." Melanctha Herbert or Jane Harden. As Stein insists, there is between them a huge emotional distance—and it shows up in their names, and in the music their names make.

The opening sentence sits by itself like a paragraph: "Rose Johnson made it very hard to bring her baby to its birth." Stein does not begin by telling us Rose Johnson had a hard time having her baby, though that might have been a normal way of putting it. If she had had a hard time having her baby, her difficulties would have appeared to have been outside her control, but no, she "made it very hard"—not "to have her baby," again, the usual way of putting it, but "to bring her baby to its birth," as if the baby were, in the womb, yet a long way off. If Mary and Joseph had taken aim on Bethlehem, then they would have had a hard time bringing their baby to its birth. Of course, Rose Johnson made it very hard for others to help her have her baby. She made it particularly hard for her friend Melanctha Herbert.

This baby will not have a long hard Negro life. Neglect will see to that, and matters of fact will describe it. Dead is dead. That's how the story will be told: directly, simply, bluntly, symmetrically, and in a style quintessentially American.

The name Melanctha is itself a melody. Melanctha Herbert

tended Rose—she sprayed and pruned and weeded and watered—
and she was, while tending Rose, "patient, submissive, soothing, and
untiring," although Rose was "sullen, childish, cowardly, black,"
matching each fine quality Melanctha had with a flawed one of her
own. A pattern of three or four or five or more modifiers will serve as
a syntactical motif throughout the story, a device that was common
in the larger-than-life tales of our early nation. Mark Twain was a
master of it—one might say its pilot.

If "Rose Johnson was a real black, tall, well built, sullen, stupid,
childlike, good looking negress," Mr. Brown, whom Mark Twain met
on the Mississippi, "was a middle-aged, long, slim, bony, smooth-
shaven, horse-faced, ignorant, stingy, malicious, snarling fault hunting, mote-magnifying tyrant" (*Life on the Mississippi*. New York:
Harper & Brothers, 1917, p. 164). Good try, Mark, but "why did the
subtle, intelligent, attractive, half white girl Melanctha Herbert love
and do for and demean herself in service to this coarse, decent,
sullen, ordinary, black childish Rose, and why was this unmoral,
promiscuous, shiftless Rose married, and that's not so common
either, to a good man of the negroes, while Melanctha with her
white blood and attraction and her desire for a right position had not
yet been really married."

Try to top that, Mark. Well, all right, how about a mule race written in pure Steinline?

> There were thirteen mules in the first heat; all sorts of mules,
> they were; all sorts of complexions, gaits, dispositions, aspects.
> Some were handsome creatures, some were not; some were
> sleek, some hadn't had their fur brushed lately; some were
> innocently gay and frisky; some were full of malice and all
> unrighteousness; guessing from looks, some of them thought
> the matter on hand was war, some thought it was a lark, the
> rest took it for a religious occasion. (*Life on the Mississippi*, p. 371.)

This is the rhetoric of the border preacher and the river liar and
the hyperbole of slanging matches (not unknown among blacks) put
to another use. Both writers write simply; both writers are accom-

plished rhetoricians; both writers are very funny; both writers dislike nonsense; both writers are satirists; both writers are as American as all git out.

Indulge me in one more example, this one also employing the same rhythmic name pauses but for different rhetorical purposes. William Faulkner is opening the door of his novel *The Mansion*.

> The jury said "Guilty" and the Judge said "Life" but he didn't hear them. He wasn't listening. In fact, he hadn't been able to listen since that first day when the Judge banged his little wooden hammer on the high desk until he, Mink, dragged his gaze back from the far door of the courtroom to see what in the world the man wanted, and he, the Judge, leaned down across the desk hollering: "You, Snopes! Did you or didn't you kill Jack Houston?" and he, Mink, said, "Dont bother me now. Cant you see I'm busy?" then at the back of the room, himself hollering into, against, across the wall of little wan faces hemming him in "Snopes! Flem Snopes! Anybody here that'll go and bring Flem Snopes! I'll pay you—Flem'll pay you!"

In a letter to Mabel Weeks, Gertrude Stein allows as how the *Lives* "will certainly make your hair curl with the complication and the tintinabulation of its style but I'm very fond of it, nothing will discourage me. I think it is a noble combination of Swift and Matisse." At first, Swift seems a curious choice. Swift and Matisse because Mabel says so, Edgar Allan Poe on account of her allusion, Flaubert from the story's title, and Cézanne, since it was in that direction that Gertrude Stein was looking. Add to the crowd Stein's medical experience and her formerly lackadaisical lesbian life.

The story's recursive nature, much commented on, can be found not only in the narrative but in the syntax of its sentences, the arrangement of its paragraphs, the systematic use of epithets: Melanctha is inevitably "complex" and "unsure," her mother is "dignified," "pleasant," "pale yellow," while her father is "big, black, and virile." There is, in addition, the carefully deployed rhetoric of each speech, which often sounds sung, the fearless use of rhyme, as well as the ubiquity of contrast and symmetry. "Melanctha Herbert was always losing what she had in wanting all the things she saw. Melanctha was always being left when she was not leaving others."

As a story, "Melanctha" approaches formal perfection. Every element is artificial, its view of the Negro starkly stereotypical, embarrassing even for its time, as condescending as a cliff; and yet readers are not wrong to feel as if its author had come from the very center of her subject. It inches forward, piling up its repetitions in a high hoop before advancing, and then immediately piling them up again, meditative and analytic, looping like something sewn, not simply circling. The earthy plain simplicity of most of the diction, the slightly awkward phrasing, yet the remoteness of the summary narrative ("In these next years Melanctha learned many ways that lead to wisdom"), allow Stein to achieve a sense of the genuine and sympathetic in black experience without having to confess to an ignorance of day-to-day details. Even the prim euphemisms, almost biblical ("the ways that lead to wisdom" or "she strayed"), help Stein measure the distance from reality that Melanctha maintains even while pretending to be a prostitute and teasing the men of the yards and docks.

Melanctha Herbert is an overtaker. Jane Harden, a paler black than Melanctha, who is paler than Rose Johnson, initiates Melanctha's instruction in the sexual ways of the world, for Melanctha is not able to escape Jane's attentions in the nick of time, as she has escaped the joshing men. Nevertheless, Melanctha soon overtakes her teacher: "Then slowly, between them, it began to be all different. Slowly now between them, it was Melanctha Herbert, who was stronger. Slowly now they began to drift apart from one another." Then slowly the words shift their positions, backing always to the beginning, slowly starting again and advancing, until they begin to pass Jane Harden and ever so slowly to leave her behind.

It is languid, this ebb and flow, like a stew, a soup slowly stirred, like a groaning churn, this prose. It starts and restarts and moves like a syrup, like a slow spoon. Not meditative itself, not like Musil or Proust the most dedicated, the most profound of meditators, but as if the stirrer is elsewhere than the hand, elsewhere than the spoon that is stirring, the spoon simply going about. As if there is much to meditate upon elsewhere, so that attention leaves the hand, no thought is given to the spoon, left to move around and around on its own.

And what is it that is going on elsewhere? Elsewhere, Gertrude Stein, the student of philosophy, the student of psychology, the student of medicine, is discovering in herself the lush ornamental sensuality of Matisse, the afterlove languor of the odalisque, the imperious pleasures of whim and impulse.

Though it can be strident, too, this prose. When Jane Harden complains to Dr. Campbell about Melanctha, her lost lover, the repetitions mount, just as we, ourselves, go on when we feel aggrieved, chewing our resentments like rubber; but mere realism would be as boring as we really are when we whine, when one time is too many, when ten times become insufferable; so, to avoid realism, the prose shapes itself and takes on its own formal interest, and gives anger a chance to dance.

All good and great books are long because they must be mumbled if not sung. "Melanctha" took me the whole night the second time around, because that second reading was all sound. Where my finger—like a dactyl—was, when I went walking, was at Melanctha's name like a musical pause. "I'd never kill myself . . . Melanctha . . . just 'cause I was blue."

How little good a jam of qualifiers really does a noun. Jefferson Campbell's father, for instance, is a bunch of them, now in alphabetical order: dignified, gray-haired, good, intelligent, kind, light brown, religious, serious, steady; and his mother: gentle, little, pale brown, sweet. So he's gray-haired—so what? So she's pale brown—so what? As the words are distributed, as they are arranged, they begin to play: "Jefferson's father was a good, kind, serious, religious man." Moral values descend from "good" through "kind" to "serious," verbal accents soften into the ending of "religious." Ethical commonplaces conquer the queue.

Jefferson Campbell is the center of this story—the doctor

Gertrude Stein almost was. When he arrives, the story moves resolutely into the mind, and there it plays itself obsessively, the way an unwanted tune sometimes sticks in the head and won't be shaken off, but continues to cling like a burr to a sweater. The doctor's long speeches—customarily phatic and ceremonially polite—say little but sing much. During their duet, Melanctha pleads for passion (as if passion could be pled for) and Jeff Campbell for good sense (as if good sense could simply be summoned). He soothes. She insults. He is careful. She says he's scared, afraid to be shaken to his depths.

> "No Miss Melanctha I certainly do only know just two kinds of ways of loving. One kind of loving seems to me, is like one has a good quiet feeling in a family when one does his work, and is always living good and being regular, and then the other way of loving is just like having it like any animal that's low in the streets together, and that don't seem to me very good Miss Melanctha, though I don't say ever that it's not all right when anybody likes it. . . ."

Gertrude Stein uses words as note units, even when they have syllabic components and are clearly accented. That's why she prefers monosyllables or words that are simple enough they can be treated as musical wholes. Remove the hesitational stuffing from the previous quotation and all we have is: ". . . I know two kinds of loving . . ." Yet padding such as "just" and "like" shift their meanings, help emphasize Jeff's tentative hold on things, his polite reluctance to be blunt. In the following example, the iambs come marching in until the word "just" is reached, whereupon trochees and spondees take over. ". . . I want to see the colored people being good and careful and always honest and living always just as regular as can be, and I am sure Miss Melanctha, that that way everybody can have a good time, and be happy and keep right and be busy, and not always have to be doing bad things for new ways to get excited."

The name Melanctha is often used as a pause of punctuation, but sometimes a simple monosyllable will serve, as "now" does in this instance: "Jefferson and Melanctha now saw each other, very often.

They now always liked to be with each other, and they always now had a good time when they talked to one another." There are three parallel constructions here, with word order varied slightly for effect. "Jefferson and Melanctha" is replaced by "they"; "now saw" becomes "now always liked" which turns into "always now had"; "each other" becomes "one another." Analysis is tiresome, so I relinquish it, though reluctantly, because it has only put one toe in the water.

To view the structure of these sentences, it is necessary to rearrange the words so that repeated parts stand above and under one another. The conjunction *and* often acts as a spindle around which phrases and clauses turn. This, too, is mechanical and rather boring, except to people like me who think they suddenly see maps of meaning and structures of sound and get excited in the way Jeff Campbell constantly complains about and worries about and warns of.

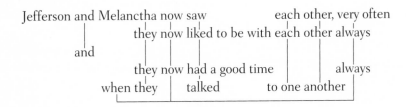

In the first clause, "very often" follows a comma and is really an add-on. It strengthens like a storm to "always" and then moves, during succeeding clauses, toward "they." When Mies van der Rohe said that God was in the details, and Paul Valéry insisted that there were no details in execution, both meant the same thing—namely that every element of the work must be made to count. That little move of "always" toward the loving couple counts for a lot.

It is, of course, an incredible courtship, carried on near the bedside of Melanctha's dying mother, delayed by the illness and the malice of Jane Harden, entirely verbal in its approaches and in its retreats, with embraces that are all air, an intercourse of thought and feeling that allegorizes the characters. As Richard Bridgeman has observed, Jeff and Melanctha sing duets, and, in Stein, we are never far from the operatic. Jeff Campbell has Hamlet's handicap. His habitual hesitations are the result of his slow thought, his constant pondering. Melanctha's passion is impulsive and headstrong. She leans near hoping to be touched. Jeff Campbell talks until she straightens up and drifts away. Or trembles. Then he puts his arms around her like a brother. The sexes continue to make war by means of mutual misunderstanding. The love/death theme is sounded on the first page when the result of love, in the body of the baby, dies of indifference. Finally, after an act or two of mutual confusion and the machinations of Jane Harden, they are allowed to enjoy their idyll, singing love and death together through the summer.

But does a dash of *Liebestod* do it? Does the psychological analysis (most of it left in the dark anyway) achieve it? Does the dance of phrases, clauses, compounds around a point establish the quality one feels here? Uniqueness may be a value, but it is not an aesthetic one. Certainly there is an amazing match in this prose between meaning and shifts of meaning, in addition to the movement, the singsong of the line; and when one hears it, maybe then that music does it: how it combines thought with flows of feeling, how it measures time, how inexorable its movement is in the direction of disaster. It is not the form, a bit of which I shall now describe, but the feeling of that form when articulated—when per-formed—that does it . . . whatever it exactly is. For instance, there are the uneasy iambs that precede the strong stresses of Jeff's fair firm love, and the bumpy fall away into its futility in this sentence (shortly to be cited); there is the modulation of "with her," "about her," "for her," and "with her" again, as we pass through this customary and customarily brilliant passage: "He was uneasy always, with her, he was uneasy when he thought about her, he knew now he had a good, straight, strong feeling of right loving for her, and yet now he never could use it to be good and honest with her."

It's what kept me up and drove me out into the street. Stein had restored prose to its formerly powerful rhetorical place, the way Joyce, of course, had done; yet more simply, less like the Irish tenor being piteous in a bar, or arranging sensualities to resemble bottles posed before their drinker in a cautionary line like, as we used to say, dead soldiers; but more the way William Jennings Bryan might have ranted, or some tent preacher might have reiterated his belief in the latest or the oldest rigmarole of his religion. It was done with the simple abstract workaday words of "yet" and "now" and "never." The most ordinary . . . the most ignored . . . "true," the most frequently repeated . . . the most modest of materials made her palate—a word like "now" for instance, a word like "one," a word like "like," or the infinitive "to go."

What would happen to "now"—that simple sound, familiar notion? It would find itself cheek by jowl with "always." Always—a stretch of great extension—always—suddenly cut short by being confined in a small tight space like an eagle in a cage—"always now." Then the space between them—"always" and "now"—is artfully lengthened, shortened, lengthened again; and a few synonyms are allowed to serve, most momentarily, in their stead, diminishing "always" to "often" for instance:

> Always now Jeff had to go so much faster than was real with his feeling. Yet always Jeff knew now he had a right, strong feeling. Always now when Jeff was wondering, it was Melanctha he was doubting, in the loving. Now he would often ask her, was she real now to him, in her loving. He would ask her often, feeling something queer about it all inside him, though yet he was never really strong in his doubting, and always Melanctha would answer to him. "Yes Jeff, sure, you know it, always," and always Jeff felt a doubt now, in her loving.

I am an organization man, and this was prose organized to matter, not just because of the importance of its sense or sentiment but also because of its art. The pace, the pause, the repeats, the loops, the variations, the apparent monotones, the pronouns, the placeholders, suddenly rose, threw off their modest roles to become riots of color, to call for new orders, and at last to assume positions of authority, majesty even; and when there, when secure in the seats of power, to turn time like a top whose turning alone kept it atiptoe: "Always now every day he found it harder to make the time pass, with her, and not let his feeling come so that he would quarrel with her."

It is customary to point out that Melanctha represents impulse and instinct; that she is reckless in her openness; and that Jeff is practical, a man of science and healing, of reason and moderation. Yet Jeff does not think a lot, if by that one means hunting for premises and driving them to their conclusion. Jeff does not investigate, if one means he collects data and forms hypotheses. No. Jeff mulls. Over and over. He hesitates; he vacillates; he suddenly, inexplicably, has a change of mind (or perhaps a change of heart has preceded and hastened it). He wonders why his attitudes have altered, and he wonders why he is wondering. Because Jeff Campbell is above all cautious. He understands the black man's world, the black man's position. He knows how easily things go wrong in it. He is in the grip of conventionality—he seeks the safe life, which is a life defined for him by the white world, its white God, its white leaders, its white laws. And every time his feelings seem to venture forth or his mind leaps like a fish to snap at a new notion, he is frightened and worried by his fear. He can look in the white man's mirror and see shiftlessness, carelessness, irresponsibility—qualities his features must not match.

Melanctha's knowledge is carnal, and she obtains it willy-nilly—through her wandering. Jeff's knowledge includes the carnal, too, for he is a doctor, after all, but it is principally knowledge of pain, not pleasure, of breakdowns in the body, not in its happy, healthy, or exuberant use. Jeff's knowledge is licensed, Melanctha's is forbidden. So Jeff Campbell stews, drawn by desire, repelled through prudence. In the wide room in his head set aside for worry, he paces, and the style Stein has given him paces with him, step for step.

The satisfaction of such sentences has stayed with me for fifty years, setting a standard that would last, for me, my lifetime; but persuading others that such sentences are as new in English as miracles, and as miraculous in themselves as miracles, too, as curative as the king's touch, their loops as thrilling as a coaster, is not easy, because quality cannot be contained in a report.

The Bridgeport Bureau of Health and its coroner can report that baby Johnson died of malnutrition on such and such a date; and the data contained in that report, said to be facts that establish the document as a true one, are open to the inspection of anyone's eye and the judgment of anyone's mind. Fresh information can always turn up, and could possibly cause us to regard the report as less than truthful. In other words, descriptions are capable of being true and false, of being added to or subtracted from; and it is to the account (and not the death of infant Johnson by itself) that we properly assign the value true or false.

Moreover, that description, if taken as true so far as it seems inclined to go, will normally give rise to feelings of moral dismay or repugnance; and even if the text is indifferent and passes over the infant's death as simply incidental, we know that Rose Johnson's callous negligence was wrong, that any social situation that requires such indifference is evil, and the author's observation that infant deaths were common in the community will not alleviate or palliate our concern. That is, moral judgments are based upon, and should attach themselves to, accurate descriptions. In this way, customarily, the law proceeds. A true account is the platform on which moral judgment stands when it proposes to speak.

But when we think of the lines that comprise the description instead of the situation they render, and call these sentences fine or excellent, or forceful or moving, or eloquent or lovely, there is no item referred to by the wording, no bit of data, no stubborn or redoubtable fact, that will help us support our judgment, nor will any analysis of the description do the trick; for, although it may be true to say a certain sentence shifts halfway in its course from iambs to dactyls, that its phrases repeat like the bells of Rachmaninoff, that there is a pun in the third clause and a curse in the last, that mouthing its open vowels makes the mouther nervously yawn and swallow hard, that it mimics, perfectly, the slow repetitious turns of interior life, none of these characteristics will give any third party a clue as to quality the way we know that a sentence that says someone saw steam turn to snow must be untrue or that a case of such neglect as was Rose's, if the account is correct, should be morally condemned.

No description of either subject matter or treatment will provide the least real clue to the actual artistic quality of the object, even if we are inclined to be suspicious of paintings of covered bridges in moonlight or of sci-fi stories or music made of metal (probabilities created by the repeated experience of so-called similar things), since lovely pictures of covered bridges are certainly possible (after all, the Madonna, among the more sentimental of subjects, has been painted magnificently untold times), while from any popular loud-mouthed medium, and possibly to great surprise, excellence might show itself like Venus riding shoreward on a dollar bill.

Accounts cannot intervene in aesthetic determinations; only the direct, informed, repeated experience of the work will serve, and therefore no one without that experience should be persuaded to admire a Mona Lisa or a pyramid, only to acknowledge its extensive and positive press.

What one can do, with description and analysis and expressions of enthusiasm, is entice, lure others to peek between the covers; to remove possible prejudices or expectations that might interfere with the experience; to provide suggestions of where best to start, what to expect, how to look or read or listen; and to give reasons why the work should be treated with seriousness and respect.

Once the quality of "Melanctha" is fully granted, and the excellence of those other two lives (Anna and Lena, neither negligible) is also admitted, then we can push our suspicious critic toward other surprises, other savors, equally ineffable, but equally there.

If Stein herself, in those earlier years, was a model for the cautious, ruminating Dr. Campbell, she learned, at least with language, to Melancthalate it, to wander with a whirling skirt among words, to play with them, to seek excitement, to risk chance encounters, to dance and sing, sing from inside, because whatever is sung from inside is yours. Readers of Stein should learn to ease up and rollick a little, to expect a good time. Here is an amusing modulation from a book called *Useful Knowledge* (p. 67): "When they are sung and sung and sung and little have to have a hand and hand and two and two hands too, and too and two and handled too to them, handed to them, hand and hands. Hands high."

Then I think we know the reason Stein is Stein—we've felt the reason, heard the reason, sung the reason why.

AN INTRODUCTION TO
AT SWIM-TWO-BIRDS

The book you are about to read—if for the first time, with delight and amazement, and if for the fourth, with delight and fond remembrance—appeared in the same year (1939) as *Finnegans Wake,* another very Irish contrivance. But the beginning of the text (there are several openings) is pure Samuel Beckett, which, for such a book as this is, seems wholly appropriate, since *Murphy* had already arrived the year before. "Having placed in my mouth sufficient bread for three minutes' chewing . . ." Brian O'Nolan, who assumed pseudonymity as eagerly as Kierkegaard, had perfect pitch and could capture and copy any tone—even before he'd heard it. Still, I shall not speak more of James Joyce, whose love of *At Swim* was well known to O'Nolan because a Joyce blurb was used to puff more than one edition, though without any apparent success. In the United States, it unanimously failed to find more than a few readers. To this day. When all shall change.

The comparison with Joyce was, I suppose, inevitable, if misleading, inasmuch as the resemblances are accidental—that is to say, Irish. "If I hear that word 'Joyce' again, I will surely froth at the gob!" O'Nolan wrote in a letter to a friend. So the publisher will perhaps paste an errata slip over this part of my remarks.

According to its author, Adolf Hitler hated *At Swim-Two-Birds* so vehemently, he started World War II in order to interfere with its sales. "In a grim irony that is not without charm," O'Nolan wrote, "the book survived the war while Hitler did not."

O'Nolan did not begin life as O'Nolan. He was born a Brian ó Nualláin, sometimes spelled Brian Ua Nualláin when apostrophed O's ran out, but he grew tired of seeing his name misspelled, especially during the public controversies in which he was so frequently but happily embroiled. He had discovered his debating skills at Dublin's University College, practiced them in the "Letters" page of the *Irish Times,* where he had begun by attacking Seán ó Faoláin and Frank O'Connor, whom he accused of pretending to "high art" (though an attack carried out under an assumed name cannot be accounted brave), and then—finding it all so much fun— polished his scorn to a high shine while contributing to other controversies, some of which his own letters had created (in company with a pal of equal waggishness, Niall Sheridan)—a sport that required the invention of many more noms de plume, including naïvely local identifications for the missive makers, such as "An Irishman from Aberdeen" or "A Glaswegian from London." It was especially delightful when honest and sincere folk were gulled into entering the fray, only to be verbally tarred and feathered by folk who did not exist.

During this period of pan-enmity, *At Swim-Two-Birds* was written by Flann O'Brien, initially of that name to deflect from his novel the anger of those he had annoyed, but now itself a conspicuous target for more recent resentments (since Flann O'Brien had been signed to his scurrilities against ó Faoláin and O'Connor), that he offered his publisher another, suggesting the innocuous and unknown John Hackett in Flann's stead. His editor, however, quite properly preferred the first choice as more grossly Irish.

The correspondence column of the *Irish Times* became so popular that its editor sought out its pseudonymous instigator, and finally offered him a column of his—that is, Myles na Gopaleen's—own. Flann O'Brien's long career as a columnist had already begun in college, where he had regularly written for its magazine under the alias

Brother Barnabas. In time, John James Doe and George Knowall would come into the world to write articles and stories for other papers. O'Nolan remained a moderate Catholic his entire life; O'Nolan toiled for eight years as a civil servant; so O'Nolan could not cast aspersions upon the character of government officials or castigate the policies of the Church or sneer at Irishness; but Brother Barnabas could, Flann O'Brien did, and, six times weekly, so did Myles.

At Swim-Two-Birds embarrassed O'Nolan, who professed to detest its youthful excesses and pretended to loathe the merest mention of the book; however, it is hard to continue to admire your first work when it turns out to be your best one, and the one on which your reputation rests, fixing Flann O'Brien to your public presence as if it were the name of someone real. Although far from a one-book author—*The Third Policeman* and *The Poor Mouth* immediately come to mind—Flann O'Brien became a one-timer anyhow, and was thus kept imprisoned in his youthful pseudonym.

Never very dutiful about the formal part of his education, O'Brien picked up ideas much as editors or journalists do—like persons met in a pub or embroilments encountered on the street. Instead of literature and grammar, he studied poker and billiards, drinking and purloining. A letter he liked, the manners of a friend, opinions overheard, a way a writer might have of putting things, places he habituated—all might find themselves hauled away to be housed in his book; and, in truth, his books were like food processors: Actual things were inserted into them and whirled about and chewed and chopped into the consistency of fiction, whereupon the mix would be poured into the world again, real once more but altered altogether.

The metafictional form of *At Swim-Two-Birds* (and how O'Brien would have loathed the term) permits its author, and the narrator he invents, and all the other writers created by the book's neophyte novelist, to be born again, to enjoy another life, to cross logical boundaries as if carried by a breeze. Here's how it goes. Brian O'Nolan begets Flann O'Brien, who begets the novel's unnamed narrator N and then places him in the real world of University College, Dublin, where he is (as his author once was) a far from diligent student. N creates, for his book, a pub owner named Trellis, who has two principal activities, writing and sleeping. Next, with the help of a cowboy romance writer, William Tracy, Trellis manages to have his archvillain appear, fully fledged, as if he had sprung, at age twenty-five, from the brow of the page. Through this strategy, Flann O'Brien makes the habit authors have of introducing characters at the one point in their life that will prove useful to the story seem strangely arbitrary, not to say weird. In the same way, he contrives his fiend's moral opposite, Sheila Lamont, who must be invented to make an edifying contrast. However, most of Trellis's characters are lured from other books, instructed as to their roles, and sent about their business.

While Trellis sleeps, his characters, both created and borrowed, like toys beneath the Christmas tree, go their own ways, eventually drugging him in order to prolong their freedom. Trellis himself cannot resist the charms of his own fair Sheila, and having brought her into being in his bedroom, he forces his attentions on her there, with the result, prescribed by tradition, that a son, Orlick Trellis, is born, and born, eventually, to write a punishing book about his father.

Although *At Swim-Two-Birds* has the form of a classic frame tale, the four books (B1:O'Brien's; B2:N's; B3:Trellis's; B4:the son's) are not hermetically sealed from one another as these designations seem to indicate. Like salvage from the sea, flotsam from this or that wrecked narrative washes up on foreign shores. How, you ask? While seated inside B1, Brinsley, a friend of B2, parodies a passage from B2's B3 in the style of B4. If authors write, as they surely must, mostly from their own experience, narrow and uninteresting as it may be, then we should not be surprised to find fictional authors doing the same thing. (What sort of experience can they have had?) O'Brien's unnamed collegian spends a good bit of his time in bed, to the annoyance of his uncle, though not in order to annoy him; so when we encounter Dermot Trellis, we are not surprised, as I said we should not be, to read him described as "flabby and unattractive, partly a result of his having remained in bed for a period of twenty years."

In this book, each plot is a digression, chaos overcomes order in a most orderly way, allusions are so plentiful, like reflections that dematerialize their mirror, who knows what belongs to what, and the narrative thread is lost in its own tangle. Anne Clissman's pathmaking study, *Flann O'Brien: A Critical Introduction,* numbers forty-two extracts in thirty-six different styles.

Among them, American readers will recognize the Paul Bunyan style, triggered by the common question: Just how cold/tall/loud/swift was the hero, the amazon, the forest critter? with its customary Rabelaisian answer: just as tall and loud as its subject—thus, if it's the sun, then brighter than; if about drink, consumption shall be measured in tuns; if on manly heroics, then of those mightier than ten thousand, of those deadlier than adders, more pitiless than bronze, especially when flung.

Here is Flann O'Brien's Finn Mac Cool:

> With that he rose to a full tree-high standing, the sable cat-guts which held his bog-cloth drawers to the hems of his jacket of pleated fustian clanging together in melodious discourse.

Now to compare this with the unmentionable rival, Jarl von Hoother, from *Finnegans Wake:*

> For like the campbells acoming with a fork lance of lightning, Jarl von Hoother Boanerges himself, the old terror of the dames, came hip hop handihap out through the pikeopened arkway of his three shuttoned castles, in his broadginger hat and his civic chollar and his allabuff hemmed and his bullbraggin soxandgloves and his ladbroke breeks and his cattegut bandolair and his furframed panuncular cumbottes like a rudd yellan gruebleen orangeman in his violet indigonation, to the whole length of the strength of his bowman's bill.

And back to Mac Cool:

> The knees and calves to him, swealed and swathed with
> soogawns and Thommond weed-ropes, were smutted with
> dungs and dirt-daubs of every hue and pigment, hardened by
> staining of mead and trickles of metheglin and all the drib-
> blings and drippings of his medher, for it was the custom of
> Finn to drink nightly with his people.

This is prose meant to be put in the mouth, then chewed, then
washed about, then swallowed, the swallow followed by a wide
smile.

Parody is what this writing is frequently called, but it is parody
with a difference, because most parody, though its original is readily
recognized, does not outdo the object of its ridicule, surpass its
excellence in any way; for normally parody grotesquely exaggerates
the outstanding and most annoying features of its victim, like a cartoon enlarging the nose, multiplying the number of nose hairs,
weighing on the flesh of the face so that its jowls, cheeks, and eye-
lids droop like curtain drapes, furrowing the brow as if to make it
ready for soon-to-be-sown seed; moreover mimicking the movement
of the original in the most mocking fashion, and making it quite
impossible for real quality to be found in either cat or copy; however,
Flann O'Brien not only mimics the salient features and fustian of
heroic Gaelic tales but supersedes them, suggesting to the reader
that *this,* his Finn, is more splendidly gigantic and mythically outrageous than the storied original.

> . . . where is the living human man who could beat Finn at
> the making of generous cheese, at the spearing of ganders,
> at the magic of thumb-suck, at the shaving of hog-hair, or at the
> unleashing of long hounds from a gold thong in the full chase,
> sweet-fingered corn-yellow Finn, Finn that could carry an
> armed host from Almha to Slieve Luachra in the craw of his
> gut-hung knickers.
> Good for telling, said Conan.

Good indeed. Where will you find—these days—as joyous a throat, so that saying the song to yourself, if not daring its full singing, will make you happier than a sniff would? Or even a check arriving in the mail?

O'Brien showed the manuscript of *At Swim* to his friend Niall Sheridan, who found it far too long, and who, according to Anthony Cronin's biography, *No Laughing Matter,* was subsequently given the job of cutting its locks and shaving its beard. Clean-cheeked, its weight less by a third, and presumably more presentable, the manuscript began to make its way through the offices of publishers, but, with uncommon good luck, soon came under the fine eye of Graham Greene, who was then a reader at Longman's, and who energetically supported its publication. The author was eagerly agreeable when it came to making changes his editor asked for, removing some "coarseness" (unwisely replacing "all balls" with "all my bum"), clarifying some scenes, and suggesting a number of alternative titles (all awful). More important were the general revisions O'Brien made on his own account, now that the book was nearing an actual existence. *At Swim's* appearance was rewarded with the reviewers' required stupidity, but was praised by Beckett and Joyce (oops, that man again), who, eyesight failing, read it with a magnifying glass.

Beckett, Joyce, Graham Greene, a few friends, later the imposter William Saroyan: Who else should be needed to satisfy the soul's hunger for support and praise? But many authors secretly disbelieve their friends or even equals, for they know how often they've lied themselves; and anyway, one's colleagues are often as unknown and pauper-bound as one's self. No. I don't blame Flann O'Brien (who wrote this wise and riotous work), but shame on Brian O'Nolan, who wanted to be a rich, famous, and widely popular author, in the very culture his book exposes as so much Irish hokum. O'Nolan, it's clear, was a conservative, anti-intellectual, provincial barfly, and pool shark, while Flann O'Brien was a Swift-eyed revolutionary, who overturned conventions the way O'Nolan turned over his poker cards, and who read every rattle in the dice cup as a menacing omen.

If I begin a book by imagining a young man (such as meself) writing a book, then who is writing the book he is writing? 'Tis still "I," of course—who else could it be? But it is not the "I" I am, with my beliefs and degrees; it is one of my other selves, who has always thought it would be fun to be generous instead of stingy, friendly and open instead of suspicious, a bit of a believer instead of a snarly skeptic. I enjoy double anonymity, having invented the author of my book as well as the author in it.

To Brian O'Nolan, for example, the theories of Albert Einstein, then being bandied about, were dark indeed, but a bit of bent light made the same things seem clear as day to Myles na Gopaleen.

His biographer, Anthony Cronin, whom we could even call a crony, quotes O'Nolan on the value of this strategy:

> Apart from a thorough education of the widest kind, a contender in this field [writing] must have an equable yet versatile temperament, and the compartmentation of his personality for the purpose of literary utterance ensures that the fundamental individual will not be credited with a certain way of thinking, fixed attitudes, irreversible techniques of expression. No author should write under his own name nor under one permanent pen-name; a male writer should include in his impostures a female pen-name, and possibly vice versa.
>
> (*No Laughing Matter*. New York: Fromm International, 1998, p. 225.)

And if, down the road, some of a writer's characters were to rebel against their immediate maker, they would do so at the writer's request; and if their names were consumed by flames fanned in their own fiction, they would forever remain in the lifeline they were given: twenty-eight when they first appeared, forty-two when cindered. Moreover, any one of them (at age thirty, for instance) could make an appearance in the operatic and movie versions of their burned-out case; posters depicting their foul-smelling faces might be tacked to dormitory walls; they would be free to lend their names to psychological complexes or even hotels or museums, to participate in discussions of their natures and functions, the futures they might have had; consequently growing more real, mention by mention, until masochism becomes as common as phlox and Sacher-Masoch as forgotten as Phil Spitalny.

Suppose I were to have a life no longer than a page; if it were the right sort of page, I might immortally reside there, frozen at five months, bawling like the baby I shall always be, bawling monumentally, bawling for all babies in all time, climes, and countries—if my bawl is bawled by an astonishing phrase.

Who remembers with fondness, or even a stretch of vivacity, one Prufrock who owned a furniture store in St. Louis?

After six months of life, *At Swim-Two-Birds* had sold 244 copies. Sales would have to slacken following such an exhilarating start. Especially when the publisher's building and book stock was destroyed by German incendiary bombs—as the novel itself seems to have foretold. Furthermore, in order to punish the persona who had created characters preferring bar life to a workaday one, and slumber in drunken beds to bars, Brian O'Nolan regularly dragged Flann O'Brien from pub to pub in the afternoon, and then staggered him to sleep in a dung brown bedroom even before nightfall—both worlds without women and soddenly safe—where piles of paper concealed the floor like the litter of a litter box, and an electric fire burned night and day, threatening to overheat and become the cause that would fulfill the calamities envisioned by a fiction.

It was a big baronial bed, but was it Brian O'Nolan or Flann O'Brien who was drunkenly lying in it? It would have to be the former, for the latter had depicted the banality of bar banter so beautifully as to end it in chagrin. It was Flann who knew most particularly the emptiness of an Irishman's saloon life, the chaff and chat and ruminations that went wetly nowhere, the liquor necessary to set one's sexuality on indefinite simmer, dull the sense of failure, fill boredom with bad jokes. Though Flann is simply poking fun, nevertheless the needled balloon bursts and out rushes its bad air.

When Brian O'Nolan assumed the self of Myles na Gopaleen, he became an occasionally clever journalist and a tart observer of society, but with the journalist's inevitable lowbrow taste and hang-around culture. The noms de plume did not get on. It was Myles, I think, who used, feared, and disliked Joyce, attacking him persistently in the papers; it was Myles, again, who repeated the old canard that art is communication, although *At Swim-Two-Birds* and *The Third Policeman* had badly wounded, if not killed, that philistine philosophy. It was Myles who wrote of Joyce what was true of Flann O'Brien: that he "was a great master of the banal in literature. By 'banal,' I mean the fusion of uproarious comic stuff and deep tragedy." On the other hand, it was Brian O'Nolan who made Flann O'Brien famous as a genius and a drunken failure (a popular Irish image of the Irish writer). It was Brian O'Nolan, not the Flann whose name was on the cover, who wrote the badly padded and excessive *The Hard Life*. It was Brian O'Nolan who, as Myles na Gopaleen, led a rascal's career, and kept Flann O'Brien's glory hidden in a darkened Dublin bedroom. As Hugh Kenner tartly remarks, when O'Nolan became "a licensed jester," a "great future lay behind him."

Flann O'Brien's sentences are always brisk and muscular and go where they are going in the promptest possible way. However, they are slowed in their own book as though held by a sleeve; they are bewildered by forms that enter every avenue like a parade; they are bedeviled by interruptions; sometimes there is a slight elevation to the diction of their pretended prose, at other times a discernable depression; they aren't often allowed to say much, although they say it directly, and frequently find themselves in heroically pointless conversations or even in the wrong mouth, and when there—in the wrong mouth—are required to speak in the pseudomythical manner the wrong mouth prefers; occasionally, some uncalled-upon critic or scholar will leave like a footprint a textual note, reminding the reader of other readers: All these forthright sentences become sillier by being sane in such precincts; yet—beware—as absurd, we must admit, as the situation often is, the absurdity is no more than a bad light in a closet making difficult one's deciding the true colors of the clothes (which does not mean the colors of the clothes are all false and dishonest), in example whereof I offer the following: "Do you know, said Orlick, filling the hole in his story with the music of his voice . . ." and I ask how often, especially in the theater where buckets of mellifluence are kept backstage to put out fires, have we heard song sing, so soulfully, a sense that isn't there?

There is . . . there was . . . a hole in the story. It is called *The Third Policeman,* Flann O'Brien's second book, certainly as brilliant as the first, a book about a dead man—blacker, more bitter than decent life, beautiful to a degree unrecognizable—which he completed during the year the work that would eclipse it—*At Swim-Two-Birds*—was published to nearly unanimous indifference. *The Third Policeman*—the great stretch of a fresh young genius—was . . . inconsolably . . . rejected; and O'Brien appears to have buried it and its dead narrator in a drawer, from whence it would not rise until 1967, when it reached print a year after its author's demise—his death allowing—nay, encouraging—the rebirth of his work. Shortly after *The Third Policeman* was turned down (and the bed of death made ready and the brown room painted the color of rye), Myles na Gopaleen began his column for the *Irish Times,* a project that ate at O'Brien's life like liquor at his liver.

It is written that "Evil is even, truth is an odd number and death a full stop." The Pythagoreans, too, thought evil was even, and truth an odd number, which is perhaps why *At Swim* begins and ends three times. Through an irony perhaps too broad to be believed, death claimed Brian O'Nolan on the first Fools' Day of April 1966, a day when Flann O'Brien was absent, participating in the celebration and drinking deep.

ON HEROES AND TOMBS

Although Ernesto Sábato's work is rather well known in Europe, where his first novel (*El túnel*, 1948) was championed by Camus, and praised by other writers of similar weight (its existential flavor went well with the mood of the day), the book did not earn him much lasting notice in the United States, even though Knopf was the first to translate it (as *The Outsider*) in 1950, six years ahead of the French. *Sobre héroes y tumbas* followed in 1961, and *Abaddón el exterminador*, completed in 1974, won him the Prix du Meilleur Livre Etranger. As if divinely arranged by the muse of prose, the great and astonishing efflorescence of Latin American literature, which the world would become aware of during the 1960s, has been blessed with English translators of exceptional skill, dedication, and literary understanding. Gregory Rabassa has translated Miguel Angel Asturias, Gabriel García Márquez, José Lezama Lima, and Luisa Valenzuela; Suzanne Jill Levine has done Julio Cortázar, Cabrera Infante, Severo Sarduy, and Manuel Puig; Margaret Sayers Peden has given us our Fuentes; while many fine writers such as Alejo Carpentier, José Donoso, and Renaldo Arenas have also been made available; yet somehow Ernesto Sábato kept slipping through the net (if any were drawn); but now Helen R. Lane, already known for her translations of Octavio Paz and Mario Vargas Llosa as well as her masterful rendering of the superb and fierce fictions of the Spanish novelist Juan Goytisolo, has brought *On Heroes and Tombs* beautifully before us—some recompense for a long delay.

Even as a sapling, Sábato leaned toward literature like an old tree long in the wind, so it is somewhat surprising to read of him studying mathematics and physics at the National University of La Plata; but one can imagine well enough how the young student, the tenth child in a litter of eleven, sent away to school and now alone for the first time in a strange city, sought clarity, order, security, and calm in the presumably emotionless realm of mathematics. It would certainly not be the first time. His human concerns, however, required an outlet, and sent him toward the Left—at the very least for comradeship and the security of shared opinions. The anarchist who figures so importantly in *On Heroes and Tombs* is based on an actual association with the movement. Harley Dean Oberhelman reports another incident of great significance for Sábato's development (in the Twayne World Authors Series). While attending a Communist Youth Conference in Brussels, and planning to leave there soon for the Soviet Union, he has a violent recurrence of his youthful insecurities, and flees to Paris, where he sinks into a stolen text of mathematical analysis.

Sábato was twenty-six when he received his doctorate, and he did well enough to be recommended for study at the Curie Laboratory in Paris, where he worked with Irène Joliot-Curie. At that time, his repudiation of science as well as his serious literary efforts began. Fragments of an unfinished novel from this period will find their way into *On Heroes and Tombs*. Under the influence of André Breton and other Surrealists, Sábato began to explore the psychic as well as the physical world. There is no question that his own illness literally turned him inward. Nevertheless, after a brief stay at MIT, he returned to the National University as a professor of theoretical physics, and remained in this post until 1943, when difficulties with the Perón government, in addition to his increasing desire and determination to write, decided him on resigning.

I draw this dim little sketch because a factor fundamental to

Sábato's concerns and career as a writer is nevertheless clearly out-lined by it. The fact that what it represents is an elementary philo-sophical mistake would not necessarily matter in the case of most writers—literature is literature, not logic—but it matters a great deal in Sábato's. Because—as it appears—Sábato had sought refuge him-self from a world of anxiety and unkempt passion by entering the field of mathematical physics, subsequently to return to that other—opposite—human field of feeling with a sense of the prodigal, and like one who has been "born again," even if unsaved; he supposed that science was such a haven for all men, and furthermore that sci-ence itself was an elaborate hypocrisy, because its vaunted efficiency and objectivity, its certainties and successes, hid a sterile emptiness; it was a pack of lies designed only to make men comfortable; first, materially, by supplying them with satisfactions and comforts (thereby binding them to pleasure); second, conceptually, by allow-ing them to believe in a knowable and orderly world, and permitting them to escape any direct confrontation with the self by substituting for it a "custom-made" character and a soil-resistant soul.

To imitate Sábato's own sort of simile: It is as if I supposed, because in my former career as a highwayman I had once hidden in a hollow tree to escape the sheriff's hot pursuit, that all trees were hollow by contrivance, and grown only for the purpose of conceal-ment by crooked arborists.

Throughout Europe, during the time Sábato was writing his first novel and divorcing himself from science, armchair analysts of the Human Spirit and our Anxious Alienated State of Absurd Existence initially felt X, and then, when a crowd came, often Y: that World War II had been fought by machines, which had then made machines of men; that the knowledge which had so improved our efficiency at murder had made us murderous; that reason, not hav-ing been employed to reason, only to rationalize, was useless; that certain ideals, never pursued, wouldn't work; that traditional values, having been abandoned, did not exist; that science, a tool of the bourgeois capitalist system certainly, was itself sick as a dog schooled in how to be vicious on command (or had it trained its keepers to growl?). They remembered, these critics of culture, that the architects and artists who worshiped the machine had also extolled speed and Mussolini, and built boxes out of the harsh modern materials of camps and bunkers; they remembered the fascism of the Futurists, the dandyism of D'Annunzio; they recalled the promises of improvement in the conditions of human life that science was said to hold out like a bouquet—and the flowers of evil that had, in fact, bloomed in our fists. They counted the lies of the politicians as if lying were new to them and the lies fresh. The long, complex, and imposing tradition of the West had failed; progress was a bad joke, business exploitive, the state corrupt, the Church an impotent falsehood; and one could not help but hear inside the painful outcries of the Communists (with whom many existentialists sympathized and with whom they stood around on streets to rattle tambourines as though playing Salvation Army) more than one kind and quality of complaint: that of the disillusioned humanist, the failed saint, the guilty technician and researcher, the embittered artist, the mournful adult, the disappointed child. Sábato gives each a voice, although each voice is his, because back in Argentina, Europe seems stale, sometimes simply an immigrant's baggage of the sort that Sábato's Italian family had brought—furniture still useful yet odd and out of place. The Communists make an effort, but they cannot collect him. Marxists pretended to worship science and they believed in progress, but for Sábato truth was personal, unprincipled but deep and demanding. For too many others—Marxists, existentialists, and pragmatists alike—truth was fluid and temporal and expedient. Soon Sábato is neither X nor Y, and alone; the whirl of opinions sickens him; he sees the wrongs of the Left and the Right like ropes around each other's necks; he accepts posts, then resigns; he writes essays and then watches events retract them.

Truth is personal because it's with*in* the person. But. But. And Sábato's doubts would fill a cave with bats. But the person is so frequently a fraud. We are dressed in deceit. Our own skin crawls to seek relief, as though all it is is a sack for shit. So when we seek, what shall we find? Perhaps the marvelous message will be, as it is in

Finnegans Wake, scratched out of a dung heap by a bird—Belinda—
whose name signifies the snake.

The novel can be a retreat and a deception, too, particularly when
it seeks the purely literary effect, extols form, plays intellectual
games (as Sábato believes Borges's fictions do); when it thinks of
itself overgrandly as Art. (*On Heroes and Tombs* contains a tasteless
attack on Borges, which is, like the dig at Madame Curie and several
of its attacks on women, contrived and petty.) Sábato's position—as
it seems from my very different yet identical point of view—is rather
well put by Marcuse: "The aesthetic necessity of art supersedes the
terrible necessity of reality, sublimates its pain and pleasure; the
blind suffering and cruelty of nature assume meaning and end—
'poetic justice.' "

On Heroes and Tombs is, in this sense, an artless book. It does not
desire to give life a meaning, a design, *that is not there.* The shape it
takes should be the shape of life. Its confusions of time and place,
style and technique, points of view, tones and intensities, its mix of
essay, dialogue, and interview, reality and dream—all are signs of
sincerity. The awkwardness of it, sometimes, is a sign. The passion is
a sign. This novel not only describes but is itself a search, a painful
passage through danger and darkness, through the interior, across
the spotted soul, the Africa of its author. But our problem is that *On
Heroes and Tombs* is a very artful book indeed—indeed, it is overly
artificial and contrived, sometimes; hammered together in a hurry
like a jakes (though not with a haste involving time); for it is also a
one-holer, with the hole's deposit—money in the bank.

Ernesto Sábato confesses to being a writer with an obsession, an
obsession that is not quite clear to him, and which he is driven to
define and to drive away by writing. The compulsive act, in this case,
is writing itself, and the aim is a kind of purification. There is a
secret inside the self, which means that the self is hiding something
from itself, is lying to itself; but the search, as Sábato sees it, is not
for some specific peculiarity that will explain his own problems with
life, but for some fundamental truth that he would, in effect, be
uncovering and uttering for all men.

The psyche that doubts itself, deceives itself, opposes itself, betrays itself, is a split one; and this novel is similarly divided into four parts and personalities, not all of whom know what others are up to—a condition that can bewilder the reader, as well. There is first of all Martin, a young innocent who becomes obsessed with a mysterious, enigmatic, somewhat older and very beautiful woman, Alejandra. With a naïveté so persistent that it becomes annoying, Martin flounders after his beloved, who deeply returns that love, but in an intermittent, almost willfully capricious way. She is a victim of epileptic seizures, religious and atheistical manias, a promiscuous eroticism from which Martin receives no benefit, and a sense of defilement that soils every act she performs and object she touches. Her father, Fernando, is the central figure of the book, dominating it even when he is not immediately present, and when we first hear of him, we read of madness and blindness at the same time. Finally, there is the wiser, more mature, but passive observer, Bruno, who becomes a confidant of Martin and his mentor.

We may grade these selves in terms of their distance from the light. Fernando lives in the world of darkness, the sewer of the self, whereas Bruno remains where he can see. Martin and Alejandra represent the offspring of these selves, one innocent, one defiled, one male, one female, one drawn toward darkness and profligate lust, the other seeking salvation. There also are, then, among the members of mankind, and among the people who populate the self, four kinds of relationship: the friendship of Bruno and Martin, the decent love of Martin for Alejandra, unsullied by selfishness, the guilty passion that Alejandra fears she will make of it, and which she experiences with her other lovers, and the incestuous, criminal kind of self-love that Fernando represents.

Just as Sábato's earlier novel, *El túnel*, began abruptly with the report of its principal event (the narrator's murder of his mistress), so *On Heroes and Tombs* commences with a laconic police notice. It appears that some woman has shot her father, and then, locking herself in a tower room with him, has set fire to it. This sort of opening is perfectly appropriate because all psychological investigations take place after the fact. In this case, an act of criminal atonement follows the sin of an incestuous love. The same report states that a manuscript in the father's hand has been found in his apartment. This manuscript is reproduced as the third, and surely the most famous, section of the novel: "Informe sobre ciegos"—"Report on the Blind."

Fernando is obsessed (as most of the characters are, in one way or other, and as Sábato admits he is), which means there is a thought that is both so forceful and so wicked that it must be displaced and repeatedly repressed; consequently, the obsessive idea is accompanied by compulsive acts. Because the pressure of the thought is so continuous, doubts always arise: Have I really done the right thing; have I rid myself of it this time? Obsessive idea, compulsive action, constant doubt, cloacal imagery, arson, oedipal fears—all are here as perfectly as Freud reported them in his famous "Rat Man" case. And the notion that drives Fernando mad is that of blindness. His part of *On Heroes and Tombs* takes the form of a memoir, scientific in intention though not in style or structure, of his penetration of that sightless world, a realm and a group that his paranoia credits with organization, power, and a limitlessly malicious purpose. Anti-Semites could substitute Jews.

This document, written separately by Sábato, capable of standing by itself, and connected with the rest of the book only thematically, is a powerful, distraught, sometimes hysterical, certainly offensive, yet magnificent depiction of the realm of the unconscious; it is a descent, like Dante's, into Hell.

In addition, there are those who like to sail alone around the world; they shut themselves up in towers to write or watch for fires; in huts encased in ice, they give up their lives to loneliness; who hunt for pelts in the mountains or are driven with aimless intensity from place to place like sand through a desert; fly solo, take to the woods. Searching for a second self, they dislike distraction. They want something to pit their strength against: angel or shade or element of nature that will assume the shape, and become the substance, of their enemy within.

Fernando is such a solitary type. He tells us how his obsession with the blind begins (innocently enough, of course), and how he starts to observe and follow—shall we say shadow?—them; how they hear him watching (the surveillance of the ear detecting the surveillance of the eye); how they lie quietly in ambush; how they plan and persevere like a wish which will never relent, but leans against the eyes like an ache. He distinguishes between those who have been born blind and lived always in the night, whose crime in that sense precedes their birth and is truly ancestral, and those who have become blind, who have been struck dark by fate, as we all shall be, since death is darkness, blindness, too; he describes the fraternal antagonism of these two kinds: It is that of the desire which has never been recognized, given a name, and the one which has had a sight of life before being sent away like the sun at the end of the day. He emphasizes their patience. You think your love for your daughter is pure, but there will be a moment of weakness and your thoughts will fly into her like a penis. They wait. They wait for that moment.

Finally, Fernando follows a blind man into a building; he passes through dark, empty rooms, discovers trapdoors and pries them up, descends into basements, moves among tunnels, has a paralyzing encounter with an imposing and silent blind woman—in the dark, we know, desire sees best of all—and then, while in a faint from his fear of her figure, endures dreadful dreams, one of which culminates in an attack on his eyes by a bird—strange, symbolic turn, because when a boy Fernando had blinded birds for sport, those creatures of eyesight and air, emblems of the spirit—so that now he has suffered the oedipal injury he fears and deserves, the law of the talon, an eye for an eye.

We are figuratively blind, Sábato seems to be saying; we fail to notice one another really; we touch only with the tip of an unfeeling cane (another phallic image); hence we live in isolation, out of all reach, surrounded by our own misunderstandings, unreceptivity, guilty passions, filth. We say we see to indicate we understand: The eye is the first circle, Emerson writes. It is the organ nearest the mind, and the sign of its sovereignty. Yet we have put it out. The eye, moreover, is instantaneous in its work. It does not see by steps and theses and deductive roundabouts. It is itself an instrument that allows others to see us, for our eyes are eloquent. They idolize. Yet we have put them out.

Fernando continues his journey through the sewers of Buenos Aires, the intestines of the psyche, suffering as he goes along various bodily alterations into early stages of evolutionary existence. At last, he finds himself in the blind woman's sealed womb, or so it seems it must be to this reader. He copulates with this grave matriarchal ghost in the gray insubstantial way that dreams permit, before discovering himself like an awakened Alice back in his above-world rooms.

Other sections of the book are at pains to place this inner search inside the public history of Argentina, which accounts for the *Heroes* in its title. Yet are they not heroes, because they are buried in the air, in the light, as is the legendary Argentine leader Juan Lavalle (whose story is told twice in this book), because his fleeing legions held his body in the saddle—a veritable El Cid—vowing their enemies would never have his head, until the flesh fell from the bones, and he became apocalyptic?

The young woman, Alejandra, is pulled between Martin and Fernando, between good and evil and all other Manichaean principles our author can invoke; but what love that contains desire like a flow of blood is not another love of one's father or mother? So Alejandra feels she can only be a temptress. Finally, in a phallic-shaped room regarded as a mirador and point of vantage, Alejandra kills her father with the symbol of his penis, and destroys herself with hers—flame—the purifying fire of a passion turned against itself.

That leaves two of us: Bruno and Martin—the innocent we are, the man we would become—free of evil only by virtue of the sacrifice of the feminine.

Which one of us remembers now that Borges was blind?

It is not a nifty conclusion, and the promise held out at the novel's close is both faint and displeasing: displeasing because the sacrifice has been too great, and the blame misplaced; faint because we know from our reading that Sábato believes deeply in the reality of evil, in the hell that each man is (and hasn't he suggested for us a punishing diet of our own continuously recycled shit?); whereas for the kingdom of heaven, or the reality of the good, he has only hope.

A DEFENSE OF THE BOOK

When Ben Jonson was a small boy, his tutor, William Camden, persuaded him of the virtue of keeping a commonplace book: pages where an ardent reader might copy down passages that especially pleased him, preserving sentences that seemed particularly apt or wise or rightly formed, and which would, because they were written afresh in a new place, and in a context of favor, be better remembered, as if they were being set down at the same time in the memory of the mind. Since these thoughts might later provide raw material for a theory about the theater or some aspect of the right life, Jonson called his collection Timber to confirm that function. Here were more than turns of phrase that could brighten an otherwise-gloomy page. Here were statements that seemed so directly truthful, they might straighten a warped soul on seeing them again, inscribed, as they were, in a child's wide, round, trusting hand, to be read and reread like the propositions of a primer, they were so bottomed and basic.

Jonson translated or rewrote the quotes and connected them with fresh reflections until their substance seemed his own, and seamlessly woven together, too, which is how the work reads today, even though it is but a collection of loose pages taken, after his death, from the defenseless drawers of his desk. The title, extended in the manner of the period into an explanation, reads: *Timber: or, Discoveries; Made upon Men and Matter: as they have flow'd out of his daily Readings; or had their refluxe to his peculiar Notion of the Times;* and it is followed by an epigraph taken from Persius's *Satires:* "To your own breast in quest of worth repair, and blush to find how poor a stock is there." With a flourish whose elegance is lost on our illiterate era, Jonson filled his succeeding page, headed *Sylva,* with a justification of his title in learned Latin, which can be translated as follows: "[here are] the raw material of facts and thoughts, wood, as it were, so called from the multiplicity and variety of the matter contained therein. For just as we are commonly wont to call a vast number of trees growing indiscriminately 'a wood,' so also did the ancients call those of their books, in which were collected at random articles upon various and diverse topics, a wood, or timber trees."

My copy of *Discoveries* has its own history. It came from the library of Edwin Nungezer (catalog number 297), whose habit it was to write his name and the date of his acquisition on the title page (2/22/26), and his name, date, and place, again, at the end of the text, when he had finished reading it (Ithaca, New York, October 17, 1926). He underlined and annotated the book as a professor might (mostly, with a kind of serene confidence, in ink), translating the Latin as if he knew boobs like me would follow his lead and appreciate his helpful glosses. I have already quoted one of his interlineations. My marginalia, in a more cautious pencil, are there now, too, so that Ben Jonson's text, itself a pastiche drawn from the writings of others, has leaped, by the serendipitous assistance of the Bodley Head's reprint, across the years between 1641 to 1923, not surely in a single bound, but by means of a few big hops nevertheless, into the professor's pasture a few years after, and then into mine in 1950, upon the sale of his estate, whereupon my name, with stiff and self-conscious formality, is also placed on its title page (William H. Gass, Cornell, '50). Even so, the book belongs to its scholarly first owner; I have only come into its possession. I hold it in my hand now, in 1998.

Out of his reading, out of texts—out, that is, of what remains of reality when old shows are over—Ben Jonson collected thoughts he thought right or wise about poetry, about good writing, and, above all, about the management of life. He wanted to save and set aside and reexamine sentences which would tell him how he should evaluate the world and its occupants.

Another book, which is also a library, but in a different way, George Saintsbury's *A History of English Prose Rhythm,* provides testimony concerning what happens when the guest is taken to a hostelry of transformatory power such as Ben Jonson's inn is: ". . . the selection, coadaptation, and application of the borrowed phrases to express Ben's views constitute a work more really original than most utterances that are guiltless of literature" (p. 205n).

In setting down the provenance of my copy of *Discoveries,* I have also done the same for the following sentence, which I put a faint marginal line beside while researching opinions about metaphor for my dissertation (now, thank God, a distant memory); it is a sentence that (having served in several capacities since) I know quite by heart, and treasure, inasmuch as it is as personal and particular to me now as its book is, having absorbed so much of myself, like the paper wrapped around fish and chips. "What a deale of cold busines doth a man mis-spend the better part of life in! in scattering *complements,* tendring *visits,* gathering and venting *newes,* following *Feasts* and *Playes,* making a little winter-love in a darke corner."

We shall not understand what a book is, and why a book has the value many persons have, and is even less replaceable than a person, if we forget how important to it is its body, the building that has been built to hold its lines of language safely together through many adventures and a long time. We have only to examine how we feel about books we own and books we borrow to begin to appreciate the character of its companionship, or consider our relation to those same texts when they've been inscribed on discs and are brought up on a screen like a miniature movie. The only thing that made return-ing books tolerable to me was my ability to borrow more.

However, words on a disc have absolutely no permanence, and unless my delete key is disarmed, I can invade our Pledge of Allegiance, without a trace of my intrusion, to replace its lines with mine: I hedge my allegiance to the United States of America and the Republic for which it stands . . . Erasure, correction, and replacement is almost too easy.

Words on a disc have visual qualities, to be sure, and these darkly limn their shape (I can see them appearing right now as I type), but they have no materiality, they are only shadows, and when the light shifts, they'll be gone. Off the screen, they do not exist as words. They do not wait to be reseen, reread; they wait only to be remade, relit. I cannot carry them beneath a tree or onto a side porch; I cannot argue in *their* margins; I cannot enjoy the memory of my dismay when, perhaps after years, I return to my treasured copy of *Treasure Island* and find the jam I inadvertently smeared there still spotting a page precisely at the place where Billy Bones chases Black Dog out of the Admiral Benbow with a volley of oaths, and where his cutlass misses its mark to notch the inn's wide sign instead.

My copy, which I still possess, was of the cheapest. Published by M. A. Donahue & Co. of Chicago, it bears no date, and its coarse pages are jaundiced and brittle, yet they've outlived their manufacturer; they will outlive their reader—always comforting, although a bit sad. The pages, in fact, smell their age, their decrepitude, and the jam smear is like an ancient bruise; but as well as Marcel did by means of his madeleine, like a scar recalling its accident, I remember the pounding in my chest when the black spot was pressed into Billy Bones's palm, and Blind Pew appeared on the road in a passage that I knew even then was a piece of exemplary prose. It was not only my book in my hands I had, as I sat on the porch steps with a slice of bread and jam; it was the road to the inn, Billy Bones in his bed, the mark on the sign, which—it didn't surprise me—was still there after all those years.

That book and I loved each other, and I don't mean just its text: that book, which then was new, its cover slick and shiny, its paper agleam with the tossing sea, and armed as Long John Silver was, for a fight, its binding tight as the elastic of new underwear, not slack as it is now, after so many openings and closings, so many dry years;

that book would be borne off to my room, where it lived through my high school miseries in a dime-store bookcase, and it would accompany me to college, too, and be packed in the duffel bag I carried as a sailor. Its body may have been cheaply made by machine, and there may have been many copies of this edition printed, but the entire press run has by this time been dispersed, destroyed, the book's function reduced to its role as my old school chum, whom I see at an occasional reunion, along with editions of Malory and Mann, Nietzsche and Schopenhauer, Hardy and Spengler, gloomy friends of my gloomy youth. Each copy went forth into bookstores to seek a purchaser it would make fortunate, and each has had its history of success or failure since, years of standing among rarity and leather, say, when suddenly, after widowhood and a week of weeping that floods the library, it finds itself in some secondhand ghetto, dumped for a pittance by customarily callous heirs into a crowd of those said, like cars, to have been "previously owned."

We all love the "previously owned." We rescue them like orphans from their Dickensian dismay. I first hold the volume upside down and give its fanned-out pages a good ruffle, as if I were shaking fruit from a tree: Out will fall toothpicks and hairpins, calling cards and bits of scrap paper, the well-pressed envelope for a stick of Doublemint gum, a carefully folded obituary of the book's author, the newsprint having acidulously shadowed its containing pages, or, now and then, a message, interred in the text, as I had flutter from a volume once owned by Arthur Holly Compton (and sold to me by the library of his own university). It was the rough draft of a telegram to the general in charge of our occupation troops in Germany, requesting the immediate dispatch of Werner Heisenberg to the United States.

Should we put these feelings for the object and its vicissitudes down to simple sentimental nostalgia? To our commonly assumed resistance to change? I think not; but even as a stimulus for reminiscence, a treasured book is more important than a dance card, or the photo that freezes you in midteeter at the edge of the Grand Canyon, because such a book can be a significant event in the history of your reading, and your reading (provided *you* are significant) should be an essential segment of your character and your life. Unlike the love we've made or meals we've eaten, books congregate to form a record around us of what they've fed our stomachs or our brains. These are not a hunter's trophies, but the living animals themselves. In this country, we are losing, if we have not lost, any appreciation for what we might call "an intellectual environment." Even when the rich included a library in their mansion plans, it was mostly for show, a display of purchased taste that is now no longer necessary.

In the ideal logotopia, every person would possess their own library, and add at least weekly, if not daily, to it. The walls of each home would seem made of books—wherever one looked, one would see only spines; because every real book (as opposed to dictionaries, almanacs, and other compilations) is a mind, an imagination, a consciousness. Together, they comprise a civilization, or even several. However, utopias have the bad habit of hiding in their hearts those schemes for success, those requirements of power, rules concerning conduct, which someone will one day have to carry forward, employ, and enforce in order to achieve them, and, afterward, to maintain the continued purity of their Being. Books have taught me what true dominion, what right rule is: It is like the freely given assent and labor of the reader who will dream the dreams of the deserving page and expect no more fee than the reward of its words.

I have only to reach out, as I frequently do, to cant a copy of *Urne Buriall* from its shelf, often after a day of lousy local prose, and to open it at random, as though it were the Bible and I was seeking guidance, just to hear again the real rich thing speak forth as fresh as if it were a fountain:

While some have studied Monuments, others have studiously declined them: and some have been so vainly boisterous, that they durst not acknowledge their Graves; wherein *Alaricus* seems most subtle, who had a River turned to hide his bones at the bottome. Even *Sylla* that thought himself safe in his Urne, could not prevent revenging tongues, and stones thrown at his Monument. Happy are they whom privacy makes innocent, who deal so with men in this world, that they are not afraid to meet them in the next, who when they dye, make no commotion among the dead, and are not toucht with that poeticall taunt of *Isaiah*. (*Selected Writings*. Chicago: University of Chicago Press, 1968, p. 154)

What poetical taunt? In chapter 14, Sir Thomas tells us, Isaiah taunts the vainglorious with vainglory. Look it up.

In the past, most people could. At one time, for many in this country, the Bible was their "Five Foot Shelf." And the "Five Foot Shelf" was their library. A few of us are fortunate enough to live in logotopia, to own our own library, but for many, this is not possible, and for them there is a free and open public institution with a balanced collection of books that it cares for and loans, with stacks where a visitor may wander, browse, and make discoveries; such an institution empowers its public as few do. In fact, it has no rival, for the books in the public library are the books that may take temporary residence in yours or mine. We share their wealth the way we share the space of a public park. And the benefits include the education of the body politic, an education upon which the success of democracy depends, and one that is largely missing from the thrill-seeking, gossipmongering, and mindless masses who have been content to place their governing, as well as their values, faiths, and future plans, in the hands of the crudest commercial interests. The myths that moved us to worship in ways preferred and planned by the Church, or to feel about things in a manner that served the interests of the state, have less power over our souls now than the latest sale of shoes, which promise, through the glory of their names, the pleasures of sex and health and social rank, and give new meaning to the old expression "leap of faith."

My high school had no library worthy of the name "book," so I would walk about a mile downtown to the public one to borrow, in almost every case, a new world. That's what a library does for its patrons. It extends the self. It is pure empowerment. I would gather my three or four choices, after deliberations governed by ignorant conjecture, and then, before leaving, I would sit at one of the long, wide tables we associate with the institution now, and read a page or two further than I had while standing in the stacks. I scorned the books deemed appropriate for my age, and selected only those I wouldn't understand. Reading what I didn't understand was, for one blissful period of my life, the source of a profound, if perverse, pleasure. I also liked to look at the card pasted in the back of the book to record previous borrowings—a card that is, like so much other information, there no longer or discreetly incomplete. It gave me a good deal of satisfaction to be taking home some rarely read, symbolically dusty, arcane tome. I checked out both my books and my pride at the same desk. See O world what I am reading and be amazed: Joyce, Wells, Carlyle. Well, Wells I could understand. That, I would realize later, was what was the matter with him.

And the Saturday that *Ulysses* was denied me because my ears were too young to hear its honesty was a large red-letter day, burned upon my symbolic bosom wherever it was then kept, for on that day I learned what righteous indignation was; I realized what libraries were really for, just in the moment my own was failing its function, because my vanity was ready for *Ulysses* even if my mind wasn't. I also felt the special pleasure produced by victimization. I left the building in an exultant huff.

Libraries have succumbed to the same pressures that have overwhelmed the basic cultural functions of museums and universities, aims which should remain what they were, not because the old ways are always better, but because in this case they were the right ones: the sustaining of standards, the preservation of quality, the conservation of literacy's history, the education of the heart, eye, and mind—so that now they devote far too much of their restricted space, and their limited budget, to public amusement, and to futile competition with the Internet. It is a fact of philistine life that amusement is where the money is: Finally, you are doing something for the community, spokesmen for the community say, saluting the librarian with a gesture suitable to a noble Roman without, however, rising from their bed of banality.

Universities attract students by promising them, on behalf of their parents, a happy present and a comfortable future, and these intentions are passed along through the system like salmonella until budgets are cut, research requirements are skimped, and the fundamental formula for academic excellence is ignored, if not forgotten. That formula is: A great library will attract a great faculty, and a great faculty will lure good students to its log; good students will go forth and win renown, endowments will increase, and so will the quality of the football team, until original aims are lost sight of, academic efforts slacken, the library stands neglected, the finer faculty slip away, good students no longer seek such an environment, and the team gets even better.

The sciences, it is alleged, no longer use books, neither do the professions, since what everyone needs is data, data day and night, because data, like drugs, soothe the senses, and encourage us to think we are, when at the peak of their heap, on top of the world.

Of course libraries contain books, and books contain information, but information has always been of minor importance, except to minor minds. The information highway has no destination, and the sense of travel it provides is pure illusion. What matters is how the information is arranged, how it is understood, and to what uses it is going to be put. In short, what matters is the book the data's in. I just employed the expression "It is a fact of philistine life . . ." That is exactly what the philistine would like the library to retrieve for it. Just the facts, ma'am. Because facts can be drawn from the jaws of some system like teeth; because facts are goods like shoes and shirts and . . . well, books. This week, the library is having a closeout sale on facts about deserts. Get yours now. Gobi will be gone soon, the Sahara to follow.

The popular description of the Internet is misguided. No one should be surprised about that. "Misinformation alley" is a more apt designation, although it is lined with billboards called "Web sites," obscuring whatever might be seen from the road. Moreover, "highway" has the advantage of reminding us of another technological marvel, the motorcar, and of all its accomplishments: the death of millions around the world, the destruction of the landscape, the greedy irresponsible consumption of natural resources, the choking of cities and the poisoning of the atmosphere, the ruination of the railroads, the distribution of noise into every sort of solitude, the creation of suburbs and urban sprawl, of malls and motor homes, of consumerist attitudes and the dangerous delusions that afflict drivers, the tyranny of highways and tollways in particular, the creation of the road-borne tourist, who drives, who looks, who does not see, but nevertheless clearly remembers "having been there." In short, blessings may be blessings, but they are invariably mixed.

Frequently, one comes across comparisons of the electronic revolution with that of writing and printing, and these are usually accompanied by warnings to those suspicious of technology that objections to these forward marches are both fuddy-duddy and futile. But Plato's worries that writing would not reveal the writer the way the soul of a speaker was exposed; that spontaneity would be compromised; that words would be stolen (as Phaedrus is about to steal them in that profound, beautifully written dialogue), and words would be put in other mouths than those of their authors; that writing does not hear its reader's response; that lying, hypocrisy, false borrowing, ghostwriting would increase so that the hollow heads of state would echo with hired words; and that, oddly, the advantages and powers of the book would give power and advantage to the rich, who would learn to read, and would have the funds to acquire and keep such precious volumes safe: These fears were overwhelmingly realized.

The advent of printing was opposed (as writing was) for a number of mean and self-serving reasons, but the fear that it would lead to the making of a million half-baked brains, and cause the illicit turning of a multitude of untrained heads, as a consequence of the unhindered spread of nonsense, was a fear that was also well founded. The boast that the placement of books in many hands would finally overthrow superstition was not entirely a hollow hope, however. The gift gave a million minds a chance at independence.

It was the invention of photography, I remember, that was supposed to run painters out of business. What it did, of course, was make artists out of them, not grandiose or sentimental describers. And the pixilation of pictures has rendered their always-dubious veracity as unbelievable as any other shill for a system. If blessings are mixed, so are calamities. I note also that, although the horse-drawn coach or wagon nowadays carries rubes in a circle around Central Park, there are more horses alive and well in the world than there ever were.

So will there be books. And if readers shut their minds down the better to stare at pictures which rarely explain themselves, and if readers abandon reading to swivel-hip their way through the inter-bunk, picking up scraps of juicy data here and there, downloading this or that picture to be stared at, and rambling on in their E-mails with that new fashion of grammatical decay, the result will be to make real readers, then chief among the last who are left with an ability to reason, rulers. Books made the rich richer. Books will make the smart smarter.

Because books are like bicycles: You travel under your own power and proceed at your own pace, your riding is silent and will not pollute, no one is endangered by your journey—not frightened, maimed, or killed—and the exercise is good for you.

Books in libraries, however awful some of them assuredly are, have been screened by editors who have a stake in their quality and their success. Once on shelves, they may receive from readers the neglect they deserve. But at the end of all those digital delivery channels thrives a multitude of pips whose continuous squeaking has created static both loud and distressing. Among the sound of a million pop-*offs*, how shall we hear and identify a good thought when it pops *out*?

Lest these remarks lead my readers to suppose I decry technological advance like some old codger whose energies are conserved for rocking, I would somewhat proudly remind them that the leaders of the literary avant-garde in this country are all over sixty, and almost alone advancing the art; that if you are eager to embrace the new cybergible boy on the block, please practice safe sex, for the children of such unions are not always the sweet apples of someone's eye. Anyhow, next to the computer, the printer sits, and spits out sheets of paper like indigestible seeds: bushels of seeds, reams of sheets, from zillions of personal computers, from millions of office copiers in hundreds of peaceful or war-torn countries, night and day.

The elevator, at first, seemed merely helpful, and the high rise splendid against the night sky—what you could see of it. Recordings allow us to hear a few elevating strains from "The Ode to Joy" several times a day, the genius long ago beaten out of it. And those miracles of modern electronics that have allowed us to communicate quickly, easily, cheaply, gracelessly with every part of the world permit us to do so in private, and in every remove from face-to-face. Air travel is comfortable, affordable, and swift (right?), and enables us to ignore geography, just as we ignore climate, because we have HVAC, and, in addition, can purchase terrible tomatoes any season of the year from stores that are open all nite.

The aim of the library is a simple one: to unite writing with its reading . . . yes, a simple stream, but a wide one when trying to cross. The library must satisfy the curiosity of the curious, offer to stuff students with facts, provide a place for the lonely, where they may enjoy the companionship and warmth of the word. It is supposed to supply handbooks for the handy, novels for insomniacs, scholarship for the scholarly, and make available works of literature, written for no one in particular, to those individuals they will eventually haunt so successfully, these readers, in self-defense, will bring them finally to life.

More important than any of these traditional things, I think, is the environment of books the library puts its visitors in, and the opportunity for discovery that open stacks make possible.

When I wish to look up a word—*golliwogg,* which I've encountered spelled with two *g*'s—or when I wish to plenish my mind with some information, say, about the ill-fated Library of Alexandria, why don't I simply hit the right keys on my machine, where both a dictionary and encyclopedia are imprisoned? Well, I might, if the spelling of *golliwog* were all I wished to know; if researches, however large or small, were not great pleasures in themselves, full of serendipity; for I have rarely paged through one of my dictionaries (a decent household will have a dozen) without my eye lighting, along the way, on words more beautiful than a found fall leaf, on definitions odder than any uncle, on grotesques like *gonadotropin-releasing hormone* or, barely above it—what?—*gombeen*—which turns out to be Irish for usury. I wonder if Ezra Pound knew that.

Similarly, when I walk through the library stacks in search of a number I have copied from the card catalog (where I can find all the information I need about my book in a single glance), my eyes are not watching my feet, or aimlessly airing themselves; they are intently shelf-shopping, running along all those intriguing spines, all those lovely shapes and colors and sizes. That is how, one day, I stopped before a thick yellow-backed book which said its name in pale blue letters, *The Sot-Weed Factor.* Though it was published by Doubleday, so there was probably nothing of value in it, I still pulled the book from its place. What did the title mean? I read the first page, as is my habit. Page one and page ninety-nine are my test spots. Then I bore it home, neglecting to retrieve the book for which I had begun my search. Instead, for two days, in a trance of delight and admiration, I read Barth's novel. Later, I repeated my initial search—for a book that turned out to have no immediate interest. But right beside it, as well as two shelves down and five volumes to the right . . . well, I discovered another gold mine. That is why I stroll through the encyclopedia, why I browse the shelves. In a library, we are in a mind made of minds—imagine—all man has managed to think, to contrive, to suppose, to scheme, to insinuate, to lie about, to dream . . . here . . . within reach of our hand.

Moreover, when I get my "information" from a book, rather than a compendium, I get it in the context of an author's thought. Which would you prefer—an olive wiped dry and placed in the hollow of a relish tray along with anonymous others, or one toothpicked from its happy haunt in a perfect martini? Location . . . location . . . location . . . haven't we heard? The dictionary itself is evidence that every word is made of the meanings it has accumulated, like delta mud, from its flow between the boards of books.

One does not go to a library once, look around, and leave as if having seen it. Libraries are not monuments or sights or notable piles: churches by Wren, villas by Palladio. Libraries, which acquire the books we cannot afford, retain the many of which we are ignorant, the spate of the new and the detritus of ancient life; libraries, which preserve what we prize and would adore; which harbor the neglected until their time to set forth again is marked, restoring the worn and ignoring fashion and repulsing prejudice: Libraries are for life, centers to which we are recycled, as recursive as reading itself.

If I am speaking to you on the phone, watching your tinted shadows cross the screen, downloading your message from my machine, I am in indirect inspection, in converse, with you; but when I read the book you've written, you are as absent as last year, distant as Caesar's reign. Before my eyes, asking for my comprehension, where I stand in the stacks or sit in the reading room, are your thoughts and feelings, hopes and fears, set down in sentences and paragraphs and pages . . . but in words not yours, meanings not mine, rather, words and meanings that are the world's.

Yes, we call it recursive, the act of reading, of looping the loop, of continually returning to an earlier group of words, behaving like Penelope by moving our mind back and forth, forth and back, reweaving what's unwoven, undoing what's been done; and language, which regularly returns us to its origin, which starts us off again on the same journey, older, altered, Columbus one more time, but better prepared each later voyage, knowing a bit more, ready for more, equal to a greater range of tasks, calmer, confident—after all, we've come this way before, have habits that help, and a favoring wind— language like that is the language which takes us inside, inside the sentence—inside—inside the mind—inside—inside, where meanings meet and are modified, reviewed and revised, where no perception, no need, no feeling or thought need be scanted or shunted aside.

I read around in this reprinted book I've rescued until I stumble on—I discover—my sentence, my marvel, my newfound land. "What a deale of cold busines doth a man mis-spend the better part of life in! in scattering *complements,* tendring *visits,* gathering and venting *newes,* following *Feasts* and *Playes,* making a little winter-love in a darke corner." What a bad business deal indeed . . . to spend a life without an honest bit of purchase.

This sentence is a unit of human consciousness. It disposes its elements like the bits and pieces of a collage, and even if a number of artists were given the same materials—say a length of ribbon, empty manila folder, cellophane wrapping, sheet of blue paper, postage stamp, shocking pink crayon—or a number of writers were allowed a few identical words and asked to form a phrase—with *was,* for instance, out of *that,* or *fair,* or *when,* and *all*—they'd not arrange them in the same way, make the same object, or invariably ask, in some wonder, "When was all that fair?" as if a point were being made in a debate. Among them, only James Joyce would write of paradise, in *Finnegans Wake,* as a time "when all that was, was fair."

In this process of constituting a unit of human perception, thought, and feeling, which will pass like every other phase of consciousness into others, one hopes, still more integrated and interesting, nothing is more frequently overlooked or more vital to language than its pace and phrasing: factors, if this were ballet, we would never neglect, because we are well aware how the body of the dancer comes to a periodic point of poise before beginning another figure, and how the central movement of the torso is graced and amplified by the comportment of the arms, the tilt of the head and smile of the eyes, and how the diagram of one gesture is made to flow into another; how the dancer must land from a leap, however wide or high, as if a winged seed; and how the energy of movement is controlled by the ease of its execution within the beat and mood and color of the music until we see one unified flow of expression; so, too, must the language keep its feet, and move with grace, disclosing one face first before allowing another, reserving certain signals until the end, when they will reverberate through the sentence like a shout down a street, and the vowels will open and close like held hands, and the consonants moan like maybe someone experiencing pleasure, and the reader will speed along a climbing clause, or sigh into a periodic stop, full of satisfaction at this ultimate release of meaning: a little winter love in a dark corner.

The books in the library regularly leave it, leave it for fresh human attentions, and the work of the institution will often take place far from its doors: at a kitchen table maybe, in someone's suddenly populated bed, amid the rattle of a commuter train, even in a sophomore's distracted head. Every day, from the library, books are borrowed and taken away like tubs of chicken to be consumed, though many are also devoured on the premises, in the reading room, where traditionally the librarian, wearing her clichés, sushes an already-silent multitude and glares at the offending air. Yet there, or in someone's rented room, or even by a sunny pool—who can predict the places where the encounter will occur?—the discovery will be made. And a finger will find the place and mark it before the book's covers come closed; or its reader will rise and bear her prize out of the library into the kitchen, back to her dorm room, or, along with flowers and candy, to a bedside, in a tote bag onto the beach; or perhaps a homeless scruffy, who has been huddling near a radiator, will leave the volume behind him when he finally goes, as if what his book said had no hold on his heart, because he cannot afford a card; yet, like Columbus first espying land, each will have discovered what he cares about, will know at last what it is to love—a commonplace occurrence—for, in the library, such epiphanies, such enrichments of mind and changes of heart, are the stuff of everyday.

MR. GADDIS
AND HIS
GODDAMN BOOKS

I

Introduction to *The Recognitions*

He had been a floorwalker at Bloomingdale's. That was one rumor. He was presently writing under the nom de plume of Thomas Pynchon. That was another. He had had to pay Harcourt Brace to publish *The Recognitions,* and then, disappointed and peeved by its reception, he had the unsold stock destroyed. He died of dysentery or some similarly humiliating and touristy disease at forty-three and had been buried, stoneless, in Spain under a gnarled tree. Among the more absurd was the allegation that he had worked as a machinist's assistant on the Panama Canal and served as a soldier of fortune for a small war in Costa Rica. He had no visible means. What he did do was traipse. He became a character in books that bore a vagrant's name. No. He worked for the army and wrote the texts of field manuals. No. He scripted films. They told you/showed you how to take apart and clean your rifle. A rather unkind few suggested he had been a fact checker at *The New Yorker.* Not at all, argued others, he was born a freelance. And became a ghost who moved corporate mouths while gathering material for a novel he would write one day about America and money. When John Kuehl and Steven Moore edited a collection of essays about him, the honored author turned artist and, for the title page, drew himself suitably suited and bearing a highball glass. The figure has no head.

In 1975, when his second novel, *JR,* won the National Book Award, his admirers, confused by William Gaddis's previous anonymity (very like the chary pronouns above), by the too sensibly priced fumé blanc, and by the customary babble at celebrational parties, frequently misheard his name, often congratulating a fatter man. Even the *New York Times,* at one low point, attributed his third novel, *Carpenter's Gothic,* to that selfsame and similarly sounding person. Yes. Perhaps William Gaddis is not B. Traven after all, or J. D. Salinger, Ambrose Bierce, or Thomas Pynchon. Perhaps he is me.

When I was congratulated, I was always gracious. When I was falsely credited, I was honored by the error.

These mistaken identifications turned out to belong in William Gaddis's book, where reality already had been arrested; for what can be true in a world made of fakes, misappropriations, fraud, and flummery? Only this: that, if we had two doorsteps, on one would stand a hypocritical holy man, on another a charlatan dressed as a statesman; that among our most revered relics, if we had some, we'd find out our local saint's pickled thumb belonged originally to a penniless neighborhood drunk, that our museum's most esteemed painting was a forgery, that the old coins we'd collected were inept counterfeits, and the fine car we'd just bought a real steal. What Rainer Maria Rilke wrote of Auguste Rodin is certainly true of the man in that headless sketch: "Rodin was a solitary before fame found him, and afterward perhaps he became still more solitary. For fame is finally only the sum of all those misunderstandings which gather round a new name." In our oddly clamorous yet silent times, to be a famous author is to be ignored not here, not there but everywhere. Similarly, *The Recognitions,* the work which wrapped William Gaddis in the cloud of its carefully adumbrated confusions, remains widely heard about, reverently spoken of, yet rarely read. It seems to lead, like a entombed pharaoh, an underground life, presumably surrounded by other precious things and protected by a curse.

Like Malcolm Lowry's great dark work, *Under the Volcano, The Recognitions* needed devotees who would keep its existence known until such time as it could be accepted as a classic; but a cult following is not the finest one to have, suggesting something, at best, beloved only by special tastes—in this case, the worry was, a wacko book with wacko fans. In fact, a cult did form, a cult in the best old sense, for it was made of readers whose consciousness had been altered by their encounter with this book; who had experienced more than its obvious artistic excellence, and responded to its neglect not merely with the resigned outrage customarily felt by those who read well and widely and wish that justice be accorded good books; it was composed of those who had felt to the centers of themselves how much this novel was indeed a recognition and could produce that famous shock: how it revealed the inner workings of the social world as though that world were a nickel watch; how it combined the pessimisms of its perceptions with the affirmations of the art it, at the same time, altered and advanced; more, how its author, though new to the game, had cared enough about himself, his aims, his skill, to create greatness against the grain, and, of course, against the odds.

Begun in 1945 without really knowing what or why, and continued in bursts from 1947, *The Recognitions* was published in the middle of the fifties, a decade so flushed with success, it could not feel the lines of morbidity which were its bones. A typesetter, it's said, refused to continue work on the text, and sought advice from his priest, who told him he was right to desist. Naturally, the novel, when it appeared, won an award for its design.

Its arrival was duly newsed in fifty-five papers and periodicals. Only fifty-three of these notices were stupid. But the reviewers' responses to the book confirmed its character and quality, for they not only declared it unreadable and wandering and tiresome and confused; they participated in the very chicaneries the text documented and dramatized. It was too much to expect: that they should read and understand and praise a fiction they were fictions in. You, too, can let your present copy rest unread on some prominent table. A few critics confessed they could not reach the novel's conclusion except by skipping. Well, how many have actually arrived at the last page of Proust or completed *Finnegans Wake*? What does it mean to finish *Moby-Dick*, anyway? Do not begin either *The Recognitions* or *JR* with any hope of that. These are books you are meant to befriend. They will be your lifelong companions. You will end, only to begin again.

It was wrong in someone young to be so ambitious, the reviewers thought; the result was certain to be pretentious, full of the strain of standing on tiptoe. If the author works at his work, the reader may also have to, whereas when a writer whiles away both time and words, the reader may relax and gently peruse. Well, *The Recognitions* will lie heavily in any snoozer's lap. (What is the weight of the one you are holding? You can compare it to the 956 pages of the first edition, which comes into the ring at two pounds, seven ounces, in order to discover how much of its substance has been leached out.)

Well, it was ambitious certainly, dense, lengthy, complex. Its author is a romantic in that regard, clearly concerned to create a masterpiece; for how else, but by aiming, is excellence to be attained? It's not often one begins a sand castle on a lazy summer morning—patty baking by the blue lagoon—only to—by gosh!—achieve, thanks to a series of sandy serendipities, an Alhambra with all its pools by afternoon. The book was about bamboozlers; the slowest wits could see that, and therein saw themselves, and therewith withdrew. This was not to be a slow evening's soporific entertainment; it was to be their indecent exposure.

They cribbed from the dust jacket. They stole from any review appearing earlier. They got things (by the thousands!) wrong. They condemned the subject, although they didn't know what it was; they loathed its learning, which they said was show-offy; they objected to its tone, though they failed to catch it; they rejected with fury its point of view, whose criminal intent they somehow suspected. They fell all over one another praising Joyce, a writer, who, they said, was the real McCoy, whereas . . . yet had they been transported to that earlier time, they would have been first in line to shower Ireland's author with deaf Dublin's stones.

Many think that it is reviewing that needs to be reformed, but I believe the culprit is the species, which surrounds itself with lies, and calls the lies culture, the way squirrels build their nests of dead twigs and fallen leaves, then hide inside. In any case, as the German philosopher Lichtenberg observed, when reader's brow and book collide, it isn't always the book that is lacking brains.

Following the hubble-bubble of its initial reception, *The Recognitions* was left in a lurch of silence, except for those happy yet furious few who had found this fiction . . . about the nature, meaning, and value of "the real thing" . . . found *it* to be the real thing. The rumor was that William Gaddis himself had published a pamphlet excoriating the reviewers of his book and citing their malfeasances one by one. The truth, when it lies down among lies, such as those falsehoods, slanders, and distortions with which I salted the opening of this intro, takes on their odor of oleo, and is soon indistinguishable from them. Gaddis did check facts for a living once. He did bananaboat out of South America. It would scarcely matter except that contexts corrupt. Bedfellows bite. Turncoats will steal from their own pockets and betray even linings. *Cozenage est un dangereux voisinage.* Actually, a pseudonymous New Yorker named Jack Green published three articles on the qualities of the book hacks who had inflicted their skills upon *The Recognitions*. He called it, rather directly, "Fire the Bastards!" and the Dalkey Archive Press has reissued it in fine form. There, in addition to much of the data I have already used, I learned that one of these gentlemen attributed the book to William Gibson.

So a slender ring of fans kept the work afloat for the next twenty years, but its neglect, I think, was due to factors having little to do with its alleged difficulty or the dubious distinction of having a cult following. If you are to remain known while writing books (for the books themselves are likely to have a mayfly's life), you must either court the media and let publicity be your pimp, à la Truman Capote and Norman Mailer, or cling like old ivy to the walls of the Academy, passing your person around from campus to campus like a canapé on a party tray. One way or another, you are thus able to appear in public often and collect the plaudits of hands that might as well clap, since they are otherwise empty. You read your work with histrionic polish, or display a practiced wit and your increasing ease on talk shows. You review. Yes, you do; you descend to your opponents' depths, where you'll be seen as just another shark. You sympose. You give interviews. All of it adding to the stuff about and by you that a student, a critic, or a scholar must consult. For you are as large as your library's catalog entries. Meanwhile, you instruct beginners on how to be a genius, giving selected students a professional boost, and forming around your tutorial self, over the years, growing rings of gratitude, your career likewise enlarging as steadily as the trunk of a weedy tree.

William Gaddis, aka Gibson, aka Green, aka Gass, did none of these customary career-enhancing things, remaining, as the politicians' escape phrase always conveniently claims, "out of the loop." Out of the network. Not in the swim. Nor did he write a new book every fortnight just to prove how easy it is, for we all know how easy it is, and how desirable, for that way you can continue to feed your few friends what they are used to, and there are publisher's parties to go to, and more and more nice notices, even raves, since now aren't we all old pals? We must remember that the same hacks who condemn, for a price also praise.

Silence became his mode, exile (in effect) his status, cunning in scraping by his strategy, while compiling data and constructing other people's niggling or nefarious plots, building another long book out of our business world's obsession with money, manipulation, and deception, composing a hymn to Horatio Alger, music made of inane, conniving, sly, deceitful speech. *JR* did okay at the store for a time, and gathered in the National Book Award, but I think it was less read than *The Recognitions,* less enjoyed, and could not produce, of course, the same surprise. Furthermore, although clearly created by a similar sensibility, and expressing a common point of view, *JR* was as different from the earlier novel as Joyce from James. But do not put down what you have to go to *JR* yet, even if it is almost as musical as *Finnegans Wake,* a torrent of talk and Tower of Babble, a slumgullion of broken phrases and incomplete—let's call them—thoughts; because there is plenty to listen to here; because we must always listen to the language; it is our first sign of the presence of a master's hand; and when we do that, when we listen, it is because we have first pronounced the words and performed the text, so when we listen, we hear, hear ourselves, singing the saying, and now we are real readers, for we are participating in the making, are moving the tune along the line, because no one who loves literature can follow these motions, these sentences, half sentences, of William Gaddis, very far without halting and holding up their arms and crying out, Hallelujah, there is something good in this gosh-awful, god-empty world.

Which is almost the whole point of what we do.

And accounts for the purity of Gaddis's artistic intentions, and the reality of the work, for he actually makes grace abounding out of fakes astounding. Furthermore, the progression from the concerns of *The Recognitions* to those of *JR* is completely reasonable. *The Recognitions,* indeed, tackles the fundamental questions: What is real, and where can we find it in ourselves and the things we do? But a generation later, there are no fundamental questions to be posed. *JR* creates a thoroughly decendental world. It is a world of mouth, machination, and money. A few reviewers of *JR,* more perceptive than most, longed for the spiritual struggle of the earlier book, but—reader—just look around: That struggle has been lost. The large has been smothered by the small. Be petty enough and the world may make you a prince. The cheat, not the meek, has inherited the earth.

Yes, we must follow the instructions we are given at the conclusion of *JR:*

> . . . remember this here book that time where they wanted me
> to write about success and like free enterprise and all hey? And

like remember where I read you on the train that time where there was this big groundswill about leading this here parade and entering public life and all? So I mean listen I got this neat idea hey, you listening? Hey? You listening . . . ?

Then, if we are properly obedient, we shall have scarcely reached the second page of *The Recognitions* before we have the hearing of a paragraph like this, which introduces us to Frank Sinisterra, at the moment masquerading as a ship's doctor, but a counterfeiter by trade:

> The ship's surgeon was a spotty unshaven little man whose clothes, arrayed with smudges, drippings, and cigarette burns, were held about him by an extensive network of knotted string. The buttons down the front of those duck trousers had originally been made, with all of false economy's ingenious drear deception, of coated cardboard. After many launderings they persisted as a row of gray stumps posted along the gaping portals of his fly. Though a boutonnière sometimes appeared through some vacancy in his shirt-front, its petals, too, proved to be of paper, and he looked like the kind of man who scrapes foam from the top of a glass of beer with the spine of a dirty pocket comb, and cleans his nails at table with the tines of his salad fork, which things, indeed, he did. He diagnosed Camilla's difficulty as indigestion, and locked himself in his cabin.

I particularly like the double *t*'s with which our pleasure begins, but perhaps you will prefer the ingenious use of the vowel *i* in the sentence with which it ends ("which things, indeed, he did. He diagnosed Camilla's difficulty as indigestion, and locked himself in his cabin"), or the play with *d* and *c* in the same section. But these are rich streets and should be dawdled down, not simply to admire the opening alliteration but to enjoy the fact that this paper money-man is made of paper, or to visualize the gesture, as suitable as a finger's, and certainly as unclean, which sweeps his pint's excessive foam away, or above all to appreciate the hidden pun that runs from "foam" to "comb," contriving the decombing of Frank's beer's head.

No great book is explicable, and I shall not attempt to explain this one. An explanation—indeed, any explanation—would defile it, for reduction is precisely what a work of art opposes. Easy answers, convenient summaries, quiz questions, annotations, arrows, highlighted lines, lists of its references, the numbers of its sources, echoes, and influences, an outline of its design—useful as sometimes such helps are—nevertheless very seriously mislead. Guidebooks are useful, but only to what is past. Interpretation replaces the original with the lamest sort of substitute. It tames, disarms. "Okay, I get it," we say, dusting our hands, "and that takes care of that." "At last I understand Kafka" is a foolish and conceited remark.

Too often, we bring to literature the bias for "realism" we were normally brought up with, and consequently we find a work like *The Recognitions* too fanciful, obscure, and riddling. But is reality always clear and unambiguous? Is reality simple and not complex? Does it unfold like the pages of a newspaper, or is the unfolding more like that of a road map—difficult to get spread out, difficult to read, difficult to redo? And is everything remembered precisely, and nothing repeated, and are people we know inexplicably lost from sight for long periods, only to pop up when we least expect them? Of course; the traditional realist's well-scrubbed world, where motives are known and actions are unambiguous, where you can believe what you are told and where the paths of good and evil are as clearly marked as highways, that world is as contrived as a can opener; for all their frequent brilliance, and all the fondness we have for these artificial figures, their clever conversations and fancy parties, the plots they circle in like carouseled horses, to call them and the world they decorate "real" is to embrace a beloved illusion. The pages of *The Recognitions* are more nearly the real right thing than any of Zola's or Balzac's.

There's no need for haste; the pages which lie ahead of you will lie ahead of you for as long as you like them to. It is perfectly all right if some things are at first unclear, and if there are references you don't recognize; just go happily on. We don't stay in bed all day, do we, just because we've mislaid our appointment calendar? No, we need to understand this book—enjoy its charm, its wit, its irony, its erudition, its sensuous embodiment—the way we understand a spouse we have lived with and listened to and loved for many years through all their nights. Persons deserving such devotion and instinctual appreciation are rare; rarer still are the works which are worth it.

It may be helpful, however, to place *The Recognitions* in the center of all stories, where it belongs, in order to get a grip on the novel's basic strategy. First, a model archetypal plot:

A baby boy is born. In former times, before equalization was achieved, the parents in our history would have been important— they were gods and goddesses, heroes and their consorts, kings and queens—because what happened to them had to be significant not just for themselves but for the whole of their society. So this child will be an heir, and, as Joseph Campbell has pointed out, he will have a thousand faces. Signs of several sorts—omens, portents, the prognostications of soothsayers—warn the father (the king) that the birth of this son endangers him, so the king has his child taken away and exposed to the harshness of the wilderness, where he will surely perish, but perish at Nature's hand and not at the hand of his father (a sophistry our signers of death warrants still practice). However, if the father in question is as forthright as Chronos (or Saturn, if you like), he simply swallows his rival. The first recognition belongs to the parents, and it is that the new generation will one day assume the position and powers now possessed by their elders. Although passing away is as important as coming to be for the health of the species, it is rarely welcomed, and is usually postponed as long as possible.

At the time the infant is borne off (if it does not already possess a mark of identity), it is inadvertently given one. Oedipus, you recall, had his feet pinned as though he were being trussed like a bird for the spit. Whether left on a doorstep, set adrift in a basket, or abandoned on a hillside, the child is found by a totem animal and raised as one (Romulus and Remus are brought up by wolves), or he is rescued by a shepherd or a fisherman, who becomes his foster parent. It is in this period of exile, during which the boy grows up in a foreign land, that the second recognition occurs, either through a slowly increasing inner conviction that he is "other" and important and has a destiny or because, at some point, his foster parents tell him something of his history. This is our "hero's" first recognition, and it is primarily negative; put crudely, he says, I am not a wolf; I am not a bear; I am not of peasant stock. "What am I doing in Akron, Ohio?" Hart Crane wonders; "Utah," Ezra Pound insists, "is not my middle-name."

Soon he sets out in search of his true homeland and his real identity. This part of the tale is in the form of an odyssey: a lengthy journey, during which the young man overcomes a series of obstacles that test his character, certify his skills, and establish his stardom, as do the labors of Hercules, or any *Wanderjahr*. His final trial, it turns out, is usually the solution to some sort of conundrum, and is a spiritual or intellectual trial rather than a physical one (Oedipus solves the riddle of the Sphinx).

Much later, after Oedipus has been rescued from his fate by his foster parents, and has wandered through the world in search of his true home (his Odyssey), he arrives in a place he has no memory of, and by chance (that is, by Fate) encounters the king, his father. His maimed feet determine his identity, the king is appropriately alarmed, and in a kind of contest (the agon) the son defeats him, and receives his reward, the hand of the queen. This recognition could be mutual, and the contest, consequently, clear-eyed, but the recognition is often put off, as in Sophocles' version of the Oedipus story, until many years have passed. The first arc of our narrative is now complete. It begins with a boy's birth and ends with his marriage, or comus; hence it is called a comedy.

The second part of the story repeats the first, but from the father's point of view, for marriage means a new rival will soon appear upon the scene. If we stay with our original protagonist, there follows for him a period of peace, during which time he establishes his rule and prospers along with his people. Meanwhile, in another country, his banished child grows restless and continues his searches. It is important to realize that from one point of view our "hero" is precisely that, from another point of view he is a unredeemable villain, and that the crimes of banishment and usurpation are repeated one generation after another without remission. The story's second arc ends, then, with the death of the hero at the hands of the son he has wronged, and it is called, of course, a tragedy.

However, a hero who is overthrown and dies is hardly a hero, especially when, as so often happens, he is torn to pieces or sacrificed or eaten. Clearly, he would not have lost the contest, the battle, the election, the war, the woman, unless he was betrayed, as Germany was by the Treaty of Versailles, as the South was in the Civil War, as every loser always is: by bad officiating, rotten luck, corporate scheming, political cabals, racial plots. We may have dropped the ball, but we did so because we were stabbed in the back. So there is usually a Judas or two hanging around, waiting to do some dirty deed, an Iago with a hankie up his sleeve. We can disloyally switch our allegiance to the new ruler—the king is dead, after all, so long live the king—but if we remain with our original character, what have we to miss and mourn but scattered bits of a disgraced corpse or a sealed tomb to pass a lifetime's vigil by? Well, the bits get put back together one way or another; the hero rolls away the stone that stoppers his grave; the followers of the betrayed and crucified king recognize him as restored and alive; whereupon, like Dionysius (his history now complete), he is pulled from the plot like the first gray hair, his name is given to a constellation, and he goes to dwell in the company of the gods.

And we—you and I—insofar as we are able to identify with the nature and life of this heroic figure, will overcome death and be redeemed as he was; For he, and the ups and downs of his career, merely embody the uncertain cycle of the seasons. "In the juvenescence of the year came Christ the tiger."

There is another section of this tale that might be mentioned, although it tends to be heretical in its content, popular rather than ensconced in any canon. While the hero of one cycle is enjoying his queen and ruling his kingdom, you remember, the son (the hero in another version) was in exile and on his odyssey. Similarly, when the king is slain, and a new king assumes command, the dead lord can be imagined as living in exile in the country of death—in the underworld—and there he will undertake another trip, and face other trials, while awaiting his resurrection. The Christian tradition describes a "harrowing of Hell": a struggle between the crucified Christ and the Lord of Hell—there, like two cocks, in the pit itself. And this phase will possess its own set of recognitions.

Poets, novelists, mythmakers rarely try to narrate the entire tale, but usually will decide to focus on one element of the story, and elaborate it (odysseys provide many such opportunities), or they will alter the ontology of the enterprise, as Sophocles does, making not action but understanding the central theme of the cycle. Because Oedipus's deeds have been so heedlessly performed, he blinds himself, once his eyes have been opened to what he's done, with a brooch taken from his lover-mother's garments. This physical blindness is, of course, a prerequisite to his now-powerful inner sight.

Suppose, now, I reenact this tale, furnishing it with details that will suit my place and time and special interests, as if none of its features had ever been seen before, as if none of its acts had ever been performed, as if none of its aims had, in any previous place or period, been realized. My rituals would be make-believe; they would be counterfeits; and their effects would depend upon the suppression of the original "once upon a time," and its replacement by my later sly reenactment. My story would be a usurper unless it recognized its kinship with all earlier versions, and it would risk overthrow the moment acknowledgment of that kinship were forced upon it. The long and unique quotation from Sir James Frazer's seminal book, *The Golden Bough,* which Gaddis inserts in *The Recognitions,* permits us to recognize (although we have now known it for some time) that the practice of scapegoating is ancient and happens often and has seasonal motives. If crucifying a monkey or a rat has an air of superstitious desperation, what quality are we to assign its Christian counterpart?

There are suppressions and recognitions, then, that are inherent in the traditional myths and tales anthropologists turn up, and that constantly occur as a part of the mechanism of their unfolding (among the suitors surrounding Penelope, it is only Ulysses' dog who recognizes him in his beggar's rags); and there are recognitions that the characters in this novel experience, too; as well as those we readers will have as we pursue its complicated course, a course whose origins it constantly alludes to in the manner of *The Wasteland*— references which make for much of its richness. Among these "epiphanies" is that special one of which I have already spoken— namely, of what it is to be a genuine work of art, and what, being genuine, "touches the origins of design with recognition."

We shall live for no reason. Then die and be done with it. What a recognition! What shall save us? Only the knowledge that we have lived without illusion, not excluding the illusion that something will save us. For the temple of our pretenses shall come down at the end in a murderous fall of its stones (just as it does at the conclusion of this novel), not from the brute blind strength of a Samson shoving great pillars out of plumb, but from an art, a music, realized in the determined performance of an organ whose stops have been pulled out to play, at last, with a reckless disregard for the risks its reverberations run it, till every stone in the vicinity trembles.

The reviews that struck William Gaddis and his book were indeed stones from an old order, but, as *The Recognitions* concludes, such genuine work "is still spoken of, when it is noted, with high regard, though seldom played."

So turn the page . . . and change that unfortunate frequency.

2

Gaddis Gets Read To

"Our immortality is made of memories and lies," Gaddis whispered to me as our group struggled up tenement stairs toward the door to Raskolnikov's room. The air was cold, the stairs were old, and Willi had the collar of his camel-hair coat up around the muffler he also wore. I knew how to say Willy but not how to spell it—certainly not Willie, for nothing about *ie* seemed right. Wasn't it Willy Brandt? Yes, Willy was more appropriately European, and where else were we? Leningrad in winter, at the frozen edge of Asia. Consequently, I said, "Willy, do you remember what Rilke wrote to open his piece on Rodin?" We could step up two abreast, but only if we sidled, so we were facing each other. Gaddis's silence told me that he never indulged in smart-ass references and didn't take tests. Which wasn't fair, because his books, his carpers said, were full of arcanity and longer than the bar exams. "Fame is but the sum of the many misunderstandings that have gathered about a new name." I recited my reconstituted quote through a cloud of aspiration. He put the red tip of his nose between the soft paws of his mittens and groaned. He put his nose between his mittens. "Pity poor Dostoyevsky," I said sotto voce. Now of course cured, I could be fatuous in my middle age. "These guys can't even leave the man's characters alone," he said upon removing his nose from his mittens. The draft, basement-born, wasn't warmth rising, but it was nevertheless filling me like an arm through a sleeve. At yet another landing, in front of a boarded door, stood a sickly green bucket, its lid thrust out like a lower lip, its wire handle flipped up the other way, as if soliciting a lift. Mary's red scarf was much admired, but, during the darkness of the afternoon, admiration for everything had died away. Except for Bakhtin, of course, who was now more important than Dostoyevsky. Ginsberg wore a flapped hat, Gaddis an inadequate gray cap, and Auchincloss was in a dark stocking. "This is it," the professor who was serving as our guide announced, allowing his arms to leave the chest they had been hugging. "The murderer's apartment." Comrade Granin had become reverence itself, like a bust on a pedestal, and now he waited for us to take it all in. "From here it is exactly mumbled steps to the spot of the crime." I was bareheaded because I am hardy and brave, eschewing stock, cap, and hat. I scorned cover because nothing could ever replace the aviator headgear I was given when ten. I was so proud of. After a time, the flaps no longer fastened under my chin. But I sported. I was Raoul Lufbery, French air ace. In snapshots, I grinned. "Is the bucket an historical marker?" Gaddis asked our guide, who gave no answer. He was, I suspect, furious with both of us. We had been disrespectful for three-quarters of an hour.

Or had I misunderstood the nature of our journey? Was this the old woman's room and had we been retracing the murderer's skittish course across the courtyard below and up these windy stairs? Had we managed to pick up an ax from beneath some handy porter's bench on the way? "And here was the fourth storey, here was the door, here was the flat opposite, the empty one." (I have just now looked up the passage.) I was certain that Gaddis understood our situation, because, for him, Dostoyevsky was as near to God as nature got. He would have been as disdainful of our guide's confusion of fiction with reality as I was, but he would have listened to every unclear word like a mole for a footstep. Then it was that our proctor, according to his guidelines, began to read the appropriate passage out of some authorized Soviet translation. My wife, Mary, standing with Adele Auchincloss a step above me, reached back a restraining hand and took my arm. Shut up, it said, with a squeeze for *please*. Gaddis had disappeared into a roll of wool. These Russians were not my idols. Well, perhaps André Bely was a bit golden-toed and his pseudonym properly accented; otherwise, my daily devotions were in Flaubert's French and Rilke's German. But the Russians spelled his first name Andrei, I remembered in the nick of time. On account of his accent, Professor Granin had turned the reading over to Mischa, one of our young translators. "Don't you think," I said to Gaddis, "that when a new character is introduced, the reader should be given more information than a long unpronounceable name?" "Just say he comes from the provinces." We stood, our feet as fixed as our expressions, in a faint urine yellow light. It was going to be a long read. Mischa held the book close to his face. His accent was excellent.

I had teased Willy a bit about his English-aping bourgeois enthusiasms early in our journey and before I realized how serious and full his appreciation was. So now he might not relish my popping off, even though his gorge was also rising through this well of iced air.

The muffler concealed his chin but not his opinions. Which I wanted to be the same as mine despite indelible differences. Though I had lost sight of the set of his jaw. How much of his youth was he carrying around now under his camel-hair coat? Remembering, as he was supposed to, while Mischa recited, his own youthful reading. The tensions of the first time. Wasn't Muriel, his beautiful companion, Russian, as well? Which accounted for just what, exactly?

Gaddis's love for the Russian novel—and for the predictable Russians at that—had surprised me, though in hindsight it shouldn't have, if I'd kept *The Recognitions* fully in front of me, because these works were nothing if not epic, with a reach as extended as their own steppes, with borders as far off as their frozen mountains. "Loose and baggy monsters," my treasured *cher maître* had said of them, a description too enviously mean-spirited to be forgotten, yet memorably on the mark. In sum, they wore plus fours, though not for golf. But if loose and baggy, *The Recognitions* was nevertheless knit. These Russian tomes were broody books, too, fundamentally melancholy, especially when, as Gogol was, they were funny. Above all, as Bakhtin had finally made us aware (bless his sainted name), Dostoyevsky at least was demonically polyvocal. He had been infernalized at an early age. Novels jam-packed with passionate ideas half-understood but as motivational as money. Every one evincing major moral concerns. Moreover, their authors were majestically indifferent to their mistakes, confident that any error would be but a beauty mark on a work of genius. Novels made of issues as well as innumerable details, richly peopled, penned in brash and innocent confidence, and written from outrage as much as ego. Worse yet, bedbugged and fleabagged by proper names. "Just say he wore a dusty overcoat and checked trousers, and came out hatless onto the low porch of the posting station at X," Gaddis said. "There is a bucket marking the spot where Mr. Hatless stood."

It was kind of Gaddis to give me my Turgenev at this juncture. "Bely was a bloody mystic," he said, withdrawing his offer of *Fathers and Children.* "Which one of them wasn't cuckoo?" I was standing on a creaky tread. "Doc. Chekhov."

Though he had crossed oceans in his youth, and run around nations in pursuit of girls, I felt Gaddis would have turned down a similar invitation to visit almost any other country now. However, the Russians would be an irresistible draw. I did remember how Raskolnikov had hung the ax head from a noose concealed beneath his coat. Present custom would advise a sawed-off shotgun. Or a malicious self-serving review. Neath his fulsome robe Phaedrus concealed someone else's speech, which he planned to deliver as his own. And I've noted since how cleverly Dostoyevsky lets the ax hang, as if swung by Damocles, over the old woman's figure while he describes her "thin, light hair, streaked with grey and thickly smeared with grease," before its blunt end arrives to bloody her head just a bit above that broken comb the author has deftly put there, as well as the rat's tail in which the wretched woman's hair was plaited. Beautifully done, no doubt about it. An ax murder by a master.

Gaddis had bade the Quad a pissy good-bye during the sad senior year of his Harvard career, so he was largely self-taught and would not be disabused of his youthful enthusiasms as I suspected most of us were who went on through the levels of snobbery one's momentary peers deemed necessary to an education. I remember having to leave Spengler and Tchaikovsky, Emerson and Nietzsche, E. E. Cummings and Thomas Wolfe behind on my journey to more elevated realms—as much as I had loved them once. And the higher one rose in the ranks of the system, the greater the sacrifice the system asked for: eventually, Verdi was dumped for Monteverdi, Tolstoy for Flaubert, and everybody for Cézanne. It took twenty years for me to return to Nietzsche, Emerson required even more self-discipline, while Dickens was recovered the day I believed I had at last learned to read.

Yet even when I was aware I had shaken off my bad ideological habits, and was actually paying attention to the words as they miraculously ran from cap to period, I never felt so special that I could call myself a Dickens reader or want to hold him to account for faults I may have feared I had. I could have complained: "Hey, don't get so soggy, and leave melodrama for the movies," but aren't we always grateful for the sins of others? His readers loved him for his weaknesses because they shared them. Gaddis's critics hated him for the strengths they didn't have.

Stendhal wrote, he said, for the happy few a hundred years ahead. It's true that the happy are always in the minority. But if you wrote for the happy few a hundred years ahead, you would certainly be scorned by the miserable many presently in dire need of fun and an absorbing story. It was pitch-dark at three in the afternoon and there was snow everywhere in the city that lay always under an alias. It was a habit of postrevolutionary countries to buy new street signs for every regime change—so the Esplanade of Friday the Thirteenth could become the Plaza of Fallen Heroes. In a wink, the Highway of High Hopes got renamed Sellout Strasse. Regally titled Königsberg was now a plebian Kaliningrad. Kant, the city's most distinguished citizen, remained *der Allzermahler,* even if there was no moral law *within* to build *without* the universal kingdom of ends.

Starless, moonless as it was on Neva's banks, you could still see by the snow's sheen where to go in search of Raskolnikov's lodgings. No. I was out of step again. Now we were hunting for Dostoyevsky's digs. His furniture would be at home even if he wasn't. I prefer movies in which people, cars, planes, and buildings are blown up and gasoline abused, because I don't have to think, then, about people, cars, planes, and buildings blowing up and dreams being misused. Could I count myself one of Andrei Bely's happy few in that case? 'Fraid not. Merciless man. Bely called his novels "cerebral play." No one reaches visceral velocity. Early in our visit, one of the bullies who called himself a host asked me whom I took to be Russian literature's most important character. Mr. Shishnarfne, I said, who enters *St. Petersburg* as an hallucination and dwindles to a dot.

Gaddis's god had never risen from the dead as so many of mine had, and I could see his youthful love glowing plainly when our group visited Dostoyevsky's apartment. The sight of the master's desk actually wet Willy's eyes. I envied him. When my eyes moistened, it was only for Bette Davis, and such a shallow show of weakness made me angry with my soul. I fancied that he was feeling the same sort of exalted state of nostalgia for an imaginary past that I had felt a few days before when our party had left Moscow in a midnight snowfall for Leningrad on the legendary Red Arrow Express. The train moved slowly from the station through a whitened landscape more literary and historical than railed, while I cooled my glass of weedy tea against the compartment window and wondered if it could really be little ole me at midnight on this train tracking a perfect Russian snow, leaving my beloved Anna, Katya, or Marfa Petrovna behind, on my way to relieve Leningrad from its one-hundred-day siege by the Huns. Dostoyevsky's room contained a table whose cloth covered all but its corners with red leaves cut into velvet. A lamp that bore a shade resembling a beaded glass crown shone on a casually opened cigarette box so directly, the case's golden bottom glowed. Gaddis allowed a forefinger to rest upon the corner of a desk where the most ordinary of objects lay—letter opener, penholder, inkwell. This—*this*—is Dostoyevsky's desk, his finger said. Or more likely: This is where those remarkable pages were made. Willy had taken his cap off as he entered, said nothing, but looked at everything as one looks at a lover at long last unclad.

I am an irreverent person because I believe reverence is usually misplaced when it isn't faked, but I felt reverence for his reverence then.

Mischa asked of some small box, "What's that?" Mary was shaking her hair out of her hat and had no hand to restrain me. "A bomb in a sardine tin," I said. Mischa was a nice young man. He laughed. Such a show-off, I said of myself to myself, but was it showing off when no one but a nice young man was shone? Maybe it was art.

Another of Willy's admirations was Samuel Butler's *The Way of All Flesh,* a work Theodore Dreiser also prized, perhaps because it gave parents a bad time, dissed marriage, was scornful of religion, and exposed Victorian institutions as guardians of privilege and power. Or because it was as pointlessly plotless as our hunt for a fictional murderer's bedroom. Or because it was fundamentally philosophical, as Dostoyevsky always tried to be. And dealt with money and property as though they were cards. Well, a book in which the Bible gets kicked across a room into a forlorn corner certainly has merit, I thought, but these reasons did not account for the supremely high regard in which Gaddis held it. I felt happier in my conclusion that Butler himself was part owner of Willy's praise, since he had kept the manuscript locked up till his death, and even if he were protecting the relatives it savages by waiting for their deaths, he could never be accused of writing this book for money, fame, or sex with a faithful reader.

For Willy, writing was a serious matter. How serious? Beckett serious. It was serious in the sense that any aim disgraced it that wasn't utmost. He never toured, read in circles, rode the circuit. He rarely gave interviews or published opinions. He didn't cultivate the cultivated, nose around the newsworthy, network or glad-hand, sign books or blurb. He didn't teach, prognosticate, distribute awards. He was suspicious of wannabes, wary of flatterers; he guarded his gates. He didn't write the way he did to prove how smart he was, to create a clique that would clack at his every move. Or to get reviewed. Or to receive the plaudits of some crowd. Or to be well paid and bathe in a tub of butter. Or to be feared or sneered at or put down by pipsqueaks. He wrote as well as he could and as he felt the art required, and he knew he would not be thanked for it. Nor would he have an ass available for posterity to kiss.

Willy followed no false gods, for he believed in none. Mankind's most universal habit was hypocrisy; its true and enduring love was money, its favorite avocation litigation, its drug of choice amusement, and the fullest expression of its fears to be found in the dogmas, trappings, and hierarchies of organized religion. He would have liked to have been an *Allzermahler*.

Gaddis knew the realities so worshiped by readers were fakes.

Instead, he created realities fashioned from their lies, their superstitions, their fatuous remarks, their pretensions, their envy, their guilty
excuses and habitual bad faith. His chuckle was the chuckle of
someone whose business was "seeing through." He knew that enter-
tainers ate the survivors of their shows. He knew what it was like to
be distasteful to tastemakers. He knew when and for whom he
should doff his cap.

How Russian was he? Had Viktor Shklovsky read him, he'd have
said that Gaddis's novels practiced *ostranenie* in its purest form—
that is, defamiliarization, placing inanities, like urinals, in hallowed
places, grocery lists in museum cases; consequently, *zatrudnyonnaya
forma,* or defacilitation, as well, by forcing the reader to pay attention and puzzle over meanings; then *zamedlenie,* or retardation, too,
sacrificing easy enjoyments to demanding strategies.

JR did for money what Butler did, but *JR* was also a music box, a
Bely-organized symphonia. You only had to open it. Then it would
start its tunes—tunes that ranged from hymns to hurdy-gurdy. How
could you not hear? It's what the Englished Dostoyevsky doesn't
have. Listen to the guy I call "the God damn man":

Sixteen years like living with a God damned invalid sixteen
years every time you come in sitting there waiting just like you
left him wave his stick at you, plump up his pillow cut a paragraph add a sentence hold his God damned hand little warm
milk add a comma slip out for some air pack of cigarettes come
back in right where you left him, eyes follow you around the
room wave his God damned stick figure out what the hell he
wants, plump the God damned pillow bandage read aloud
move a clause around wipe his chin new paragraph God
damned eyes follow you out stay a week, stay a month whole
God damned year think about something else, God damned
friends asking how he's coming along all expect him out any
day don't want bad news no news rather hear lies, big smile out
any day now, walk down the street God damned sunshine

begin to think maybe you'll meet him maybe cleared things up got out by himself come back open the God damned door right there where you left him . . . (*JR*, p. 603.)

We made our way down the stairs. They wouldn't pass the fire code, these worn wooden sticks. I put my hand on Gaddis's shoulder, not to steady either of us, but to soothe what I felt was a shared exasperation. Though muffled by his muffler, Willy snorted on my behalf. He wore the wrong kind of cap for this cold. His ears glowed like Fyodor's cigarette box would when we got there. "Sentimentality should be one of the deadly sins," I said to no one in particular, still stuck in my fatuous phase. It was especially mortifying when one's tears ran from the contemplation of a pregnant Bette Davis. "Faith is bad; bad faith is deadly," Gaddis answered to no one's question. For folks our age, Sartre was unavoidable. And during our brief span of effort and exclusion, excellence as an ideal became romantic.

Well, excellence is inconveniently difficult. Moreover, as Aristotle argued concerning virtue, it is neither guaranteed nor rewarded by any external sign. We shall all go to our graves in ignorance of our work's worth. Our aims may be as perverse as our group's search for Raskolnikov's room was that dark afternoon, and our comfort as cold as a Leningrad winter, but perhaps we can say with some honestly earned pride that during our most minor and marginal lives we did not dishonor our gods.

3
When It Was Over

In 1955, a writer with no record, no resources, and few connections published a novel called *The Recognitions*. Great novels are never merely "about" something, but certainly one theme of this unexpected beast of a book was counterfeiting—forging, faking, aping, impersonating, conning, duping, misleading, pretending, lying, misrepresenting, spinning, dreaming—a continuum that travels almost perversely from the cheap knockoff to the creation, by the imagination, of the ineffably real. Its reviewers didn't read *The Recognitions*, but they hated it anyway, verifying, by means of their own vilification, the novel's vision of America as a land where the flimflam flag waves . . . from "me" to shining "me."

While its author, who had scarcely surfaced, sank out of sight once more, the few who loved the book circled protectively about it. Critics said we were a cult, as if, at midnight, we gathered in abandoned barns to tear out pages of Herman Wouk while chanting from *The Recognitions* especially loved lines like "Merry Christmas! the man threatened," a sentiment that belongs alongside Ring Lardner's treasured "Shut up! he explained." There were bits of poetry also worth memorizing, but it was not true that we recited them in dark stalls. I remember, particularly, sweet Norah Winebiscuit:

> Pride drew her garments up, and swathed her face
> In lineaments incapable of disgrace.
> Slipped then away, her face bedewed with do,
> Beyond the glass, and knowing all, she knew
> That the immortals have their ashcans too.

So in the absence of the author, in the absence of the audience, we, the faithful, did create an icon, and make the sudden appearance of this skull-busting, heartbreaking book—its sordid reception, the ensuing silence—into an emblematic cause célèbre; because what *The Recognitions* proved was that great ambitions were still possible, were not just instances of romantic futility; that the real, the original, the genuine work of art could be accomplished; that the novel was not dead, as many liked to think, but had only taken a brief nap, a short snooze; that the book's bleak outlook could be shared with something like a wry smile rather than the suicidal funk the sad seaminess of its worldview suggested.

The novel's motto became our motto: No Counterfeits, No Fakes, No Imitations, No Compromise.

And twenty years appeared to pass. We began to fear that solicitude was scarcely enough to sustain such a work forever. Then, quite coincidentally (for coincidence is the real ruler of all things), I was asked to be a judge for the National Book Award during the very year in which *JR,* William Gaddis's second novel, would appear. Mary McCarthy, also on the jury, simply shoved the third judge (a worn-out hack reviewer) into the corner as you would an unnecessary chair, and the award went to "Junior," as she liked to call it. This did not mean the war was won. The war against mediocrity is never ending. Mediocrity is like the salt mill of fable: It keeps on turning, and a sea of brains goes brackish. For decades, Gaddis had endured our culture's obdurate resistance to excellence, but now he would have to endure more. George Steiner pronounced *JR* "unreadable," and Alfred Kazin, bless his bourgeois heart, wrote that it was "like nothing else around, and is not a masterpiece." Well, he was half right. It *was* like nothing else around.

JR is about that great depersonalizer, money, and is written in speech scraps, confetti-like wiggles of brightly colored cliché. As a medium, it would appear to be as unpromising as might be imagined. And the reader has to ride in the parade and organize all that fluttering that's come down from on high. *JR* takes time. *JR* takes patience. *JR* takes faith. But unlike other faiths, it does not put off salvation until some weekend after all who have lived are dead and only their bones dance; it is immediately and continuously redeeming.

Reading it, I could see Gaddis with his scissors, slicing another instance of inanity and foolishness from the news, lining up this imbecility above that one, or should this jackass sit over here, nearby still another numbskull. The world convicted itself of lunacy almost daily, and Gaddis had his chuckle and his scissors ready for it.

As time goes by, the mysterious Mr. Gaddis is actually seen in public, is elected to the Academy, earns a MacArthur, writes a book in less than twenty years. He must be slipping. *Carpenter's Gothic,* the briefer, more accessible novel, breaks the cult's hold on his appreciation and gives him a larger audience. This is certainly true in Europe, especially in Germany, where *Carpenter's Gothic* and *A Frolic of His Own* have been acclaimed. Reviewers read no better than they ever did, but they are respectful now. Damn, did we, the faithful, want him to have this kind of approval?

When *A Frolic of His Own* appeared, and after the Lannan Foundation awarded William Gaddis their Lifetime Achievement Award, those earlier works quietly became classics, as if they had never been thunderclaps, as if they had always been applauded, as if his artistry, his stature, had never been in doubt, as if he had never exposed America as the land of the fraudulently free, as he was doing once again—this land of the litigious, of the suer and the suee—in a depiction so farcically funny, so absurdly interconnected, so bottomlessly baroque, it reads not like something scissored from the *New York Times* but bits rescued from a *National Enquirer* that's come apart in the rain.

Given their material, and each book's point, these novels ought to be gloomy and sour, but they manage to achieve quite the opposite effect. I have found myself momentarily happy that man has been such a mean and selfish small-time huckster, because he has thereby furnished William Gaddis such a satisfying target.

His death did not catch me altogether by surprise. Sarah Gaddis had reached my answering machine with the message that Gaddis was in the hospital, that he was being brought home soon (a disheartening phrase), that he wanted to talk to me. She gave me two numbers: the hospital, where he would be no longer by the time I rang; and another, presumably "home," where he wouldn't be, either. That second number was a wildly wrong one. A voice had been misheard or misconstrued. Perfect. If Gaddis could still chuckle the chuckle he had perfected, he'd chuckle—this artist of missed, of broken, of imperfectly made connections.

Number was one of Gaddis's tic words, too. He would say he had someone's number, or that so-and-so had done a number on him, or that another's number had come up, or that a lovely young woman, just observed, was quite a number. He allowed these mostly faded uses to place him, to tell us when he had been young and with the crowd, and to say he wasn't ashamed that a part of him was still of that time and that place.

Chuckle he surely would, too, if he were able to see that on the back of his *New York Times* obituary there was a list of mutual funds and their performance. Remember how *JR* opens: "—Money . . . ? in a voice that rustled." And the response: "—Paper, yes."

Opening the *Times,* I half-expected to read of my own demise. Our names—Gaddis and Gass—were so frequently confused. The first time was during the babble of voices that make up cocktail parties, and provide for the participants decent cover. At the awards ceremony for *JR,* I at last met Gaddis. In the din of artificial levity and the crush of mostly insincere congratulations, I was mistaken for him so many times that evening, I finally began to accept sweet nothings on his behalf with a benign smile and a modest nod.

This confusion could not always be put down to static and a bad connection, because, later, the *New York Times* credited me with the authorship of *Carpenter's Gothic,* and *Books in Print,* confusing my introduction with the text, listed me as the author of *The Recognitions.* I could enjoy these mistakes, since Gaddis seemed equally amused, but I couldn't help notice that no one mistook Gaddis for Gass, only Gass for Gaddis.

There was no other place from which a mix-up might emerge, because if I was shabby, shaggy, and paunchy, Gaddis was dapper and thin, even a bit gaunt in his gray days, a face from which good looks had gone, but only after a long stay. He was quiet, and, though opinionated, did not feel the need to advertise or argue or orate, whereas I (at the same age Hercules had throttled a serpent in his crib) was lecturing my parents on the art of bringing up baby.

We saw one another on the rare and brief visits I made to New York, at this or that occasion of award, sharing an L.A. earthquake once; or, by odd chance, on trips we took abroad together: to the Soviet Union, in Cologne. Offered a second vodka, Gaddis would give me a gleeful roguish look: We're on a junk-ket . . . a junk-ket . . . a term reserved for pointless trips by politicians on padded expense accounts. In Leningrad, forced by our hosts to follow Raskolnikov's footsteps up and down a dark and bitterly cold stairwell while being read to from *Crime and Punishment,* Gaddis and Gass heard themselves muttering in concert, "But it's fiction; it's fiction." Then walking by a bookstore window in Germany and seeing there, as large as life, Gaddis pictured on a Key West porch, accompanied by the announcement, formerly appropriate only for God, "Gaddis *kommt.*" Best of all, though, was the moment, with Matthew, in Cologne, after riding through the dark in a limolike car to Gaddis's great German celebration, when Gaddis slowly emerged into a starfall of flashbulbs worthy of the Academy Awards, the popping of a hundred corks. It was so impressive that I said, to cover my glee, "I must be riding with Jimmy Stewart," and Gaddis replied, to cover his, "William Holden, I think." It was a wonderful evening, fully worthy of him, which he nevertheless had to go to Germany to enjoy.

When the bad news came, that his number was up, I was able to take it. I had seen him sitting in a window a world away, so I knew: Gaddis didn't went. He *kommt.*

THE ROAD TO THE TRUE BOOK

Elias Canetti was a short, slight, then pale-gray-mustached man I met in Berlin years ago at a festive German writers' party. From three insufficiently separated places in a large ballroom, three bands were playing colliding tunes. Umpahpah rammed jazz, roll hit rock, and watermelons spilled their seeded juice and soft red pulp all over the road. In the wreck, some broken loaves of Wonder Bread Blues lay soaking. I tried to tell Canetti how much I admired his novel *Auto-da-Fé*. Jack Barth was executing a storklike dance step. I was fascinated. Canetti could not hear me, of course. A person between us (it was Christopher Middleton, the poet and translator, I believe) passed our words back and forth like notes in bellowed code. "He wants to know where you're from," Middleton yelled. "The USA." "What?" "Eh?" "The USA." Shout it forward. Pretend it is the flag. Do not drop the flag. A tuba ran into the grand piano with a crash. Spoons of soup spilled. I think Canetti said he didn't much care for the USA, but I can't be certain. He refused to raise his voice, and my intermediary was reluctant to continue in such a futile role. I was irritated by the braying of instruments about me—the deplorable saxophone, the hateful amplified guitar—annoyed both by the need I felt to say something significant to this remarkable man, and by the impossibility of saying anything. An accordion, for

Christ's sake, began breathing heavily, its costume predictably Bavarian. Canetti seemed bemused, reduced even further by the din, as if his vest gave us the glimpse of another shrunken suit beneath the one he wore. Jack Barth was concluding some complicated flourishes of foot. I was fascinated. The bands brayed on. They bombinated. They blared. They baaed. I moved. That caused one kind of noise to rise. Was that preferable?

Were I to write my autobiography (were I to find myself handsome, rich, young, famous, dancing on the moon), should I include this trivial little incident? After all, it is stuffed like a pillow with important names. And I have managed, with the customary arrogance of the autobiographer, to attach this deeply thoughtful and dedicated writer to me, quite offhandedly, as if he were a mitten I've removed. He is—if you want him identified—short, slight, pale, glassed-over, gray, and simply a man I met one noisy evening in Berlin. No more considerable importance can be conferred upon him. And, in addition, now you know I knew of his work and its importance well before Canetti received his Nobel Prize and passed from one obscurity to another like a low moon among clouds. Besides, my admiration is as interesting to me as his novel—anyone can see that. My admiration is my precious gift. Fortunately, Canetti will not have to walk it home, shelve it somewhere out of sight, leave it with the Samaritans to be shoveled on the poor. Yet my account shows me to be modest enough. We met, I merely say. We shouted (I shouted), but we didn't speak. I am not puffing myself, making much of it. The incident is all nicely underdone, like a properly roasted leg of lamb. I am, however, dropping names like melons on the road, even nicks: Jack this, Jack that. Is no one who happens along to have any protection from me and the private diaries I am eager to hurry into print; the journals, like johns before whose mirrors I parade my pride, bowls in which I relieve my spite? And the impatient, hence incautious, reader (so slyly sounded are my description's undertones) may believe that Saul Bellow has also been mentioned.

Then the word *I*—that moist reedlike letter that makes the winds sing, that wonderful word for *me*—takes ten typical bows in our specimen paragraph, while *my* and *me* get one each (it could easily have been oftener for all); although, at the party, I was less than one really, a quarter of one perhaps, when I left, and I remained unknown in the noise the entire time—my name blown away from Canetti's ear—alas!—as overlooked as the rug upon which nothing more was spilled than a little ash, wine, wads of napkin, foams from German beer.

I think back, but thinking back is a bad business, because doubts immediately begin to nibble on the edges of my images, and I cannot allow these doubts to dim the clarity of my account. My text must smell of certainty, if not with success. Yet was it a vest, or a sweater, Canetti was wearing? And isn't that my present self—the self that since has seen Canetti photographed in a cardigan—standing there is the midst of the din I'm repossessing? His pictures suggest a man more birdlike than he was. Then were there really three bands playing simultaneously, or did it simply seem (and sound) so? I may have told the story several times to friends, adding orchestra to band as I played for the attention of the dining table. No, I stood in front of each of them in order to hear what they were individually playing. But does that prove there were three? Well . . . to remember is to give limbs to a new lie.

As the autobiographer in this experiment, I must balance the self I am with the several selves I was, nor dare I scant the selves I shall become as the writing of my life goes on and alters me; I must furthermore not conceal the disparities there are between the "I" I look through and the "me" you see, even while I seek an essential harmony; therefore, I must never omit myself, my things, the things of others, or the others who own them, and I must carefully place my lonely consciousness down between the blaring of the bands and the many figures who stand stiffly about like bearers of cups; because I had come to this party hoping to meet Günter Grass (why—to make *him* a present of my admiration?); consequently, as I searched for him among these strangers whom I assumed were located somewhere in German writing like oil in an engine, I looked about for a fiercer face, another kind of mustache; hence my encounter with Canetti was wholly unexpected: I hadn't thought to think he was alive. And did these feelings of mine—my prickles of irritation, my brief whiff of surprise—did they dance a bit of a jog like Jack's while I stood to one side and watched with fascination? Already our incident has become uncontrollably complex. I must know more than I know in order to render my insecurity, fix floating images, outline my ignorance. Where am I to put my smothered startle when Canetti's name was said, a hand from somewhere shaken?

Many writers, novelists especially, use up their pasts until there is no more paint in the can when they come to cover their lives, only in the rim of the lid, and Canetti is quite aware of this. Many of the experiences that went into the writing of *Auto-da-Fé* are missing from his autobiography. But once you have falsified fact and made it fiction, it is impossible to go back and re-cover the case, as it was, intact and untouched—to reverse the metamorphosis—and that is because you have meddled with your memory, and to meddle with memory, either in the service of art or from a fear of the unexamined, alters it; it is no longer "your" memory; it has been reconstructed, just as you were being rebuilt when you cleared away the obscurities of the past, overcame its biases, filled everything evenly in; for "your" memory was dirty and broken and incomplete from the beginning. Now that you understand it, it is no longer yours; it belongs to your analysis. Your dreams have become oedipal, like everyone else's.

In his autobiography, Canetti writes:

I bow to memory, every person's memory. I want to leave memory intact, for it belongs to the man who exists for his freedom. And I do not veil my dislike for those who perform a beauty operation on a memory until it resembles anyone else's memory. Let them operate on noses, lips, ears, skin, hair as much as they like; let them—if they must—implant eyes of different colors, even transplant hearts that manage to beat along

for another year; let them touch, trim, smooth, plane everything—but just let memory be.

Now, as I continue to dance about the memory of my foolish
encounter with Canetti in Berlin, imitating Barth's felicitous foot-
falls, the moment becomes as full of significance as it was noisy
then, because it is noise that Canetti hates—social static, gabble,
chatter. He says of Hermann Broch, but it is also true of himself,
that he is most interested in the specific way a man makes the air
shake; yet the air we stood in on that evening was already pulsating.
The air we tried to shape and give voice to was a trembling air,
beaten till bruised by a concerted instrumentalized huffing, by flatu-
lent sounds called tunes, by arrangements that would never reach
music, by the commercial culture that has consumed our everyday
life. And in that eloquent 1936 tribute to Hermann Broch, Canetti
speaks of the air as if it were free, unowned, "the last common property." Today, however, our air has been subdivided, built on, leased,
rented. Today, we know that when we breathe our last, that last
breath will have been a chimney's smoke before we breathed it, or
the fume in an exhaust, a radioed wave, smoker's cough; it will be
wet with a clarinetist's spit; it will have taken shape in a subway,
somewhere between a paunch and a hip; it will have been bought,
sold, renovated, washed, reused; and even then we'll have to pay
well in advance for it, like a seat for the World Series. Our last breath
will be brought to us, very likely, through a rented plastic tube. Perhaps we won't be able to put sufficient funds up front. In that case,
our last breath may be denied us.

Elias Canetti begins his autobiography (the first volume of which
he has entitled *The Tongue Set Free*) with a characteristically arresting and symbolic episode that he says is his earliest memory. Every
morning, as he steps out into the hall of the house where he is staying, in the company of the girl who is taking care of him, a smiling
young man confronts him with a jackknife he has withdrawn from
his trousers, and after commanding the boy to stick out his tongue,

he places the cool blade alongside it, threatening to cut it off. Each morning the young man refrains—folds and repockets the knife—but promises to carry out the operation the following day. Suddenly (as it must have seemed), both young man and maid disappear from Canetti's life. Much later, he learns that this knife-smiling youth has been having a vaguely defined affair with his nannie, and uses this frightening gesture to ensure the little boy's silence. "The threat with the knife worked," Canetti writes, "the child quite literally held his tongue for ten years." A page later, we learn he was two at the time.

This vividly drawn vignette is more than merely an apt and gripping beginning to the first volume of Canetti's memoirs. It foreshadows many of his fundamental themes: the critical importance of the tongue and its freedom to speak, the intercourse of minds through conversation, hence the evil in lies, in misdirection, in enforced silence, in verbal mystification and every other offense against speech and its moving element, the word, especially death's offense against it, against creation (since for all of us, it was the first curse cried; for each of us, it is the last curse carried out), because Canetti hears death as silence, the final flight of the breath, the triumphant rattle of the snake. However, there is also the evil born in the howls of the mob, the shrieks of the insane, who lost the ability to converse and cannot convey to others the condition of their consciousness. These are Canetti's subjects—in sum: utterance and its inhibition, learning, listening, and the terrible dangers of the deaf ear.

The deer is alert and turns to catch the wind and every sound. Our ears turn, too, always away from the signal. So that we shall not smell rot, we wear perfume; we spice our food to disguise its blandness or, contrarily, its decay; we fill our souls with sensation so we shall not have to see. Headphones smother our ears.

Canetti's use of this little adventure is typical of his technique as an autobiographer, too, because he concentrates on those events of his life that were to become models for others—prototypes—and that would therefore reappear often, much as a persistent thought does: this first fear, for instance; yet he does not pretend to write of it in the ignorance and simplicity of its onset and scant survival (although the child recalls only the red of walls and stairs, the knife and its threat, and not a bit of the hanky-panky he was presumably a witness to); nor does he use it to prognosticate, subjecting it to analysis and noting an early connection between tongue and phallus in his psyche, talk, and intercourse, or an alliance of power and *interdiction,* which later became severe; instead, he strikes a perfect balance between his present knowledge and his childhood ignorance, and allows us, his readers, to learn of his life as he does. Canetti's tact with time and knowledge is one of the artistic triumphs of these memoirs.

The idea of the model, moreover, is important to Canetti in other ways. He is a seeker and builder of them, a worshiper of heroines and heroes: initially his mother, then the cultural critic Karl Kraus, next his future wife, Veza (who will receive the dedication of *Auto-da-Fé*), still later, writers like Hermann Broch, Isaac Babel, both of whom he meets, and Franz Kafka, whom, of course, he cannot. All his models are people who teach, whose speech or writings are their blackboard, chalk, and rod. Similarly, then, he treats the events of his life as instructors, as occasions to be "lived up to" in reliving them, to be passed through like phases of one's education, and to be freed from finally, so that others, always higher, more excellent, more demanding, may be met, heard, spoken to, learned from, and, possibly, surpassed.

Canetti was born to proud and well-to-do Sephardic Jews in Ruschuk, a port city on the lower Danube, in 1905. It was, as he notes, a city full of the babble of many tongues, not simply Bulgarian, but Turkish, Romanian, Russian, Greek, and Armenian as well, in addition to the Ladino dialect that his family spoke, a Spanish Yiddish of, to me, unimaginable exoticism and oddness. His parents, however, had spoken German to each other during the days of the somewhat difficult courtship, and they continued to do so after their marriage, linguistically preserving a privacy and a past that meant much to them. Young Canetti is angry with those who can read and appear to be denying him this accomplishment (it provides him with one of his archetypes: first feeling of murderous rage), and he is jealous of a language he cannot understand, phrases of which he begins to memorize without knowing what they mean. Language is something for which he has an exceptional need, and he associates, from his earliest years, his basic passions with it. Not only that, he also links various of life's activities with different tongues: Ladino, for instance, with all the dramatic events of his upbringing, Bulgarian for fairy tales and the world of the peasants, German for intimacy and love. Only later do many of these areas of existence *become* German.

He is six when his father moves the family to Manchester, where the Canettis had a profitable business, and seven when his father dies suddenly of a stroke, a newspaper reporting the outbreak of a war in the Balkans in his hands. His father's horror at reading of the war had killed him, people said. That was the first lie, a solicitous one, to protect a child from a truth he could not, it was said, understand. The truth bespoke a different calamity. Shortly after their arrival in England, his mother, clearly of a high-strung, even hysterical, somewhat cruel nature, fell ill and was sent to Bad Reichenhall for a cure. Young, intelligent, attractive, well-read, she charmed and was charmed by one of her doctors, who urged her to leave her husband and become his wife. She is too frank with her husband about the doctor's attraction to her, and he orders her back to England, where, on the morning following her arrival, and after a serious quarrel the night before, he continues to refuse to speak to her until she finally confesses the whole affair (which he insists must have occurred, although there was none), and dies abruptly in the midst of his silence. The boy, who has never fancied his mother much and has not especially missed her, is gathered to her with an oedipal ease, which must account for some of Canetti's dislike of Freud, for if ever a psychology seemed best understood in those terms, it is his. The boy had learned English while in Manchester, of course, and begun lessons in French, but his mother now takes him away to

Vienna; begins to teach him the native language of her marriage; feeds his neurotic hunger for knowledge; becomes his demanding tutor, confessor, führer finally. Their conversations are exhilarating, exhausting, loving, cruel, interminable. Canetti grows up to be a book, but his mother meanly teases him, too, accusing him of knowing nothing because he knows only the word and nothing of the world.

His mother's mysterious malaise returns; she goes off to a spa, so their complex affair now has to be carried on through the post, though with undiminished intensity, until she begins to reenact her little play of seduction with yet another doctor and with her son now in the role of the jealous husband. When mother returns from the sanatorium, her suitor soon follows, and his attentions are torture to Canetti, who behaves like an inspired brat in order to defeat his opponent. Mother and son collapse into reconciliation and flee further intrusions into their life and love by traveling to Zurich, where Canetti's studies are continued in still another country, in yet another temporary lodging.

These developments are rendered with great honesty, humanity, and understanding, in an uncharacteristically lean, straightforward German prose. Canetti's style is almost continuously declarative, and his comprehension of human affairs remains amazingly outside any system, for he does not psychoanalyze his relationship with his mother, but simply, wisely, *has it*; and this is one reason why his account is so unmuddled, immediate, and moving.

Canetti, like his scholarly sinologist, Professor Kien, the central figure of *Auto-da-Fé*, seems to remember clearly everything he wants to, although his recall of conversations brings to mind Thucydides' marvelous oratorical inventions in which historical figures are allowed to speak as they ought to have, rather than as they probably did. Still, I feel no uncertainty about their essential truthfulness, and this accuracy of fact (also a characteristic of Professor Kien) has no doubt been greatly helped by Canetti's habit of making personal memoranda, taking notes, and keeping diaries, inscribing the latter in a coded stenographese to ensure privacy. (These types of writing he distinguishes for us in a charming essay, "Dialogue with a Cruel Partner," collected in *The Conscience of Words*, a volume that also contains his magnificent study of Kafka's letters to Felice, as well as his thoughts on Karl Kraus, Hermann Broch, Georg Büchner, Hiroshima, Speer, and Nazi architecture. The musings, notes, aphorisms, and reflections Canetti set down during the decades of the composition of *Crowds and Power* [1942 to 1972] have been gathered together in a very stimulating volume called *The Human Province*.)

It seems clear that this autobiography was intended to be a major work: first on account of its length (*The Tongue Set Free* takes his life only to its sixteenth year, *The Torch in My Ear* brings it barely to 1931 and the composition of *Auto-da-Fé,* while the physiognomy of *The Play of the Eyes* puts us in Vienna from the crucial years of 1931 to 1937, and ends, as the work ends, with the death of his mother); and second because of the quality of its conception and composition. What Canetti says of the Analects of Confucius is also true here: ". . . everything it contains and indeed everything it lacks is important." Now the three volumes have been handsomely boarded together as *The Memoirs of Elias Canetti* by Farrar, Straus and Giroux.

Episode after episode is drawn with unforgettable vividness, and although literature and painting continue to provide him with permanent objects of study (Kafka, Gilgamesh, Grünewald, Bosch), Canetti's sensitivity to the external world has been sharpened to the point of pain by the taunts of his mother, who has accused her sixteen-year-old son of being "a coward who refused to look life in the face because of mere books, an arrogant fool stuffed with false and useless knowledge, a narrow-minded, self-complaisant parasite, a pensioner, an old man who hadn't proved himself in any way, shape, or form."

Canetti was as convinced as I am that this rough reality we are so often urged to confront, as though it were our fate, is not always worse than the word in its harshness, or greater in its degree of reality; because the word, whether it merely scrapes the nerves or shatters the soul, can live through many seasons in its sentence, even in the shortest phrase; it does not sting singly and die like the bee, but it multiplies throughout history as though lengths of time were its queen; it stings, therefore, incessantly; it poisons with a vicious persistence. Still, Canetti feels compelled, like a sissy who seeks fights, to go out against the world, to yield it pride of place. Yet the glare of that world affronts the cloistered eye: A woman faints in the street; the face of a friend suddenly registers for you the profoundest hate; a protesting crowd is fired on and figures fall softly in the street; you wake to find your landlady, a widow, in your room, quietly sniffing and licking the backs of the photographs of her husband that normally honor the walls. So have you gone out of doors to go mad, as Professor Kien does? Have you slipped from between the covers of your books to be dazzled by daylight and blinded by things? In any case, Canetti's tenderness toward existence, his shock, his surprise at the way the world is, his grave and humorless naïveté before facts he already knows and has read about, continues to yield him epiphanies and prototypes of all kinds, riddles and knots and confusions he will spend the rest of his life patiently trying to understand—unravel and sort out.

Although there are brief, sharply drawn portraits of Brecht, Grosz, and Babel, three other figures dominate the second volume. The first is Karl Kraus, a professional dominator anyway, whose magazine, *The Torch,* Kraus writes entirely himself, and which gives to this period of Canetti's life its name, *The Torch in My Ear;* the second is Veza, the woman we know will eventually become his wife, whom he meets at a Kraus "concert" the way, almost too perfectly, one might meet one's future spouse at church, or a Communist cell meeting, and the person who will soon replace his mother in those endless conversations that, for Canetti, are surrogates for courtship, and, as far as we know, every kind of caress; while the third is a paralyzed young man, a student of philosophy it turns out, who lives near Canetti in Vienna and whom he encounters being wheeled by his mother through the street.

Our author does not have to put asterisks at either end of this conjunction of signs: mother, helpless body, philosophy, active mind.

Many were drawn to Karl Kraus. Some, like Canetti and Adorno, Adolph Loos and Alban Berg, came to study his scorn, and grew to admire his moral and intellectual courage, his hatred of everything cheap and vulgar, of stupidity, violence, and death. Others came to experience the movement, like a dancer's, of a fine mind. Karl Kraus was a moral model by profession, a rhapsode in the old Greek sense, a speaker of insidious power, a reviler who condemned his enemies out of their own mouths. He whipped them with what they wrote, stoned them with their own sounds. Kraus believed that Vienna's corrupt society could be read like the periodicals it published; that cliché and carelessness and lack of taste ought to burn the pages they were placed on; and he taught Canetti to look for human weakness in words, and to demand a style that made no concessions to sect, sex, or marketplace in its pursuit of sincerity, honesty, and truth.

Nowadays we are likely to think, so far have we fallen, that ideals of this kind are only useful to stuff a shirt.

To Thomas Marek, the paralyzed student, Canetti begins to speak, for the first time fully, of his obsession: the crowd, its character, control, significance (it is a subject Canetti has come to in the same way he has all his others—through an initial shock, a prototypical experience of riot and violence); but Canetti is impressed by the triumph of Marek's mind over his body, by this man who must turn the pages of his philosophy texts with his tongue (more of the same symbolism); and with Marek, Canetti learns to listen, too, for Marek is almost pure voice, a living anticipation of Samuel Beckett.

Karl Kraus despised the trivial; he was satisfied to expose the fraudulent, the glib, to nail the hypocrisies of the Viennese to the local trees; but there is something easy about all that, even though it is necessary. Canetti begins to hear a real heart beating in that silent pudding we so often are; he starts to discover, in the trivial and fleeting, the steadfast human things; and perhaps he even heard my irritation at the noise that murdered our meeting, even sensed my tendency to shrivel like a spent balloon in people-packed places.

While working in a chemistry lab (for he is obediently pursuing a

useful career), Canetti is, of course, surrounded by the tics and
japes and oddities of others. But, as he writes:

> I did not realize how much I learned in the laboratory from
> seemingly absurd or insignificant conversations. I encountered
> advocates of all opinions that were affecting the world. And
> had I been open to all concrete things (as I mistakenly imag-
> ined myself to be), I might have gained a good number of
> important insights from these supposedly trivial conversations.
> But my respect for books was still too great, and I had barely
> set out on the road to the true book: each individual human
> being, bound in himself.

Thus the conflict between life and art, writing and reality, the library
and the street, is solved, but at no expense of respect for the book,
because each person is ennobled and set free by being, in the book's
way, bound.

A deceased Nobel laureate, Elias Canetti has now achieved such
fame as to be unknown all over the world. His obscurity is a part of
his character, and is a credit to him, for he might be more widely recognized if his thought were sly and riddling, got up in a seductive
lingo all its own so as to seem complex and problematic, not simply,
plainly, and vertiginously deep. A quizzical look would not always follow the saying of his name if he had established a school of intellectual knaves to keep that name alive, his logo lit. If he had adopted a
posture like a dog's the more fulsomely to piss against whatever
noble tree might be embarked; if he had been an idolater, an ideo-
logue, a fanatic, a terrorist, instead of a fiercely candid critic and
generous yet shrewd admirer; if he had simply *joined* something,
he'd have had a considerably greater play in the press. If he had softened his scorn, rather than giving it a hard and endless edge, or run
out of anger like water while fighting a fire, instead of drawing on an
abundant store with which to combat the fresh catastrophe each day
presents, we would perhaps love him more, because we are flattered
by the failings of others; we prefer weakness, especially in our moral-
ists. And if he had not finally fallen silent from respect for the word,

and learned to listen—that lost art—learned to listen to *us*—to our most trivial mutterings, our conventional complaints—in order that his own writing might bear witness to the leprous condition of our consciousness, the sorrowful state of our lives, we might have kept our own bound volumes shut and out of reach of this grabby, voracious rabbi of our word.

HUMORS OF BLOOD & SKIN

I
The Sentences of John Hawkes

We feel, first of all, that we—you and I—that we can't miss it: fine-
ness, excellence, quality; it is there like an address at the end of
some elaborate directions we've been given: larger, more bovine,
than life; and we believe that although, conceivably, others may be
obtuse or spiritually absent on occasion, certainly we (it is ourselves,
after all, of whom we speak) won't overlook Eden, Etna, or their
equivalences; yet—alas!—at one time or other we surely shall: We
shall fall asleep in the train window while, beneath the trestle, a
painted canyon opens like a lily; we shall blink in the middle of a
beautiful pirouette; blunder into the wrong street and never find the
duomo; pick the squid out and shove it to the side of our plate; yawn
in the face of the vast Pacific; sneeze on the president's hand as he
fastens the medal to our chest; quarrel about love in Syracuse and
thereby miss Sicily, a land our embittered memory can't return to;
yet, similar incidents will happen often: Ancient, medieval, modern
history, as well as present life, continually repeats and records such
oversights, such nodding, such detumescence; there is a coolness

that clings to us sometimes even when we are wrapped in flames and pretending to be a phoenix.

I record with shame the several times I failed to complete the first chapter of *Under the Volcano,* my tardy appreciation of Turner's burning boats and smoggy sunsets, the jokes I made about a Gertrude Stein I hadn't read, the deaf ear I turned to *Eugene Onegin* just because it had been composed by Tchaikovsky, the foolish idea I had that Ford Madox Ford had hung around Conrad's neck like a ten-cent Saint Christopher's medal. My grudging regard for Walt Whitman is still a blot upon my escutcheon. And in 1959, while reading manuscripts for a little magazine named *Accent,* I nearly fell asleep over my first pages of John Hawkes. In the tall, sloppy stack of stories that were victimizing me, I had turned up a piece called "A Horse in a London Flat," by an author whose name was unfamiliar. It was a title not strange enough, by itself, to make me sit up, though it should have. Afterward, I found excuses for myself: It was winter in Urbana; an infant had mewled its misery throughout my night; the stories in the slush pile I'd been assigned were artless and awful. So my eyes had run over perhaps five pages like rain down a window, when somehow my consciousness was penetrated by his prose. There was fog on a river, I remember. What else was going on? They—dim figures, men—were lifting a horse by means of a sling from the bottom of a barge to a place on the quay . . .

The whistles died one by one on the river and it was not Wednesday at all, only a time slipped off its cycle with hours and darkness never to be accounted for. There was water viscous and warm that lapped the sides of the barge; a faint up and down motion of the barge which he could gauge against the purple rings of a piling; and below him the still crouched figures of the men and, in its moist alien pit, the silver horse with its ancient head round which there buzzed a single fly as large as his own thumb and molded of shining blue wax.

. . . and I woke as if something scalding had fallen in my eyes. I did not complete the paragraph that followed. My cheeks were burning with embarrassment. The pride I took in my taste, as well as the protective arrogance of an unbudded artist, were, in that moment, removed. I found myself in dirty underdrawers at the scene of an accident and about to be arrested.

He stared down at the lantern-lit blue fly and the animal whose ears were delicate and unfeeling, as unlikely to twitch as two pointed fern leaves etched on glass . . .

I don't know why it was this particular passage which woke me rather than another; it should have been the brilliant opening paragraph that did it, the paragraph to which I now returned in order to enter a beautiful and dangerous new world. From the first, John Hawkes's prose had sounded what Henry James would have said was "the right note," and I had not heard it. As I read the pages I had previously dozed through, those two leaflike ears were etched on my imagination, and image after image went to join them. The lines of *The Lime Twig* are alive as few in our literature are. They compose a prose of great poetry, a language linked like things in nature are—by life and by desire. This prose is exploratory without being in the least haphazard or confused; and, for me, at least, it is fundamentally, and in the best sense, exemplary: It shows me how writing should be written, and also how living should be lived.

So I shortly went next door with the shock of my recognition, its author's pages beating in my hand like a fresh heart, only to have a choral scatter of voices say:

"Oh yes, John Hawkes. Of course. Haven't you read *The Cannibal?*"

"Or *The Goose on the Grave,* for God's sake."

"What about the beginning of *The Beetle's Leg?*"

"That's *The Beetle Leg.*"

"He's like no one else. I'd recognize his work in a minute."

"Hawkes was still practically a baby, you know, when he wrote

The Cannibal; right after—like the infant Hercules—he strangled a snake in his bed."

So I suffered, in a matter of moments, my second humiliation. I didn't know; hadn't read; wasn't up. Yet it is true, as I told myself, that in our society a major writer can work for years, and have a hardy and devoted following, even achieve an international reputation, without interrupting the insipid flow of the culture by scarcely so much as a comma. Hadn't Faulkner been safely sealed in indifference for three-quarters of his writing life? There comes a time, for most of us, when, with respect to some fine filmmaker, novelist, poet, or painter, the seal gets broken. Originality escapes like a genie from a jar.

The secret is in the sentences. Of course, the sentences must add up; they must amount to something more than themselves; they must create that larger sentence which every fine fiction passes upon us in the course of its composition; but if those phrases which form a face, for instance, have not themselves some features, if there's no "look" to them, no character, then the unremarkable will remain as unremarked as it deserves to be; just consider when you last regarded with love some inclining head, and ask yourself if it was ever true that the eyes were without allure, the nose without distinction, the mouth not worth a mention, its smile without consequence, while the whole, on the other hand, was wonderful: attractive, generous, appealing?

In a sense, the pieces that make up this reader, which Hawkes has called *Humors of Blood & Skin,* are fragments, and can only beg us to restore them to the complete text they somewhere else are; to return us, as my eye was returned, to the beginnings of all these endings. But the fragments we have here, like the even smaller shards that are the sentences themselves, are not useless nothings like bits of broken bottle; rather, they are "details" as details are depicted in the careful study of a painting: magnifications, points of focus, centers of concentration. They invite the closer look, the savor of the silent reader's inner tongue; they invoke that special state, the literary reverie, which, unlike the daydream, as Gaston Bachelard has argued, circles its subject and returns us repeatedly to places of thoughtfulness and appreciation. I draw out a few sentences from here and there in this book or that:

> The damp smell of the river rolled over soldiers' leggings and trousers that had been left in doorways, and a cow lying dead in a field looked like marble.

> Even the dialogue of the frogs is rapturous.

> Precious brass safety pins holding up their panties, and then I saw the pins, all at once saw the panties, the square gray-white faded undergarments of poor island girls washed in well water morning and night and, indistinguishable from kitchen wash-rag or scrap of kitchen towel, hung on a string between two young poplars and flapping, blowing in the hard island wind until once more dry enough and clean enough to return to the plain tender skin, and of course the elastics had been worn out or busted long ago and now there were only the little bent safety pins for holding up their panties and a few hairpins for the hair and a single lipstick which they passed from girl to girl at country crossroads or in the high school lavatory on the day of the dance.

> For a moment she stood there waiting, allowing him to see through his tears and his swollen lids her chest, her knees, the little belly that was the same shape as her face.

Though taken almost at random from several novels, don't they call for fresh intensities of inspection, these extraordinary combinations? And the nature and effect of each is quite different, for our author knows many modes and can be breathless and romantic or harsh and succinct, as seems best—formal or colloquial, circumspect or blunt. The use of "and" in my first example, we might settle on it, our eye like a fly made of blue wax; or we might consider the character of those trousers that have been left in doorways, repeating the expression until its oddness is engraved upon us; or we might simply listen to the dialogue of the frogs; or match, as we move our minds from word to word, the pace of the beautiful sentence about the panties, with its characteristic Hawkesean slide, in this case, from pins to hairpins, hairpins to lipstick, lipstick to lavatory, and lavatory to dance; or we might appreciate the sight Hawkes has permitted us of a belly the same shape as a face.

Each such sentence, and there are thousands of them—thousands—creates not a new world so much as a special and very alert awareness of one; and that awareness is so controlled, so precise, so intense, so angular while remaining uncomfortably direct, so comic, too, as if a smile has been sliced by a knife, that many readers have recoiled as though from reality itself, and pretended to be running from a nightmare, from something sur- or unreal, restoring the disguise that Hawkes's prose has torn away. In Rilke's great novel, *The Notebooks of Malte Laurids Brigge,* there is a passage in which Malte perceives an old woman with her face implanted in her hands, as if put there by Rodin, so that when—startled by a sudden sound in the street—she pulls her hands away, her face must adhere to her hands, and she (and Malte, too) must then look down at the inside of herself as one might at the inside of a mask or the inner peeling of a fruit. Above the compote of the palm, the peeled face Malte cannot confront is presumably moist. This is the effect of Hawkes's fiction: It sees the world from just inside its surface, a surface at which it looks back the way Orpheus so dangerously did, thereby returning an unlamenting Eurydice to Hades. It is as if a wall were examining, from its steadfastly upright side, the slow peel of its paint. The position is unprecedented. And the final result is the merging of two surfaces, as if the print of this page were bleeding through the paper to shadow the obverse side; or, again, we might imagine a stained-glass window made of what could be simultaneously seen from both sides. We cannot pretend that the world has only one "out" or one "in." There is a second skin. So those panties we encountered a moment ago are observed not only from the point of view of a voyeur who might enjoy their innocent flaglike

alignment, but from the vantage of the flesh which will wear them—
the two contemplations pressed together then as though by thighs.

Rilke wrote that beauty was the start of a terror we could barely
endure, and I think the reader will feel that tension, that double-
ness, here; but I want to rejoin those thighs for a moment, pay heed
to the warmth they generate, for among the more prominent qualities of John Hawkes's prose is its glorious sensuality:

> So while the spring kept Oscar cool, the five of us sprawled
> close together and held out our hands to the fat black arm that
> disappeared inside the pot and came up dripping. Calypso her-
> self couldn't have done better. Sweet guavas and fat meat that
> slid into the fingers, made the fingers breathe, and crushed
> leaves of cinnamon on the tongue and sweet shreds of coconut.
> We are together under the dark speckled covering of the tree,
> sprawled together, composed, with no need for wine, and the
> cows stood about and nosed us and a blackbird flew down and
> sat on Sonny's cap. We ate together among the smooth green
> oval calabashes that were as large as footballs, and lay among
> the calabashes and licked our fingers.

Such language nourishes more certainly than lunch, and within its
context the song it sings contains a smile, for Oscar is a vial of
sperm, and this—for the cows—is artificial insemination day.

2

When It Was Over

I once wrote, about some of Jack Hawkes's sentences, that their
language was more nourishing than lunch, but for Jack himself,
lunch always seemed more important than anything else except perhaps dinner. Mary and I were traveling with the Hawkeses and the
Barths and Heide Ziegler from Tübingen through the Black Forest
to Meersberg, on Lake Constance. Naturally, there were many
lunches, many dinners. In the Black Forest, we got tipsy on West-
phalian ham and *Spargel,* then in season, while sobering ourselves

with the local champagne. Hawkes kept insisting that nearby were advertised baths of mud in which we might wisely, while holding one another's hands, immerse ourselves, allowing hot mud to seep into our secret cracks and remove them, I supposed, like unwanted warts. Wrappers of ham so tissue-thin that you could see through them must have suggested such an adventure to Jack, surely not the champagne or the thick white spikes of asparagus. To me, Jack seemed a puzzling combination of the naïve and the knowing, the cautious and the daring, a dangerous guide whose love of the sensuous might lead my mind into thoughtless pastures—the green and obscene together like grasses. The term *mud bath* was, for me, a serious contradiction. But his imagination—so incarnate—was already giving himself up to the warm embrace of the earth, while I thought only of the grave: hot or cold—who cared in a casket? And had I communicated my undertakerish concerns—think what caskets cost these days!—Jack (if he found himself in such a closet) would have felt the shiny satin lining like a suit inside himself, as though his own skin were the sheets. Have another helping of pale plump *Spargel*, Jack, and dream a different dream.

Which he did. Which he was always doing.

Fiona with the empty sweater clinging to her back like the cast-off skin of some long-forgotten lover, Catherine with her eyes tight shut and hair awry and broad cheeks brightly skimmed with tears, I shading my face and easing off the uncomfortable and partially opened rucksack, Hugh holding aloft his prize and leaping through the weeds to a fallen pediment, Hugh turning and facing us with the little copper rivets dancing on his penitential denims and his mouth torn open comically, painfully, as if by an invisible hand—suddenly the four of us were there, separated, disheveled, blinking, and yet reunited in this overgrown and empty quadrangle that now was filled with hard light and the sweet and salty scent of endless day. I dropped the rucksack, squinted, fished for a fat cigarette. Fiona caught hold of the sleeves of the sweater at the wrists and pulled the long empty sleeves wide and high in a gesture meant only for the far-off sun. Catherine sat on a small white chunk of stone and held her head in her hands, Hugh tipped his prize onto the altar of the fallen pediment and flung aside the torch, reared back, and waited. (*The Blood Oranges,* pp. 205–206.)

Fortunately for the rest of us, there are other ways to see, to dream, to write, to persuade four characters to climb; we had better seek them out, because this way was Jack's way, a prose that breathes what it sees, and marshals its gerunds like a general.

We might have lunch in some kitschily glamorous *Stube* where the tables were enclosed in huge wine barrels. Jack would have Heide Ziegler translate the menu for him—no easy task because equivalents are never readily come by—and to each description she offered, he would ask, "Does it come with a big hunk of meat?" because that's what Jack wanted—meat, a huge still-quivering slab.

Early one morning in a town famous for the growing of some grape, I arose from my bed in the inn and stepped outside alone to the automobile. I smelled the odor of flowers thirsting early for the sun; deep green fields stretched to either side of the road, wet and silent; it was the cold dawn of the traveler and I wished suddenly for a platter of home-cooked sausage. ("The Traveler.")

That was my guess: that one sense keyed up all the others; if he were looking, his ears would wiggle; if listening, his mouth would water; if in a tub of mud, who knew what else would demand an oiling?

My wife, Mary, had her heart set on seeing the Church of St. George, a ninth-century structure at Oberzell, on the island of Reichenau, so naturally I had mine set on seeing it, too. Shelly and Jack Barth were committed to sailing, so we persuaded Heide and the Hawkeses to come with us on a voyage to Reichenau Island. It turned out to be a frustrating, hot all-day tramp in full sun over flat, dull, unshaded terrain—an island as magical as monotony, with Jack frequently reminding us how the Barths must be feeling a blue breeze and beneath them lulling swells. In fact, we had scarcely started our walk when Jack thought it time to stop—for a beer. But true tourists do not stop. True tourists trudge. And we did, promising Jack, as often as the prophets promised the Israelites, the swift coming of his kingdom, a cool dark saloon. Of course the kingdom never came. They never do. Jack peeled and handed the peelings to Mary, who bore them before her. When we found the church, it was . . . well, okay, if you like ninth-century stuff. Jack still had most of his clothes.

I suggested to Jack, who was now silent and stooped as a parched plant, that this island seemed the perfect exotic spot to write his next book, since his books and their spots seemed so attuned. "Like Lesbos," he said. "I've been here already."

The heat was leaden, the sea flat and gray, at the end of a short quay made of cracked concrete were hung dead and drying infant octopi from a sort of clothes line. The Turkish coast was a flat and ominous smudge on the horizon; there was a ruined fortress atop a bleak hill, a few tortured olive trees, a beach of pebbles and shards of rusty iron.

It didn't do to disappoint Jack. You'd be led to hell behind a troop of surly adjectives. But Reichenau Island, I thought, was nicer than the inside of an army ambulance, or nicer than Fort Peck, Montana, where he and Sophie were married, and even though it could hardly compete with Grenada or Vence, it was at least as lovely as the blackfly-filled farmhouse in Brittany he chose for a while to write in. Later, there would be Venasque, of course, where *Virginie* was composed, a work I much later taught to a roomful of innocent college kids in an act of pure revenge. They were not innocent of sex, of course, but of sensuality. And got even with me by making me explain everything—twice.

Jack tried hard to be an innocent. He marveled, when we reached Berlin, that there were Russians there. We marveled that he marveled. How could he be innocent, I thought—though he wrote of innocence—since his prose knew everything. Innocence ends early in life; it ends with the awakening of the senses. Jack wanted his always just about to be aroused: alert, hungry, filling, overflowing, yet somehow not yet full.

I wrote about Jack's work once, and concluded my remarks by summing up my own sense of it, as if putting words in his mouth.

The world is not simply good and bad on different weekends like an inconsistent pitcher; we devour what we savor and what sustains us; out of ruins more ruins will later, in their polished towers, rise; lust is the muscle of love: its strength, its coarseness, its brutality; the heart beats and is beaten by its beating; not a shadow falls without the sun's shine and the sun sears what it saves. These are not the simplicities my saying has suggested. In our civilization, the center has not held for a long time; neither the center nor the place where the center was can now be found. We are disordered, arthritic fingers without palms. Inside the silence of unmoving things, there are the sounds of repeated explosions. Perhaps it is catastrophe breathing. Who has rendered this condition more ruthlessly than Hawkes has, or furnished our barren countrysides with their hanging trees and human sluices more honestly, yet with wealth, with the attention one lover has for another? For his work has always refused ruin in the act that has depicted it, and his life's labor was the joyful showing forth and celebration of such a healing art.

THE PUBLIC BURNING

You are about to read the one real book about Captain America. Written in the 1970s, published finally in 1977, about actual and imaginary events of June 1953, it could not be more current, more relevant, more right on than it is now (on whatever date the reader finds herself immured).

Before Watergate and Whitewater and all the other gates that have opened and shut in recent decades, the United States had many a witch-hunt, political trial, congressional investigation, retaliatory leakage of private papers, as well as periodic waves of general harassment, with their associated villains and victims: the Sacco-Vanzetti case, for instance, that of Alger Hiss, Klaus Fuchs and Harry Gold, the McCarthy hearings, the ordeal by committee of the Hollywood screenwriters, the confinements of suspicious persons after December 7, and, among the more notorious, the trial of Julius and Ethel Rosenberg.

Our country is as rich in scares as Halloween. They have come in almost every color, and conspiracy theories have not been confined to rural right-wing gun toters. Nor have our politicians been above the use of fright and intimidation to gain votes and influence policy. Assassinations occur with the frequency of business cycles and provide the paranoid with many hours of happy conjecturing. Although we still dig up traitorous moles from the grounds of the CIA, the Red Menace has largely gone back to the comics, from whence it came. We cling to the Yellow Peril, though, and fear various cults of the ungodly, such as Castro's Cubans, plague-bearing gays, ghetto gangs, drug lords, and immigrants in general. Then there are the terrorists to trouble our sleep, and all those rogue nations manufacturing chemical weapons and planning to build the bomb, which, now that it's no longer scary, has become hairy scary indeed.

In *The Public Burning*, the fright wig is worn by the Phantom, who is naturally invisible and everywhere—all ears. Huge hunks of the book are narrated by Dick Nixon, Eisenhower's VP at the time, though thinking and conversing with more pith and eloquence than the real one managed, since we have now read the tapes and are acquainted with his style. The book's Tricky Dick is nevertheless blessed with sufficient hypocrisy, self-delusion, and opportunism to suggest his connection to the historical vice president. But not to cement it. Coover's Richard Nixon is a rich and beautifully rendered fictional character. The real Richard Nixon is a caricature. That is one of the profound ironies of Coover's achievement. In evidence thereof, here is a passage in which Nixon is describing his peacemaker's role as Eisenhower's second in command:

> I was Eisenhower's salesman in the Cloakrooms, that was my job, I was the political broker between the patsies and the neanderthals, I had to cool the barnburners, soften up the hardshells, keep the hunkers and cowboys in line, mollify the soreheads and baby tinhorn egos, I was the flak runner, the wheelhorse, I had to mend the fences and bind up the wounds. I'm a lot like Lincoln, I guess, who was kind and compassionate on the one hand, and strong and competitive on the other.

The allegedly real Nixon does not speak in sentences, but in sputters and jabs. His clichés are mostly scatological. He talks like a mob boss. Concerning Ted Kennedy, Nixon orders his henchmen: "Plant one. Plant two guys on him. This will be very useful. Just might get lucky and catch that son-of-a-bitch and grill him for '76."

As the novel proceeds, the text will furnish us with ample evidence of Nixon's treacherous, self-serving, delusional character, and would do so even if Nixon's name were changed to Fred Smith. The reader does not need to know Nixon's history of paranoia to understand the Nixon of *The Public Burning*. This Nixon, like the historical Nixon, like politicians generally, speaks in pat phrases, employing epithets, if not of Homeric quality, at least of Homeric frequency. He needs to fool himself ("I'm a lot like Lincoln") before he can fool others. But the rhetorical range and energy of the fictional figure, the psychological complexity of his personality as pictured, reach a level far surpassing the historical Nixon's pandering curse-laced drivel and Lionel-sized two-track mind.

The same can be said of Uncle Sam, the slick salesman of snake oil. As an American symbol, he has almost outlived his usefulness, a weak finger-pointing rube on enlistment posters; but here he is America's cutout boy, described in a dozen resplendent but tacky, hence circuslike, lingoes, everywhere larger than anyone's life, a liar but a go-getter, proud as spiked punch: The tall-tale teller and backwoods braggart, the glib salesman, the sideshow barker, the Fourth of July politician, the ringmaster, the circuit rider and tub-thumper, the inspiring coach, the corn-fed orator, the bullyboy roughrider, the shoot-'em-dead cowboy, the patronizing educator and preacher, the soldier of your fortune, the mealymouthed savior of souls and robber of the poor box . . . they are all here in their linguistic glory; and you will meet Sam—created, top hat to coat tales, by all of these cartoon creatures in a newsreel-rolling prologue whose satiric energy and savage musicality are simply unequaled in our literature except by some other passages, constructed on similar principles, in *The Public Burning*.

This novel—the interior history of a history—is consequently dense in detail, fragments drawn together like a crowd to an accident (or a mob to an execution); disparate pieces suddenly become one and massive and in motion, which is just as it should be for a fiction that intends to alarm history and ourselves by demonstrating how the Unreal rules, that must immerse us in many facts and figures—data dancing to a clown's song in Kay Kaiser's Kollege of Musical Knowledge—because around any one character whirls another dozen and all their doings, each a Jack Benny, a Rochester, a Charlie McCarthy.

Drenched in data, fantasy becomes reality. Because at one level, it is real. If Nixon is going to become president of his country, then he will have to be united with Uncle Sam the way a state is admitted to the union—joined by being buggered. The logic of this is impeccable. The voice of the chronicler, in a device that reminds me of John Dos Passos's Newsreels in *USA*, sums up the state of the nation and the world, describing situations that are inherently hard to believe, if inspected thoroughly. Eisenhower and Nixon play golf at Burning Tree. *Burning Tree?* Nixon is the consummate duffer. Baseball may be the sport of America's ordinary guy, but golf, and golf alone, is the game of the successful man: presidents, actors, bankers, heroes of other sports. They tee off. . . . They pitch; they drive. . . . They hole out. . . . They toss them down—their scotches and waters—at the nineteenth green . . . still wearing their nail-soled shoes. Facts, which are dumb, resonate when they enter fiction, and fantasies, when acted on, become factified. When she was a girl, Ethel Greenglass starred in a prison melodrama. A *prison* play? She is starring still—but only while we read, since in stir she scarcely stirs. And Richard Nixon gradually becomes enamored of the woman he wants to electrocute in the square of burning signs called Times. Then she—this duchess of darkness, she—(he comes to feel)—she wants—(as he does)—someone to love. Before the final hour, he will go to her in her cell in Sing Sing. *Sing Sing?* The book begins with a quote from Mrs. Nixon about how much fun they used to have at parties, sometimes reenacting "Beauty and the Beast." Guess who the beast is; think whom a transposed Ethel plays.

At one point, as Nixon works amid a scatter of papers on the celebrated case, he finds himself thinking about the names of its principals.

> . . . all the colors. Strange. Green, gold, rose . . . which nation's flag was that? I played with the street names, codenames, names of the lawyers, people at the edge of the drama— Perl, Sidorovich, Glassman, Urey, Condon, Slack, Golos, Bentley. I realized that the initial letters of the names of the four accused—Sobell, Rosenberg, Rosenberg, and Yakovlev— would spell SORRY were it not for the missing O. Was there some other secret agent of the Phantom, as yet unapprehended, with this initial? Oppenheimer? Oatis? This kind of thinking may be crazy, but it is common; it is customary, everyday; its catastrophic consequences are quite ordinary and certainly to be expected.

Throughout Robert Coover's career, he has been trying to come to grips with commercial deceit, political lies, and religious myths, the better to strangle them. He empties out fables and received beliefs like frequently used spittoons. His fine first novel, *The Origin of the Brunists,* concerns the creation of a millennial cult awaiting the end of the world (as here it is an execution). In *The Universal Baseball Association, Inc.,* a sport sets sail for the sacred. His book of stories, *Pricksongs & Descants,* pops many a cultural cliché, reducing them to raddles of split rubber. Then there is his short play, *A Theological Position,* (playlets crawl out of cracks in *The Public Burning*), and several political send-ups like *A Political Fable* (or, as I prefer, *The Cat in the Hat for President*) follow it, as well as Coover's manipulation of the stereotypes featured in Hollywood's films (*A Night at the Movies*).

Coover's prose is occasionally leisurely, like a sailing ship, bobbing along on the waters of history, but then it will shift suddenly into high gear, zip away, and rocket off. Diction rises and falls like an elevator. There are floors for High Art, Religiosity, Bamboozle, and Scatology, as well as Porn. Good guys—villains to the villains—for instance, Justice William O. Douglas, who, with an opinion, saves, at least momentarily, the Rosenbergs from burning—are nevertheless greatly outnumbered. Lawyers run loose like packs of wild dogs. Orators are apuff with pomposity and deliver themselves of their opinions in slow and heavy southern drawls. "Ah see no pahticulah point in sendin' mey-un to Ko-REE-ya to dai, Mistagh Cheymun, whahl aytomic spies are allowed to liy-uv heah at HOME!" Above all, there is Uncle Sam, constantly trying to come to terms with constraint, calumny, and disappointment. Hearing his voice, I know that I love Uncle Sam—this Uncle Sam, that is—a creature of unending criminentlies (expressions of surprise).

Politicians talk. They talk to their colleagues, endeavoring to strong-arm them with verbs and frighten them with nouns. They speechify, I suspect, within their own heads, and hear themselves in sleep squarely praise and roundly denounce the talk of other talkers. Though their words reach newsprint, and memos always have to be circulated, it is still the press conference, the convention floor, the smoky cloakroom, and the halls of Congress where the politicos live and lie and babble. Appropriate to its theme, then, is the insistent and successful orality of Coover's prose. The reader cannot hurry and still hear; because an entire nation's mendacity is given rhythm by its political marches, by the brasses of its big bands, through its swoony hymn singing; and Coover's sentences sing similarly, becoming another sort of sentence, another kind of verdict.

Whatever the justness of its final judgment, the Rosenberg trial was a show trial. Coover's Times Square setting for their execution is scarcely an exaggeration. The nation's taste has eagerly lowered itself in the direction of public executions—at least ones that the vengefully aggrieved may observe and enjoy—so that the idea of achieving death through electrical illumination in the fashion of a flashing sign is not so wildly satirical as it once might have been. The description of the Rosenbergs' ordeal is full of deft and devastating touches. "Julie had to have two teeth pulled out (Warden Denno in his economy-minded way making sure he got temporary plates only) . . ." This garish and vulgar "chair in Times Square" is meant to remind us of the behavior of the Inquisition, which held public burnings on a regular basis—not for punishment but for edifying educational purposes. In their yellow robes and conical hats, they could have been clowns. *The Public Burning* envisions a Roman carnival, a Roman circus, as well as a witch-hunt. But the ceremony is mostly one appropriate to the pagan pomp of some secular religion. Gertrude Stein once declared, when she decided that General Grant was a leader of the American Church, that "there is no up in American religion."

Power, when it has to rest on public opinion instead of relying on policemen and armies, is compelled to express itself differently from the way it does when secrecy and silence are its henchmen. Early in their steps to power, both the fascists and the Communists opened their courtrooms to public gaze and edification; however, later, their positions secure, they tended simply to have their enemies quietly disappear.

In the United States, the court of public opinion has always been a busy one. Now, with TV technicians focusing on the court's proceedings, judges preen, juries dress up, while lawyers listen to the roar of the crowd and try their cases on, instead of in, camera. Vanzetti's noble last words to the court concerning his friend Sacco, which the local press probably carried, cannot be imagined for this case, because the Rosenberg trial was bourgeois from top to bottom. It was, in a way, a family affair. We have, no longer, even ears for such words as Vanzetti uttered. "Sacco is a heart, a faith, a character, a man; a man, lover of nature, and mankind; a man who gave all, who sacrificed all to the cause of liberty and to his love for mankind: money, rest, mundane ambition, his own wife, his children, himself and his own life."

It has become customary for journalists to jive up the lives, the crimes, the conditions they write about with fictional flourishes, but, until recently, it was not acceptable for novelists to deal with the present in a similar way, allowing living figures to walk their fictional streets, figures modified from their real-life roles so that their actual natures could be better recognized. *The Public Burning* does more.

It puts Very Important People in the center ring of a circus, in the highlighted square of the editorial cartoon, and I am reminded of the fierce satirical images of Félician Rops, George Grosz, of Hogarth and Daumier, as well as the unintentional parodies of Horatio Alger. The lawyers of allegedly real life worry about the cut and fit of impending suits of libel.

Nor does our history speak well of our moral improvement, now that we enjoy a president who daily issues new smeary blue lies like an old-fashioned mimeo machine.

Coover's manuscript has suffered as many ups and downs as some of the novel's characters. Prudently, he shows a swatch of it to his editor, who is alarmed but valiant. So Coover continues working on the book, although with less confidence now about its eventual reception than could be considered helpful. Suddenly, tragically, the editor, young and at least morally strong, dies during a tennis match. *The Public Burning* is without a champion. But shortly another publisher appears, full of confidence and good cheer. The editing of the manuscript proceeds without incident. The book seems ready for publication in 1976, appropriately during the nation's bicentennial year. Copyediting is completed and the manuscript returned to the publisher, where it falls into a well of silence. Finally, the truth is wrung from the wet suit of reluctance. The company's legal team is scared, and has Nixoned the novel's publication. He, the Most Feared Tricky Dicky, is most feared because he is a lawyer with a skin thinner than a condom, and is believed to possess a vindictive streak so wide, it would turn a skunk white. After difficult negotiations, it is agreed to submit the manuscript to an impartial jury for judgment. This group, headed by the dean of the Columbia Law School, sees some potential problems but decides that they are not serious enough to prevent the book's publication. Virtue appears to have triumphed.

The story goes—speak of Burning Tree!—that the publisher's bossman was playing golf with a legal iron, and while fairwaying (certainly not while on the green), he described the book to his eagle. You'll land in a trap, the Kingpin was told. Since the Bigman's loyalties to the party opposing Nixon were well known, the legal mashie warned that the Topper could be sued for malice as well as libel and invasion of privacy. The decision to publish was reversed as quietly as possible (don't tell the author) so that the Head Honcho might receive, undisturbed, a freedom of the press award from New York City journalists.

The truth had to be wrung once more from the formerly enthusiastic editor, who then watered Coover well. Of course the book was not going to be published, because it was an immmoral work. With three *m*'s. That bad. Why? Look at it this way, came an answer: Suppose you had written the book about Eleanor Roosevelt instead of Richard Nixon. The editor, proud of his rationale—a triumphant non sequitur—was not amused by Bob's offer to work Eleanor in.

Looking for a home, *The Public Burning* went on a long and unpleasant odyssey from one set of corporation lawyers to another— from Siren to Circe to Polyphemus—racking up refusals—five, ten, fifteen, more—there aren't as many major publishers left as had the opportunity to say no in their lawyer's Latin. Like a spill of oil, rumors of impeding suits began to pollute the book's possibilities. Backstairs shenanigans increased. Everywhere, front stairs stood unused. Until finally a fine publisher bit. The phone rang. Bob picked up. Bob's agent reported: It's a done deal. Why was the author reluctant to pop a cork just yet?

The phone rang again—minutes later. Bob picked up, but his heart sank. Bob's agent now said: It's an undone deal. The publisher's ear had been tickled by a spiteful tongue, on whose tip was another legal warning.

The tunnel of love is not yet just ahead. It is the Valley of Despond and Misery's Mountains that loom. There was one editor left with any worth to turn to, and Coover explained to him the nature of the threats that had been made against the manuscript. The head of the publishing company, a neophyte as well as someone important's nephew, was persuaded that the book would make only the right waves, and wash lots of ruck ashore. Contracts were finally drawn and actually signed. Who should be away on summer vacation during all of this progress but the firm's chief lawyer? Who, of course, cried "ruination" when he got the news. However, there was that damnable pair of signatures. The contract had to be honored. A few changes, which the publisher had to insist on (to retain its honor), arrived in Coover's mail: six to ten pages of them in uninviting single space, like an invasion of ants. The opening "request" was that all living persons be removed from the novel. Perhaps they might be ceremonially murdered in Times Square. But somehow on the q.t., so that no one would ever know they'd been there.

Push back the furniture now for acrimonious discussions. These delayed the book a year. By now, Bob had his own lawyer and the text was fought over like the fields around Verdun. One doesn't have to be an author to imagine Coover's state of mind by this time, for he could no longer trust the intention behind any suggestion. Meanwhile, publisher number one wanted its advance back. Coover's present publisher—reluctant, angry, and frustrated—would not only not advance him the necessary money (spent in a distant decade) but threatened to pauperize him if the company were sued, so Coover had to borrow against his slim estate a sum sufficient for any of us to live a year on, a debt that took ten years to pay off.

Fearing an injunction, which would halt publication after production costs had been met, the firm announced *The Public Burning*'s August/September appearance, and then pushed it out of the house during May/June, where it sold well enough its first week to reach the *New York Times* best-seller list. That was not good, for it was felt that if this infamous book became widely read, legal action would be certain. The novel's name was removed from the publisher's catalog, no advertising was permitted, and copies were quietly withdrawn from the stores.

The book probably wouldn't have been sued anyway, but—look around—what book? It was nowhere to be found.

This book has suffered a seemingly endless series of intolerable blows. Yet in hindsight . . . in hindsight what a convincing confirmation of one's work, what joy to have unsettled the nerves, and exposed the craven hearts of so many immmoral minions, stalwarts of their glorious high-minded industry!

Now at last, *The Public Burning* will reemerge like the ground-hog and see its shadow. And the reader will get to know the real Richard Nixon, and learn to understand Uncle Sam, who, even young, was ". . . lank as a leafless elm, already chin-whiskered and plug-hatted and all rigged out in his long-tailed blue and his striped pantaloons, his pockets stuffed with pitches, patents, and pyrotechnics . . ." and he will discover just how the world works here, because *The Public Burning* is an account of what this country has become. It is a glorious, slam-bang, star-spangled fiction, and every awful word of it is true.

MORE DEATHS THAN ONE

Chronicle of a Death Foretold does not tell, but literally pieces together, the torn-apart body of a story: that of the multiple murder of a young, handsome, wealthy, womanizing Arab, Santiago Nasar, who lived in the town where Gabriel García Márquez grew up. The novel is not, however, the chronicle of a young and vain man's death, for that event is fed to us in the bits it comes in. It is, instead, the chronicle of the author's discovery of the true course of the story as well as, simultaneously, a rather gruesome catalog of the many deaths—in dream, in allegory, and by actual count—that Santiago Nasar is compelled to suffer. Had he had a cat's lives, it would not have saved him.

It is his author who kills him first, foretelling his death in the first (and in that sense final) sentence of the novel: "On the day they were going to kill him . . ." We are reminded immediately of García Márquez's habit of beginning his books in an arresting way, perhaps a by-product of his long journalistic practice. "Many years later, as he faced the firing squad . . ." *One Hundred Years of Solitude* commences, and *The Autumn of the Patriarch* is no less redolent with death or its threats: "Over the weekend the vultures got into the presidental palace by pecking through the screens on the balcony windows . . ." Santiago Nasar's death is first foretold in the way any fictional fact is, because the fact, of whatever kind, is already there in the ensuing pages, awaiting our arrival like a bus station.

Santiago Nasar also dies in his dreams—dreams that could have been seen to foretell it, had not his mother, an accomplished seer of such things, unaccountably missed "the ominous augury." Before the day is out, his mother will murder him again. Unwittingly, and with the easy fatality we associate with Greek tragedy, Santiago dons a sacrificial suit of unstarched white linen, believing that he is putting it on to honor the visit of a bishop, just as he has celebrated the day before, along with the entire town, the wedding that will be his undoing. So attired, he stands before his mother with glass and aspirin and tells her the dreams she will misunderstand. Santiago Nasar is then symbolically slain and gutted by the cook when Nasar takes a cup of coffee in his mother's kitchen and has another aspirin for his hangover. His father has mounted this woman, and she is remembering Santiago's father as she disembowels two rabbits (fore-telling his disembowelment) and feeds their guts, still steaming, to the dogs.

The cook's daughter does not tell Santiago that she has heard a rumor that two men are looking to kill him, for he continually man-handles her, and she wishes him dead; the town, it seems, knows, too, and participates in the foretelling. Attempts to warn Santiago are halfhearted: People pretend that the threats are empty; that the twin brothers bent on his death are drunk, incapable, unwilling; that it is all a joke. But Orpheus has his enemies in every age. Dionysus was also torn to pieces once, Osiris as well. The women whose bod-ies Santiago Nasar has abused (the metaphor that follows him throughout, and that appears just following the title page, is that of the falcon or sparrow hawk) await their moment. They will use the duplicities of the male code to entrap him. The girl whose wedding has just been celebrated goes to her bridegroom with a punctured maidenhead, and he sends her home in disgrace, where she is beaten until she confesses (although we don't know what the real truth is) that Santiago Nasar was her "perpetrator." And had not her twin brothers believed that the honor of their family required revenge, Nasar would not have been stabbed fatally, not once but seven times, at the front door of his house, a door his mother, believing him already inside, had barred.

The coroner is out of town, but the law requires an autopsy—the blood has begun to smell—so Santiago Nasar is butchered again, this time while dead. The intestines he held so tenderly in his hands as he walked almost primly around his house to find a back door he might enter in order to complete the symbolism of his life by dying in the kitchen he had his morning aspirin in—those insides of the self of which the phallus is only an outer tip—are tossed into a trash can; the dogs who wanted them, and would have enjoyed them, are now dead, too.

Santiago Nasar's mother's last sight of her son, which she says was of him standing in her bedroom doorway, water glass in hand and the first aspirin to his lips, is not, we learn, her last. Her final vision, which she had on the balcony of her bedroom, is of her son "face down in the dust, trying to rise up out of his own blood."

One man is dead, and hundreds have murdered him. The consequences of the crime spread like a disease through the village. Or, rather, the crime is simply a late symptom of an illness that had already wasted everyone. Now houses will decay, too, in sympathy. Those people—lovers, enemies, friends, family—who were unable to act, now act with bitter, impulsive, self-punishing foolishness, becoming old maids and worn whores, alcoholics and stupid recruits, not quite indiscriminately. The inertias of custom, the cruelties of a decaying society, daily indignities, hourly poverties, animosities so ancient that they seem to have been put in our private parts during a prehistoric time, the sullen passivity of the powerless, the feckless behavior of the ignorant, the uselessness of beliefs, all these combine in this remarkable, graphic, and grisly fable to create a kind of slow and creeping fate—not glacial, for that would not do for these regions, but more, perhaps, like the almost imperceptible flow of molasses, sticky, insistent, sweet, and bearing everywhere it goes the sick, digested color of the bowel.

Gregory Rabassa has rendered García Márquez's rapturous reportorial style in poignant, precise, and stabbing English. *Chronicle of a Death Foretold,* like Faulkner's *Sanctuary,* is about the impotent revenges of the impotent; it is about misdirected rage; it is about the heart blowing to bits from the burden of its own beat; yet the author, Santiago Nasar's first murderer, goes patiently about his business, too, putting the pieces back together, restoring, through his magnificent art, his own anger and compassion, this forlorn, primeval, little vegetation god, to a new and brilliant life.

OPEN ON THE SABBATH

I

The Franchiser

You do not write a foreword to the novel of a friend, and the man, among men, you admire and love most, with an easy conscience or a restful mind. To place any words ahead of a work like this is the act of an upstart, an interloper, an interventionist; so I shall say briefly what moves me most when Stanley Elkin's prose becomes my consciousness, and simply hope that others will be drawn to it, and find, if not my pleasures, others equally important and enduring.

Stanley Elkin puts his imagination to work by placing it like a seed within the soil of some vocation. *Vocation:* That is no trade-school word for him. What is your name? Where are you from? What do you do? Among those who survey the habits of Americans, there are many who find these questions, which are likely to be among the first beckoning blanks we fill in on forms, and the first we put to strangers, indicative of our indifference to the essential self. Should men and women, after all, be defined in any important way by their work? The answer is, of course, yes; otherwise, the activities that largely support our lives and consume our time would be unfriendly, foreign, and irrelevant to us. Our occupation should not be something we visit like the seashore in summer or a prisoner in a prison, despite the fact that the work may be unpleasant and dangerous and hard, like that in a mill or a foundry or a mine. Even if it is like speaking a foreign language we haven't mastered, that incapacity itself is totally defining.

In *Boswell*, Elkin's first novel, the occupation was that of a celebrity seeker, but it may be a merchant's, as it is in *A Bad Man*, or a bail bondsman's, as it is in the brilliant novella of that name. Again, a gloomy grocer may be his concern, or a debt collector, the disc jockey of *The Dick Gibson Show*, or a franchiser like Ben Flesh—jobs that are often seedy or suspect in some way. Elkin does not wonder what it would be like if he were a professional bully, or an elderly ragman, though new to the nation, a peddler trundling a cart down the street and crying "Regs, all cloze." He does not say, What if I were running my own radio show?—and then write. His fictions are not daydreams; there is no idleness in them, no reveries. They are not acts of ordinary empathy, either, in which the novelist listens in on some way of life and then plays what he hears on his Linotype. Instead, Elkin allows the activity itself to create his central characters, to find its being in some gainly or ungainly body, and then he encourages that body to verbalize a voice.

Voice: For Elkin, that's no choirboy's word. Just as in Beckett, the *logos* is life. There is not a line in *The Franchiser* that doesn't issue from one. And what is this occupation it speaks for, but acts and their names, agents and their frailties, the textures of their environments? . . . things, words, sensations, signs—all one. And the mouth must work while reading him, must taste the intricate interlace of sound; wallow, as I now am, in the wine of the word. With the whole book to follow, one is still compelled to quote:

> He loved the shop, the smells of the naphthas and benzenes, the ammonias, all the alkalis and fats, all the solvents and gritty lavas, the silken detergents and ultimate soaps, like the smells, he decided, of flesh itself, of release, the disparate chemistries of pore and sweat—a sweat shop—the strange woolly-smelling

acids that collected in armpits and atmosphered pubic hair, the flameless combustion of urine and gabardine mixing together to create all the body's petty suggestive alimentary toxins. The sexuality of it. The men's garments one kind, the women's another, confused, deflected, masked by residual powders, by the oily invisible resins of deodorant and perfume, by the concocted flower and the imagined fruit—by all fabricated flavor. And hanging in the air, too—where would they go?—dirt, the thin, exiguous human clays, divots, ash and soils, dust devils of being.

"Irving, add water, we'll make a man."

And this is precisely how Elkin makes a man—out of the elements he lives in, the body he is confined to, the world he works in, the language he knows.

From time to time, the voice halts, fills its trunk, and sprays us with speech. How long has it been, how far back must we go, to encounter such speeches, such rich wild oratory? If I were to hazard a guess, I would say we should find it again in *The Alchemist,* in *Volpone,* in *Every Man in His Humour,* and if that seems an extreme claim, simply compare Jonson's characteristic rodomontade (as wonderful as the word that is supposed to condemn it) with the piece you will shortly encounter, the speech that begins: "How crowded is the universe . . . How stuffed to bursting with its cargo of crap." And goes on: "A button you could be, a pocket in pants, a figure on print." And on: "I am talking of the long shot of existence, the odds no gambler in the world would take, that you would ever come to life as a person, a boy called Ben Flesh." And on: "You weren't aborted, you didn't end up in a scum bag. You survived the infant mortality stuff. You made it past measles, polio, mumps. You outwitted whooping cough, typhoid, VD. God bless you, boy, you're a testament to the impossible!" And on, page after page: "Ben, everything there is is against your being here! Think of get-togethers, family stuff, golden anniversaries in rented halls, fire regulations celebrated more in the

breach than the observance, the baked Alaska up in flames, everybody wiped out—all the cousins in from the coast. Wiped out."
Until it ends:

> So! Still! Against all the odds in the universe you made happy
> landings! What do you think? Ain't that delightful? Wait,
> there's more. You have not only your existence but your edge,
> your advantage and privilege. You do, Ben, you do. *No?* Every-
> body does. They give congressmen the frank. Golden-agers go
> cheap to the movies. You work on the railroads they give you a
> pass. You clerk in a store it's the 20 percent discount. You're a
> dentist your kid's home free with the orthodontics. Benny,
> Benny, we got so much edge we could cut diamonds!

Central to the theme and movement of the book, this harangue is
one of fiction's finest moments.

The Franchiser is engaged, then, in the naming of names, the
names of places and people, of course, but above all the names of
things: commercial enterprises of all kinds, name brands, house
brands, brandless brands, labels, logos, zits. Elkin composes a song
from the clutter of the country, a chant out of that "cargo of crap"
that comprises our culture, the signs, poles, boxes, wires, the stores
along the roads and highways, our motorcars. He writes with the
stock-in-trade and with the salesman's slang. About the tissues, rags,
and wipers that are appropriate to every fixture and furnishing—
bowl, screen, or clock face, asshole or cheery cheek—he knows, and
taps out the call sign, grasping the peculiar argot of every agency, the
specific slant of every occupation, the angle, the outlook—the edge.

There is, in Elkin, only the "rich topsoil of city asphalt"; there are
no lisping winds or drooling streams. He dances to a wholly urban
oo-la-la. He cannot see the forest for the picnic tables, the cookout
pits, the trash containers with their loose heaps of bottles, Dixie
cups, and paper plates; and on those plates he spots the catsup
smears, the mustard marks, the crumbs from cookies and potato
chips, and he understands at once whether they were reconstituted,

ruffled, extra-hearty, baked, or Mexicanized. Nature is a Kodacolor picture wall in one of Ben Flesh's Travel Inns. It is where you go to get wool for fine suits, wood for boardwalks, walls, ceiling joists, food for fast foods, electric warmth for blankets, power for power tools. There is one moment—you will reach it—when Ben Flesh finds himself in Nature (ominously in, as though she really were the Mother of Us All). "In nature. His scent in the thin air like a signal to the bears, to the cougars. Out of his element, the franchiser disenfranchised. Miles from the culture, from the trademark and trade routes of his own long Marco Polo life."

Elkin is not concerned with high culture, either. He knows it not. The city, itself, is his Smithsonian, and there is real lust in his love for it, not merely the usual honor and respect, let alone awe and fear. He has been happily captured by this vast dump of dreck the city has become, and the country has become as it has become a city. He adores this spill of drink and splat of spittle, this rind of flesh, dry ash, and peel of paint, this loud honk the city is, and all its elements; even if it is a steel shaving, this mother of muggers and vulva of vulgarity, this hospice for rape and every kind of wretchedness—the city; although it is only a loud shout, a long hurt, and place of enlarging hate—he loves it, its objects, its stone scapes, lit ways, and glowing windows, this shag of hair and shard of glass the city is; the bag, can, weed, and bitter litter it makes; the cold smoke, the poisoned air it holds; this dog leaving that the city is: Elkin has an embracing passion for it. He celebrates it as no one has done or has been able to do (if we except only Augie March), and although he knows motels, as habitable space, are like the shaven cunt of a packaged whore, still he hums his hymns; although he knows how many streets are ugly, foul-smelling, and dangerous, as full of E. coli as a lower intestine, he warbles away; even though he knows money is society's perfumed, silver-plattered shit, he goes on loving the prime rate; he knows fame is a faded billboard now for rent, and yet he goes on touching the famous as if they were kings who could cure; he knows, and yet he goes on loving the menace and the waste, the tacky, cheap, lovelorn, gimcrack life our modern lot has all too often come to; he loves it exactly as the saint loves the leper—*despite* and *because*—not in blindness or through any failure of taste, but because it is all so deeply and dearly human to him; because, as Rilke put it, it is good just to be here—*"Siehe, ich lebe"*—since existence itself is outrageously chancy and strange and stable and ordinary (it is like that flameless combustion of gabardine and pee); and all of it—our whole cornpone commercial culture—becomes so transformed by Elkin's attention, his love and his writing, so changed, altered beyond any emblem, that even an enemy of crud such as I esteem myself to be—grim, bitter, and unforgiving—is won over, and I walk through the dime store in a daze of delight.

Here then we have no namby-pamby style. The roll call rolls on: wristwatches and lamps, you name it and Elkin will name it; the rhetoric rises like a threatening wind, and the effect is like that of a storm on those who like them: exhilarating, and a little scary.

It was a hotel, dark except for the light from an open elevator and a floor lamp by one couch. The Oriental carpets, the furniture, the registration desk and shut shops—all seemed a mysterious, almost extinguished red in the enormous empty lobby. Even the elevator—one of four; he supposed the others weren't functioning—seemed set on low. He looked around for Mopiani but the man had remained at his post. He pressed the button and sensed himself sucked up through darkness, imagining, though it was day, the darkened mezzanine and black ballrooms, the dark lamps and dark flowers in their dark vases on the dark halved tables pressed against the dark walls of each dark floor, the dark silky stripes on the benches outside the elevators, the dark cigarette butts in the dark sand.

There is no fear of excess here, either, because Elkin oversubscribes to everything. Centers will not hold him in spite of his academic training, his professional position. He goes to extremes simply to have his picture taken standing at an edge. His language carries him away (there is a pileup of images at every corner, like a crash of cars); his characters get carried away; his words first explore, then explode the world.

He is not content with nice precise observations, in which, for instance, a policeman's long holster looks like an animal, "its pistol some bent brute at a waterhole, the trigger like a visible genital" (wonderful and radical enough), but the uniform itself becomes a weapon, and then parts of this new mechanism are beautifully described: "the metal blades of Mopiani's badge, the big key ring with its brass claws, a tunnel of handcuffs doubled on his backside, the weighted, tapered cosh, the sergelike grainy blue hide, the stout black brogans, and the patent-leather bill of his cap like wet ink."

He is not satisfied with the simply sensuous (Ben Flesh standing in his tux, "his formal pants and jacket glowing like a black comb, his patent-leather shoes vaulted smooth and tensionless as perfect architecture," as though he "might be standing in the skin of a ripe bright black apple"). It does not matter that apples are every other color, or that eggplants come close to patent black in their most ebullient moods; just try *eggplant* instead of *apple* and feel the effect of the change.

Not satisfied, never content, Elkin presses beyond his mountains of apparently realistic detail, with their dangerous slides of wit; he passes safely through the misleading forests of simple fun, the satiric gibes, the sirenlike lists; he pushes on into the nuclei of his various vocations (the dance studio, for instance, one of Ben Flesh's failing franchises), pushes, presses, until they are more than metaphors, more than merely the nice idea that "work for rent" has been set up on signs. He searches inside of whatever one of them possesses his imagination at the moment to find the form—the spreading itch—of the image itself: its finality, its limits, its outer edge; for then that occupation, because it is the wholehearted consequence of a thought that has put on a pair of pants and found a passion that they conceal like an excited penis; this work, with all its learning and its lingo, dreams itself back over the whole world of the fiction like a cloud, settles over us all like a communal hallucination; whereupon we realize that Elkin is a visionary writer; he is Brueghel or he is Bosch; he pictures people at picnics, at weddings; Icarus falls suddenly through the white sky; in the middle of a figure eight a skater dies, a sodden sleeper floats out of the nervous corners of our eyes; and the exuberance with which Ben Flesh has traveled the cloverleafs, generously giving hitching thumbs a ride; his and our relish for existence, for the least as well as the most, for the sweet names of things, turns to dumb drunkenness, to petty meanness, to slobby gluttony; vice emerges like a viper from virtue's smiling mouth; the dance of life becomes the dance of death, but—more than that— the dance of death is no better off: The bones play like tickled ivories some sugary welcome to the spring or some soft September song.

The dance develops, step by step, as Ben Flesh decides to honor his losses with a gala, and trays of slivered turkey and skin-thin beef are bought with a Diner's Club card and taken to the studio. People are lured in off the street by bribes, and the Wurlitzer is applauded to get in practice for the time when there will be a real band. "Night and Day" is played, and "Happy Days Are Here Again." A bottle of catsup falls from a shopping bag and spills its blood on the floor, where it soon shows Flesh the paths of the dancers, its "beautiful red evidence" making the music visible. It isn't long before this mess is mixed with bits of pork and rice, assorted hors d'oeuvres, soft crusts, and chunks of chicken that explode "like delicious gut under the dancer's weight." It is a nightmare made out of reality by adding more: Do people tend to put out butts on the ballroom floor? Then let fall a thousand cigs like flaming stars. Do guests incline to crumb their canapés, spill their drinks? Let litter float down upon the party like the ash that preserved Pompeii. Do old folks like to love the old songs? Then let them be set upon by "On the Road to Mandalay." Elkin plays the real world *loud*; and by turning up the volume, he has already rendered the hellish glow many a heaven casts before he gets around, in *The Living End,* to depicting our conventional ones— depictions, however, that rival, recall, revive Brueghel, Bosch.

The machine plays "The Night Was Meant for Love." It plays "I'm Sitting on Top of the World." The dancers continue to turn through their own slop, and Flesh makes a great and crazy speech presumably about convenience (complete convenience, not just that of convenience foods), the total ease of chemical creams, the relief afforded by flowered sheets and pretty pillowcases, the comfort control he calls the real measure of mankind. It is an astonishing replay of the earlier "oration" I mentioned, and there will be others, later, even more amazing. "Nobody, nobody, nobody ever had it so good. Take heed. A franchiser tells you." Liquor continues to leak from the plastic cups. "Smile, you fuckers, laugh, you shitlings. I come from Fred Astaire, *everybody dance!*"

Flesh, in effect, foams at the mouth; he represents America at its best; he is the word become Ben; he utters pure pop; he speaks lite beer; his verbs are coated with a secret recipe, and Vic Tanny keeps his prepositions slim, though his nouns are all frozen custards and spun milk; yet what his long rant is really about is the movement, the form, the true table turning of this incredible novel.

Vision, I said. For Elkin, it is no visionary's word, no politician's promise, preacher's ploy. It is the unerring instinct of the verbal eye.

Ben's name knows the worst: The flesh fails, and Ben is stricken with a scribbler's sickness; he is MS'd up, to put it as poorly as possible; nevertheless (our author notes), though as illnesses go, MS is truly big-league—while one is sitting down (as authors do), it is an invisible disease. In-visible. Our language, in Elkin's hands, opens like a paper flower. The symptoms of this sickness are drawn inside out with an unfailing artistry of line. Once again, they circumscribe a vision. It involves the unity of hell and heaven—this vision—even a nervous interplay; it is a vision of value, to complete the *vs,* of how life is nurtured by decay; it is a victory for the material, for the carnal spirit, because even as Ben weakens, as both his flesh and his Fotomat fold, and the hyperreal world of the novel completes its business and makes its final sale, its hero is having an ecstasy attack; and because love is finally Ben Flesh's forte, he retains his edge to the end.

To turn to account . . . to disable disabilities by finding their use . . . to celebrate circumstance . . . to turn on a light in the heart of darkness . . . well, all flesh is grass, as the prophet said, but the word of the Elkin shall franchise it forever.

2

The Living End

Many of the beliefs mankind enjoys—and we certainly do enjoy most of them—are held like a pan above the fire, close enough to warm them but not so near that any will singe, sear, char, or fry. We are inclined to back off from our beliefs when they begin to turn ugly or unmanageable. Like that face in the morning mirror, it's there but we no longer look at it. For instance, a lot of us like to believe that we (in some sense that's comforting) are immortal, that the death that is essential to this life will be overcome and defeated. We may, in addition, be convinced that our life after life could be unpleasant as well as pleasant, disagreeable in the extreme if we aren't baptized or badly misbehave; and that Dante has pictured it rather well, this pit in inner earth where sinners shall burn for ages like coal-mine fires sometimes do—with implacable anger against their fuel. Of course, we cannot imagine the pleasures of heaven or the pains of hell in other than human, body-borne terms. So we say "it will be *like* this" but "it will not really *be* this," because the fires of hell do not consume or even singe, sear, char, or fry—not really—since a few poor souls must fry forever, seared and seared again, requiring some tatter of spirit to remain to be singed afresh, some cut of body and sliver of sense to survive and relay the pain to that corner of consciousness set aside for the torment intended.

The damned are forbidden to forget, sleep, or faint.

Dante often imagined metaphors made mundane and hammered flat in the inferno's forges so that those who, in effect, ate their children little by little while they lived would be forced, in fact, to eat them bite by bite the way the starving Ugolino, like a constipation clogging the bottom of the universe, is compelled to gnaw the skull of his own betrayer—an archbishop no less—and wipe his blood-smeared mouth with the prelate's hair, because he was suspected, while nailed with his kids in a castle tower for his several treacheries, of becoming a cannibal to his children. There is always this problem with literalizing a figure of speech: All its aspects should be dealt with equally; but we never . . . we never do that . . . because, as in the case before us, if our flesh is not really fuel, if it burns but does not burn up (and just imagine the amount of oxygen with which Hell must be constantly supplied), then it isn't fuel, isn't burned, and cannot consequently cause the pain we might have experienced when nipped at the stove by a pan lid, for instance, an affliction that could be cooled and soothed and a smart that was mean but momentary. So this pain we are promised is a fiction, and the fires are fictions, too, since our flesh is not like gas to be charged for by the BTU, but is returned to its body to be burned again as though an eyeball, muscle, lymph node, or rib had been rented. Yet even a rental—tux or car or folding chair—will wear out. In Hell, everyone is in poor health, yet no one may die. Our corpses may lie in ruins, but our ruins dare not rot . . . well, not utterly. Eternity won't let them.

To live on endlessly . . . all of us . . . How often do we seriously contemplate what that might mean? Boswell hoped that Hume would keep his atheism on a short leash when death knocked, and went to the philosopher's bedside when illness was apparently winning its war with him to hear what Hume thought about his future at such a crucial hour. Indeed, Boswell hoped to be comforted by Hume's expected backslide of mind, but when asked whether "it was not possible that there might be a future state," Hume replied that "it was possible that a piece of coal put upon the fire would not burn," and added that immortality was "a most unreasonable fancy." Boswell tells us that this answer made him feel "like a man in sudden danger eagerly seeking his defensive arms." The arms he found were his mother's and Dr. Johnson's.

Stanley's divinity calls upon all the dead who are somehow missing, and not properly interred, to congregate on the last day, but who knows in what condition? Wet as we first were when we fell into the sea? Or cold as we've been in glacial ice? Or in the same scattered bits to which a car bomb blew us? If and when the earth throws back its covers, coffins pop their lids, and we are resurrected, will it be in our prime, as we died, with the cancer that gnawed us nearly in half still greedy? Or with the erection we were sporting when our heart failed? We do not inquire. Or if, after death, we are only souls, as immaterial as time is said to be, what will distinguish mine from yours? My memories? At five, when I had little to recall? At eighty-five, when I no longer knew my name? We do not inquire. If souls are all the same, as some believe, then It, not I, is immortal. For *It,* I do not care a fig. I want to know what screams while it roasts in Hell or strums the strings in Heaven—tirelessly—and for whose ears?—whose agony and whose inattention?—forever and ever.

Perpetuities, eternities, infinities, immortalities: troublesome concepts, worse realities.

What if . . . Stanley Elkin wondered on his way to and from the bathroom in the middle of the night. "What if all this stuff about heaven and hell were true? Literally." It was a middle-of-the-night idea, flown in from dream, so was it as wonderful as he thought? And would he even remember it in the morning? He woke his wife, Joan, to verify its value and, lest he forget, to bear it for him in tomorrow's mind. He needn't have troubled her, for the next morning the words that went with the idea lit like pigeons on the page, and the first story, "Conventional Wisdom," already conceived to be the left panel of three, began its confident unfolding. The ultimate result, a fan made of three sections, called *The Living End,* is, at this writing, twenty-six years old, which makes it middle-aged by fiction's count, because novels not only age more rapidly than dogs; their first years are measured in review days and remainder weeks. It is the final volume of the Dalkey Archive Press's reissue of Stanley Elkin's fiction. *George Mills,* Elkin's most ambitious work, keeps it company, as it did in the beginning, since *The Living End* popped up in the midst of *George Mills* like a volunteer in a formal flower bed. Even its composition, brisk as it was, took two years, because it was written during lulls in the long novel's more tortuous course.

Conventional wisdoms are like dodgem cars—ineptly steered

and always colliding. Good deeds will not go unrewarded, in the next life if not in this one, but we had better read the deed's fine print, for it is also true that no good deed goes unpunished. Nor are our most immediate notions of what might be a fit punishment for a particular crime to be trusted or that authority granted to W. S. Gilbert's divine Mikado, an expert, like Dante, in these matters. Ugolino, we need to remember, is placed on Cocytus, Hell's frozen lake, by Dante's decision, and therefore for treason and not because he may have eaten his children. The teeth he has sunk in his enemy's skull are his revenge and the archbishop's punishment, but both of these practiced betrayers are cold in Cain's country because, in a feudal society, fealty is more essential than blood to the life of each fief.

Hell—defined as the most unpleasant place its inventors can imagine—is consequently the best depository for human bile and vindictiveness. It is also the goblin that is going to get us if we don't do as we are told. It exists, but only in the chambers of the human heart. When it comes to envisioning Hell, details are never lacking. Heaven, on the other hand, is always vaguely rendered. Nearly everything is white, like a Richard Meier museum. In Elkin's account, of course, it must contain celestial choirs, gates of pearl, and streets of gold. Aside from the chance to walk over hills as woolly as sheep, we shall see few fields of wheat or barns of hay or arbors heavy with grape—no signs of work—perhaps some shining cities, sugar plum fairies, or big rock candy mountains. I think that is because, if we were to give it its due as the pleasantest place its inventors can imagine, we would be embarrassed by the common quality of our wants—women, sweets, silks, wine, luxurious surroundings—so we make no mention of being able to gorge ourselves without ever being sated, of being perpetually in heat so we can be repeatedly pacified, hitting the opium pipe to benefit from dreams better than sleep, or enjoying the opportunity to peek below the balcony while various injuries are inflicted upon our enemies— to watch without weariness, remorse, or fear of reprisal. To go to

Heaven is to be put in charge of Hell. It is to get unevenly even. In this regard, Dante and Milton were the last living divinities.

These days, just to show how much things change even in Heaven, many immortal souls as well as a raft of angels, previously unemployed for ages, if not left to twiddle during eons of idleness, have rewarding roles on TV, and bodies given them for the occasion that the heavenly would long to have if longing were allowed up there. Of course, what do the heavenly have to do but meddle in earthly affairs?

Actually, when political and religious leaders try to con other people's children into going to war or committing suicide for them, the suckers' rewards are often described in just such embarrassingly hedonistic terms and often include the offer of camera coverage. If God were on our side, He would warn us to be wary of causes that ask us to die for them. If we have not read *The Living End,* we might complain that God should do Himself what He wants done instead of handing out assignments. He is the progenitor of the illocutionary act. After "let there be light," "let there be peace" should be easy, "shut up" a snap.

Because the first panel is given over to our common saws, Elkin reins in his language, renders his narrative's actions with the broad strokes of low comedy, and forms his dialogue from a continuous stream of clichés. Irony is thicker than Christmas pudding. The tradition mandates this approach. My Bible dictionary is quick to affirm it for Job, one of Ellerbee's precursors.

> Two prominent features appearing throughout the book [of Job] may offer keys for one's hearing of the divine speeches. These features are the use of irony and of questions. Ironic speech abounds, in which the obvious sense is subverted and another implicit sense emerges through them. Often the device serves to mask and reveal dissenting views in the garb of conventional wisdom, which is thereby left intact for the imperceptive but exploded for the keen listener. (*Harper's Bible*

Dictionary. Paul J. Achtemeier, gen. ed. New York: HarperCollins, 1985, p. 493.)

Ellerbee, who is given no other name than Mister, has been going through a bad patch in his and his family's fortunes. He will be a Job without a job description. Elkin's rhetoric, of which he is a stair master, makes fun of our daily recital of complaints. Nothing is so trivial that it can't be worth a good hand-wringing. There is (1) the loss of loose change (2) between the cushions of other people's couches; there are (3) bottles broken (4) on which a deposit was receivable; there are (5) other coins that phones or vending machines refuse to return, as well as (6) expensive tickets that Ellerbee cannot use because he must be out of town or is iced up or snowed in, and (7)—a characteristic step—there is his habit of overtipping in dark taxis: all this before we reach the first landing, a level of hell set aside for reversals in the stock market.

For openers: Ellerbee's house is reappraised for tax purposes at a lesser value, which is a lucky break, but the house promptly burns down. His Minneapolis liquor store is robbed and two of his clerks are shot—one killed, the other crippled, and, oh yes, brain-damaged to boot. A worse fate is to befall Ellerbee. He is a good and kindly man. He feels obliged to help both the sick and the dead—against his wife's wishes.

"Idealist," May said. "Martyr."

"Leave off, will you, May? I'm responsible. I'm under an obligation."

"Responsible, under an obligation!"

"Indirectly. God damn it, yes. Indirectly. They worked for me, didn't they? It's a combat zone down there. I should have had security guards around the clock."

Ellerbee is done for. Hell is his destination. But there is worse to come. At his clerk's funeral, the fetching widow kisses him on the lips. His body responds with a boner. Can she be counted a neighbor's wife? Can a boner be a case of covetousness? Ellerbee is toast.

For sure, Hell is where he's headed. But there is worse to come. He starts up another store. This one is in St. Paul and it is called High Spirits.

The business flourished—doing so well that after only his second month in the new location he no longer felt obliged to stay open on Sundays—though his promise to his clerks' families, which he kept, prevented him from making the inroads into his extravagant debt that he would have liked.

If it took three strikes to be called out in this game, Ellerbee would be, but he needn't have stayed open on the Sabbath, or had what Elkin has elsewhere called a soft-on, for taking God's name in vain was whiff enough.

Our author is on theologically sound ground here. God's laws are to be followed to the letter. Some readers will remember the fate of Uzzah, the son of Abinadab, who, while accompanying the Ark of the Covenant as it was being moved from his father's house, put out a saving hand to keep the Ark from tipping when it bounced about in its cart on a rough road, and was struck dead on the instant his unsanctified fingers touched it. Nor was it Ellerbee's fleeting desire that did him in, but the boner, however fainthearted, because it was a real, if covert, act. The widow's name, after all, is Mrs. Register, and Ellerbee might as well have signed in. Moreover, he failed to keep the Sabbath holy when he kept his store open, even if his intention was of the kindest, because intentions of any kind don't count.

The letter killeth. The complaint's been made—by some of the wiser prophets. But the Divine Commandments are modeled on Natural Law. Had Uzzah touched a live wire, he would have died regardless of his character or his designs. The water that fills a drowning man's lungs does not ask for his résumé. It would be a mistake to think that regulations regarding adultery were of less concern than those involving a loss of life, for the laws, being those of God, are all equal, are frequently expressed as taboos, and can be summed up in a word: obey. In time, since there were lawyers abounding, these laws multiplied, until there were so many only the scribes had any clear idea of what they were or what they meant. Anyone interested in keeping the Sabbath holy might have felt the usefulness of an itemized list. This multiplication, especially of ritual requirements, was an enormous source of power.

Perhaps literature's most brilliant representation of the strength and glory of biblical law can be found in Kafka's novella *In the Penal Colony.* The commandant of the colony is especially proud of his instrument of punishment, which literally etches upon the condemned person's body the letters that spell out his crime, putting period to both life and sentence with an emphatic spike. This officer disapproves of the new commandant, who apparently supports the spirit of the law, values love and forgiveness over justice, pleads insanity or good intentions, introduces degrees of importance and other niceties, as well as endless legal delays, just as the prophets did, dematerializing Israel's Kingdom to Come into something within, circumcising the heart, and paradoxically, by pushing sin past act and intention into instinct, ensuring that we are all guilty of something . . . or other . . . all the time . . . dirty-minded though clean-shaven. There were little sins and big sins, forgiven sins and deadly sins, crimes of passion, conscience, and calculation, sins of omission and commission, ancestral curses, private as well as public vices, with Love and Justice so tightly wound around each other's throats, neither could breathe or cry. Ellerbee fell victim to beliefs prominent in earlier ages, still active, however, in this one; for these are times when times are out of joint, with people living in different centuries, not just in different places.

Ellerbee will be shot and killed during another holdup—a stickup of his new St. Paul store. An angel of death will accompany the robbers but be taken as a bystander because he just lurks. According to conventional wisdom, the angel of death is an escort service. We are compelled to infer that they—the powers that be—expect Ellerbee to be murdered. They don't do the deed themselves, however, though they have sent an emissary. Rather, they allow a pair of klutzes to perform that service. One is an ace abettor named Ladle-haus, whom Ellerbee will meet in Hell when he gets there. The other is a gunsel whom Ladlehaus, a blabber, calls Ron. In the meantime, Ellerbee goes up to Heaven, as souls do, and is overwhelmed by the rightness of it all: shining cities with shining streets and a populace of families advertising their reunions in the afterworld with radiant faces. Supernaturally, there are angels attached to wings larger than they are, God drowning in aura, halos gleaming like lightning bugs, not a beard untrimmed or a wig askew. Inevitably, there is ambrosia, manna, and music. Ellerbee decides, as he and the angel beam up, that seen from afar, Heaven looks like a theme park. Then, having arrived, he thinks it still looks like a theme park. Strikes four and five. In the World of Law, your actions put you at risk; in Love City, your unspoken opinions can take you down. Heaven has always resented having been designed by Disney.

So Ellerbee catches it from both sides, as though the Old and New Testaments were the closing jaws of a vise. But there is trouble from yet another direction. In Hell, where he has been abruptly sent, he learns from the main man Himself still another reason for his plight. Since he was an orphan, he has never had the chance to honor his father and his mother as he ought, and the filial pieties he has practiced toward his adoptive parents don't count. Strike six.

Life may not be fair, but afterlife is more so. Ladlehaus, accomplice in crime, the pettiest of crooks, lives to be nearly a hundred and dies "an organic, unbleached death like something brought back from the Health Food Store." He does go to Hell, though, and even gets to see God on one of God's Ubiquitous Training visits. It is Elkin's opportunity to have some fun with the "omnis"—the four great properties that conventional but also theological wisdom give to God: the all-powerful, all-knowing, everywhere-present, and perfect Being. God admits that "Omniscience gives Me eyestrain. I'll let you in on something. I wear contacts." But readers who enjoyed Philosophy 101 can point out to the Almighty that His omnipresence makes eyestrain unnecessary. He is a part of everything that happens, so of course He knows about it. God also complains that "omnipotence—that takes it out of you. I mean if you want to work up a sweat try omnipotence for a few seconds." You mean trying to create a rock He can't lift? the quick student invariably wonders. Logic is the devil's pitchfork, and when Elkin has God claim to have squared the circle, we know that either the deity or His draftsman is fibbing. There are limits to omnipotence, and that is one of them. Contradiction is the careless thinker's catastrophe.

The "omnis" are enemies of one another, but God's perfection is an intolerable nuisance. Elkin's God is arbitrary, mean, selfish, ruthless, and vindictive—where is the goodness in that?—moreover, He makes mistakes which His perfection and His knowledge can't permit, even if He does say "oops!" His indifference to the feelings of Mary (engendered), Joseph (cuckolded) and Jesus (sacrificed), as Elkin ruefully renders the foursome, is appalling. And are the sufferings of Hell His sufferings, as well? Because He's there in every lick of the burning lake, in the agony of every hamstring pull. I wag my philosopher's finger at our author, but Stanley has an answer that will satisfy me when—at the conclusion, of course—he offers it.

With a song in its heart, theology marches on. The reader will doubtless remember those frequent movie scenes in cemeteries when, before a simple cross or forlorn stone, a husband kneels to commune piously with a loved one prematurely lost. When he is not vowing revenge, he is seeking forgiveness for having fallen in love again, or he needs some advice, his nerve annealed, his blunted purpose pointed. The focus is soft, the wind calm, the moment in the movie crucial. Sometimes the lady's image is superimposed; sometimes we hear her voice in the hero's head; sometimes he speaks out loud, as if they were in conversation; sometimes a brief breeze will move the flowers he's brought, indicating a ghostly presence. These clichés represent conventional wisdom, but in the central panel of this triptych, called "The Bottom Line," Elkin has it his own way— as always.

Open on the Sabbath

God has mistaken Ladlehaus for a smart-alecky back talker and flung him impulsively out of Hell to be retombed in what is now, because eminent domain has grabbed the graveyard, a high school athletic field in St. Paul—"his consciousness locked into his remains like a cry in a doll." Everywhere in Elkin's work the reader will run into electrifying lines like this one, so perfectly, so powerfully accurate and apt, so directly yet desperately phrased, that what might have seemed a bit of kidding around can only be taken as the somber chuckling of a malign fate.

"For he felt that that was where he was, somewhere inside his own remains, casketed, coffin'd, pine boxed, in his best suit, the blue wool, the white button-down, the green tie pale as lettuce." There he manages to catch the attention of Quiz, the school's caretaker and groundskeeper, when that not-nice man finds that his wife has medicated his lunch by adding oatcakes. *Oatcakes* is the word that reaches his grave through the cleat-scarred ground, and by chance arrives at the end of an eloquent monologue by Ladlehaus in time to seem to be the answer to its question: "What's the bottom line, eh?"

Quiz has heard Ladlehaus but hasn't fancied hearing tales of woe from a lot of lawn. He's the John Wayne who should be communing with this stone, and not a member of the supporting cast attending to the whining of an afterthought burial plot. So he begins a series of charades designed to give the body below the belief that St. Paul is now at war with its twin city. It is a characteristic of all of Stanley Elkin's work that at critical moments reality is roughly shoved aside and lengths are gone to as if they brought you to a cottage on the Cape or a castle in the Balkans—steps are more than taken; steps taken are not returned; the shoes worn on the feet that took the steps are put back in their boxes and shelved according to wearer weight and tread size—lengths are measured off like cloth in order to compel the customary to give up its hypocrisy—so that what has passed for real grows larger than life, like a six-ton pumpkin, a modest personal quirk is decked out like a float on parade and preceded by a band just off a steamer from New Orleans. The bubble we live in is blown till it bursts. That is to say: All Hell breaks loose.

Ladlehaus is regaled. His sacred ground gets peed on. With the help of an unruly bunch of boys, Quiz puts on war games. There is a brisk session of Q and A. Then Quiz and his wife convince Ladlehaus he isn't dead but on life support. The pair threaten to pull the plug. And no one involved—Quiz, the Quiz kids, Quiz's spouse—question the phenomenon—after all, they are familiar with the phrase "a voice from the grave." A world in which children play where the corms of death are planted makes Ladelhaus, who can feel nothing by definition, shudder despite his incapacities; he, who "had lived in Hell and seen God and who had, it was to be supposed, a mission," gets the willies; he who "represented final things, ultimates, whose destiny it was to fetch bottom lines" feels some qualms, because, as a consequence of their frolics and charades, "appearances had not been kept up" and his grave was littered with "candy wrappers, popsicle sticks, plugs of gum." But after all, if you get sent to Hell for doing business on the Sabbath, there is nothing strange in those who are buried cursing little boys who vandalize, picnickers whose leavings litter the cemeteries, or lovers who experience their delicious little expirations nearby the stones of those who know death at some length and by and large.

The mock triumphant final panel, "The State of the Art," is a painting of an unhappy Holy Family. Here all pretense of following conventional views is abandoned for the sake of the tough questions, though some of the questions are conventional enough if asked of you or me—as, indeed, they inevitably are: Was Jesus lonely as a child with no brothers or sisters to play with? Jesus does sit at the right hand of God, but on a hinky-dinky stool. However, there are unique questions, too: What must childbirth be like for a virgin? No picnic. And a life without what we call love? No picnic, either—nor for her husband, who isn't even a figurehead, fuming forever at the object of fun he's been made. Jesus resents having been offered up, and, in addition, mourns the loss of His worldly life. Joseph can't stand this imposture of a kid who claims to be the Messiah. Jesus wears jewelry celebrating His sacrifice, but He is "a surly savior," and cherishes His limp. God seeks forgiveness of the Forgiver for the murder of Quiz, whom He smote in a fit of annoyance when that man interrupted a concert by the high school band with his complaints about the talkative ghost who's inhabiting his grounds. Nonetheless, God does not ask to be shriven for the death of a boy whose playing God so liked He ordered him to Heaven. There are many such revelations. However, the conclusion of all things is too satisfactory to be spoiled by some secondhand account, for this is a story with a punch line—a profoundly sound one, in my opinion.

One page of *The Magic Kingdom* says this:

> . . . everything has a perfectly reasonable explanation. Everything. Wars, earthquakes, and the self-contained individual disasters of men. Courage as well as cowardice. Generous acts out of left field and the conviction that one is put upon. Everything. Man's fallen condition and birth defect too, those San Andreas and Anatolian, Altyn Tagh, and Great Glen faults of the heart, of the ova and genes. They're working on it, working on all of it: theologians in their gloomy studies where the muted light falls distantly on their antique, closely printed texts, as distant as God (which, God's exorbitant aphelion, outpost, and mileage—the boondocks of God—also has a perfectly reasonable explanation); scientists in their bright laboratories where the light seems a kind of white and stunning grease.
>
> *Everything* has a reasonable explanation.

3

After Everything Was Over

When Stanley Elkin's heart finally failed, it killed his MS. Multiple sclerosis is a pitiless disease. It deserved to die. Gone, too, were what I imagine were his daily humiliations: trying to get out of bed, trying to shave, to dress, to face another day of pain and physical incompetence. The smooth board which, like a spatula, helped slide him from wheelchair to sofa or car seat could now suffer some idleness, as did the tram which hauled him up and down the stairs. The wheelchair itself can remain folded in a closet out of sight. MS is cowardly. It weakens you, and encourages other organs to fail, but like the parasite which destroys itself when it destroys its host, is itself done in by its own nefarious doings. Stanley's lungs would occasionally collapse. He would fall ill of pneumonia. His heart had been repaired more than once. Stanley wrote about all this—wrote wonderfully about it; that is the irony. Illness, his own, others', had come to occupy a central place in his work. MS sneaks up on you. It leaves you for a while, only to return like an unwelcome relative. It goes about its business more slowly than a postal clerk. There is no present cure, and hopelessness must invade its victims, dull every activity like a storm of dust. Another irony (not lost on Stanley—ironies never were): Its initials form the singular for *manuscript*.

However he dealt with it in private, I never heard a single note of self-pity from Stanley Elkin. He got about, as hard as movement had become, with a resolve I could admire but never really comprehend. Such adversity would destroy me in minutes.

For years, we treated his increasing infirmities as a joke. When I returned from a journey, I would take him yet another cane. I'd complain at having to snail along at his pace. In Europe, when we occasionally attended a conference together, he frequently could not get his chair into the narrow elevators, and would have to be left behind while the group visited a library or museum. From a balcony, I would sometimes describe our good times in jovial shouts. These exchanges were childish, clumsy, but a comfort. Stanley made it easier for his friends to endure his illness, the sight of his hardships. I call that courage of a very special kind.

He held his classes at his home, and I had participated in several oral exams. When he sat, his breath would be forced from his lungs like a bellows. There was no way to make light of that. And his body had begun to bend, as if it were thinking of bowing. But Elkin's spirit was not bowing down; it was working, though he complained that

268

his new book was proceeding slowly. I expressed surprise that he was embarked on another project so immediately after sending a new novel to his publisher, but his firm, direct look told me what I should have known. Writing was literally life.

Writers in romantic moments like to talk that way. If only, they say, if only writing were the one thing in their life, how much they would accomplish! Stanley did not make such a wish, but it was granted him anyway. How awesome the burden, how awful the boon! Clichés, I guess, can no longer comfort, and the sense of accomplishment does not accompany you to the grave, but it is nevertheless true that Stanley's pages will remain alive as long as literature is allowed to; that in the midst of the most disagreeable of destinies, in pain, and personal decay, Stanley Elkin created a language that rises from the page to celebrate life in a way no one of us who are scribbling now can rival.

Stanley was an intimate of undeserved misfortune. It made a theologian of him. He even wrote about a rabbi—*The Rabbi of Lud*—a rabbi whose incompetence is so finely honed, he only serves families he does not know in a town whose chief industry is cemetery plots. It is a city—rather, a town—of the dead, but the whole earth is a grave, and in *The Living End* we shall hear from one who is buried beneath a high school athletic field. What about that final book that he told me he was pushing out? It was to be called . . . *Mrs. Ted Bliss*. Of course. How ironic, even in its music: missus Bliss. Yet how wholly meant in all the ways it went.

Stanley Elkin loved excess. More is more, he quite correctly said. Sometimes he sounded like a sideshow barker. His was the Greatest Show on Earth. Here, inside the covers of his books, would mysteries be revealed: Behind this jacket flap, ladies and gentlemen, you will see wonders—the hairless bearded lady, the anorexic fat man, the sword swallower who is made, himself, of shiny metal—and why shouldn't he be, with that steady diet of steel?

For him, it was the nomenclature of the world which was its wonder. From drugstore, dance studio, cosmetics counter, dry cleaner, hospital, motel, jailhouse, Hell—he gathered his words. And released them at the right time, the way the magician does his birds. Illness—his, kids', country's—he visited like a doctor, a consoling friend, a doubting Thomas. When Stanley did illness, he did the illness in. The illness was a curse, of course, but a curse like that uttered by one of Mark Twain's river pilots, a curse so elaborate, it had, by its end, forgotten the pain that had provoked it.

And when he did health, what happened? Health soon had the snivels and a rough cough. In this passage from *The Franchiser,* his paean to "convenience" comes down with a fever.

> Maybe all that distinguishes man from the beasts is that man had the consideration to invent garbage can liners. What a convenience! We die, yes, but are compensated by a million conveniences. Hefties are just the beginning. We perfect ourselves, we reach toward grace—I foresee a time when there will be flowered sheets and pillowcases in motel rooms. This is a deflection to convenience and the magnitude of the human spirit, the leap to comfort. The chemical creams . . . the chemical creams. You know, the little sacks of powder you put in your coffee. I foresee the day—someone may be working on this right now—when non-dairy creamers shall be mixed with saccharine in the same packet! There you go: convenience! And do you think for one minute that the man now waiting for this great idea's time to come will have thought it up for mere money? *No.* Unthinkable. It will hit him on an airliner like an inspiration, for the grace of the thing, only that, for the convenience it would make, and if he profits by his idea, why the money will be only *another* convenience. Someday a visionary shall come among us. He will lobby Congress to legalize pot on the principle that it would be a terrific boon to the snack-food industry! Oh, friends, the quality of all our lives shall rise like yeast. I love this world, this comfortable, convenient world, its pillow condition.

And Stanley did love this world, he loved it well, even when it did badly by him, even when he became bedded and pillowed in awkwardness and pain; and when we read him, our lives really do rise. He used to pretend—and he did a good job of it—that money was the only measure that mattered; but had he wanted money, he would have made it. He wrote—as Ben Flesh imagines his inventor of conveniences invents—he wrote for the grace of it, for he was an unmatched celebrator of the world, and most particularly of its unseemliness, its vulgarity, its aches and envies, its lowlifes, its absurd turns, its apparently ineradicable superstitions—still, for the grace of it . . . only that.

THE SENTENCE SEEKS ITS FORM

I have always thought more about writing than I have written about writing, and even when I was writing about things a world away from writing, I was thinking harder, longer, more eagerly about writing them than anything the writing aimed to address. Even putting down these first few words makes me aware of an emerging rhythm, a pattern of repetition, and consequently of an attention to what has been written that will tell me what to write, as if the first few words were seeds already intending the plant they would become, as if they were anticipating the earth they would occupy and own, if not adorn, the nettles they would form, the allergies they would eventually exacerbate. That is: the sentence seeks its fulfilling form.

Naturally, since the form it seeks can be realized only through the agency of its author, the direction it seems to be taking must be agreeable to him, please him in a no doubt deeper way than chowder. See that? The word *chowder*, lowborn and jobless, has shouldered its way into the middle of this half-formed thought, unasked and unannounced, simultaneously to energize a handful of typing fingers—who knows why?—so many others could have done the trick—*chocolate,* say—however, *chow* was hiding there like an ingredient in the soup, even though *chow* signifies a class of which *chowder* can represent but a member—a situation that would not change even if it were the dog that was meant. (I cannot prevent my ego from admiring the way the phrase "even if it were a dog that was meant" passes smoothly from the subjunctive demanded by all contrary-to-fact conditionals into the passive past.) (Self-congratulation is the only sincere form of flattery though it has but a mayfly's life.) In sum: The sentence, seeking its form, must pass through belly and bowel without irritation, as though it belonged in that dim hallway, as though it was—as though it were—on skis, on rails, on call, on a mission.

Well, that was the wrong image, although characteristic of the low slope to this author's mind which impelled the text to embrace such a misleading and evacuational metaphor. The nose will do us better service. When we breathe, we take in the oxygen we need to live, but we also acquire at the same time the air necessary to form words, and these are sent forth, when we exhale, in the same way that the lion growls or the hyena chortles. Breath *(pneuma)* has always been seen as a sign of life, and was once identified with the soul. Don't fall for phrases like "gut feeling" or "coming from the heart." Language is born in the lungs and is shaped by the lips, palate, teeth, and tongue out of spent breath—that is, from carbon dioxide. That is why plants like being spoken to. Language is speech before it is anything. It is born of babble and shaped by imitating other sounds. It therefore must be listened to while it is being written.

So the next time someone asks you that stupid question, "Who is your audience?" or "Whom do you write for?" you can answer, "The ear." I don't just read Henry James; I hear him.

Breath that has sustained a life has been shaped into words useful to communicate a life. This breath is otherwise waste, which may be another reason why the text wanted to intestinalize itself. These words hope to find companions called a sentence, and the sentence, too, is seeking a paragraph it may enhance. The writer must be a musician—accordingly. Look at what you've written, but later . . . at your leisure. First—listen. Listen to Joyce, to Woolf, to Faulkner, to Melville. And to the poets, above all.

Ah, but I have a story to tell, characters to create, a plot to contrive, you may, with incautious confidence, insist. No. That's what moviemakers do. They make hokum. You do not tell a story; your fiction will do that when your fiction is finished. What you make is music, and because your sounds are carriers of concepts, you make conceptual music, too.

What can we do to find out how writing is written? Why, we listen to writers who have written well—wondrously well—because that self through which the sentence passes—those eyes, those ears, that nose—is made not of flesh and bone and their dinky experiences, but of pages absorbed from the masters, because that is what writing comes from: It comes from reading. It is not acquired by taking the lift to a slippery peak, by breaking up with yet another boyfriend, by being miserable from thirteen until now. Nor would you have been miserable from thirteen until now if you had sheltered yourself with books.

You must pay attention; but you can pay attention to anything. Experience is constantly being egged on to surpass itself by descriptions that lie on its behalf, achieving an accuracy of perception rarely reached, a complexity and depth of feeling normally unavailable, and a thoughtfulness too considerate of its object to be common or comfortable in the self-absorbed consciousness that writers tend to possess—or rather, be possessed by.

"My Lord," Jeremy Taylor writes to his patron, the earl of Carbery, by way of introduction to his new book, "I am treating your Lordship as a Roman Gentleman did Saint *Augustine* and his mother; I shall entertain you in a charnel-house, and carry your Meditations awhile into the chambers of Death, where you shall find the rooms dressed up with melancholy arts, and fit to converse with your most retired thoughts, which begin with a sigh, and proceed in deep consideration, and end in holy resolution."

Taylor wrote what some believe to be the most enduring monuments of sacred eloquence in English, and this passage only gets better as it goes along; but did Taylor ever entertain such a conceit as this is? Was it a thought he had while also wondering how to impress the man whose chaplain he presently was? In this charnel house, they (you, I, Lord Carbery, Saint Augustine, and Jeremy Taylor) will find the body of Caesar "clothed with all the dishonours of corruption that you can suppose in a six month burial." Not: There we shall find Caesar's badly decomposed (that is, rotting) corpse. No, not in a room dressed up with melancholy arts. Not where we might speak with our most retired thoughts, a sigh preceding our considerations, and in such meditations as will reach an edifying and holy conclusion. No, these were never the musing of any man; they were constructed; they were built and rebuilt; they were sought before they were seen, and seen only after their period had been put down, and the mind had gathered up its words and brought them like raiment's to the noun that ruled them, and laid them gently down there.

The sentence, through you, seeks its form, and its form is the endeavoring of a desire, the outline of a feeling, the description of a perception, the construction of a concept, the dreaming of an image.

Between Shakespeare and Joyce, there is no one but Dickens who has an equal command of the English language. He can be a misleading guide, because if you pay attention to what is usually said about Dickens, you will miss his gifts altogether. David Copperfield has just met his new landlord, Mr. Micawber, who offers to show the young man the way he must take through the city to reach his new lodgings. Mr. Micawber always endeavors to condescend, but he must do so from such a helpless height, he is always looking for a stool on which to stand himself; consequently, he puts on airs—verbal flourishes—and adopts, like a dog not his own, a highborn tone. This tone is particularly necessary when something embarrassing must be admitted; in this case, that the Micawbers are so strenuously up against it they must rent out a room they can scarcely spare.

Like many of Dickens's delinquent creatures, Mr. Micawber is made of Mr. Micawber's speech, which customarily characterizes him, rather than some subject or sentiment that may be on his mind. Here he has designed his speech to do (to accomplish) just the opposite—to hide his status, conceal his plight—but it regularly fails of its purpose. " 'I have received a letter from Mr. Murdstone, in which he mentions that he would desire me to receive into an apartment in the rear of my house, which is at present unoccupied—and is, in short, to be let as a—in short—. . . as a bedroom . . .' "

Mr. James has the very highborn tone that Mr. Micawber strives for, and if he were to read Mr. James (which, as fellows common to the Universal Library, he might), the right airs could be donned and doffed as circumstances required. The right airs include a measured gravity, a mouthfilling motion and stately rhythm that suggests that every word is formed out of the politest consideration for every other, and that a Latinated diction has been chosen, which is so full of itself, so free of the contaminations of commonness, it can hardly bear to touch any subject whatever, and lights upon one, only to leave immediately for another, which it approaches with the same trepidation.

In scarcely less than a moment after he appears upon the page, Mr. Micawber becomes the famous W. C. Fields figure we all pity, sunshine our smile upon, and sentimentally love.

> "Under the impression," said Mr. Micawber, "that your peregrinations in this metropolis have not as yet been extensive, and that you might have some difficulty in penetrating the arcana of the Modern Babylon in the direction of City Road—in short," said Mr. Micawber, in another burst of confidence, "that you might lose yourself—I shall be happy to call this evening, and instal you in the knowledge of the nearest way."

There are words so workaday they have no class, no special niche or station, and the phrase "that you might have some difficulty" is made of them, at least up to "difficulty," which is firmly middle-class; "trouble" would be a mite lower, while "that you might have a hard time" is lower still. Words have their class and their occasions: "Hey, Davie boy, since you don't know the town, I'd better show you around or you'll get as lost as Shirley's sheep."

A little later, Davie boy is bemoaning his impecunious circumstances; his lot in life has made him hungry as a hound, so he thinks often of food and how little money he has to buy any. He makes (earns, receives) seven shillings a week for his work (labor, efforts, contributions) at the warehouse, and this sum he must stretch like a thin length of rubber till it snaps (breaks, stings, deelasticizes, rebukes him). "From Monday morning until Saturday night, I had no advice, no counsel, no encouragement, no consolation, no assistance, no support, of any kind, from any one, that I can call to mind, as I hope to go to heaven!"

"I had no advice, no counsel . . ." is a move Micawber might have made. Mark the noes—to the sixth power: They measure the rhetoric's pace, teaching us what energy is—vehemence—and Dickens is masterfully energetic; his prose has more muscles than Mr. Universe. The sentence is composed of short bursts—"of any kind, from any one"—and is a bit of a whine. But we should also watch the way the noes are re-formed, turned inside out, in the *o n* of "Monday," the *o r n* of "morning," the *o u n* of "counsel," the *o n*'s of "one" and of "consolation." No consolation for us either when *on* reverses *no* (after all, it is a yea-sayer, consolation is), lets *so* rhyme with that same *no*, and finishes with another *on*. "Con so lat ion" offers to us little of its nature, since it is sister to "iso" as well as "deso." A "console" is likely to hold a radio. "Consolation." The word brings none of any kind I can call to mind, not for a person wishing desperately to be a writer—yet another lesson for the learner.

We can gather nearly everything from Mr. Dickens, but here is just one more passage to ponder, containing a device that, in the hands of Henry James, becomes transcendent. The sentence sometimes moves as its meaning moves; in this case, like a camera in terms of what it perceives. This camera is able to say what it is doing: I am now backing, tracking, zooming, closing in. A younger, smaller Copperfield is looking down the hall from Peggotty's kitchen into a churchyard, although the eye's move (following a blatant pun on "passage") is an imaginative one:

Here is a long passage—what an enormous perspective I make of it!—leading from Peggotty's kitchen to the front-door. A dark store-room opens out of it, and that is a place to be run past at

night; for I don't know what may be among those tubs and jars
and old tea-chests, when there is nobody in there with a dimly-
burning light, letting a mouldy air come out at the door, in
which there is the smell of soap, pickles, pepper, candles, and
coffee, all at one whiff. Then there are the two parlours; the
parlour in which we sit of an evening, my mother and I and
Peggotty—for Peggotty is quite our companion, when her work
is done and we are alone—and the best parlour where we sit on
a Sunday; grandly, but not so comfortably. There is something
of a doleful air about that room to me, for Peggotty has told
me—I don't know when, but apparently ages ago—about my
father's funeral, and the company having their black cloaks put
on. One Sunday night my mother reads to Peggotty and me in
there, how Lazarus was raised up from the dead. And I am so
frightened that they are afterwards obliged to take me out of
bed, and show me the quiet churchyard out of the bedroom
window, with the dead all lying in their graves at rest, below the
solemn moon.

I shall rest my case with "soap, pickles, pepper, candles, and coffee."
If you switch "pepper" with "pickles," retaining both meter and the
pattern of alliteration, you will immediately hear why Dickens had it
right: "soap, pepper, pickles, candles, and coffee" is hard to say
because the two *l e*'s aren't as easily articulated when placed that
close together, yet their closeness pulls "pickles" into orbit with
"candles and coffee" rather than leaving it with the "soap," where it
belongs.

Just a detail, don't I hear a critic complain? There are no details in
execution, Paul Valéry wisely said. He said everything wisely. Even
when what he said wasn't wise, it was wisely said.

So smell the moldy air of the storeroom and then the doleful air of
the Sunday parlor, and let those memories dance a Proust for you.
The dead are no comfort unless doornailed. The paragraph (written
in the key of *p* and rich in Peggotty's doubled letters) occupies precisely the spaces it makes. And suggests the reason why we compose

278

and perform requiems. And fasten down coffins with lids, and weigh down graves with earth and with heavy headstones. And keep store-room doors closed. Our instructor's paragraph has its own stone, exquisitely fashioned from *mn*'s and *o*'s: "below the solemn moon." One can browse this paragraph like a meadow, there is so much that is tender to be chewed. Would poetry were so regularly on its way to milk.

So the sentence, in search of its birth, is passing through the company of writers the writer has stored like so many bars of soap, barrels of pickles, sacks of coffee, candles connected by uncut wicks. It wants a rhythm the way infants need feet; it hopes for a satisfactory rhetorical shape; it curses its bad luck and low-class diction; it likes to hum a tune as it rolls along.

I know that you expect decadent authors like myself to cite *Nightwood*, so I shall, in this instance in order to demonstrate what a bit of delicious diction can do. This is Felix's father, from the first page, dead already:

> Guido Volkbein, a Jew of Italian descent, had been both a gourmet and a dandy, never appearing in public without the ribbon of some quite unknown distinction tinging his buttonhole with a faint thread. He had been small, round, and haughtily timid, his stomach protruding slightly in an upward jutting slope that brought into prominence the buttons of his waistcoat and trousers, marking the exact centre of his body with the obstetric line seen on fruits—the inevitable arc produced by heavy rounds of burgundy, schlagsahne, and beer.

The word *belly* will not appear here, *stomach* is the preferred term, as is *trousers* over *pants*, but there are plenty of "buttons" discreetly placed to remind us of its self-satisfied shape. Djuna Barnes's observation of the "obstetric line" is worthy of Marianne Moore, and her Germanized whipped cream is a masterstroke. Mister Micawber would have liked to use such language about himself. In any mouth, it will say "fraud."

A description is an arrangement of properties, qualities, and features that the author must pick (choose, select), but the art lies in the order of their release—visually, audibly, conceptually—and consequently in the order of their interaction, including the social standing of every word. To accompany Djuna Barnes, here is Flem Snopes in *The Hamlet* in his bow tie:

> In addition to the gray cloth cap and gray trousers, he wore not only a clean white shirt but a necktie—a tiny machine-made black bow . . . a tiny viciously depthless cryptically balanced splash like an enigmatic punctuation symbol against the expanse of white shirt which gave him Jody Varner's look of ceremonial heterodoxy raised to its tenth power and which postulated to those who had been present on that day that quality of outrageous overstatement of physical displacement which the sound of his father's stiff foot made on the gallery.

The gray cloth cap, the clean white shirt, the machine-made black bow—ordinary nouns and their simple modifiers that live almost out of sight in the crowd—are succeeded by another triad, this time of abstract, subjective, and judgmental adverbs—"viciously, depthless, cryptically"—capped by "enigmatic punctuation," "postulated," and "ceremonial heterodoxy," before the sentence falls back at the sound of the father's stiff foot. We recognize this rise and fall in diction to be as typical of Faulkner as is the heteronymous collection of terms for the tie: a viciously depthless splash (the latter a measure that suits most splashes) and a cryptically balanced one, like a punctuation mark on the white shirt.

As for punctuation, Faulkner very carefully doesn't give us enough. The words that make up the description of the bow tie come at us without pause, like thrown stones. We are bound to be bumped about on our first try, but then we pick ourselves up and insert the pauses where they belong: "a tiny [pause] viciously depthless [pause] cryptically balanced [pause] splash." Then we sail along smoothly enough until we hit more rough swells: "ceremonial heterodoxy"—one word like a waltz step, one like the bunny hop.

Lest we imagine such fancy writing is an accomplishment of the dead alone, here is a final example of language's social structure, taken from Alexander Theroux's satirical masterpiece, *Three Wogs*.

> Touching a finger to her chin, Mrs. Cullinane pondered the frightening aspects of seeing a bread line five miles long filled with beggars, schinocephalic pygmies, gypsies, old men in tatters, imported grobians teetering on the edge of some evolutionary mishap, and Negroes with eyepatches and their bronze-age cutlery, stropped, blood red and as long as broom handles, all marching with their ferocious wives and polydactylic offspring into Buckingham Palace where, in a stroke, they would chew past the carpets, do the buttery, weasel into the state bins and wardrobe, and devour everything in sight, up to and including the Queen's Candles.

This is a style, snobbish to the nose, directed against social prejudice. It describes what it is feared the great unwashed will do if given a chance to use a lavatory, and does so in a highbrow style full of scorn for those who fancy themselves superior while wearing attitudes that bring them below rags. The acerbic Theroux (not to be confused with his glib and unenviable brother) once replied to a reviewer who had dared to demonstrate against one of his sermonious sentences by reminding the author that "less is more," a lie no more countenanced on the page than in the countinghouse. "More is more," Stanley Elkin once replied to such a squit. Theroux's rejoinder in *Metaphrastes*, because he is an Alexander, was more elaborate:

> To the wood-hewing Gibeonite, the mis-educated snool in factory shoes, it's [my style is] irksome and my less than homeric reviewer visibly had no patience for it, she, poor thing, with small Latin, less Greek, and an utter void apparently when it comes to knowledge of what we today have inherited from the beautiful Franco-Latin-English trilingualism of the Norman Period.

As if Pinocchio had lengthened his nose only to look longer down it at earthworms, Theroux's lines are triumphs of tone, a topic we now wearily arrive at after a long walk through diction, rhythm, rhyme, and even some reason. Theroux, quite put out, goes on to get even angrier at Samuel Clemens, who hasn't any longer the energy required to resurrect and read *Three Wogs*, let alone *Darconville's Cat*:

> "Eschew surplusage," snapped Twain, that anti-European, anti-Catholic pinchfist from the American midwest, with his unlovely spray of scentless botanicals. Blink the incidentals! Fract that chicken! Scumble that depth-of-field! Rip off that wainscotting! Slubber that gloss! Steam down those frills!
> (*Metaphrastes*, p. 4.)

Alexander Theroux does not find the periphrastic Mr. Micawber funny, possibly because both are shopping for the same bargain: a stool to stand on, a place where one may feel superior even to the lake of the same name.

The tone of most writing is that of neglect born of indifference, with the consequent loss of much possible effect, but tone need not be an absent feature of a style that is plain, direct, and Anglo-Saxon. Twain would have repealed the Norman Conquest if he'd had a genie to grant his wish; otherwise, he can tub-thump with the best of them, and against every kind of cleric. He is Amurrican, all right, sage of the whittle stick, a teller of tall tales and a lay-about liar, otherwise a skeptical son of the King James Version, with enough tone, enough attitude, to hay a horse.

The example to which I now turn—the example of examples—is printed on the obverse page, where a sentence from Henry James's *Italian Hours* is reproduced as a spindle diagram. One is to imagine a stake driven through the sentence at its core in order to show the spine upon which the sentence hangs—namely, the infinitive and its repetitions: "to dwell," "to have," "to be able," "to gallop," "to look," "to come back," "to lead," and "to gather," along with the ghost "to dispose." The second spindle skewers fifteen "and"s and the one "with" that joins them, to disclose a vertically organizing hinge. Two

The Sentence Seeks Its Form

To dwell in a city which,
much as you grumble at it,
is after all very fairly a modern city;

with crowds
and shops
and theatres
THE CITY   and cafes
and balls
and receptions
and dinner parties
and all the modern confusion of social pleasures and pains;
to have at your door the good and evil of it all;

and yet
to be able in half an hour
to gallop away and leave it a hundred miles,
         a hundred years, behind,
and
to look at the tufted broom blowing on a lonely tower top in the
         still blue air,
and
THE COUNTRY   the pale pink asphodels trembling none the less for the
         stillness,
and
the shaggy-legged shepherds leaning on their sticks in
         motionless brotherhood with the heaps of ruin,
and
the scrambling goats and staggering little kids treading
out wild desert smells from the top of hollow-sounding mounds;
and then
to come back through one of the great gates
and a couple of hours later find yourself in the "world,"
         dressed,
         introduced,
THE CITY   entertained,
         inquiring,
         talking
about "Middlemarch" to a young English lady
or
         listening
to Neapolitan songs from a gentleman in a very
low-cut shirt—

all this is

to lead in a manner a double life
and
to gather from the hurrying hours more impressions than a mind of
         modest capacity quite knows how to dispose of.

283

opening and closing latches can be found at "it" and at "of," the preposition with which the sentence and its trip daringly concludes.

The sentence and its subject leave the bustle of Rome for the quiet countryside. Three clauses open the city section, which is populated by eight descriptive phrases and ends with a one-line summary—the good and evil of it all. A couple of clauses front the escape into the countryside, which is made of four poetical descriptions, packed like a picnic with assonance, alliteration, consonance, and metaphor until, having eaten all its images, the prose returns through some gates to a six-propertied, less public, Rome again, before making its final falsely modest summation.

> To dwell in a city which, much as you grumble at it, is after all very fairly a modern city; with crowds and shops and threatres and cafes and balls and receptions and dinner parties and all the modern confusion of social pleasures and pains; to have at your door the good and evil of it all; and yet to be able in half an hour to gallop away and leave it a hundred miles, a hundred years, behind, and to look at the tufted broom blowing on a lonely tower top in the still blue air, and the pale pink asphodels trembling none the less for the stillness, and the shaggy-legged shepherds leaning on their sticks in motionless brotherhood with the heaps of ruin, and the scrambling goats and staggering little kids treading out wild desert smells from the top of hollow-sounding mounds; and then to come back through one of the great gates and a couple of hours later find yourself in the "world," dressed, introduced, entertained, inquiring, talking about "Middlemarch" to a young English lady or listening to Neapolitan songs from a gentleman in a very low-cut shirt—all this is to lead in a manner a double life and to gather from the hurrying hours more impressions than a mind of modest capacity quite knows how to dispose of.

A mind of slender capacities like his own, James suggests, may be bewildered by this double life. In which case, what will ours hold? We may have a brain the proverbial size of a pea, but perhaps our brain can manage to be the sort of pea that makes a princess uncomfortable.

Of course most sentences need not, nor should, be built like a museum or a palace, but built they will be, well or ill or so-so, and their paragraphs, like towns they partially comprise, will also be commodious or cramped—a Paris Texas or a Paris France.

Henry James always repays study, not simply because he knows what his vowels are about ("hollow sounding mounds"), but because he pays the best attention to everything, including the paragraphs that follow, for which this sentence is a preparation. An extended anecdote, like the country ramble, leaves the main road of the text and takes us to a farm where horses may be had for an exhilarating gallop. Why are we here? To illustrate the "double life" and confirm the presence of so many impressions, of which one bundle makes up the owner of the stables: "We talked with the farmer, a handsome, pale, fever-tainted fellow with a well-to-do air that didn't in the least deter his affability from a turn compatible with the acceptance of small coin . . ."

We must notice, with an admiration we should have used up by this time, what James does not write: He does not write "with the acceptance of a *few* small coins," and he does not write "with the acceptance of *some* small coins," or, even more unlikely, he does not write "with the acceptance of a tip"; rather, he elevates what might have been a by-the-way occurrence into a prescribed part of the farmer's profession: "the acceptance of small coin." The farmer must remain a farmer, not a servant, in his own freeholding mind, while his grand air, his affability, compatibility, and acceptance all hover, like tethered balloons, at the same altitude (I almost wrote "height") of genial abstraction.

The discreet tug of James's *f*'s and the competition between the fellow's fever and his well-to-do-ness help keep the farmer at a distance the writer will measure only with his walking stick.

What are all these bucolic pages up to, after all? This is travel prose; we are seeing things, hearing things; our life is full of both nature and—rather high—society. My specimen sentence maps its represented journey, and disposes of the impressions it has gathered—despite modest protestations to the contrary—with a skill so practiced and secure, a form so perfectly adapted to its aims, that the reader forgets for a moment where she is: in a bit of prose written for the magazines in order to redeem the luxury of travel and the pleasures of high society from accusations of pure indulgence, and, by the by, to make a little money.

To worship now, another god. How often, from a high window, did some unacknowledged widow watch for the return of her husband's ship? Melville knows, and Melville will furnish me, in the eighth sketch of *The Encantadas*, with my final example of some of those aspects of writing whose neglect, in favor of the famous "plot" and "character" and "moral aim," has so often fatally damaged just those prized factors. The "image" is the element I mean: the sudden transformative lens through which a commonplace can become as mesmerizing as a religious mystery. Here is a widow similarly preoccupied both with a window and one of its trappings, a venetian shade (I avoid the customary word here because Melville will pun upon it), waiting for a seaman who has not returned, as if "not returning" were a sail itself on an empty horizon. Properties of the shade are selected. The rhythm is recalcitrant.

> The panel of the days was deeply worn, the long tenth notches half effaced, as alphabets of the blind. Ten thousand times the longing widow had traced her finger over the bamboo—dull flute, which played on, gave no sound—as if counting birds flown by in air, would hasten tortoises creeping through the woods.

The bamboo blind is fingered as though it were Braille worn down by a learner, or as if the tracing finger were lingering on, and moving off, the double *o* and *ou* stops of a flute, and this futile enterprise, longing's Sargasso Sea, is compared to counting birds, as if their numbers and the frequency of their passage would hasten the tortoise—perhaps in its futile pursuit of the hare.

The panel of the days turned into an alphabet—good—the alphabet, when fingered, became a flute—grand—the whole repetitive procedure by a leap refigured: as if counting hours were like counting passing birds, as if fingering the slats of a venetian blind spelled something, played something, a tune to urge turtles, symbols of longevity, on their laggardly way—a desperate non sequitur, but one of genius.

There is so much more to be said about the mouth and its music, the pen and its pentameters, tone and temperament, as well as the small society of the sentence, but perhaps these few remarks may recommend to us the virtues of the soundless flute. In any case, we (readers and writers alike) should learn from every example that we have time for, but we shouldn't try this kind of Melvillean mind leap at home. You will break things that belong to you.

RILKE'S RODIN

We can pretend to know precisely. At three o'clock on the Monday afternoon of September 1, 1902, bearing the appropriate petitions of entry, although he had arranged his visit in advance, the twenty-six-year-old poet Rainer Maria Rilke appeared on the stoop of Auguste Rodin's Paris studio and was given an uncustomarily gentle and courteous reception. Of course, Rilke had written Rodin a month before to warn of his impending arrival. It was a letter baited with the sort of fulsome praise you believe only when it is said of yourself, and it must have been an additional pleasure for Rodin to be admired not only by a stranger so young but one with a commission to write of the sculptor and the sculptor's work as handsomely as, in his correspondence, he already had. Rilke was enthusiasm in a shabby suit, but Rodin, who paid little mind to social appearances except when he was mixing with potential clients, was willing to set aside some time for a chat, while suffering the foreigner's fledgling French without complaint. He could not have realized that he was going to be the victim of a role reversal, because it was the artist who would play the sitter for a change. Rilke had arrived with an antici-patory portrait well advanced, and his tireless pen immediately began making mental corrections. ". . . it seemed to me that I had always known him," he wrote his wife, Clara, the following day. "I was only seeing him again; I found him smaller, and yet more powerful, more kindly, and more noble. That forehead, the relationship it bears to his nose which rides out of it like a ship out of harbor . . . that is very remarkable. Character of stone is in that forehead and that nose. And his mouth has a speech whose ring is good, intimate, and full of youth. So also is his laugh, that embarrassed and at the same time joyful laugh of a child that has been given lovely presents." (Letter to Clara Rilke, Tuesday, September 2, 1902. *Letters of Rainer Maria Rilke,* vol. 1, *1892–1910,* trans. Jane Bannard Greene and M. D. Herter Norton. New York: W. W. Norton, 1945, pp. 77–78. Hereafter, *Letters* in any given citation refers to this work.)

Released to explore the studio and its holy objects, Rilke discovers, almost immediately, a hand: *"C'est une main comme-ça,"* Rodin says, gesturing so impressively with his own broad, blunt peasant hands with their plaster white fingers and blackened nails that Rilke fancies he sees things and creatures growing out of them. In Rilke's steamy state of mind, Rodin's every word rises in the air, so that when he points to two entwined figures and says, *"c'est une création ça, une création . . ."* the poet believes, he reports to Clara, that the word *création* "had loosed itself, redeemed itself from all language . . . was alone in the world." (Ibid., p. 78.) Everything small has so much bigness in it, he exclaims to his page.

Rilke tries to take everything in, as if there will not be a next day, but there is a next day, and at nine he is on the train to Meudon, a twenty-minute ride to transformation. The town clings to a hillside from whose crest the Seine can be seen snaking its way to Paris. He walks up a "steep dirty village street" to Rodin's home, Villa des Brillants, which the sculptor had bought in 1895. Rilke describes the journey to Clara with the sort of detail one saves for wonders of the world: over a bridge—no voilà yet—down a road—no voilà yet—past a modest inn—no voilà yet—now through a door in the villa wall that opens on a gravel path lined with chestnut trees—still no voilà—until he rounds a corner of the "little red-yellow house and stands"—voilà now!—"before a miracle—before a garden of stone and plaster figures."

Rodin had transported the pavilion from the Place de l'Alma, where he had exhibited his work in Paris in 1900, to the small park surrounding his house, where there were already several studios set aside for cutting stone and firing clay. The pavilion was a heavily glassed, light-filled hall full of plaster figures in ghostly confabulation, and it also contained huge glass cases crammed with fragments from the design of *The Gates of Hell.* "There it lies," Rilke writes, already composing his monograph, "yard upon yard, only fragments, one beside the other. Figures the size of my hand and larger . . . but only pieces, hardly one that is whole: often only a piece of arm, a piece of leg, as they happen to go along beside each other, and the piece of body that belongs right near them. . . . Each of these bits is of such an eminent, striking unity, so possible by itself, so not at all needing completion, that one forgets they are only parts, and often parts of different bodies that cling to each other so passionately there." (Ibid., p. 79.)

Rilke had brought a sheaf of his poems, which Rodin dutifully fingered, although he could only admire (as Rilke imagines) their pose upon the page; otherwise, he left Rilke to roam about the place, examining its treasures. The poet poured out upon these figurines and fragments a bladderful of enthusiasm, as was his pre-Paris habit ("each a feeling, each a bit of love, devotion, kindness"); but the city's unyielding and indifferent face and the sculptor's dedicated work habits would teach the poet to see his surroundings as they were in themselves and not simply allow his glance to fall like sunshine on surfaces where it could admire its own reflection and its glitter.

Then it was lunchtime. And the first lesson, *en plein air.* They sat five at a trestle. No one was introduced. There was a tired-looking, nervous, and distracted lady, whom Rilke assumed was Madame Rodin. There was a Frenchman notable for a red nose, and "a very sweet little girl of about ten" who sat just across from him. Rodin, dressed for the city, is impatient for his meal. Madame replies with a torrent of apparent grievance. Rilke begins to observe—*Regarde! Regarde!* is the new command—and sees Madame giving forks, plates, glasses little pushes that disarray the table as if the meal were already over. "The scene was *not* painful, *only sad*," he writes. The master continues to complain as calmly as a lawyer until a rather dirty person arrives to distribute the food and insist that Rilke partake of dishes he did not desire. The poet should have been hungry—he was on his uppers, but he was also finicky to a fault, a vegan of a sort, a fancied sign of his ethereal nature. Rodin rattled on agreeably. Rilke spoke of his art-colony days in Worpswede and of the painters he met there, few of whom Rodin had heard of, although that would not have surprised the poet had he realized that his acquaintances, his friends, were nobodies. And as a poet, he was invisible in this space.

Because it was full of blazing plaster casts in a pavilion that gathered light as if it were fruit. "My eyes are hurting me, my hands too," he wrote to his wife. Madame Rodin was gracious after lunch, inviting him back, as we say, "anytime you're in the neighborhood," little realizing, I imagine, that for Rilke that would be tomorrow.

And so ended the second day.

Nothing is more fragile than adoration, yet Rilke's adulation might have remained that intense, agreeably decorating a dirty pane like a window's curtain, had he not sunk into an outcast's life. Poor, alone, he sought refuge from the friendless Paris streets in the Bibliothèque Nationale, often from ten to five; or he fled by train to Meudon and its sheltering plasters, kinder to his eye, though they blinded him, than the beggars who would offer him their misfortunes for a franc; while evenings he passed in the squeeze of his room, writing letters to his wife as forlornly beautiful as letters get. The poet was, among other things, an inadequately educated youth who would play the poet even on those days he wasn't one, and who sought to unite his spirit with the spirit of his poems, so as to live several feet above the ground. Yet the great sculptor would eventually prove to be a crude, rude clown, a satyr in a smock, who was losing his strut, caught in the curves of female connivance and flattery, only to be led around eventually (in Sir Kenneth Clark's estimation) like a dancing bear. (Kenneth Clark, *The Romantic Rebellion*. New

York: Harper & Row, 1973, p. 353.) So loyalty would demand that Rilke separate the man from his art, a split easier for a Solomon to decree than a babe to endure, and an act at odds with his inclinations.

Moreover, the fragments he so admired in Rodin's workshops, alive in every brief line that defined them, were confronted by the ugly realities of the avenues, poor creatures who every day looked more like himself.

> They were living, living on nothing, on dust, on soot, and on the filth on their surfaces, on what falls from the teeth of dogs, on any senselessly broken thing that anyone might still buy for some inexplicable purpose. Oh what kind of world is that! Pieces, pieces of people, parts of animals, leftovers of things that have been, and everything still agitated, as though driven about helter-skelter in an eerie wind, carried and carrying, falling and overtaking each other as they fall. (Letter to Lou Andreas-Salomé, July 18, 1903. *Letters,* p. 109.)

In these lines, written in Worpswede during the following summer, he relived for his former mistress's benefit his Paris suffering. Rilke was also rehearsing what would become the magical opening pages of his novel, *The Notebooks of Malte Laurids Brigge.* It is worth quoting a bit more in order to demonstrate the psychologically stressful difference between the euphoric celebrational style of the first Rodin monograph and its author's daily state of mind.

> There were old women who set down a heavy basket on the ledge of some wall (very little women whose eyes were drying up like puddles), and when they wanted to grasp it again, out of their sleeves shoved forth slowly and ceremoniously a long, rusty hook instead of a hand, and it went straight and surely out to the handle of the basket. And there were other old women who went about with the drawers of an old night stand in their hands, showing everyone that twenty rusty pins were rolling around inside which they must sell. And once of an evening

late in the fall, a little old woman stood next to me in the light of a store window. She stood very still, and I thought that like me she was busy looking at the objects displayed and hardly noticed her. Finally, however, her proximity made me uneasy, and I don't know why, I suddenly looked at her peculiarly clasped, worn-out hands. Very, very slowly an old, long, thin pencil rose out of those hands, it grew and grew, and it took a very long time until it was entirely visible, visible in all its wretchedness. I cannot say what produced such a terrible effect in this scene, but it seemed to me as if a whole destiny were being played out before me, a long destiny, a catastrophe that was working up frightfully to the moment when the pencil no longer grew and, slightly trembling, jutted out of the loneliness of those empty hands. I understood at last that I was supposed to buy it. (Ibid., pp. 109–110.)

In the novel, Malte eventually realizes with horror that he has become an accomplice . . . another shabby person of the street.

. . . when I noticed how my clothes were becoming worse and heavier from week to week, and saw how they were slit in many places, I was frightened and felt that I would belong irretrievably to the lost if some passer-by merely looked at me and half unconsciously counted me with them. (Ibid., p. 111.)

Perhaps, when you beg only from the best families and the finest foundations, you can call yourself a development officer, but where Rilke was living at the time, there were no banks, no fancy estates occupied by susceptible titled ladies, just *aisles de nuit*, the Hôtel Dieu, and *hospices de la maternité*.

The path to Paris had been a circuitous one, the result of flailing more than plan. At Christmas, two years before, Rilke had returned to Prague to visit his mother, always a trying time for him, although Santa brought him a new briefcase, and on his way home he stopped in Breslau to visit an art historian, Richard Muther, who he hoped might agree to tutor him in this vast field, since Rilke was now considering a career as an art critic. He thought that perhaps Muther might help him combine this fresh but desperate interest with a trip to Russia that Rilke was planning. It would be his second. (Ralph Freedman, *Life of a Poet: Rainer Maria Rilke.* New York: Farrar, Straus and Giroux, 1996, p. 108.) Muther was presently the editor of some pages on art for a Viennese weekly called *Zeit,* and he suggested that Rilke write something on Russian art for its pages. Rilke promptly did so and composed another article after he had completed his trip.

When they met again, it was at the newly married couple's cottage near the art colony of Worpswede, outside Bremen. Rilke's second essay was about to appear. Muther had just completed a monograph on Lucas Cranach and sent a copy in advance of his arrival. His hosts showed him studios and introduced him to painters as a part of their mutual cultivation. A few months later, Muther would get his review and Rilke receive the Rodin commission. In that regard, he had an edge his youth and inexperience could not dull: His wife, Clara, was herself a sculptor and had studied with the master, and for that reason they had initially planned to do the piece together. Clara's previous relationship might be expected to make entrée easier.

Rilke was eager to get out of his honeymoon house, a cute thatch that had lost a good deal of its charm after Clara had given birth. Babies often allow wives to feel they have done their sexual duty and husbands to feel they have been warned: What the house now holds will hold them. *Housebroken* is the customary word. Clara was also anxious to return to work and would eventually join Rilke in his Paris penury after she had dumped little Ruth with her grandmother. (The word *join* suggests more intimacy than was sought, since they maintained separate lodgings.) The commission was urgent because the couple's funds were nearly exhausted, and, although Clara insisted on paying her own way, Rilke's sources of charity were drying up.

Rilke was learning on the run. He had no scholarly skills. Confronted by a mass of materials, he tended to freeze. "Instead of taking notes on a text with concentration and efficiency, he was forever tempted to copy the entire book." (Wolfgang Leppmann, *Rilke: A Life,* trans. Russell Stockman. New York: Fromm International, 1984, p. 174). There were many things about his subject he would have known, for they were in the air as well as in the newspapers or came from Clara's recollections. But some of the things he thought he knew were wrong and some of the things Rodin revealed about himself weren't true: that he had married *"parce qu'il faut avoir une femme,"* for instance (Letter to Clara Rilke, September 5, 1902. *Letters,* p. 84.), since he would not marry Rose Beuret, the woman he had—unlicensed—lived with from 1864, when she had become his model and his mistress, until their approaching deaths made such legalities matters of concern. (Rose died in February of 1917, he in November of that year.)

Rodin had been born a profligate and it had apparently always been necessary to have a woman . . . or two. Waiting to pose, nude or nearly, a pair of models might lounge around the studio. When they did, they often had to assume and maintain athletically strenuous erotic postures for extended periods while he drew—comfortably wrapped—in a room Rose kept cool to save sous and suppress inclinations, although often, nearer his models and more discreet, Rodin worked at the Dépôt des Marbres in Paris. "Moving constantly around him as he worked were several nude models. He watched them as they moved, like Greek gymnasts, establishing a familiarity with the human body, and with muscles in movement." (Sue Roe, *Gwen John: A Painter's Life.* New York: Farrar, Straus and Giroux, 2001, p. 55 passim.) Occasionally, he would insist they caress one another. His artistic excuse for these practices was that through them women were psychologically laid bare, not merely their thighs and bosoms. Rilke, predictably, put a feminist spin on these images. Speaking of figures on *The Gates of Hell,* he says: ". . . here the woman is no longer an animal who submits or is overpowered. She is too awake and animated by desire, as if they had both joined forces to search for their souls." During such times that the models moved or froze in the midst of a gesture, the artist worked with great rapidity, sheets of drawings literally flying from his pad to litter the floor. At a more leisurely moment, he would apply a light wash of color to the graphite. (Albert Elsen, *Rodin.* New York: Museum of Modern Art, 1963, p. 165.) Rodin did not conceal his erotic drawings from less candid eyes, but exhibited them more than once. The Musée Rodin has many thousand such sketches. Later, Picasso would exhibit a similar unremitting libidinous energy.

Without warning, the maestro would disappear for weeks from beneath Rose's eye. These absences sometimes corresponded to brief encounters with one of his models or with one of the innumerable society women whose appetites were aroused by his reputation as a lover. But when, to excuse himself, Rodin put up a sign on the door of Studio J of the Dépôt des Marbres that read THE SCULPTOR IS IN THE CATHEDRALS, it was sometimes true he was visiting them. (Robert Descharnes and Jean-François Chabrun, *Auguste Rodin,* trans. Edita Lausanne. Secaucus, N.J.: Chartwell Books, 1967, p. 118).

Four years before Rilke's arrival, Rodin had broken off an extended affair with Camille Claudel, the gifted sister of the great poet and playwright Paul Claudel, and a splendid sculptor herself, with disastrous consequences for Camille, who had to be institutionalized, though there were doubtless other reasons for her paranoid delusions. She and Rose had passed through words to come to blows, and it is said (by those who say these things) that Camille had a habit of lurking about the grounds and that Rose had once fired a shot in the direction of some concealing plants. Camille's brother, whose Catholicism was central to his work, was not Christian enough to forgive the sculptor such a prolonged misuse of his sister, but in this case, forgiveness might have been a fault.

As for Rodin, he was nearsighted: he had the big bulging eyes of a lecher. When he worked he had his nose right on the model and on the clay. Did I say his nose? A boar's snout, rather, behind which lurked a pair of icy blue pupils. In all his sculpture, what you have is his nose working together with his hand, and sometimes you catch the face emerging from the very middle of the four fingers and the thumb. He tackles the block as a whole. With him everything is compact, massive. It is dough that gives unity. His limbs tend to get in the way.

How different from my sister's light, airy hand, the sense of excitement, the perpetual presence of the spirit, the intricate and sensitive tendrils, the airiness and play of inner light! (Ibid., p. 130.)*

While Rilke was in attendance, Rodin took up with Gwen, another sister, this time of Augustus John. She would survive the experience to become a talented painter, though she never married and the little village of Meudon held her fast her entire life. (Roe, pp. 47–81.) Through Gwen John's letters, we can follow the progress of their affair and get an idea of how many of these amours must have taken a similar path, because, if it was a unique romance for each woman, it was an established routine for the artist, who was consequently always in charge. As girls, they came to Paris to make art their career; they sought work as models in order to pay their way; sometimes they would pose for a painter who posed for Rodin and that way achieve an introduction. In Gwen's case, it was her suppleness that initially appealed to the master, though other women doubtless had their own special qualities. Soon he would be singling her out, lending her books, asking her to make copies of certain passages he would mark for extraction, and then—la coup de coeur—requesting to see her work. One day, while she was in a half-naked prancing pose—knee up, head bowed—for the Whistler memorial statue, the kiss arrived. "I can feel, rushing across my lips, sensations of mystery and intoxication," she told him. (Ibid., p. 56.) Gwen would dream of giving up all for him (especially her career), of

*In L'oeil écoute (The Eye Listens), Claudel had written extensively about Flemish art and praised it in particular for capturing "the movement of human life toward its conclusion." In contrast, Rodin's art would have had to seem profane.

becoming his wife, of taking his material tasks in hand and, though not a tidy, enterprising person, organizing his life. For this last task, Rodin would solicit and seduce Rainer Maria Rilke.

In his two monographs, Rilke will touch on such matters so discreetly, not even he will avow his knowledge of them; but the contradiction between Rodin's life of quarrelsomeness, deceit, and sensual indulgence and his consuming artistic dedication; the difference between the studio's dusty physicality and its apparent product—abundant beauty and grace arising out of clay, marble's serene cool glisten like light in a water glass, lofty ideals caught in casts of plaster—these militant contrasts govern every line of the poet's essays—where Rilke enlists awe to ward off consternation—just as they control every surface of the artist's sculptures, including the version of the Balzac memorial that depicts the novelist with an erection. After George Bernard Shaw sat for his bust by Rodin, he wrote, "The most picturesque detail of his method was his taking a big draught of water into his mouth and spitting it onto the clay to keep it constantly pliable. Absorbed in his work, he did not always aim well and soaked my clothes." (Quoted in Elsen, p. 126.)*

On Rilke's next visit Rodin held class. After a lunch which resembled the first in everything but menu, they sat on a bench that had a fine view of Paris while Rodin spoke of his work and its principles. Rilke has to run after Rodin's rapid French as though for a departing bus. The sculptor's work is manual, like that of a carpenter or mason, and produces an object unlike the memos of a office manager, consequently, to the young, the calling has lost its attraction. They don't care to get their hands dirty, but *"il faut travailler, rien que travailler,"* he likes to repeat. In fact, Rodin did little if any carving (or welding either, of course), although it is said that he liked to greet people at the door head-to-toed with dust and fisting a chisel. His bronzes

---

*Rodin's impact on Rilke, from the French point of view, is thoroughly discussed by J. F. Angeloz in *Rainer Maria Rilke: L'evolution spirituelle du poète* (Paris: Paul Hartmann, 1936), and by K. A. J. Batterby in *Rilke and France: A Study in Poetic Development* (London: Oxford University Press, 1966).

were cast, his marbles carved, by workers he rarely saw. (R. H. Wilenski. *The Meaning of Modern Sculpture.* Boston: Beacon Press, 1961, p. 25.) Henri Lebossé enlarged the sculptor's plaster models to the dimensions proper for a public monument.* Rodin complains that the schools teach "the kids nowadays" to compose—to emphasize contour rather than to model and shape surfaces. ". . . *ce n'est pas la forme de l'objet, mais: le modelé* . . ." (Letter to Clara Rilke, September 5, 1902. *Letters,* p. 84.) Rodin's hands were his principal tools, and with them he plopped and punched and gouged and smoothed, making both curves and straight lines wavy, allowing shoulders to flow into torsos and torsos to emerge from blocks (even when they hadn't), encouraging elbows to establish their own identity, his fingers everywhere busy at fostering the impression of life, giving strength and will to plaster, ethereality and spirit to stone.

Not to everybody's taste: Rodin's hopes for his work were revolutionary and, at first, few shared them. Lovers of the antique saw in the figure of Aphrodite the embodiment of Love. She was a god of mythology and therefore never existed, so she could only be regarded as ideal. Her thighs were to be as smooth as a peeled stick, though fleshier and amply curved. Since, like Hamlet, or Jesus, for that matter, no one knew what Love looked like, her form and all her emblems eventually achieved a generic status (Jesus is blond and thin, tall and handsome, not in the least Semitic); but this stereotype was never of a particular, an instance of which you might meet on the street, instead its entire being was devoted to the service of the universal. For fanciers of Christian figures, however, Mark and the other Testament teachers, while remaining within the type that had been cast for them, and representing the ideals of the religion as well as figures in Christian history, were nevertheless to be depicted as actual persons. Jesus may have been a scapegoat, but he must

---

*See Albert Elsen's "Rodin's Perfect Collaborator, Henri Lebossé," in *Rodin Rediscovered,* ed. Albert Elsen. (Washington, D.C.: National Gallery of Art, 1981, pp. 249–259.)

not be so idealized he becomes nothing but sacrifice. Another example: Many sopranos must be able to play Mimi; if one of them cannot make Mimi's emaciated weight, then cast, crew, and customers will pretend they are watching the role sing rather than the occupant of it. Rodin's departures from these norms were felt before they were formulated. Where would we locate the walk of the *Walking Man?* in "walking itself"? in this sort of stride among many? in the habitual gait of someone exercising? and particularly during his morning constitutional? This amazing figure is the expression of a specific kind of muscular movement in which the determination of the walker's will, even without the walker, is evident. These legs walk by themselves. Across meadows. Down streets. Through walls. The battered torso is the handle of their fork.

> The *Walking Man* as finally exhibited is the antithesis of the nineteenth-century statue, for it lacks the old values of identity, assertive ego, moral message rhetorically communicated, completeness of parts and of finish, and stability. More than any other of Rodin's works, this sculpture overwhelms the viewer by the power of movement. . . . No sculptor before Rodin had made such a basic, simple event as walking the exclusive focus of his art and raised it to the level of high drama. (Elsen, p. 32.)

As Rodin's style developed, so did the complaints. *The Age of Bronze* was felt to be so lifelike that it must have been made from a body cast. *Walking Man* convicted the sculptor of dismemberment. *The Man with the Broken Nose, The Crouching Woman,* and *The Old Courtesan* were attacks upon their subjects, deliberately disgusting, or perverse attempts to make the ugly attractive. *The Kiss* was too sexy or too pretty, and *The Thinker* banal—or worse, a schoolboy bathroom joke. *The Gates of Hell* had ended up an expensive hodgepodge. *The Burghers of Calais* were too sorrowful; the monument didn't depict them as behaving bravely enough. And yet his terracotta sketch for *The Call to Arms,* proposed to commemorate the Franco-Prussian War, was so vehement, it failed consideration. The great draped *Balzac* didn't look like Balzac, while the naked *Balzac* was an affront to the writer, his art, and his public. The *Balzacs*, in particular, called for outrage.

He was accused variously of having depicted his subject as a penguin, a snowman, a sack of coal, a menhir, a phantom, a colossal fetus and a shapeless larva. Other criticisms included the charge that Balzac had been reduced to the role of an actor in a gigantic Guignol, that he had just gotten out of bed to con- front a creditor, or that exposing the public to such maladroit handling of proportions and physical distortion was equivalent to the dangers of a live bomb. (Ibid., p. 103.)

As late as 1932, R. H. Wilenski would claim, in *The Meaning of Modern Sculpture,* that "Rodin's interest when he modeled the Balzac was concentrated in the head. Remove the head and we have nothing but a shapeless mess." Wilenski provides an illustration in which he has done the decapitation. (Wilenski, p. 23, illus. 1b.)

It was claimed that Rodin's impressionistic style was better suited to painting than to sculpture, although the Impressionists weren't initially approved of, either; moreover, he appeared to disobey the modernist rule that the work should reflect the nature of its materi- als and manufacture, yet in what but clay would his kind of modula- tions occur? Or his mingling of limbs be easy? This much was true: Rodin's aim was to transform his materials into something ontologi- cally alive—after all, had not God made mud into man?

Elie Faure enlists his eloquence, honed through a thousand pages of his *History of Art,* to register Rodin's errors.

Often—too often, alas!—the gestures become contorted, the unhappy idea of going beyond plastics and of running after symbols creates groups in which the embracing figures are disjointed; the volumes fly out of their orbit, the attitudes are impossible, and, in the whole literary disorder, the energy of the workman melts like wax in the fire. Even in his best days, he lives and works by brief paroxysms, whose burning sensation runs through him in flashes. (Elie Faure, *History of Art:*

Modern Art, trans. Walter Pach. New York: Harper and Bros., 1924, pp. 402–403.)

A good many of the misapprehensions that Rilke says constitute Rodin's fame were fomented by social scandals, as I have tried to suggest, and the sculptor's name continued to collect scurrilous rumors for the remainder of his life; but at the same time his renown drew to him many who were also famous, each bringing with them their own bounty of slander, gossip, and glorification. Isadora Duncan claims that she wants to have children of genius by him, and Loïe Fuller would love to wind multicolored ribbons round her body while he draws her.* Eleanora Duse will recite poetry at the Hôtel Biron, and Wanda Landowska play Bach upon a harpsichord trucked in for the occasion. Meanwhile, the press enjoys publishing lampoons of various kinds, and caricatures by Sem and Belon amuse their publics. In one, Rodin is depicted pulling the arms and legs off a female figure. I think we are to imagine she is not alive at the time. Another, called *Terrain Rodin,* shows a garden of disembodied heads and embracing bodies. (Descharnes and Chabrun, p. 216.)

The Meudon days begin to pass. Rilke reads Rodin's press clippings in the villa's little park and enjoys the garden's postcard views, or he walks up the village slopes to a thick wood where he can brood in a solitude free of Paris's insistent presence or Rodin's impalpable one. Among his wishes: that he could take the forest's lofty fresh air back with him to the city, where the heat is oppressive, the atmosphere odiferous, stale, and heavy. He presses his face against the

---

*Lest we forget Mrs. Fuller's talent—namely, her skill with illusion—here is a juicy bit from Cocteau: "Is it possible . . . to forget that woman who discovered the dance of her age? A fat American, bespectacled and quite ugly, standing on a hanging platform, she manipulates waves of floating gauze with poles, and somber, active, invisible, like a hornet in a flower, churns about herself a protean orchid of light and material that swirls, rises, flares, roars, turns, floats, changes shape like clay in a potter's hands, twisted in the air under the emblem of the torch and headdress." (Jean Cocteau, *Souvenir Portraits,* trans. Jesse Browner. New York: Paragon House, 1990, p. 81.)

fence of the Luxembourg Gardens like one in jail, and even the flowers in their beds feel constrained to be there.

On September 11, Rilke does something so transparent, it almost
ceases to be devious. He writes Rodin a letter. Like a lover, he
explains that his poor French makes it difficult for him to express
himself as he would like, and the care with which he prepares his
questions make them seem contrived and inappropriate for the
occasion; so he is sending on a few verses in French, with the hope
that they will bring the two of them a little closer. After some customary fulsomeness, Rilke confesses, "It was not only to do a study
that I came to be with you,—it was to ask you: how must one live?"
The answer we've heard: *"Il faut travailler."* However, Rilke says he
has always waited for the beckon of the muse, waited for what he
calls the creative hour, waited for inspiration. He has tried to form
habits of diligence, but now he knows he must try again, try and succeed. Sadly . . .

> . . . last year we had rather serious financial worries, and they
> haven't yet been removed: but I think now that diligent work
> can disarm even the anxieties of poverty. My wife has to leave
> our little child, and yet she thinks more calmly and impartially
> of that necessity since I wrote her what you said: "Travail et
> patience." I am very happy that she will be near you, near your
> great work . . .
>
> I want to see if I can find a living in some form here in
> Paris,—(I need only a little for that). If it is possible, I shall
> stay. And it would be a great happiness for me. Otherwise, if I
> cannot succeed, I beg you to help my wife as you helped me by
> your work and by your word and by all the eternal forces of
> which you are the Master. (Letter to Auguste Rodin, September 11,
> 1902. *Letters,* pp. 87–88.)

The verses in French Rilke wrote for Rodin have a German
brother, because on the same day, doubtless after the same stroll
through the same park, he also penned one of the two better-known

autumn poems from *The Book of Hours*. His state of mind could not be better represented.

Autumn

The leaves are falling, falling from far away,
as though a distant garden died above us;
they fall, fall with denial in their wave.

And through the night the hard earth falls
farther than the stars in solitude.

We all are falling. Here, this hand falls.
And see—there goes another. It's in us all.

And yet there's One whose gently holding hands
let this falling fall and never land.

Despite his misery, his anxiety, Rilke is greedily gathering material. These months will be among his richest. Incidents of no apparent moment will crystallize and coalesce. Here is one. At the end of September, he writes to Clara:

Rodin has a tiny plaster cast, a tiger (antique), in his studio . . . which he values very highly . . . And from this little plaster cast I saw what he means, what antiquity is and what links him to it. There, in this animal, is the same lively feeling in the modeling, this little thing (it is no higher than my hand is wide, and no longer than my hand) has hundreds of thousands of sides like a very big object, hundreds of thousands of sides which are all alive, animated, and different. And that in plaster! And with this the expression of the prowling stride is intensified to the highest degree, the powerful planting of the broad paws, and at the same time, that caution in which all strength is wrapped, that noiselessness . . . (Letter to Clara Rilke, September 27, 1902. *Letters,* p. 90. Rilke refers to the little tiger again in a letter to Lou Andreas-Salomé, August 15, 1903. *Letters,* p. 128.)

Auguste Rodin

The panther Rilke will study in the Jardin des Plantes began to
find its words, I suspect, as a tiny plaster tiger with a prowling stride
and broad paws; the bars of his cage were borrowed from the Luxembourg Gardens, and his gaze from the poet's own, as well as his
sense of desperation. The abbreviated sonnet, J. B. Leishman suggests, was the earliest of the famous *Dinge,* or "thing," poems, whose
nature has been ascribed to Rilke's Rodin experience. (J. B. Leishman, ed. and trans, *Rainer Maria Rilke: Selected Works,* vol. 2. *Poetry.*
New York: New Directions, 1960, p. 178. These translations are from
William H. Gass, *Reading Rilke.* New York: Knopf, 1999.)

The Panther

His gaze has grown so worn from the passing
of the bars that it sees nothing anymore.
There seem to be a thousand bars before him
and beyond that thousand nothing of the world.

The supple motion of his panther's stride,
as he pads through a tightening circle,
is like the dance of strength around a point
on which an equal will stands stupefied.

Only rarely is an opening in the eyes
enabled. Then an image brims
which slides the quiet tension of the limbs
until the heart, wherein it dies.

Rodin's surfaces are there to suggest a reality that can only be
inferred, just as fingers or a face, by gesture or expression, disclose
a consciousness that would otherwise be indiscernible. Sculptures
are things: they start as stuff, stuff taken from stuff like rock or clay,
and they stay stuff until the artist gives them a determinate form so
that, through that form, they may have life. The poet's problem is
precisely the opposite. Language is our most important sign of elevated awareness, but language has weak presence. Though often on

paper, it possesses no weight. A poem is like a ghost seeking substantiality, a soul in search of a body more appealing than the bare bones mere verses rattle. It is consequently not the message in a bottle that Rilke previously thought it was, nor a young man's feelings raised like a flag. All of us have emotions urgently seeking release, and many of us have opinions we think would do the world some good; however, the poet must also be a maker, as the Greeks maintained, and, like the sculptor, like every other artist, should aim at adding real beings to the world, beings fully realized, not just things like tools and haberdashery that nature has neglected to provide, or memos and laws that society produces in abundance, but *Ding an sich,* as humans often fail to be, things in themselves. In a strange way, Rilke's new Rodin-induced resolve will unite the poet's most primitive impulse—in this case, animism—with his most sophisticated inclination—art as an end, art that stands apart from nature and in opposition to it, since nature does not and cannot produce it.

If we look at *She Who Was Once the Helmet-Maker's Beautiful Wife* (sometimes called *The Old Courtesan*), we shall have to pass through several necessary shifts in point of view. The woman Rodin depicts is old, bent, clinging to a rock as if the river of life were about to sweep her away, skinny and scarred, all bone and tendon, her dugs pendulous, shrunken, and flat, her belly bunchy like a wrinkled bag; whereas once, we are asked to believe, her skin was smooth, her body lithe, strong, bearing breasts that were perfect bowls and boasting hair that fell across her back like lines of music; but the body's beauty, the sculpture unoriginally says, comes to this: the condition of the prune, a figure formed from suffering and age, alive only to wonder why.

Facile feelings of pity and regret are available from this site as stamps from a post office, yet what is piercing about the piece is its beauty, a beauty that we could sentimentalize by thinking, for a moment, that even decrepit whores in this wonderful world are lovely, when, of course, they are not; abuse takes its toll, hard living, too, and the body is our first grave. It is the bronze that is glorious; it is the bronze that reminds us that age and dying, death itself, have their own life, their own stages of fulfillment, their own value and measures of success. Baudelaire's poem "A Carrion," for which Rodin and Rilke shared an admiration, is of the same genre as Villon's snows of yesteryear, Rochester's dust that has closed Helen's eyes, and Yorick's dug-up skull, whose chaps are now quite fallen. It begins:

> Remember now, my Love, what piteous thing
> We saw on a summer's gracious day:
> By the roadside a hideous carrion, quivering
> On a clean bed of pebbly clay,
>
> Her legs flexed in the air like a courtesan,
> Burning and sweating venomously,
> Calmly exposed its belly, ironic and wan,
> Clamorous with foul ecstasy.

Rilke's animism is poetical, of course, but is also, in its way, religious, for it requires respect for all things equal to the respect we tend to show now for only a few, since we prize so little even in the things we prize. It gives value, as Rodin did, to every part of our anatomy, to each muscle movement—stretch, twitch, and fidget; our physical features—a silk soft earlobe, tawny limb, or crooked finger; or facial expressions—grimace, smile, or howl; as well as the very clay we come from (at least in his workshop)—wood block, slab, and plaster pot. Moreover, it endows even the accidental encounter of different parts—my hand on your shoulder—with its own dignity as a legitimate state of affairs. Gestures, expressions, postures, moods, thoughts, sudden urges merely change more rapidly than habits, attitudes, convictions, dispositions do, and can be slowed by stone to suit our scrutiny throughout a homemade eternity.

> The flies swarmed on the putrid vulva, then
> A black tumbling rout would seethe
> Of maggots, thick like a torrent in a glen,
> Over those rags that lived and seemed to breathe.

(Allen Tate's wonderful translation. Charles Baudelaire, *The Flowers of Evil*. Selected and edited by Marthiel and Jackson Matthews. Norfolk, Conn.: New Directions, 1955, p. 38.)

It was not simply in the shop, among the fragments and the figures, that Rilke saw this willful independence and fullness of life. He encountered it on the streets of Paris. That thin pencil that rose slowly out of an old crone's fist was alive, as were the rusty pins that ran from side to side in their proffered drawer as if to escape your eye when you looked down on them. In the early morning, the water from the water wagons "sprang young and light out of their pipes," the hoofs of the horses struck the street "like a hundred hammers," and the cries of the vendors echoed while "the vegetables on their handcarts were stirring like a little field." But his most indelible encounter was with the man suffering from Saint Vitus' dance whose gyrations and frantic coping strategies he vividly describes in a letter to Lou Andreas-Salomé (another rehearsal for passages that Rilke includes in *Malte Laurids Brigge*). Rilke follows the man for several blocks as the poor fellow's shoulders twitch, his arms fly about, and his legs jig. (Letter of July 18, 1903. *Letters,* pp. 112–115.) The man's will is at odds with his limbs, each of which has its own plans, and all four would hop off by themselves if they had their way like the fragments in Rodin's cases.

So the surfaces of Rodin's work, which his studio light makes lively, implicitly rely upon a philosophical principle of great age and respectability—one that has been seriously entertained by Galileo, Hobbes, and Spinoza, through Freud up to the present. Since the effect in question is one of animation, it may seem odd that the principle involved is that of inertia. A body at rest will remain at rest—a body in motion will remain in motion—unless something else hectors or hinders it. When that interference occurs, the stone or the ball or the dog at the door will resist; it will attempt to restore the status quo, strive to save its situation, maintain its equilibrium, preserve its life. Spinoza called the tendency to stay the same the object's *conatus*. It is popularly thought of as the principle of self-preservation. All things would be self-sufficient, as windowless as Leibniz's monads, if they could. The condition of the fetus, which is automatically fed, protected from every outside shock, surrounded by an embalming ocean, growing as it has been programmed to grow, is ideal. We are pushed out into the world; we are forced by circumstances both inside us (hunger and thirst) and outside (sensation and harm) to cope, and, as Freud argued, we are repeatedly compelled to reduce the unsettling demands of our desires to zero.

A limp that tells the world we are compensating for an injury becomes a habit hard to break even when its cause has healed and there is no longer any "reason" for it. Except that the limp wishes to remain. Our stutter wants to stay. Our fall from a ladder would be forever like a cast-out angel if we didn't fetch up in a lake of fire or at least on a floor. The fire, moreover, eats its way through every fuel it's offered only because it is eager to stay burning like that bright gem of quotation fame. As the naked models move about Rodin's studio, he observes the participating parts of their bodies until he can catch, in the middle of an action, the very will of the gesture, its own integrity and wholeness. The consciousness that inhabits us (and, as Rilke likes to imagine, inhabits even the so-called least thing) refuses to age. As we all have surely noticed, only the body gets old, and does so reluctantly, while each creak, each ache and pain, comes to stay if it can, as vigorous as a virus, youthful as our death will be, buoyant and hopeful. Dying does not want to die. Dying would make dying a career. And death has its own designs.

We can call it war if we like—Hobbes did—we can call it competition, but unities create their own momentum, complex states of affairs resist disenabling influence (what are bureaucrats for?), and all of the figures that make up a sculpture like *The Burghers of Calais*, each eloquent in its own way, must feel the influence of so powerful a composition. The man with Saint Vitus' dance had lost control of his Commonwealth. Which is what happens when parts of the body politic no longer feel safe to pursue their own plans and the grip of the state police grows weak. The group must ensure the safety of its members if it wishes to survive. Otherwise, it will explode or choke itself to death. Similarly, the elements of a work of art must form a community which allows each element its own validity while pursuing the interest of the whole. A word, if it could have had a choice, must feel it would have chosen just the companions it has been given, so that when it glows with satisfaction, it also makes its line shine.

Moreover, the unity of a sculptural fragment, when imagined alongside a correspondingly severed limb, insists upon its own superiority, for it can flourish quite apart from any body, whereas both amputation and amputee are damaged possibly beyond repair.

October was filled with Rilke's work on the essay, but now Clara had arrived in Paris and had her studio in the same apartment building as his, according to an arrangement he had finally worked out with his conscience. Their economic circumstances remained dire; the couple's dislike of Paris, now shared, increased; they endured their separate loneliness through the gray city's winter, living on roots and water, or so it seemed. The essay at last concluded, Rilke came down with the first of several bouts of flu and a gloom that obscured the upper half of the Eiffel Tower. By March, he was ready to return to his itinerant ways, and fled for Italy, the first of many nations in which he would find refuge.

It would be three years to the month of his first meeting with Rodin before Rilke would return to Paris and Meudon, this time as an invited guest. The master had read Rilke's monograph by this time, since it now extolled him in French, and he welcomed the poet warmly as a trusted friend and fellow artist. The visitor was well housed, with a nice view of the valley. Rilke offered to help with some of Rodin's overwhelming paperwork and was soon hired on, as it were, full-time. Often he, Rodin, and Rose Beuret would rise early to visit the city or enjoy Versailles, and once they dared Chartres in the dead of winter, where terrible winds, because they were envious of such grandeur, Rodin said, tormented the towers. (Some details have been taken from Ruth Butler's *Rodin: The Shape of Genius*. New Haven: Yale University Press, 1993.)

Rilke seeped into the role of Rodin's secretary, a position he wanted because it cushioned him in Meudon, because he was paid, because the work was expected to be undemanding; yet a position he did not want because it confined him to Meudon, his French might be inadequate, because it put him below stairs in Rodin's service when he had his own fish to hook and fry—the poet as ambitious as the sculptor.

Rilke planned a lecture tour on behalf of Rodin, a project that would take him to Dresden late in October (the talk becomes part 2 of the Rodin book), but the response to his first appearance disappointed him because, although there were "six hundred people," they were "not the right ones." Then in Prague he twice performed for a small crowd of mystified officials and sleepy old ladies whom he imagined were more concerned with the digestion of their dinners. When Rilke asks, a few paragraphs into his text, "Are you listening?" is the question entirely rhetorical? Worse than their inattention, his take wasn't covering costs. In Berlin, there were visits and readings before he repeated his Rodin lecture a final time—on this occasion with some success. (Freedman, pp. 233, 242.)

Spring of 1906 would find him back in Meudon, where his work, fatter than he remembered, sat upon his shoes like a heavy dog. In one of his poems, he likened himself to a swan out of water, waddling his way "through things still undone." The personal epistle was an art form at which Rilke excelled, but the business letter in French was boring, intractable, foreign, and frustrating. The poet had become dilatory and the sculptor impatient. Moreover, Rilke had begun answering mail without taking the trouble to inform Rodin of the fact or the nature of the exchange, assuming an authority he did not have: once to Baron Heinrich Thyssen-Bornemisza, a wealthy German patron, once to Sir William Rothenstein, an important English art administrator and academic painter. Upon learning of these presumptions, Rodin fired Rilke with a force that expelled him from his cottage and the grounds as well as from his secretarial position. He was soon back in his little Paris room, a spent shell. (Ibid., p. 245.)

The poet had recovered his perilous freedom, his personal space, a space, one suspects, that was very like the space he believed Rodin's figures required, not only one that allowed you to inspect them "in the round" but a space that was theirs by right of uniqueness, that distinguished them somehow "from the other things, the ordinary things, which anyone could grasp." A small statue could, therefore, seem large. Rilke, too, required such room as respect conferred, where he might stand "solitary and luminous" with "the face of a visionary." (Rainer Maria Rilke. *Auguste Rodin,* trans. Daniel Slager. New York: Archipelago Books, 2004, p. 36.) Yet Rilke's rhetoric, when he writes about Rodin's work, is not simply a reflection of his need to enhance his own importance; it also expresses the necessity for any work of art to lay claim to the appropriate arena of its enjoyment, hence the close placement of paintings in some museums above, below, or beside one another on the same wall or the squeezing of a bust into a corner or the dumping of a figure at the end of a narrow hall that leads to the johns, the elevators, or the shops is a sign of catastrophic overcrowding, a show of curatorial contempt, or evidence of feeble artistic force. Even a fragment should stand in its space like Napoléon, and there is ample testimony to the imperial effect of Rodin's sculptures whatever their size. In his essay collection *Leonardo's Nephew,* James Fenton quotes Aristide Maillol—as his talk is recollected by the ubiquitous Count Kessler:

> When you view a Rodin from afar, it's small, very small. But sculpture forms part of the air all around it. Rodin has a Buddha at his place, well placed on a socle, in his garden, in front of a circle of small shrubs. Well, it's as big as that [showing it very small] and yet it's as big as the sky. It's immense. It fills everything. (James Fenton, *Leonardo's Nephew.* New York: Farrar, Straus and Giroux, p. 171. *Berlin in Lights: The Diaries of Count Harry Kessler* [New York: Grove Press, 1999] is an abridgement of the diaries and does not contain this quote, so don't hunt for it there or in the corresponding English edition.)

Rilke was similarly taken with this piece.

Buddha

As if he listened. Silence. Depth.
And we hold back our breath. Yet nothing yet.
And he is star. And other great stars ring him,
though we cannot see that far.

O he is fat. Do we suppose
he'll see us? He has need of that?
Sink in any supplicating pose before him,
he'll sit deep and idle as a cat.

For that which lures us to his feet
has circled in him now a million years.
He has forgotten all we must endure,
encloses all we would escape.

Rodin's preeminent biographer, Ruth Butler, suggests that some additional factors were at work in Rilke's dismissal. When Rilke returned from his leisurely lecture tour, Rodin was ill with what was called the grippe. Rose Beuret was in a foul mood, which didn't improve his. So he asked George Bernard Shaw, whose bust he had been commissioned to sculpt, if he and his wife would take the train to Meudon to sit for it so that the ailing artist wouldn't have to travel to his workshop in Paris. At first, the Shaws came unencumbered, but when Shaw learned that Rodin didn't mind being photographed (the playwright had tried his own hand), he asked permission for a friend, the American photographer Alvin Langdon Coburn, to visit, as well. Shaw, not easily impressed by anyone farther from himself than his beard, was aware that Rodin's thumb was a greater imprimatur than the Pope's seal, and told Coburn, "No photograph taken has touched him. . . . He is by a million chalks the biggest man you ever saw; all your other sitters are only fit to make gelatin to emulsify for his negative." (Details of this meeting are from Butler, p. 390, and the quote is from *Alvin Langdom Coburn Photographer: An Autobiography*. New York: Dover Publications, 1978, p. 22.) Rodin could not have been disappointed with Coburn's customarily lyrical view of him sporting a beard that resembled a river and a hat we now call "a pillbox." There is a slight upward tilt to his head that resembles the heroic pose he fashioned for Balzac.

To watch him pose for his immortality, Shaw gathered a crowd, also calling the curator of the Fitzwilliam Museum, Sydney Cockerell, to his side.

Rilke joined them, almost immediately impressed with Shaw as a sitter—the entire squad eager to write brilliantly about a glittering constellation they underestimated even while trying to exaggerate it.

In the newspaper *Gil Blas* for May 24, 1912, Shaw wrote:

> Rodin worked laboriously. . . . When he was uncertain he measured me with an old iron compass and then measured the bust. If the nose was too long he cut off a section and pressed the end to close the wound with no more emotion or affectation than a glazier replacing a window. If the ear was not in its place he would cut it off and lay it on correctly, these mutilations being executed cold-bloodedly in the presence of my wife (who almost expected to see the already terribly animated clay begin to bleed) while remarking that it was quicker to do it thusly than to make a new ear. (Quoted in Elsen, p. 126.)

Rilke wrote to Shaw's German publisher, Samuel Fischer:

> Rodin has begun the portrait of one of your most remarkable authors; it promises to be exceptionally good. Rarely has a likeness in the making had so much help from the subject of it as this bust of Bernard Shaw's. It is not only that he is excellent at standing (putting so much energy into standing still and giving himself so unconditionally to the sculptor's hands), but he so collects and concentrates himself in that part of the body which, in the bust, will have . . . to represent the whole Shaw,

that his whole personality seems to become concentrated essence. (Quoted in Butler, pp. 390–391.)

They all took a break to attend the celebration for the installation of *The Thinker* in front of the Panthéon. Shaw, not to be outdone (and as excellent at sitting as standing), persuaded Coburn to photograph him the very next day, naked following his morning bath, in the pose presently before the Panthéon. The photo exists for posterity's wonder. Rilke was visibly taken with the English genius, who didn't mind adulation even from callow unknowns. Apart from that, during Rodin's week of work, and, worse, during his week of triumph, Shaw had clearly been competing for attention, if not glory, with a sundry that included Rodin's secretary and Rodin's statue. Butler says, "It was Rilke who paid the price for the mischievous Englishman's visit." (Butler, p. 191.)

Although Rilke would suggest to Rodin the purchase of the Hôtel Biron, later the Musée Rodin, and for a time live in that building (as Cocteau would, who claimed to have a role in its preservation), his intimacy with Rodin was over. Two days after Shaw's departure for London, on May 10, 1906, Rilke was "dismissed like a thieving servant." We can pretend to know precisely.

RILKE AND THE REQUIEM

ENTER Ghost

"Thou art a scholar; speak to it, Horatio," Marcellus says, because he knows that Latin is the language of the exorcist, a tongue he cannot use himself. Nevertheless, Horatio does not resort to ritual speech when questioning this specter he had, merely moments before, disbelieved in. That Horatio is unsure of the ghost's nature is clear enough. He accuses it of usurping the night and assuming the form of Denmark's previous king; perhaps it is a devil in disguise, or some omen of disaster, as when, before Caesar's murder, the sheeted dead did squeak and gibber in the Roman streets. Whether annoyed by Horatio's tone, the lack of deference in his address, or simply because he is not the person sought, the ghost stalks away without a word.

The play has opened with a hint of what's to come—the ghost foretold in a phrase—when Bernardo asks "Who's there?" of Francisco, who is standing watch and should have been the one to challenge. "Nay, answer me. Stand, and unfold yourself," he properly replies, whereupon Bernardo says, "Long live the king!" The real king, however, has only a half-life now; he remains unavenged, his sins still soiling his unpurified soul. Marcellus will see this figure four times, Bernardo three, while Horatio and Hamlet will meet it on two occasions each; but the ghost will speak only to its son, even refusing, in act 3, to frighten Gertrude when, in her bedroom, it chastises Hamlet for his inaction. The spectral husband feels some lingering propriety, perhaps, when he appears in that place. Certainly the ghost is full of concern for her . . . but are they real concerns or merely ghostly ones?

To Hamlet, the immaterial presence of his father says much. Although the king was not properly shriven ("Cut off even in the blossoms of my sin," the wraith complains), a service would certainly have been performed (among the populace, there would have been many observances, most likely); but even such an official ritual as the state would have called for has clearly not succeeded in putting to rest the soul of the departed. Hamlet wants to know "Why thy canonized bones, hearsed in death, have burst their cerements."

The Protestant Church had insisted that such intercessions were improper, denying Purgatory as a site and a condition, but the king claims to be imprisoned by day in a place that, were he to describe it, "would harrow up [Hamlet's] soul, freeze [his] young blood," and "make [his] two eyes like stars start from their spheres."

But maybe, in a Lutheran country, no requiem would have been performed, despite the king's bones having been "canonized." If so, then the king's ghostly presence confutes the Protestant claim that there are no ghosts; there are no penitential prisons; and therefore no priest may receive money for saying a Mass on anyone's afterlife behalf.

Purgatory, if there were one, was not lacking in those needing a good word—one to improve their condition, another to bail them out. As in our world, some were said to be well-off, feasting like lions, but there were many, to be sure, in need of any push a prayer might give. Fortunately, the Church has thoughtfully provided ample intercessors, whose prayers matter more than most: bishops, mitred and majestic, whose devotions are worth acres; abbots whose priors and deacons can be persuaded to bend a knee on the right behalf; priests, monks, canons, friars who will often work for a full bowl; summoners, suffragans, and pardoners whose sole business it is to empty Purgatory for the price, per soul, of a few pence. But what of those who want not prayers but penalties, who wish that some yet alive would feel hellfire's lick ahead of their appointed roast? A fancied injustice still appears most likely to stir up their disquiet.

Of course, ghosts are notoriously indistinct, their presence temporary, so we cannot be certain that the one who confronted Horatio was Hamlet's father's; it might have belonged to Andrugio in Marston's play, *Antonio's Revenge,* to mention merely one other resentful and commanding spirit of the many who could have been left behind on the stage from an earlier performance, when the battlements represented a cemetery and the action proceeded between stones rather than upon them.

Seneca's ghosts always got things going, and some of his might be hanging about us still, representing to our proud modern period of exile, genocide, terrorism, and assassination their own perilous past. History is always the true ghost, invariably requesting that its own wrongs be avenged, however prolonged the wait, as if shooting an archduke could cure a single social ill, as if, his usurper slain, the bones of a poisoned Claudius would cease their jig.

Even before Hamlet's play is performed, the anonymous author of *A Warning for Faire Women* (1599) complains

> How some damn'd tyrant to obtain a crown
> Stabs, hangs, impoisons, smothers, cutteth throats:
> And then a Chorus, too, comes howling in
> And tells us of the worryings of a cat:
> Then, too, a filthy whining ghost,
> Lapt in some foul sheet, or a leather pilch,
> Comes screaming in like a pig half-stick'd,
> And cries, *Vindicta!*—Revenge, Revenge!

So—ENTER Ghost

From the dim rear of the dining room at Urnekloster, "a slender lady in a light colored dress," as though borne by a castle draft, floats toward the young Dane, Malte Laurids Brigge. A path is cleared for her by Count Brahe, who holds back Malte's frightened father to prevent a confrontation. The lady, who is Christine Brahe, passes indifferently through another door without a word.

Here is a ghost with ancestors, the most significant, no doubt, being Tycho Brahe, a contemporary of Shakespeare, who built a castle near the sea to royally ensconce himself, and an observatory in which to mount his telescope. Losing some of his privileges, he went off, in a huff, to Prague, providing us with a less fictional connection to Rainer Maria Rilke.

Some ghosts, as we shall see, are no more than faintly lingering presences; others, like Hamlet's father's ghost, wear both armor and a frown. How came the light-colored dress to *its* demise, and what has it done to deserve a purgatorial state? The king was not wearing a buckler when he was poisoned, yet he shows himself to Hamlet and Horatio in full armor, suggesting more his present intent than his dress at death; whereas, when he appears in Gertrude's bedroom to sharpen Hamlet's blunted purpose, he is "in his habit as he lived"—in short, the ghost has changed from the metals of war to a king's everyday ermines, something more suitable for a visit to a lady's bedroom. Certain social amenities are being preserved beyond the grave. The pale glare that the ghost shows Hamlet, though, is so persuasive, it could energize stones.

ENTER Ghost

Or a remnant of one. It is a winter evening in the Brigges' town apartment. Malte is so small, he must kneel in the chair that hoists him to the table where he is coloring a knight astride a strikingly caparisoned horse. He reaches for a much-used red crayon, only to see it roll slowly off the table and fall softly into the long-haired rug below. Clambering awkwardly down, and blinded by the reading light, whose retinal burn his eyes will bear to the base of the table, Malte gropes with his right hand through the rug's nap, searching for the color. Gradually, his eyes recover from their afterimages, so that he sees his hand and its outstretched fingers, a little like a strange aquatic animal, stirring about as if in remotest independence. Suddenly, out of the wall at the dim rear of the room, comes another hand, larger, thin as its bones, similarly in search of something, and now the two hands slide slowly over the carpet toward each other as if intending to meet by accident. Malte's initial curiosity turns to terror. He wills the withdrawal of the hand he believes is his and somehow regains his seat in the armchair, only to shiver there, so pale that the look of him causes Mademoiselle, his companion, previously preoccupied by her own reading, to kneel beside him, to shake him still further in her concern, and to cry out his name. Malte tries to speak, but he cannot say a word.

He has no name for what has happened to him now, but what happened has a description nevertheless, and that description will bide its time—these ghost words will wait their moment—and they will return, forcing him to relive the fall of the crayon, and his vision of the two hands blindly searching the carpet for it, as if the color belonged to both crayon and account, and was therefore equally missed.

ENTER Ghost

A large mirror stands in the corner gable room at Ulsgaard, along with closets containing many clothes. Young Malte Laurids Brigge has opened the closets and is trying on some of the fascinating garments—dress coats, uniforms, gowns—as well as masks, Turkish trousers, Persian fezzes, and other masquerade materials, subsequently admiring his costumed figure as it raises its arms and turns gaily around. However, in so doing, Malte bumps a small table, overturns it with all its fragile objects—two porcelain parrots that die in shatters, a candy box that throws its lid, and a vial of perfume whose shivered pieces scatter their scent and spot the floor. In a guilty panic, Malte tries to free himself from his disguise, only to have it cling more tightly to him. The mirror, he thinks, may help him see what he is doing. But then, enormous, an unknown figure faces him, as if a genie had been released from the bottle. It stares from the glass at a Malte who is no longer there; rather, it is this weirdly got-up creature who runs out from the mirror and stumbles down the stairs, fainting into the arms of laughing servants, merely a wordless piece of "whatever" among a crumple of package wrappings.

ENTER Ghost

This ghost's name is Jens Peter Jacobsen. In Schwabing, the university district of Munich, in 1897, Rilke met a dark, short, shabby wannabe novelist, Jacob Wassermann, who was as full of opinions as he was ambitious, hungry, cold, and thin. Rilke had read some Tolstoy, and Wassermann pressed Dostoyevsky and Turgenev upon him, as well. Surprisingly, given Wassermann's social and historical aims as an artist, he also spoke persuasively of a psychologically centered high-style novel called *Niels Lyhne,* written by a Dane, Jens Peter Jacobsen. Certainly the two additional Russians encouraged Rilke's romantic identification with that country, but it was Jacobsen whose personal history intrigued young Rilke, and whose literary practice and artistic aims were enormously appealing.

Jacobsen regarded most thesis novels, in his words, as "lawyers' pleadings." He wouldn't claim superiority for either the Right or the Left, and was well aware of his elevated artistic status. "I happen to belong to the family of the best," he said. His father was wealthy, so Jacobsen could afford to be marginal, and was happy to remain in his northwest Jutland village of Thisted. Unfortunately, he contracted tuberculosis, a disease he fought bravely but futilely for twelve years, until his death at the age of thirty-eight in 1885. For the young Rilke, this tragically short life, with the melancholy and pessimism the disease encouraged, was a further encouragement to think well of the Danes. Jacobsen's scientific interests, which were serious, allowed him to throw off superstition and to make atheism a central issue in his work, as Rilke would, although for more familial reasons.

Jacobsen's second novel, *Niels Lyhne,* is one of the many texts that haunt *The Notebooks of Malte Laurids Brigge.* It depicts the inner states of a unsuccessful poet and persistent daydreamer, while its language celebrates the writer's failure to find love. Niels is clearly a precursor of Rilke's Dane. Its namesake has a moony role-playing mother, too. Above all, *Niels Lyhne* celebrates style. Sensuous and discerning, it could have taught Malte himself how to see. This botanist had an animistic imagination that matched Rilke's, and it was in his work that Rilke would find human loneliness given metaphysical status. The novel also argued for the hypothesis that we carry our own death deep within us. The novel, which Rilke carefully carried from château to castle, hovel to hotel, helped him finally to accept Ellen Key's invitation to visit Scandinavia, where, in addition to visiting castles with ghosts, he picked up some of the country's language, and translated a little of Jacobsen himself.

Niels Lyhne was not a secret to young artistically inclined Germans. Stefan Zweig said that it was the *Werther* for an entire generation of German writers, and he extolled Jacobsen as the "poet of poets." The painter Paula Becker chose the book as her first gift to Clara Westhoff, who would become Rilke's wife; and Rilke gave Paula his copy of another Jacobsen novel, *Marie Grubbe,* on whose flyleaf he inscribed some lines in praise of the author. Jacobsen stood for genius unrealized, and his character, Niels, was the specter of such failure, a ghost who said, Remember me: I, who let others lead my life.

ENTER Ghost

Our death is born when we are born. Then it will begin to grow as we grow, in our wombs if we are women, in our chests if we are men, as Rilke has written:

For we are nothing but the bark and burrs.
The great death we bear within ourselves
is the fruit which every growing serves.

The same previously mentioned company of Danes is dining at Urnekloster when Christine Brahe enters again, bearing once more the story of her death into the presence of her appalled family and their friends the way she bore the boy whose birthing killed her. This time, though, when the old chamberlain lifts his glass to the level of his gray chin, Malte's father masters his emotions, and just as her figure passes behind his chair, he returns the toast, raising his goblet from the table as though the wine were heavy—as though the wine were laden—to the height of a hand.

ENTER Louis Onze, the Duke of Burgundy's Fool, in the guise of a dog

After Rilke had written *The Notebooks of Malte Laurids Brigge,* Death, through its badly abbreviated teeth, was allowed to breathe upon the pages, and alter every one of them the way a feeling changes behind a face as fixed as stone. The principal theme of the first Notebook is death, and that of the second love, but the love in this inverted *Liebestod* has been marinated like the *coq* in *vin.* The deaths of part 2 are simply more literary than those that occur in the Danish castles or in the Paris hospitals of the first part. Death can be said to dog our footsteps because dogs do dog them. They are our faithful companions who will bring their love back, though it's been thrown like a stick, even to our unworthy ghost, whether it haunts invisibly or is sheeted like a sofa for the summer.

Young Malte comes into possession of a slim book of stories bound in green cloth (a book of the dead, though not in name—its name has been conveniently mislaid), and he recalls for his pages two stories that were willing to be read. I shall permit only the second to trouble us here: that of the downfall of Charles the Bold, the last reigning duke of Burgundy, a man made from the cliché "hot-blooded" by the simple expedient of taking that commonplace quite literally, if only as far as his hands, which would blush when the duke's high-pitched veins poured into them, putting his fingers in such a fever, each sought cool stone tables and winter benches to rest their tips upon. It was his bloodline languishing within him, and he feared it as he feared no other enemy. This blood distrusted his achievements; there was nothing good enough for it; and it began to want out of the duke's body the way someone shamed seeks to escape the cause. Other than those intemperate hands, his face remained in one expression, as if it were attached to a cathedral.

After his catastrophic defeat at Nancy in the Swiss wars, the duke went missing, turning up neither in the carts of the dead nor on the cots of the wounded. His life was so much on everybody's mind that his reality grew in his absence. And the deep cold froze each memory. One of the duke's pageboys claimed to have seen the great soldier fall, and he led the searchers over crusted snow to the spot. The earth ground its teeth where they walked. The duke's fool, whom the court called Louis Onze, ran ahead, pretending to be a dog, leaping and coursing on all fours, nosing the corpses, demanding one of them rise and assume the self they sought, but apparently the dead were satisfied with their situation.

At last the duke is found facedown and frozen in a pond, one hand hard by, its stiff fingers in a fan. A wolf's jaw, a sword's wound, the bite of the ice, had deprived the head of its features; nevertheless there were clues beyond a few snuffed fingers to be looked for— a scar on the throat, an ingrown toenail—but the fool objected to so intimate a search, squeamish about such an intrusion, for he felt that his long face, where all the duke's true virtues were now written, was evidence enough.

EXIT an Actual Dog

There are the blind, ill, impoverished whom Malte meets on the streets; there are buildings whose walls are ruinous and provide the poet with paragraphs of surpassing beauty; there is the silence that overcomes a used-up life; there are odors that stay the night in darkened doorways, sounds that give away the location of someone in sorrow: These are the ghosts of what they will become—the ruinous before the ruin. They precede, they presage, they herald a deed before its perpetration the way a pistol's shot recedes into its wound. There are our memories, ghostly, too, as the duke's memory was, when his followers looked for him in their imaginations like a pair of lost gloves. There are, of course, the ghosts that hover over the recently departed, released with the last breath from a weary lung; and there are the ghosts who dwell in us, the somewhat living, and greet the ghosts whose roaming time has come. They listen when commanded—List! List! as Hamlet's own ghost did—and bite the conscience, like a terrier, on the calf . . . ghosts in plenty . . . searching . . . uneasy . . . but are there purgatories suitable to each kind or requiems sufficient to bring peace to all of them?

Ingeborg, beautiful, much loved, a lady bountiful—we need know, at this moment, no more—has died, and it is now the Thursday following her funeral. Malte's mother, who was a mourner and a witness, tells her son the story, what Maman saw: She was taking tea on the terrace, which gave her a view through the trees of the family vault. The table's setting was designed to disguise Ingeborg's absence, her place divided among the rest like property at the direction of a will. Malte's aunt, Abelone, was pouring. It had been Ingeborg's habit to bring the mail out of the house every day at this time, although she hadn't been able to do so during the final weeks of her illness. Nevertheless, at that instant, as expectation nearly placed her name on Malte's mother's lips—"*Wo bleibt nur . . .*" The family dog, who always ran to meet her, bolted from beneath the table toward where she should be, if she were coming, mail in hand as she always did, twice turning his head quizzically from side to side before rushing headlong till he reached where she should have been, if she'd been coming, jumping around and up near her face to lick it where it would have been bent when she leaned down to pet him, if her face had been there for him; the dog leaping and licking so exactly the way he always did that the mother felt Ingeborg must have been there, inside the circle of his loving, until Cavalier, as he was called, spun, howling, and collapsed like a balloon that's suddenly lost its air.

The dog is borne from the stage in Malte's father's arms. There are no drums, only the sound of the father's footsteps on the terrace.

ENTER Ghost

What else are we to call this count in eighteenth-century dress whom Rilke has imagined is sitting on the other side of the fireplace in a corner of his castle room at Berg am Irchel, and who dictates ten poems, each wholly unexpected, during a fortnight at the end of November 1920, and then completes the cycle with eleven more in early February of the following year? Colonel Richard Ziegler and his wife have lent Rilke their château for the winter, and his friend Nanny Wunderly has found him a housekeeper. The poet shall enjoy a solitude like that he'd had at Duino eight years before. Indeed, if he does not complete the *Elegies* now, what will be his excuse?

Whenever Rilke installs himself in a new lodging, he looks at once at the library, but in this instance the bookcases are bare. Well . . . bare but not bare: A dog-eared Stendhal, a lone Goethe are there (according to one biographer; a Molière and two Stendhals, according to another; while Goethe, Molière, and Stendhal is the opinion of a third). Rilke will have to create a few volumes himself in order to have something to read, so he imagines an author, one Count C.W., also thought of as a former owner of the *Schloss*, now deceased, whose style hovers between very clumsy and much too clever, and whose wishes Rilke obeys with an immediacy Hamlet might have employed to his profit. Yet, like Hamlet, Rilke obeys only to put off his obligation to those elegies as yet unwritten, hanging about, waiting for their words. As was his wont, he writes too many long letters. These letters were composed, and the words placed upon the page, with a pastry cook's care, never to be eaten or otherwise disturbed, but to sit in a window and advertise the baker's wares. With difficulty, he researches the history of the house he has been given, as also was his habit. He works on his translations of Paul Valéry and writes a brief preface in French for a book of narrative drawings by the twelve-year-old son of his present lover, Baladine Klossowska. The book is called *Mitsou* and we shall know its artist by the name of Balthus.

Of all abstractions, the Truth is the most ghostly and the most frequent cause of guilt. One evening, while Rilke was undressing (he told his publisher, Anton Kippenberg), verses began arriving, though they were never the first of anything final: "Mountains rest, splendored by stars;—though time sparkles in them too."

The count, as Rilke remembers him in correspondence, begins as an amusing fiction, soon is guiding the poet's pen, and finally feels personally present to him—as it were, growing more fully a ghost through each account of the case. Perhaps "Publish me!" is this ghost's command. So Rilke insists on his charade and never issues the poems under his own name, since they are not only uncharacteristic; they are so clearly sad substitutes for the remaining elegies that didn't arrive. There is one exception to this reluctance: he permits the poem "Karnak" to be published, though anonymously, perhaps because it is too much his. The poem begins with an arresting positioning of its phrases.

> In Karnak. We were driven,
> Helen and I, dinner dispatched.
> The dragoman pulled up at the Pylon—
> never was I so in the middle
> of the moon's world.

The remains of Egypt's ancient past both measure and dismiss our shallow, fleeting present. This poem shoulders the others aside, and when the count begins offering Rilke lines in Italian, he is summarily dismissed.

ENTER Ghost

The death that enveloped and became Chamberlain Christoph
Detlev Brigge grew so huge, it was feared that wings would have to
be added to the manor house to hold it. His death required that it be
carried from room to room by wearying servants until there
remained but one place it had not lain and bellowed like an angry
animal. This was, as tradition insisted, where the chamberlain's
mother had died twenty-three years before, and it had been reveren-
tially left intact and untouched all the seasons since. Finally, the
chamberlain's death, refusing—outgrowing—every bed, lay in the
middle of the floor, bulging between the buttons of a dark blue rum-
pled uniform. For ten weeks, it stayed there, waxing slowly, demanding to see others who were more thoroughly dead than it was, and
calling for its own doom. Imagine: a death demanding to die. The
roaring of the chamberlain's death frightened the dogs that at first
had howled in concert with its groaning. The noise seemed, in the
village, like thunder, and pregnant women, hearing it as if it were a
growl in their own stomachs, hid in remote rooms, fearing for their
infants and themselves, wordless as statuary, their hands resting
upon a double swelling, their features full of motherhood's melancholy and its mysterious beauty.

ENTER Ghost

It is a poem, this ghost, that puts the words of a requiem into the
voice of an eight-year-old boy, Peter Jaffé, who died in Munich in
October of 1915, a boy who would consequently have to have at least
a shred of still-embodied spirit; for if a detached hand can come out
of a wall like a mouse, why can't a disembodied mouth manage a few
lines?

> *Requiem on the Death of a Boy*
> I impressed so many names upon myself
> that cow, dog, elephant, the whole ark

Rilke and the Requiem

might have filed by without remark
as far as zebra. And . . . for what?
    The element that bears me now
rises like a tidal line
above all that. What comfort can there be
in knowing I existed there in me
but never got so far inside my face
to form a feature?

And these uninitiated hands—

The father, Edgar Jaffé, a political economist, played a significant
role in the movement for peace that came to realization in 1918. He
would later serve as Bavarian minister of finance. Yet this "Requiem
on the Death of a Boy" would scarcely provide the parents solace. As
in all of Rilke's requiems, a bitterness resides there, turning farewell
into an accusation, an accusation so unfair to the Jaffés, whom Rilke
knew only remotely—politically, not socially—that one has to conclude another speaker really speaks it—again a ghost behind a
ghost—namely, the poet's own youthful self addressing another pair
of parents, Phia and Josef Rilke.

        You sometimes said: I glimpse a hint of promise . . .
        I promised, yes—but what I promised you
        was never overwhelming.
        I would huddle near our house for hours
        watching the skylark scale the sky.
        If only I could have risen with my gazing,
        had a look that lifted me right up there!
        I held no one dear. Affection was anguish—
        you understand—
        then I was not we,
        but bigger than a man,
        I was the only risk I ran,
        the seed of my own anxiety.

Rilke had been a replacement for a female infant who had died a year before his birth. For many years, he was dressed as a girl called René, or Sophie sometimes, when she was good, and played with like a doll to please her mother, only to be abruptly sent away to military school to satisfy his military-minded father, and deprived of childhood altogether, according to Rilke's frequently voiced complaint. No wonder Rilke saw himself sometimes as the ghost of a girl.

A tiny seed. Let it sail down the street;
let it whirl in the wind. I give it gladly.
That we were all so cozy together
I never believed. On my honor.
You talked, you laughed, yet none of you
were in your language or your laughter. No.
How you all shillied, how you shallied
as neither sugar bowl nor wine glass would.
The apple lay. How happy it would make me
to hold a firm full apple in my hand,
or the table's edge where breakfast stood
in its sturdy bowls—they pacified the year.
And my playthings were sometimes good to me.
They could almost be as other things were,
as staunch, though more excitable.
In terms of unwavering watchfulness they stood
somewhere between my hat and me.
There was a wooden horse, there was a cock,
there was a doll with one leg;
I have done a lot for them.
I shrank the sky when they wanted it
because I understood how alone
a wooden horse is. How one can make
a horse of wood into something possibly great
by painting it and pulling it by a string
over the bumps of a real road.

Why was it not a lie to call this stick a horse?
Because one felt oneself grow maned and muscular,
fourfooted, with glistening flanks,
so one might run to manhood as in a race?
But wasn't there wood in oneself as well?
Didn't one quietly grow hard for its sake,
and go about with a diminished face?

As a ghost-gowned girlboy, René would visit his mother in her
room; but her false piety, as he saw it, her hypocrisy and dissem-
bling; her selfish manipulations, fondling him and ignoring him by
turns; her dissatisfactions with her life, so frequently expressed; her
social pretentiousness, her petty mind: that is what of his mother, he
remembered. In the costume of another sex, he saw another self, as
Malte saw another self in the mirror of the manor house. The loss of
identity, hence his autonomy, was horrifying. Yet the merging of the
self with what it saw and felt and knew was a much-sought escape;
it sufficed for his mysticism, and effected his salvation.

It would almost seem, each time, that we
    swapped selves.
I would murmur when I saw the stream,
and when it murmured I would rush pell mell.
When I saw a ringing, I would be a bell,
and when it rang, I was its reason.

I embraced everything impetuously,
yet everything was everything already,
and made sadder by my company.
Now I am abruptly bid good-by.
Must I relearn my letters, ask anew,
or is my task to tell of you? That troubles me.
The house? I never understood it.
The rooms? There were too many things in business there.
. . . You, mother, do you know who the dog
    might really be?

Even that we gathered berries in the woods
seems now a strange discovery.

"I am I because my little dog knows me," Gertrude Stein wrote
scornfully, and Rilke frequently agreed that he knew who he was
when, as Ulysses was nosed, the dog greeted him; but here he turns
that moment of recognition around: The mistress does not know her
pet. In his life, memory has so highlighted its many miseries that the
thought that he was happy once, and enjoyed familial feelings,
seems as odd as an early photograph in which one is wearing a page-
boy haircut and golfing knickers.

―――

There must be some dead children
who can come and play with me.
There are always new ones, dying.
Same as me. After a long spell
of lying still and never getting well.

Well. How silly that sounds here.
Does such a thing make sense?
Here, where I am, no one is ill.
Since my sore throat, already so long ago—

Here each of us is like a refilled glass.

Yet who shall drink us I've not seen as yet.

―――

Peter Jaffé, the eight-year-old son of Professor Edgar Jaffé, died in
Munich in October 1915.
The poem is dated November 13, 1915.
Rilke read this poem frequently during his first lecture tour
through Switzerland following the war. In all but one of his requiem-
like poems, he preferred to memorialize individuals he scarcely

knew. It allowed him more easily to cry out "rest, perturbed spirit" to restless pieces of his own past.

ENTER Ghost

For an interrogation. The first questions usually are: Who are you really? Why are you bothering me? What do you want?

Almost no one asks: How do you know?

There you were, Father, adrowse in your orchard, as you just said, when Claudius poured henbane, fiercely distilled, into an unheeding ear, where, like quicksilver, it sped through your sleeping form and in an instant took away its life. Now, ghost father, I can readily understand how you might have learned you were a cuckold, having lately hung near the royal bed of pleasure like a curtain, or how the story that you'd been stung by a serpent had been featured in the popular press; but how came you to know it was henbane, that it was carried in a vial, and when did you wake and rise and turn and see Claudius steaming with guilt like fresh dung? By your own account, since you and he were without witnesses, you could not have then learned anything, nor could you later have found such shocking facts out, lest you climbed through a window into Claudius's head and there heard him confess it to himself.

Methinks, Father, you have made this business up, angry as you rightly are over your wife's betrayal and how eagerly she now takes her plump pleasures from another. So—bad beguiling ghost—begone! The dogs of day do woof!

When Hamlet's father's ghost appears upon the battlements; when Christine Brahe floats her form past the dining chairs at Urnekloster as slowly as a sick person; when the chamberlain's death oozes out of his coat between its buttons; when Count C.W. materializes at Rilke's fireside to read to him from a yellowed manuscript: How a ghost can bear arms, sport a frock, roar commands, keep a manuscript around so long the pages sour—yes, where is the lung that lets Death bellow so?—are questions poetry is as reluctant to tackle as theology, because, presumably, little Peter Jaffé's words are as ghostly as Hamlet's father's are hollow. It is, in fact, the unsettled soul that must find some countenance to be seen in, some sounds to make itself heard; it must inhabit a body as it once did its own, and make unfamiliar organs groan.

"Mountains rest beneath splendoring stars, but in each of them it's time that twinkles" was the first sentence of Count C.W.'s dictation. Whose mouth made it, whose larynx shaped the syllables? Surely not the one still rotting in unison with the count's corpse? How then can Christine Brahe's borrowed body pass through the wood of a broad door if it is flesh, and if it be immaterial, how can a gown hang where there is no hanger? How can Peter Jaffé say "mütter" without the teeth to make the *t*'s? Because Christine Brahe's body is an image, the same as she would be to me in my consciousness if I were attending the birth of her death when the baby split her.

The aged pages from which the ghost reads suggest that the poems were written by the living count and not the dead one, yet the lines wear incoherence like a winding-sheet.

What is most worrisome to those who have been confronted by ghosts is that it is not merely a leftover bit of life like a stale odor Hamlet or Malte's father or the reader has encountered, but an altered world where specters may read from spectral pages spectral words, because the door through which the ghost of a dead mother passes must widen the spaces between its molecules in an accommodating way, as immaterial in that moment as a dead king's armor; because ghostliness is contagious; I am made a phantom, too, when the count, through Rilke's agency, pours the poem's words into the porches of my ear. "Never was I so in the middle of the moon's world." When the ghost departs, Hamlet is left with obligations from another realm, and in the grip of his father's dream. How insubstantial does that make him? Yet is his sword now insubstantial, too? When C.W.'s figure fades, Rilke has in hand some problematic poems in place of the remaining elegies he was hoping for—an insufficient and inopportune substitution. If he does not lend them his name, do they remain as ghostly as their author? And how do their whispered words ride toward us on real air?

ENTER Clara

Westhoff. Not a ghost, of course, but the poet's future wife, and the mother-to-be of his daughter, Ruth. Our stage cannot too long bear the weightlessness of so many specters. It needs a person of real substance to tread upon its boards and push them back aground. It is November 20, 1900, and Rilke is earnestly courting this young sculptor whom he has met at the artists' colony at Worpswede, at the same time enjoying the attentions of, and attending to, her friend, the painter Paula Becker. Clara has just written him about the death of another friend, and Rilke enters in his diary a report on the contents of her letter.

Clara writes today about a black ivy wreath, and what she recounts is again a work of art. The way she speaks of this heavy black wreath that she took down unsuspectingly from the gable of her house and brought in out of the gray November air and that then became so monstrously earnest in the room, a thing unto itself, suddenly one thing more, and a thing that seems to grow constantly heavier, drinking up as it were all the grief in the air of the room and in the early twilight. And all this shall lie then on the thin wooden coffin of the poor girl who died in the South, in the hands of the sun. The black wreath may cause the coffin to cave in, and then its long tendrils will creep up along the white shroud and grow into the folded hands and grow into the soft, never-loved hair and grow into the heart that, full of congealed blood, has also become black and dulled and in the twilight of the dead girl will scarcely be distinguishable from the heartlike leaves of the ivy. . . .

And through the empty corridors of the blood the ivy will make its way, leaf by leaf on its long tendrils, like nuns who lead themselves along a single rope and pilgrimage to the dead heart, whose doors are lightly ajar. ["The Worpswede Diary," from *Diaries of a Young Poet*, trans. Edward Snow and Michael Winkler. W. W. Norton, 1997, pp. 245–246.]

Enter Dante Gabriel Rossetti like a smell. Enter Edgar Allan Poe. Rilke writes a requiem for Clara to address to this friend, Gretel, who, the poem says, has had a brother and a sister die before her so that she might know in advance what her own dying would be like. This is—I think—a novel explanation. The poem begins:

> In the last hour the world was made richer by a wreath.
> A while ago it was a few leaves. I wove them:
> and now this ivy is particularly heavy,
> and as full of dark as if it had drunk
> out of my things their future nights.
> I am fearful of my next night
> alone with this wreath that I wove
> not realizing that something happens
> when the tendrils wind themselves around the hoop;
> needing to understand one thing;
> that something can cease to be.

And the wreath breaks into Gretel's coffin, creeps into her corpse, crawls through her emptied veins toward her heart, as if it wished to justify my definition of decadence. Life is a dream, the poem not very originally reminds her, but the rest of that short line is Rilke marching to his own theme: Life is a dream, but we wake from it elsewhere. Moreover, Gretel is firmly admonished:

> Your death was already old
> when your life began;
> therefore he attacked it,
> lest it outlive him.

In the German, her life is an "it" (*es*), her death a "he" (*er*).
Being outlived is one reason for the maliciousness of ghosts,

and often their only way of surviving is to hang on to some fragment of the living like a barnacle to a ship bottom. "You know,"
Ruskin wonders, "if there are such things as souls, and if any of
them haunt places where they have been hurt, there must be many
about us, just now, displeased enough." Christine Brahe, as one who
haunts, is rejuvenated by the gasps she can cause, by the recognition that in some way she remains in the frame of life. You will
remember me, like it or not. You will see me, hear me, feel me
against your will; your awe, fright, guilt, astonishment will prove
I've made my mark and am in the real world still. The poem makes
Clara say:

> I am lost in thoughts I've never entertained,
> although wondrous things stand there
> that I must have somehow seen.

ENTER a Day Dead for a Long Time

> Let us remember May 31, 1578, when a peasant digging
> for *pozzolano,* or volcanic sand, slipped through a sud-
> den subsidence of the earth into the catacombs.

Rome was amazed when these passages were rediscovered. Since
the days of the Apostles, Christians had put not just their graves but
their graveyards underground to save the bones of their families
from the hostilities of persecuting mobs. The living said Mass
there, and delivered homilies in the close dark halls, scratched
words on walls, and painted faces and figures on the coffins that
torches would disclose. Though the living often prayed that those
whose death was now behind them would be forgiven their sins,
equally often they directed a "remember me" to one deceased: "Pray
that we may be saved," they begged. Even a dead infant was considered to be "over there" and in a position to intercede. "Anatolius,
our first-born, ours for a little while, pray for us," one such petition
began.

Raising the dead for such purposes has not always been regarded a difficult thing. Robert Graves has written:

> To bring the dead to life
> Is no great magic.
> Few are wholly dead:
> Blow on a dead man's embers
> And a live flame will start.

Over there, yet in a position to intercede . . . but not much comfort would mom and dad receive if their child were a boy like Peter Jaffé, who used Rilke's words to speak to them of loneliness and loss instead of forgiveness, and insisted that their parental love was a gaudy mockery—in short, to say what no child would have been allowed the words for while alive, and still so young, and still a victim.

What a good thing, then, to be a ghost, to say what you dared not say in daylight, to order acts of vengeance on your own behalf, to urge the merely physical to follow you even to the precipitous edge of a castle's battlements, or, at least, to trouble the conscience of a lover who had not mourned for you sufficiently or felt sadness to your satisfaction.

ENTER Erik and a Parade of Images

At Urnekloster, as was the custom in castles of that time and place, there was a gallery set aside for a lineup of ancestors: A regal row of rogues, it often was, and it meant as much not to be as to be there. For some painters, this bit of family pride provided a paltry livelihood because not all black sheep could be banished and have the household still pretend to a flock. Malte, increasingly curious about Christine Brahe and her appointment in the hierarchy, leaves a sleepless night to fret his bedclothes while he climbs the stairs with a tapered light that flickers with apprehension. In Rilke, space is as palpable as perfume and can cling too—for instance, like a collar or a sleeve. Now the deep corridor comes toward him; he feels the windows pressing against him as they must be pressing against the night, so he elevates his candle on the side opposite where the paintings hang in a single rank, awaiting review. Rilke's poetic animism is rarely more evident than in passages like this one, for now the faces observe him with a fixity that demonstrates their interest in him, not with a stare that's the result of the implacable settlement of paint.

Perhaps the ghost of a king to come has had the living king's portrait painted so that the ghost will have a place to inhabit in its afterlife, where it may be visited as one visits grandmother on high holidays, and where a conscience can be pricked by a stern look that perhaps it has waited generations to inflict.

Malte's intention was to watch for women only, but the gentlemen in their frames jostle the candle's shadows for position. Hair, cheeks, eyes slide by as slowly as scenes from a departing train. Until the children. The candle is passed before them like a priest's blessing, but that is how this reader imagines it, since the reader has been brought there, too, just as the audience is on guard at the battlements, and sees the shape of the king, huge in his armor, hoarse because the director demands it, stalk slowly toward Horatio, who is shrunken with surprise. Are these also ghosts then, these renderings of past pretensions? Unlike a figure that leaves an actual indentation of its form in any light that offers itself—any light a camera is poised to gather—these portraits have traveled through the thoughtful eyes of artists, layer by layer in their composition, and not in an instant, but over time, so that something more may be expected of them than mere nose and mustache can manage. But ghostliness? Are they uneasy, too, these wives of kings and paragons of doubtful virtue who dare to parade their laces and their braids before the course of history?

A little girl has forgotten the pert bird standing on her palm. And the small dog seated at another's feet is being ignored, along with the color of its ears. A ball, like an apple, lies nearby, incapable of roll. Though they are not yet ladies, they are waiting, waiting in their dresses, waiting . . . but not for buses.

Then, that abruptly, he bumps into Erik.

Mind your light, Erik whispers.

This is a Disney world, where teapots talk and candles dance; but it is also where yet another female relative, primping like a princess before her mirror, amply lit on both flanks, has her filmy gown ignite and consume her while her reflection remains unburned and ready for the ball to begin. You here? Malte exclaims, wondering whether their encounter is a good or evil omen. The candle flame wavers to the music of his mind. Erik laughs. Then tells him that the woman he seeks, her portrait, is not here, but another floor up, in the attic—probably packed away—and that Erik and Christine are looking for it.

This Erik is a cousin Malte's age, who might have become his friend, for they shared melancholy looks like notes in school, and had seen Christine Brahe step weightlessly across the dining room together. Erik, Rilke tells us, was based on a childhood chum, Egon von Rilke, and was therefore given Egon's squint, small neck, long chin, and early death. Egon was awarded an Orphic sonnet, no doubt on account of the shortness of his life, always, for Rilke, an odd plus. Odd here because Egon's stand-in is not nicely treated by the text, and is given the name of a historically (1722–1756) ill-fated monarchist and military man who was executed for his part in a plot to extend the powers of the king,

In the sonnet (part 2, number 8), however, Egon is honored in the culminating line as someone who understood the estrangement of the poet and his playmates from our grim run-of-the-mill grown-up world. The emblem seen to be suitable for his fate is, as it often is in Rilke, the ball—round, rolling, bounding—which establishes a relation of pitch and catch that's cooperative, connecting, and distant at the same time. Though what happens when you fail to catch it?

> You, rare playmates from a childhood far away,
> in the city's scattered parks we played.
> Shyly we discovered one another,
> and like the lamb with the speaking banner,

spoke without speech. Our happiness
belonged to no one, like a sweet we shared,
but how it melted among the pressing throng,
and from the anxieties of a long year.

Carriage wheels rolled indifferently around us,
houses embraced us, their hugs firm but false.
What knew us as we knew us from that unreal realm?

Nothing. Only the balls. Their glorious roundings.
Not even other children . . . But sometimes one,
one frail and failing, stepped under the descending ball.

In memoriam Egon von Rilke

What do children know that we now know no longer? What makes
them unreachable, except by Lewis Carrolls? They know that everything is alive, will remain alive in one realm or another, both stay and
alter like a rhyme. When our toys dance while we sleep, it is merely
playful romance; when the wind kisses their cheeks, they may blush
at its advance.

How had Erik come to know that Malte was in the gallery? How,
for that matter, had he come to know Christine Brahe—to be, as it
were, in cahoots with her—so chummy they had become search
partners? After the fact, we might imagine that it was because Erik
was half a ghost already, near to his own death, and practicing the
art, but Malte cannot have had such a premonition.

Erik blows out the candle. Giggling, he hangs on Malte's arm.
Malte protests the darkness while trying to disengage. Erik hisses. A
spray of spit wets Malte's ear. Shall I tell you? He giggles again. I
brought her a mirror, a gazing-glass. Because she has no portrait
here. Now he punches the muscle of Malte's upper arm. *But she
wasn't in it.*

Malte remembers, from a narrator's distance, that Erik Brahe was
sitting for his portrait at that time in a suit of velvet heliotrope. And
he wonders if the painter knew that his subject might die before he
was done, or patiently went ahead, his concentration on catching

the squint in the right light. Then (in a passage protected by parentheses) Malte wonders whether, when the portrait is at last in line, visitors will confuse this small youthful Erik with the larger older one who was executed for serving too well the interests of an eighteenth-century Danish king.

ENTER Ghost

As an afterthought. Count Wolf von Kalckreuth was a nineteen-year-old nobleman who shot himself (for love, according to one biographer, because the failures of his art broke his heart, according to another) while in military service in 1906. Rilke had heard about the case from his friend Anton Kippenberg, who had published Kalckreuth's poems and translations of Baudelaire at the Insel Verlag. Almost immediately following Rilke's completion of the greatest of his requiems, that for Paula Modersohn-Becker, he embarked upon another. Like the one for Peter Jaffé, it would be as detached as Paula's anonymously titled "Requiem for a Friend" was personal, although the mode of address and some of the poem's tone would be carried over from hers. Moreover, they would form a polite pair while filling a little book to be called, simply, *Requiem,* as if there were only one.

Strictly speaking, this count does not deserve a requiem, because he deliberately killed himself. Ophelia should receive no music, says the priest in charge of her burial. "We should profane the service of the dead / To sing a requiem and such rest to her / As to peace-parted souls." Her death, the priest thinks, was doubtful—whether by accident, from madness or intent, who knew? And When in Doubt, Deny Service: That seems to be his motto. But Rilke is not a priest, not even Catholic any longer, and has more things on his mind than orthodoxy. He has his own career on his conscience, a place where he finds both guilt and pride; for he has succeeded many times in turning suffering to good account, and he has sacrificed many on the altar of his art, and given up much of what he could have had in his own life lest it flower too fully—captivate, oblige, consume, and thus destroy him: his own wife, his own child, numerous lovers—indeed, every attachment—many pleasures of the palate and the flesh, the condition of being a person—a lawyer or a teacher, a loving husband, a dutiful son—rather than a poet. Wolf, the count, has relinquished life because, like a netted fish, he could not escape human relationships, hence failed his art; but this point of view, we must remember, is pure conjecture.

The official excuse for a requiem is the peace it is supposed to bring to the soul of the deceased, but in many cases its reason may be the relief it brings to those who grieve. The tragic choice the count could not successfully make still haunts the poet who made it.

> Is it true I really never saw you? My heart
> is heavy with you the way reluctance makes hard
> a difficult beginning.

The requiem recapitulates common themes; its objectivity is only methodological. Death is a state like living is, not merely an end of life. It is properly *"being* dead," as some are in love. The young count clearly expected to go to a better "world"; however, where he went is simply different: He hoped to possess what he wanted more purely in a place where wants are unknown and possession is impossible; he believed he would finally find himself in the picture, instead of standing outside it like a gallerygoer; he would approach his beloved from within, and pass lightly through everything, perhaps as the ghost of Christine Brahe does. The count was too impatient; he should have waited until the hardness of life was broken by its own weight, and new uses for suffering could be found. Instead, he destroyed when there was so much to build; some woman or work-man might have saved him, and had either love or labor succeeded in arresting his fatal course, then he would have read the words he had been engraving in himself since childhood—as Peter Jaffé maintained:

> I impressed so many names upon myself
> that cow, dog, elephant, the whole ark

might have filed by without remark
as far as zebra.

He would have found a space for feeling, experienced that saintly
gaze that accepts everything and desires nothing, and, had he lived,
he would have achieved his own chosen, homegrown, fully ripe
conclusion.

Most poets fail (and Rilke means his former self and practice)
because they bewail their state instead of describing it; they evaluate
their feelings instead of forming them; and although they believe
their joys and sorrows should be known, they are unable or unwilling
to transform their consciousness into an adequate poetic language,
they fail to make of their poem "a thing" that can sit in the world as
fat and steamy as a teapot, or the way, in Peter Jaffe's poem, the
apple simply lay.

If the young man's inadequacies were as numerous as his requiem
suggests, we should not need to seek reasons for his suicide. How
could he have called himself a poet and continued to live? Of
course, he could have been sensible, given his probable level of talent, and have chosen to be a count instead.

The count is forgiven his impetuosity and the inflation of his feelings, but, as always, his requiem is scarcely his, nor is the famous
summing up: "Who speaks of victory. To endure is everything." Or, as
I sometimes prefer to think: "To survive sums it up."

ENTER a Lineup of Ghosts

"List, list, O, list! If thou didst ever thy dear father love—"
Rilke has heard them, the Ophelias, the women who loved in
vain, who perished in puberty, pure as an unbitten peach, women
who went mad, young men who murdered themselves, children who
simply succumbed: Gretel, Peter Jaffé, the sister he never knew, his
boyhood chum, Egon von Rilke, as well as this young count whose
cause he has taken up, and then Wera Ouckama Knoop, the young
dancer who would die of the same leukemia that would kill

Rilke later, and to whom he dedicated the *Sonnets to Orpheus* (yet another requiem in intention, if not in form), and of course Paula Modersohn-Becker, who was, after all, only thirty-one when an embolism took her. To listen, the "First Elegy" tells us, is a moral requirement, and the elegy asks them what they want, these voices, and the answer is, in effect, a requiem Mass.

> Voices, voices. Listen, Oh, my heart, as hitherto only
> holy men have listened, listened so the mighty call
> lifted them straight from the ground, although they kneeled on,
> these magicians—and paid no attention,
> they so utterly listened. Not that you could bear
> the voice of God—far from it. But hear the flowing
> melancholy murmur which is shaped out of silence
> wafting toward you now from those youthfully dead.
> Whenever you entered a church in Rome or in Naples,
> did not their fate speak insistently to you?
> or a lofty inscription impose itself upon you
> as lately the tablet in Santa Maria Formosa?
> What do they want of me? that I should gently cleanse them
> of the tarnish of despair which hinders a little,
> sometimes, the pure passage of their spirits.

The Reformation may have made intercession impossible, but these ghosts don't know it. They howl, they complain, they argue, they dictate, they command, some merely prowl, but most of them seem to think this will cause a living being to do their bidding. However, there are not a few wraiths who are creations of the pen, for Gretel and Wera and Wolf, as far as we know, are unaware of their ghostly status, and never immaterially appear. They have already received, or did not need, their requiem. Count C.W. is part invention, part ghost, part joke. Who knows if Christine has a thought in her head, but merely floats along as witless as the air in a balloon? And the chamberlain's bellowing ghost is Death itself. Fully sprung from the body of life.

Rilke's requiems are rarely pure in intention. They give the poet an opportunity to praise, but also a chance to complain on behalf of the deceased, or even to berate the deceased on behalf of Art; because it is clear that the principal reason for living is one's work, which should not allow itself to be interrupted either by bourgeois institutions or human suffering, the demands of family, or the enticements of pleasure and power.

If Death itself were to die, would it have a ghost, and would the ghost of Death visit the dead in the guise of someone alive, if only to fright them from any temptation to return?

From Pindar to Pope, from Archilochus to Larkin, eulogies have been made of both encomium and invective. In Rilke's case, complaint tends to exceed praise, but the mixture is the result of his belief that not only are life and death intertwined but guilt and goodness as well—shame and pride—so that, as Simonides saw, pure praise (and praise was an essential part of the poet's business) was delivered despite reservations, in their—through their—teeth, because human heights are fashioned almost solely from shortcomings. Bruno Gentili's description of Simonides' practice as involving "a poetics of tempered praise" seems apt.

The way Rilke writes about death suggests that there are three kinds of demise. A moment ago, I said that the chamberlain's ghost was Death itself. That was carelessly put: It was only *his* death, though finally and fully realized. It was not pure impersonal death—its distilment, the famous "a blue residue in a cup without a saucer"—any more than a single Mephistopheles or Beelzebub makes up the whole of Satan, who has many names and forms. Both of these meanings (death in the abstract and someone's death in particular) are different from the state or condition of *being dead,* which Rilke says we should recognize as a matter of degree in a continuum that includes life like a color, for as different as blue is from red, they are companions in the same spectrum—indeed, life and death are mingles of each other. Accidents and errors sometimes prevent it, but one should die one's life and live one's death. The "First Elegy" is eloquent on this point:

True, it is strange not to live on the earth any longer,
no longer to follow the folkways you've only just learned,
not to interpret roses and other promising things
in terms of a rich human future;
then to be no longer the one who once lay
in ceaselessly anxious hands, and to have to put aside
even one's proper name like a broken toy.
Strange, to wish one's wishes no longer. Strange,
to see all that was one time related, fluttering now
loosely in space. And it's difficult to be dead.
There's all that catching up to do before one feels
just a little eternity. All of the living, though,
mistakenly make these knife-like distinctions.
Often Angels (it's said) cannot say if they linger
with the living or the dead. The eternal current
carries every age through either realm
forever, and drowns their voices with its roar in both.

ENTER the Ghost of a House

When the Schulins' manor house burned down, the fire was confined to its central rooms. Two wings of the building survived, and
the Schulins divided themselves in order to live in the uncharred
portions. Their passion for entertaining guests remained undiminished, but it sometimes meant, if company arrived on a foggy
evening, or while it was snowing heavily, and if they failed to remember that the core of the mansion had been consumed, they would
drive their carriages to a front door no longer there to respond to rap-
ping or swing open in welcome. Neither of Malte's parents could get
used to the main building's absence, and would call themselves
ghosts to be knocking at a door that wasn't there, or stubbornly
affirm the house's former presence behind a concealing scrim of
flakes. Malte, a child when these occasions occurred, was convinced
that the old place was still nearby, so he would slip away through bil-
lows of party skirts (like a dog, he says), though, in this singular case

he was caught by one of the family's many sisters and restored to the group, where, moments later, the odor happened.

Count Schulin was in mid-anecdote when the countess apparently said something that stopped him long enough to issue a condescending pooh-pooh; but the countess hissed like a librarian in reply, and everyone listened so hard in the silence that followed that the furniture grew larger, and everyone looked about so intently, the family silver shone without uncertainty. One of the many sisters explained—"my mother smells with her ears"—herself becoming all nose. Then the company began to sniff hither and thither the way we do when trying to follow a scent with our scanty equipment. The reader, from a superior stage of development, will imagine that smoke from the fire, still caught in a curtain or soaked up by soft wood or lingering in upholstery inadequately cleaned, has escaped as one would expect it to do, to fill the mind with an unwelcome remembrance of the tragedy; however, young Malte, observing the grown-ups flummoxed by something invisible, begins to fear its power to bend a roomful of busy talkers to its will.

Malte's apprehensions increase—Is he the source? Will it burst from him? Will all noses point in his direction?—and when he observes his mother as if waiting to embrace him, he goes to her trembling side, though others twit him for it. There, mother and son remain to comfort each other until the ghost of the house finally returns whence it came.

Requiem aeternam dona eis, Domine

When Rilke met Clara Westhoff and Paula Becker at the Worpswede art colony in 1900, he was in emotional flight from his surrogate mother and former lover, Lou Andreas-Salomé, who had regretfully but with relief freed herself from the boyish demands and tantrums of her poet. Rilke immediately saw Clara and Paula as shapes in a painting—two women in white, he said—and stepped into the middle of their friendship, courting them with thoughtful attentions, observations, and beautifully crafted notes and letters—methods of seduction of which he was a master. He apparently fancied the painter, Paula, more than the sculptor, Clara, although the fact that the latter had been a student of Rodin piqued his interest.

Rilke appears, however, to have been indifferent to Paula's art, while she was already drawn to a painter, Otto Modersohn, who admired her work and won her hand. I suspect that Paula Becker at first saw marriage as a refuge. Her own family as well as Modersohn's were pushing her in that direction; otherwise, what could she do to earn a living but teach schoolchildren or become a governess?

Rilke sought stability, too, but he could no more come to rest than a robber on the run. After a year of penurious confinement in a romantic cottage, he used his Rodin commission as an excuse to move to Paris, and although he is initially miserable there, he hangs on, if not for dear, then for dire life.

A young man, far from fully formed, he had made a series of major mistakes. He had married Clara Westhoff, thereby obligating himself as a husband; he had agreed to have a child, thereby obligating himself as a father; he had, in doing so, deflected his wife from her work as well as inhibiting his own, wrapping them both in a bourgeois cottage romance—a mutually enhancing narcissism that scarcely survived the first months of the nesting routines customary for the recently married.

Then Paula Becker, perhaps to save herself from the life of a governess, married Otto Modersohn, in the belief that he would help her further her art. Instead, she obligated herself as a wife. Nevertheless, she refused to have his child, refused to be drawn into that world where women were livestock, bore calves, and moo'd o'er the lea. Twice she left her husband (and his importuning family) for Paris, painted in increasing privacy, and slowly altered Rilke's initially indifferent estimation of her work into one of admiration.

This was, however, only Rilke's view of the situation, because, as Eric Torgersen points out in his wisely balanced account, *Dear Friend: Rainer Maria Rilke and Paula Modersohn-Becker*, Paula had always wanted children and had remembered with some longing the comforts of her own middle-class family. It was her poet friend who had a horror of it. What she no doubt thought possible, when she did decide to have a child, was the presence of household help sufficient to free her for her art. Still, she put off this ultimate acceptance of her marriage, dropping a heavy anchor outside that harbor.

So Rilke was encouraging, supportive, kept Paula company in Paris during her runaway days, sat for that openmouthed, olive-eyed portrait she painted of him; but the moment she seemed seduced to his side, Rilke grew as cool as Mama Bear's porridge. Finally, Modersohn and Modersohn's family put such pressure on her to return that she did fall back into their hopeful arms. And filled them with a girl.

We do not know the details of Christine Brahe's death, but Paula Modersohn-Becker's was more melodramatic than any soap, for she dies only minutes after doctors have released her from two weeks of recuperation and bedrest. She stands; she combs her hair before a mirror (not unlike the mirror she used to paint her self-portraits); she sits in a chair to cuddle her child, and dies of an embolism with the baby still in her lap. *Schade*—what a shame—she says.

ENTER Ghost

Purely as a presence the poet feels her. She brushes a shoulder, bumps a table or a chair, not because she's taken on awkwardness in the other world, but just to let him know: She's there. Like the odor of burned wood, like the brisk touch of an unexplained breeze, like a gray glint of armor in those moments before dawn. The poet says: "I've had my dead, and I let them go / and was surprised to see them so consoled, / so soon at home in being dead, so right, / so unlike their reputation." They became—these other, different dead—much like the Eurydice of myth and of that other poem, "Orpheus, Eurydice, Hermes," which retells the time Orpheus, accompanied by Hermes (his safe conduct), went into the Underworld to retrieve his wife; and did so, but on the return journey, with the gates in sight, had to look back, contrary to Pluto's injunction; had to see if she were happily behind him, eager as he was, his impatient strides gulping down the journey. Lot's wife looked back and never knew the consternation that befell her. Orpheus also never saw how plump Eurydice was, as preoccupied as a pregnant woman, ripe as the ripest fruit, and so full of her own death there was no room for recognition. Who? Eurydice vaguely wonders when Hermes tells her; he . . . he has turned around. Who?

"I thought you were farther off." Paula's presence is contrary to Rilke's own consoling myth: that death is another form of existence, a transformation of the self into a sort of soul, satisfied simply to be, without wants and worries, all relations removed, dare we say, a *Ding an sich*. It's wrong, the poet complains,

> that you are giving up some of your eternity
> to return here, friend, here again . . .

And then, that it should be she, of all those dead the least likely to be still troubled because, the implication is, while alive she had transformed herself from a woman into an artist, and therefore should find the shift from the experience of life to the experience of death rather easier than most. Worse . . . she comes bearing a petition . . .

> that from the circle that received you,
> the stubborn pull of some past discontent
> has dragged you back into calibrated time—
> this starts me from sleep like the break-in of a thief.
> If I could say that you only come out of your
> abundant kindness, that because you are so sure
> and self-possessed you can wander childlike here and there,
> unaware of any risk from harmful places—
> but no: you are beseeching.

"Was bittest du?" Literally: "What pleases you?" The tone is flat and challenging. What do you want?

She might have arrived like Hamlet's father's ghost to chide the poet, to indict or blame:

> A grim rebuke, borne to me by your ghost,
> might weigh on me at night when I withdraw
> into my lungs, my guts,
> into the emptied chambers of my heart—
> such a protest would not be as grotesque
> as this pleading is. What do you want?

The sarcasms that follow contain some of the most powerful lines in the poem. The poet guesses that Paula has returned in search of the ordinary things of life she lost—female things—since she apparently chose *Kinder, Kirche, und Küchen,* but also drearily conventional things: "oh to have seen Tuscany just once before I died!" Or visited India or read the walls of the Alhambra.

> Tell me, should I travel? Did you leave some
> Thing behind that runs after you now in vain?
> Should I set out for a country you never saw,
> though it was the other half of all you knew?
> I shall sail its rivers, search its earth, and ask
> about its oldest customs, speaking with women in their doorways,
> and watching when they call their children home.
> I shall see how they wrap their world around them
> when they work the fields and graze their meadows.
> I shall ask to be brought before their king,
> and bribe the priests to take me to their temple,
> so I may prostrate myself before their most powerful idol,
> and have them leave me there, after latching the gates.

Does she regret not having had a peasant woman's life of nursemaiding, tending, of toil and subjugation, with superstition her sole solace? The poem then drops its tone of scorn and shifts in the direction of praise.

> I shall have gardeners recite to me
> the many flowers so I can bring back
> in the pots of their proper names
> some trace of a hundred scents.
> And I shall buy fruits, too, fruits in whose juice
> a country's earth will rise to join the sky.
> For fruit you understand . . .

Becker learned from Gauguin, van Gogh, and Cézanne. The hues she chose were earth tones, those of clay, the blown rose, euonymus leaves, apple and pear, bananas both ripe and green. She preferred to give women Fayum faces—supremely sad-eyed—and paint peasants, ungainly nudes, pottery jugs and plates of fruit, her pre- and pregnant self. Only thirty-one when she died, she was already painting with power and originality. *Schade.* Shame. Indeed.

The poem remembers those still lifes and impersonal nudes, and celebrates Paula's success with art's powers of transformation: that process that is its essence, and whose very name—*Wandlung*—is Rilke's talisman.

> Peeling from your clothes, you brought
> your nakedness before a mirror,
> and waded in up to your gaze . . .

The mirror, as we know, alters all our visible relations while leaving us under the impression that nothing has changed. This transformation represents, when Paula wades into the glass, her achievement of an artistic self; it is not now merely a woman who wields the brush, any more than the Cézanne who signed his paintings was simply a man. So when she paints herself, model, paint, and canvas become a single new thing. Who died, then, when Paula Becker died—woman or artist, giver of life or creator of being?—tell us, that the poet may know which ghost has breathed into his ear, tugged upon his sleeve, and made him start as though he's heard a thief.

> Come into the candlelight. I'm not afraid
> to look the dead in the face. When they come back
> they have a right, as much as other things,
> to the hospitality of our gaze.

As much praise as the poem contains, as much of Paula's struggle as the poem struggles to understand, its conclusion is, nevertheless, inescapable.

> And so you died as women used to die,
> died in your own warm house,
> died the old-fashioned death of childbearing women
> who try to close themselves again but cannot do it,
> because that darkness that they also bore
> comes back again and bullies its way in like a callous lover.

Incestuous rape is the shadow that this sentence casts. And the poem now turns plainly mean. The ghost is accused of making petty complaints about her mourning rites.

> Even so, shouldn't someone have rounded up
> a few wailing women. Women who will weep for money,
> and if well-paid will howl for you all night,
> when otherwise all is quiet.
> Customs! We haven't nearly enough customs.
> All gone and out of use.
> So that's what you had to come back for:
> the mourning that was omitted. Do you hear mine?

Rilke is the restless one. He is, when he composes this poem, but one year older than Paula Modersohn-Becker would have been had she not lost the struggle between life and art, the battle with her

354

body, biologically bent upon a different kind of birth than gratifies the artist. A year later, Rilke wrote these explanatory lines in a letter to Hugo Heller:

> The fate that I tried to tell of and to lament in the Requiem is perhaps the essential conflict of the artist: the opposition and contradiction between objective and personal enjoyment of the world. It is no less conclusively demonstrated in a man who is an artist by necessity; but in a woman who has committed herself to the infinite transpositions of the artist's existence the pain and danger of this choice become inconceivably visible. Since she is physical far into her soul and is designed for bearing children of flesh and blood, something like a complete transformation of all her organs must take place if she is to attain a true fruitfulness of soul. (Stephen Mitchell's translation in *Selected Poetry of Rainer Maria Rilke,* New York: Random House, 1982, p. 305. Letter to Hugo Heller, June 12, 1909. *Letters of Rainer Maria Rilke,* vol. 1, 1892–1896, trans. Jane Bannard Greene and M. D. Herter Norton. New York: W. W. Norton, 1945, p. 345.)

In a series of astonishing lines, Rilke describes how Paula, having reformed her birth-bearing body and become a painter, now devours the green seeds of her proper artist's death, and orders her blood to return to its normal maternal course. Her blood obeys, but sullenly.

> Do you know with what hesitation,
> what reluctance, your blood, when you called it back,
> gave up its commitment to an incomparable circulation?
> how confused it became when asked to take up
> once again the restricted circuits of the body?
> how, full of mistrust and astonishment, it flowed
> into the placenta again, exhausted suddenly
> from the long journey home?

The poem blames the poet, blames Otto Modersohn by implication, but more enthusiastically blames men in general for the wrongs

done women, who have been subjugated, co-opted, and denied their
creative opportunities. Rilke is only too painfully aware of his early
condescension, his own serious falls from grace, his fearful failure to
support Paula's efforts at independence, his own Modersohn role.

> Look, we inadvertently
> slip back from what we've labored to attain
> into routines we never intended, where
> we weakly struggle, as in a dream, and die there
> without ever waking. No one will be any wiser.
> Anyone who has lifted his heart for a lengthy task
> may discover that he can't keep on, the weight
> of the work is too great, so it falls of that weight, worthless.
> For somewhere there's an ancient enmity
> between ordinary life and extraordinary work.
> To understand, to express it: help me.

So the petition turns out to be in the poet's, not the painter's,
hands, though hers are ghostly and his fictitious. It is he, all along,
who has needed rest, and for whom all his requiems were written. To
remain ordinary is his failure and his fear. No high Mass here, either,
with music by Mozart or Berlioz or Verdi. This is the low Mass, a
Mass said, not sung, for those who have accused themselves of
hypocrisy and contradiction, a Mass to be spoken in the catacombs.
Kyrie eleison. It is not for the victims, but for the victimizers. *Christe
eleison.* Clara Westhoff's pregnancy might have ended with a
Schade, and she might now be haunting that dismal just-married
cottage as Christine Brahe haunts her castle. Have mercy on the living, then, who must sit upon their swelling conscience, trying to
cry out as loudly as the chamberlain's death did. It is not Hamlet's
father's ghost, but Banquo's—a ghost that guilt has sent for—that the
poet faces. Where were the poet's principles when, in Paris, Paula
appeared to be approaching him, and he helped send her, instead,
back to her marriage, child, and deathbed. Now he charges her with
a lack of courage. "Don't come back," the requiem's last lines read.

Rilke and the Requiem

> If you can bear it, stay
> dead among the dead. The dead have their own concerns.
> But help me, if you can, if it won't distract you,
> since—in me—what is most distant sometimes helps.

Life is a series of embroilments; living is entangling; hell, as Sartre said, is other people; that is why Rilke always had a preference for things and made his best love by post. The artist must deny life in order to celebrate it. He must transcend the ordinary altogether. It is a sort of death, a freeing of the soul. Death dissolves these worldly relations, and those who die young, especially as virgins (for love is a knot made of knots), have less disengaging to do. The great series of sonnets to Orpheus that Rilke dedicated to Wera Ouckama Knoop, and that serve as her requiem, contains one (part 2, number 13), addressed directly to Orpheus himself, that can serve as a summing up and a welcome to the world of wraiths, phantoms, and almost holy . . . ghosts.

> Anticipate all farewells, as if they were behind you
> like the winter that's just past, for among winters
> there will be one so relentlessly winter
> that in overwintering it your heart will be readied to last.
>
> Remain with Eurydice in the realm of death—rise there
> singing, praising, to realize the harmony in your strings.
> Here—among pale shades in a fading world—
> be a ringing glass that shatters as it rings.
>
> Be—but nevertheless know why annihilation
> is the unceasing source of your most fervent vibration,
> so that this once you may give it a full affirmation.
>
> To the store of copious Nature's used-up, cast-off,
> speechless creatures—an unsayable amount—
> jubilantly join yourself and cancel the count.

SACRED TEXTS

Exemplum

1. And God decided to write the world. He wrote the words **round vast empty dark.** They made a line He liked. He wrote the word *vast* in triplicate because He wanted the world to be very, very vast. He wrote the word *empty* twice because he wanted the world to be mostly empty, so that one might turn tens of thousands of its pages and find them all blank and black. The word *dark* he doubled for the same reason. There was no point in writing the word *round* more than once, because whatever was round (and surely round was round) could not become any rounder, even by rolling. God appointed one *vast* to accompany the darkness like a friend, and another to confront emptiness like an enemy, for what is it to be vast if your vastness is for rent?

2. **round vast empty dark**
   vast dark empty vast

was the way it went. Then He wrote **revolve** so there might be a place for time, but nothing did, for there was nothing but a vast emptiness, as He had decreed; moreover, had that vast dark emptiness turned, no one would have noticed. God had thought He could write down whatever He wished. But the Creator was corrected by His creation. God had thought He was omnipotent until He began to write. He thought about adding ***erase,*** but what was the point of erasing Nothing to get nothing? Vexed, God decided to let those vast black pages curl from exposure and disuse. He didn't write another word for what would have been a long long time.

3. And then, still miffed, He wrote the word ***revolver.*** The chambers did, but the chambers were empty.

4. And then, still more miffed, he thought about mixing ***meaningless*** in, or ***pointless,*** or ***aimless,*** but why should the Future know? Let it remain ignorant as the cows that would come to be.

5. God remembered, being omniscient, how Plato's Demiurge would one day do it. When the Demiurge (who had fashioned the world's soul and set the planets moving in perfect circles, and who, using the harmonic mean as a recipe, had readied the rational light that was to be set in man's head) was confronted by the problem of creating the lower parts of the human soul, he realized that he had better outsource that aspect of the job (as we say now), because the lower parts of the soul called for imperfection, and imperfection was exactly what was beyond the Demiurge's abilities.

So he turned the task over to the planets, inadvertently giving astrologers a big boost, for these lesser gods, striving to do their best, would still be unable to surpass or even equal their own natures, and thus, though aiming high, create just the lowness necessary. Man's whole soul in a sense would have three authors: (1) Plato, who created the Demiurge, (2) the Demiurge, who created the planets and their rational paths, as well as, out of the leftovers, man's mind, and (3) the planets, who would supply the soul with its darker dimensions.

God then remembered that it would get worse. Among men, some would be poets. There'd be Hesiod, for one. And he would invent gods by the dozens and give them hierarchy, home, and history. Valleys would be haunted, woods, too, cliffs and caves. There'd be

Olympians, Titans, Fates, and Furies, Nymphs and Naiads, Sprites and Lemurs, bugbears aplenty.

6. Instructed by the future, then, God wrote **host of angelic scriveners** in His very long hand. Let them do the writing, which is damnably hard, God silently, inside Himself, said; I'll just publish. These were God's last words, even to Himself, since He wished to remain Omnipotent.

> *round vast empty dark*
> *vast dark empty vast*
> *host of angelic scriveners*

God's last thought, however, was a bit of rearrangement.

> *round vast empty dark*
> *host of angelic scriveners*
> *vast dark empty vast*

He wanted his writers to be in the thick of things.

7. Soon the Heavens were full of Bards creating all kinds of creatures, including a class called prophets, through whom the Bards liked to scream and bellow, rant, promise, and threaten. Thus, as in past times Plato told it, did sacred books come into being: first as the word of God, told and retold, memorized and related syllable by syllable, through generation after generation of prophets, seers, oracles, sibyls, gurus, and rishis, and then set down in various forms of writing, which would be finally gathered, compiled, and anthologized to make the sacred texts.

The pages and paragraphs, the verses and chapters, the sentences and lines of these books were divinely revealed; therefore, they were at once good, true, and beautiful. And those who lived under their spell received the name Hindu or Moslem or Christian or Buddhist or Jain or Jew.

The Hindus had the Rigveda, the Samaveda, and the Yajurveda, the Atharva, the Brahmanas, the Aranyakas, and the Upanishads, just to begin with, for fully sacred texts soon lent a little of their aura to other works that gathered around them, such as the Kalpa-sutras, the Srauta-sutras, Grhya-sutras, and Dharma-sutras, which grew more and more divine over time, the way the holy men grew their beards. Even epics became canonical in order to please the public. The Mahabharata and the Ramayana, as well as the Puranas, made the grade.

The holy book of the Jains is called the Agama, and contains eleven Angas, twelve Upangas, ten Painnas, six Chheda-sutras and four Mula-sutras. The Hinayana Buddhist books are called "baskets," which even God would have to find charming: the Sutta-pitaka, the Vinaya-pitaka, and the Abidhamma-pitaka. The Mahayana Buddhists appeal to the Maha-vastu, the Buddha-charita, and the Lalita-vistara, but they have their sutras, too, among them the Saddharmapundarika, the Prajnaparamita, the Dasabhu-misvara, the Samadhi-raja, the Karandavyuha, the Gandavyuha, the Lankavatara, the Suvarnaprabhasa, the Sukhavativyuha, and the Tathagata-guhyaka. The sacred book of the Sikhs is the Adi-Granth.

The Hindus, like the Romans and the Greeks, set about inventing gods even faster than the seraphim could inspire them: Siva and Kali and Agni and Atar . . . as well as Et Cetera . . . the deity of endless lists.

The canon of the Zoroastrian faith got badly knocked about during its first thousand years and exists now only in fragments: the Yasna, the Visparad, and the Vendidad, among them. They made up for this lack later by adding the Dinkart, the Bundahishn, the Arda Viraf Nameh, the Sayast la-Sayast, the Datistan-i-Dinik, and the Shikand Gumanik Vigar.

They invented Ahura Mazda, and let Atar be his son. They also invented his opposite and equal, the dark star, Angra Mainyu, so that the condition of the world would always be one of war.

Muhammad believed that the One Book has existed eternally (which gets around God's writer's block), and has been revealed in the Jewish Torah, in the Christian New Testament, as well as by him in the 114 surahs of the Koran, which his followers collected after the Prophet's death.

Despite the fact that there is but one God called Allah,

Moslems managed to give him ninety-nine names, and plenty of companions—angels, jinns, genii, and prophets too numerous to number. Sanctity spreads as swiftly as some plagues.

This aggrandizing tendency, in which Yahweh, for example, is promoted from local chieftain to God Almighty has been praised by theologians, who regard monotheism as a kind of religious and intellectual progress; but every such Grandfather God harbors a multitude of lesser beings, not all of them nice, in His heavenly house. Monotheism is just a rock under which polytheism lurks like a crowd of roly-polys.

The early Christians created God the Father, then Jesus Christ, and then the Holy Ghost. Although technically Mary is not deserving of worship, but should properly receive merely adoration, the highest degree of veneration due saints, the reality is that as the Blessed Virgin she is treated like a god. There were all those angels, of course, and plenty of saints, who were all but deified, and whose pickled body parts both healed and inspired.

Western philosophers lamely offered the Absolute, the One, or the élan vital, while some politicians tried to Bible-ize *Das Kapital*.

Shinto principally depends on the Kojiki and the Nihongi. The Chinese regard their books as simply the work of wise men; however, that has not prevented them from being as dogmatic about the contents of these wise writings as everybody else is about theirs. Their canon contains Five Classics and Four Books. The Classics are the Shu-Ching, the Shih-Ching, the I Ching, the Li Chi, and the Ch'un Ch'iu. The Four Books are the Lun-Yü, or the Analects of Confucius; the Ta Hsüeh, the Great Learning; the Chung Yung, the Doctrine of the Mean; and the work we call Mencius on the Mind.

I have always admired the Yezidi, who have tried to isolate themselves from the rest of mankind, since the rest of mankind sprang from the intercourse of Adam with Eve, whereas they are descendants of Adam alone. They have two sacred texts, the Black Book and the Book of Revelation. Their supreme God is passive (perhaps fed up, see above), and He has turned the management of the universe over to seven angels, the most important of which is the peacock angel, Malak Ta'us. He fell from Heaven along with the rest of that disobedient crowd, but repented so copiously, his tears quenched the fires of Hell. Like many others, the Yezidi do not utter his name, although I can—he is, but is not called, Satan.

For our part, returning from Kurdistan to the USA, we have fathered the Book of Mormon in addition to Oashpe, Science and Health, *The Joy of Cooking,* and *Dianetics.* Is everything sacred? . . . How many volumes, then?

Perhaps not so many as stars.

Exegesis

Every significant religious system stands upon a sacred text. This text is indeed its temple. Inside, its heroes and their history are enshrined. Although leaders of varying degrees of divinity are always involved in the creation of a new sect, they usually have short lives, often come to bad ends, and their influence, diluted by disciples, soon disappears as water does in sand. What the leader leaves behind is *Mein Kampf* or its equivalent: his testament. Occasionally, by the indolent, an existent text is chosen, or a compilation selected—a golden treasury. From time to time, other writings may be dubbed divine, as though knighted. This is not a simple social thing, however. It is more important than a nation adding to its territories. Any addition to the divine canon will approve, proscribe, or admit new thoughts, new practices, and, in consequence, elevate different people to positions of privilege and power.

Once, the Word, almost any word, if written somewhere, was an object of wonder. Previous to its materialization, the word was like air that dare not be let out of its chamber—some tribal member's memory—lest it escape for good. Cast in language full of devices to aid its retention—the descent of the gods, or the history of the clan, with its founding heroes, its notable triumphs, the lessons of its history, including, of course, an account of the legitimate passage of power through persons and families—each was enshrined in the poet/archivist's head, and sections of the great saga sung on appropriate ritual occasions, its lessons taught to kids, and periodically reinforced by being dinned in every nearby ear.

Lest there be unseemly alterations (which was likely in any case), great emphasis was placed on retaining the history word for word, and variations of any kind were forbidden. Apprentice bards listened, and learned, and sang the same story generation after generation. Since all lore lay in either tribal memory or in what the skilled hands of hunters or weavers or magicians remembered, this caution made splendid sense.

Nevertheless, mistakes were bound to be made. We just don't know what they were. Additions and revisions and omissions would be certain to occur over time. And as stories spread, floating like weather-driven clouds over regions foreign to them, the need for literalness would be loosened, and updating would not be entirely unwelcome. The Homeric epics, based on tradition, acquire a patina of contemporary lore and custom. Like a tall drink, they are repeatedly refreshed.

Although the poet is supposed to pass on, like a professional gossip, what he's heard, and is properly to be appreciated for his performances, the aura of the gods hangs round his head, the great song issues from his mouth, and the deed depicted enhances its reciter, so that it is natural that the poet should borrow a little of that divinity his text has so much of, and, as actors often are, be identified with his role.

The Greeks believed the *Iliad*. They cited Homer to settle all sorts of disputes, both legal and moral. The poets were in touch with matters beyond mortal ken. The rhapsode, as Ion claimed, was inspired, and so spoke the moving word, supported prescribed beliefs, and incited proper action. Plato was apparently of the opinion that Homer's poetry was self-validating; that is, its "poetic" power convinced its listeners of its truth. It did not require letters of recommendation. It did not need to wear the halo of tradition, or become oracular (and therefore ambiguous), or furnish a list of its past successes. And of course that made it dangerous. What it said was unclear, and equally secure from rebuttal or test, but its emotional appeal easily overwhelmed reason. In short, it was a sacred text.

Even now, though examined and exposed and explained, sophistries have their charm, like roués, and continue to seduce. Imperfect arguments are often more persuasive than perfectly sound ones. Sad, we may say, but true. Yet it is human ignorance that permits many a millionaire to make his millions, and many a tyrant to prosper, too, and reelects politicians rotten at core, pulp, skin, stem, seed, and juice.

I don't want to sound like the gun lobby, but was it poetry that was at fault here? Was Homer a Mussolini eager to bomb Abyssinia? A Bush burning to free Iraq? Or was his poetry used for such purposes by the unscrupulous, who sought to employ Homer's charm, his genius, his moving language, his cultural vision to win over already-tipsy souls to some completely personal plan and policy? Plato's objection to the poets was really a condemnation of his society—a society of people eager to have their fears at the same time provoked and calmed, their greed promised figs and pigs, their stupidity praised, their bigotry encouraged, their failures extolled as achievement, their hatred allowed, indeed furnished, a helpless object. In short, a society like any other.

Nor could Second Isaiah, as "he" is now called, have any idea to what low aims, profitable schemes, and sentimental dreams his beautiful language would be put to praising.

In any case, the devas have been busy, whether in the guise of Gabriel in his shiny togs, or the serpent in his slithers, because revelation is as common as the cold, and the word of God, on and in and from so many tongues, has become a Babel.

Yet each book, to be a proper revelation, and worthy of the trust of the faithful, and in order to sustain itself, and preserve its message, must claim certainty, exclusiveness, a single unwavering interpretation, and an authority which remains total and undiminished. That's why so many such texts are books made of many books, which allows the sacred to enlarge its territory and cope with changing times without admitting any limitation, weakness, or unclarity.

Surrounding the book, guarding and profiting, are the priests, its professional readers and propounders, as well as institutions like the Church, which outlast mortal time, and serve as material centers for the sacred teaching.

Surrounding the surrounders is a society that supports both the book and its holy men; is ruled and blessed by them; defines its members in terms of the book's beliefs, the religion's rites, its preferences in morals, food, and dress; and is structured according to the values it places on its several sorts of people, and its attitudes toward life.

The Aztecs offered hearts still warm with blood and the cover of the chest to Huitzilopochtli, their god of war.

Books about the book, about the readers of the book and preachers of the word, about the institution based upon its truths, emerge from semi-inspired pens, and soon are semi-sacred, making similar claims and requiring similar protections. But the one rule to remember is: The sacred text is actually an enemy of every other. It is the monotext that makes even sycophantic and adoring volumes obsolete and unnecessary.

Particularly dangerous are those "friends" of the God-like work, who offer to explain the Word, to interpret it; because in short order the monotext is a polytext again, and it is being read anagogically or allegorically or metaphorically or symbolically, and there is no longer one message, but many, and sects and cults and other divisions appear in the once-closed ranks of the faithful until the Faith becomes faiths, and is thus destroyed.

Paradoxically, dogmas in a plural world often make common cause, because they all fear the same things. An attack on any sacred text, even of an enemy, endangers their own. Heresy needs to be punished and heretics extirpated. Between different, even warring, religions, there are many silent and secret connections.

Logically, if any scripture is the word of God, and if God is all-seeing, all-hearing, all-speaking, all-knowing, all-willing, all-powerful, all-good, and all-over, then his revelation should be plain, clear, unalterable, and complete. It should need no interpretation. Those who believe otherwise than the Glorious Gift are wrong, wrong in the worst way, because any contrary opinion constitutes a denial of the One True Text. And if the word of God is false on any point, however trivial, God is fatally impugned.

Of course, that's what theologians are for—the spin doctors of the sacred. They explain how three can be one, and one, three; how wine becomes blood; how we rise as we died from the dead on the last day; how a good God and his evil creation are compatible; how sin is transmitted in the semen; how God's son was conceived by a virgin; why reason is useless in matters of faith; and why the infidel should be slain, and heretics burned alive, and converts created by the threat of the sword.

Sacred texts are not accepted as sacred simply on the seerer's say-so, although the history of revelation offers examples of some pretty thin claims. Sincerity and conviction on the prophet's part are standard, and sometimes the text is supported by miracles and other extraordinary occurrences which give its contention credence. But sacred texts are held against the believer's heart because they offer him something. If they demand, they also deliver. They make rules and hand out prizes and penalties. They put people in their proper places and teach them the duties and satisfactions of their station. They create the concept of sin, which could not exist without religion. And then provide methods of redemption, and salvation. Above all, sacred texts supply the illusions which suit the powers that be, and calm the fears of the general population. That heart-eating god of war, Huitzilopochtli, was said to maintain a realm of delight to which fallen warriors were taken, finally, for a good time. The manipulative nature of Valhalla myths is obvious, as are so many others.

The guardians of the sacred stand to gain a great deal, as well. Not only are the sacred books in their charge, and for that they have the esteem of the people, but they enjoy the protection and bounty of the system, often much wealth and considerable power.

Sacred books are often signs of revolt against other sacred books, especially when the administrators of the holy become corrupt or when they support social policies increasingly felt to be burdensome and mistaken. Such was the case with the founder of Sikhism. Nānak was a disillusioned Hindu, disgusted by the caste system and the Brahman priesthood. He was also a poet and the follower of Kabir, another poet. Many of their songs were later gathered into a kind of hymnal, which became the sacred book of the Sikhs. As political and religious leaders, poets rarely have such luck. Despite being the offspring of a poet, the Sikhs became fierce warriors, and some sold their services to the internationalized city of Shanghai as police.

In the United States, a democracy of demonology has occurred, and splinter groups splinter both weekdays and weekends, as Christianity is numbered, weighed, and divided. For instance, Mrs. Alma White founded the Pillar of Fire, whose headquarters became located in Zarephath, New Jersey. Already blessed, and the wife of a Methodist preacher, Alma received a second blessing in Kentucky. Her sect stresses holiness, and is fundamentalist, therefore literalist, and premillenarian.

The phenomenon of speaking in unknown tongues, very popular in America, is pure Borges. Here, the sacred text is delivered in a language no one knows, the language of God Himself, perhaps. Usually, revelations come packaged in the newspapers of the region, so this is a switch.

In Plato's day, priests, poets, philosophers, and politicians were competing to be the most authoritative voice in Greek society. The poets pretty thoroughly lost out, but they continued through the centuries to claim many characteristics of the sacred texts for their own. In particular, they often insisted on inspiration as an explanation for the excellence of their poetry, and insisted that poetry was a way of reaching and expressing and persuading people of the truth.

They shared with sacred texts the belief that the truth existed in a certain inspired set of words, through which, from the gods into the poet, and from the poem to the people, revelation flew like a frightened bird.

They also maintained that the choice, order, and music of their language should not be altered by jot or tittle. It was, as the commandments were, to be considered carved. Like the law on the secular side, and revelation on the other, the poet's wording must not be reworked or reworded, not a rhyme redesigned, not a meter altered. And as religious belief in the West shattered into sects, and lost credibility at least among the educated, the Romantic poets took upon themselves the seer's role again, and made a religion of art. It was no longer the church that represented God, but the mural in the cathedral.

> Michael Angelo left a proof
> On the Sistine Chapel roof,
> Where but half-awakened Adam
> Can disturb globe-trotting Madam
> Till her bowels are in heat,
> Proof that there's a purpose set
> Before the secret working mind:
> Profane perfection of mankind.

It is Yeats's indecorous diction that demonstrates the change, and the cocky attitude of someone like Lawrence.

> Stand up, but not for Jesus!
> It's a little late for that.
> Stand up for justice and a jolly life.
> I'll hold your hat.

After all, it wasn't Muhammad alone who enjoyed trances, nor Euclid, despite the poem, who looked on Beauty bare. Blake and Yeats had visions, and Merrill owned a Ouija board that could versify.

Around the freshly elected poets/prophets rallied the professors, priestly in their mien and mission, which was to explain, protect, and serve the divinity in art, provide themselves with a career, and an opportunity to discover and talk about the Truth the way the school-men had—by reading books and releasing their revelations. This Truth was not the province of science, which only told us how the world worked; it was the same Truth that religion had once revealed: the Truth about life. But art, and especially literature, did so by means of quite different sorts of myth—the myth of Anna Karenina or the brothers Karamazov—in the way in which such novels repre-sented life, they uncovered life's meaning.

Just as religion's perks and privileges had drawn many to it who had no more interest in the spiritual world than the whale in Jonah, but were nevertheless required to swallow hard, so art as a unique form of knowledge had great allure for those who found exegesis easier than experiment, and tenure more comfortable than the rigors of exploration.

Sacred books are as dangerous as snakes, but what makes them particularly poisonous is their sophistical methods of argument, and consequent abandonment of reason, their rejection of testing and debate, and their implicit disparagement of experience, since they, not life as lived, contain all that really needs to be known.

The wannabe works of the writers employed rhetoric, sophistry, and example no less artfully than the preacher or the politician, and persuaded their readers by methods no logician could countenance. They were particularly good at cozying up to their audience, encour-aging identification, and suggesting that, yes, David Copperfield's story was their history, too.

Sociology, psychology, history, morality, philosophical understand-ing, all were lifted out of poems, plays, and novels, like cans from a cupboard. Balzac undertook to laugh and cry at the entire human comedy. Novels fattened in scope and detail as they became swollen with philosophical pretension. The lives of the poets resembled the lives of the saints: promise, purity, suffering, genius, and martyrdom. After all, what was the point of reading literature, other than to pass the time till death arrived, unless it was to learn about living? Why were they written, if not for this? And the critics were there to declare which works were sacred and which weren't, and to set forth what each really meant: anagogically, allegorically, metaphorically, symbolically.

It may be that the Browning Circle, the Bobby Burns, the Henry James, and the James Joyce societies do not have quite the weight or the historical interest that the Rosicrucians or Knights Templar have. And it may be that the disgrace which befalls Henry when it is learned that he disparaged Jews is not in a class with the slanders put about by Philip the Fair concerning the Templars because he wanted their wealth; but the fact that a book may be traduced because its author is a parlor bigot (or bigot of a bigger kind), or that ill-writ works like those of Sinclair Lewis and Theodore Dreiser are esteemed as literature because they rake muck pretty well, suggests the sanctimonious, if not sacred, atmosphere in which they dwell.

And so it came to pass that poets, playwrights, and novelists became the enemies of God because they had their genius, were inspired, revealed the truth in rhymes and stories, and invented icons, like Hamlet and Madame Bovary, around whom thought revolved as around a complex living human being.

Adjuration

1. What gets into people? God wondered. He wondered only as an exercise, because He knew, knew everything perfectly well. Fantasies get into people—fictions—falsehoods that avoid prosecution by calling themselves myths. All these celestial scriveners blowing their verbal bugles through prophets from here to Tibet and back to Toledo . . . they get into them. Fantasies cannot be refuted. We may tire of them; they may lose their charm, effectiveness, or purpose, but you cannot bruise a cloud, only wait until it blows over. The fact is that there are people who will believe anything. The Mormons "believe" that immediately following His Resurrection, Jesus paid a visit to the Indians of America. If you can believe in the Resurrec-

tion, the visit to America should be a snap. Speaking of Indians, there are people who believe there are real Mohicans in Cooper's novel concerning the last of them.

Irenaeus says Papias says Jesus said, "The days will come, in which vines shall grow, each having ten thousand branches, and in each branch ten thousand twigs, and in each twig ten thousand shoots, and in each one of the shoots ten thousand clusters, and in every one of the custers ten thousand grapes, and every grape when pressed will give two hundred gallons of wine." This is the kind of promise one wants the next millennium to fulfill.

2. It is also said that when the Buddha was born, the music of the angels filled the air, the earth quaked, causing streams of water to pour down for his bath. Four great kings, from the four quarters of the earth, and a company of divine beings, paid homage to him. Baby Jesus was only worth three magi, a cow, and a star.

3. Such goings-on, God thought, when only **round vast empty dark** were the four words written. Did no one find themselves troubled by the contradictions among all these truths, or about the secular profits the sacred has tended to amass, or the wars holiness has hosted, or the crimes which have been committed in some god's name, or the ignorance and inhibiting conformity which sacred texts impose on their believers?

4. Poets and the followers of poets are relatively innocent of monetary gain. They often praise war, but they do not foment it. They are occasionally guilty of De Sades of one sort or other, but they do not burn, hang, crucify, imprison, or mutilate people, and rarely recommend these practices. "Smite the Philistines!" is, for them, a mostly metaphoric exclamation. Yet if truth be at the heart of their success, then it is difficult to explain Milton's greatness in company with Dante's, or Goethe's with Sophocles', since their worldviews differ so widely. The moralities that we may feel are implicit in Henry James and then in D. H. Lawrence do not lend themselves to harmonious resolution. Perhaps Shakespeare's are the only sacred texts. But from these plays can we draw one scheme, one plan, one way of life, even a single prophecy?

5. But perhaps the opposition between the secular sacredness of art and the spiritually sacred works of religion that I have been harping on is only an apparent and not a real one. To be sure, our material world worships things, and builds temples to objects, not to ideas or aspirations anymore, but these errors are to be attributed to our terrible times, just as the awful consequences of belief lie in the believers—in how they believe, not in what. "Love my God, or die" is not a commandment.

But efforts to reach the underlying One, or Tao, beneath all religious doctrines, or to penetrate to the ultimate Logos of Literature, if not Art itself, have been no more successful than efforts to reach the center of the earth: in dreams, in descriptions that make mystical mush, in simplifications so silly astral projections seem serious.

6. Learning what the four great words were, an ant exclaimed, "The universe is a bit more hilly than round," and "No universe is any larger than an area an ant can scurry across" and "It can't be dark because the sun is warming the piece of banana I'm crawling on" and "It can't be empty because I'm here and so is the banana." Whereupon God said, "Not for long." And put his foot down. Alas, there were more ants, exactly like the smart aleck. Then God said testily, "The universe is vast because even I've not yet got to the bottom of it, and it is empty because the amount of blank dark space is so great it makes an ant of matter, and it is dark because suns are infrequent, and it is round because Albert called it curved, and it is very very vast because then anything can claim it is the center, as an ant may, or man."

7. Anyone who remembers God's former vow of silence may think now that He has not kept it. But removing such worries is what theologians are for. When God decided to keep quiet, He meant only to ration His outbursts of creation. He could speak all He liked so long as he avoided anything ex cathedra.

8. God was not without his warts. He knew it. In addition to the four great words, He had said **host of angelic scriveners,** and now he shouldered the blame. Better by far was the host of human ones, because they filled libraries instead of burning them, and when one

of their works was done and found its place on some shelf, indexed and alphabetized, and sometimes even opened, they didn't try to elbow one another out of all gaze. Artists may shame themselves by competing for fame and prizes, but the excellence of one book never diminishes the excellence of any other; excellence begets excellence more often than not. We might strip sacred works of their rank, for they certainly have disgraced themselves, and return them to common decency—an action all to the good—but I fear those who favor them will not have it. Because they contain the word of the One God. If we cannot make scripture into history, myth, and literature, we should not be allowed to lower literature into the inky realm of the sacred.

9. God had created the scriveners for a not entirely laudable purpose. It made Him less responsible for all the divinely inspired balderdash they'd filled the earth with, but the glut had grown embarrassing. Not all of these fellows had Chrysostom's golden throat. He thought about tossing the lot out of heaven and into some fiery pit, but He remembered in time that there was no heaven in His system, only in theirs, and no hell in His, either. Hell was their damn doing, as well. He could have cried *erase,* as He had considered crying earlier; however, He remained tied to His vow like a pony to a post, and docile and content in regard to Himself. So He spoke through the forks of the scriveners' tongues and wrote them off. Go roast your toes in your own lies, He said, stroking the beard some said He had, letting the no-longer-holy host be swallowed up in the fog of their own illusions. I'll catechize the four I can count on.

10. *round*
    vast
    empty
    dark

SPECTACLES

Mr. Barnum has carefully sectioned a few grapefruits for use in a salad and refrigerated them in a glass bowl. Later, when he retrieves the bowl from the refrigerator, it slips from his grasp and falls to the tile floor, shattering there in a violent spray of sharp nasty pieces. The break is spectacular: the burst shockingly noisy, the shards innumerable, the distance they fly astonishing, as are their complex ricochets and the obscure small places in which their evilly intentioned edges have sought to hide. Grapefruit juice forms a sticky splash upon the floor, where chunks of fruit seem to float now in a circle of glistening fins. The plastic film he had stretched across the top of the bowl has been shredded and lies beside the puddle in a damp shrivel. If the mischance took seconds to complete, searching for slivers and scrubbing up the gummy juice will steal a valuable half hour from Mr. Barnum's dinner-party preparations. Are the grapefruit sections so important to his salad he must repeat their extraction? He settles for canned mandarin oranges. A bit too sweet for watercress, but what the hell.

The bowl was a servant. It would chill the fruit, endure the dishwasher, then return to its cupboard to await reuse. Any plastic container could have performed as well—or better, because the fall would not have broken it—better, because its surface would not have been as slippery. None of Mr. Barnum's guests would have said, with uncalled-for cruelty, "Humphrey, this grapefruit tastes as if it had been chilled in plastic." Or mocked him with smacks of satisfaction: "Nothing beats good French glass for chilling the hell out of grapefruit." Like good help, such implements make no sound and leave no trace. Unlike the set of Royal Copenhagen china Mr. Barnum had been willed by his grandmother, they are not destined for the stage. On hand-painted salad plates, oak-leaf lettuce looks glorious, the cress is positively girlish, while rounds of radish, white as wash, stay confidently crisp. There will be several rooms to tidy, linens to wash and iron, silverware to polish. These dinner parties, always a bit theatrical, will need many hands backstage, many invisible participants.

Neither the juice that spilled nor the fruit that fell, not Mr. Barnum himself, who uttered a half-completed *oooh* as the bowl fled his hand, no . . . only the damnable dish has, as we say in English, made a spectacle of itself. Had Mr. Barnum, in a fit of pique, thrown the bowl, he might have been thought to be causing a scene. Of course when we speak so, we speak loosely, for spectacles depict catastrophes without consequences, or they are the performance of symbolic rituals intended to impress an anticipated public. The coronation of King Edward VIII, with its marching bands and men on horse, its caissons and carriages, its solemn ceremonials, was an extravaganza in the purest sense, while the spectacle the king was about to make with Wallis Warfield Simpson, a commoner thin as her scruples, a divorcée and an American to boot, was a spectacle only metaphorically—just a screaming headline for the tabloids; since the general opinion later was that Edward was compelled by the archbishop of Canterbury to choose between sin and sovereignty, and wasn't disgracing the monarchy on purpose. When the United States smart-bombed Baghdad, they hoped to produce a spectacle: A population reduced to watching, unharmed by the explosions though shocked by their damage, and in awe of American marksmanship, might, and expertise. But spectacles do not bear frequent repetition. Fear departs as awe recedes, and soon the population is back about its business and ready to complain if a single rocket goes astray. Anyone who has doubts that the official war was theatrical should consider how its victory was used to threaten other nations with the same show of considerately deadly force: awe for Egypt, shock for Syria, foreboding for Iran, and unsettling suspicions for the Saudis. During World War II, the bombing of London was tactical, that of Dresden a crime of spite, but neither were spectacles.

It was a war meant to be heard and seen, enjoyed in an old Roman way, reported in medias res like a tennis match or a football game, although it had no Handel to write new music for its fireworks display.

This century looks to be a short one, one of spectacle, a *Gotterdämmerung* for camera crews, so it might be wise to consider the place of spectacle in the scheme of things, in as much as spectacles need more than a lot of artful plotting for their realization, though they do want that; they need an audience to shake up and amaze, countless invisible participants to prepare the scene, great quantities of cash, actors and objects who can be seduced to perform, and interests, however poisoned or perverse, to satisfy and serve.

Spectacles are a branch of visual rhetoric, since they are constructed according to an understanding of what their audiences are and the precise effects on them such spectacles are desired to produce. The challenge that the promoters of the war on Iraq so triumphantly met was to carry out an invasion of another country while suffering minimal damage to their own forces and such minor injury to the enemy's civilian population that it would not seem to its spectators that a war had been fought at all, but, rather, that something merely warlike had occurred; while at the same time impressing the rest of the world with the overwhelming might and destructive power of their forces. Brevity is the soul of war as well as that of wit. Gertrude Stein, with her usual prescience, declared that "war is dancing." She may have had American Indians in mind. After the drums had got the warriors' dander up, fiercely painted faces and howls for blood might frighten their enemies away. To avoid the lack of seriousness for which this remark was criticized, she could have said that war "would be dancing"—the Baghdaddy Bounce perhaps. In any case, it was a tune to suit the temper of the times.

After the war was over, after the bombs were gone, after a few stores were looted and some significant statues pulled down, a riot broke out—entirely unanticipated, though what happened at the first performance of Igor Stravinsky's *The Rite of Spring* might have been instructive had it been remembered. On that occasion, heads were umbrellaed, ears were boxed by handbags, faces slapped with rolled-up programs. Not for the first time had an organized spectacle been followed by an unruly one. Innovation tends to be underappreciated.

Spectacles have no moment of origin in human history. Where society is, they are, with suitable ceremony knitting groups together while dismaying others, producing displays of wealth and power, making knights out of knaves and murders into executions, validating sovereignties, creating gods, and certifying the mergers of families, financial houses, even nations. Yet when the king is crowned or God is praised, the point of the procedure is presumably not the requisite posture of obeisance, the imposing presence of the Grenadier Guards, or the quality of the gems sewn into the hem of the royal robes, but reverence proper to the Lord, fealty due the state, the security promised by a safe succession. Nevertheless, it was spectacle that gathered the crowds. It was spectacle that solemnized the occasion. It was spectacle that reassured loyalty and strengthened convictions.

Some periods and places in history have been more inclined to see their world through spectacles than others. Let us for a moment leave Humphrey Barnum to his mopping up so we may revisit the English court during the early seventeenth century in order to get a seat at one of its major amusements: the masque. Like Stein's image of modern war, the masque was mostly dancing, but, like opera, it called upon all the principal arts to achieve its effects, and was as collaborative in its creation as film. All of us have seen Fred Astaire and Ginger Rogers waltzing away on a crowded floor, and how the other dancers have drawn a circle of admiration around them. In some such similar way, a chosen few of the masqueraders would suddenly command the scene (to no more real surprise than the extras have for Fred and Ginger), and interrupt the ball's intrigues with a play whose parts were kept simple enough, at first, for amateurs to enact. Ben Jonson wrote a number of these for Queen Anne, who was disposed to spend the sums they required, provided that she got to play the lead. He might have initially thought that a young architect fresh from Italy and intriguingly named Inigo Jones was to assist him, but he came to be annoyed by Jones's emphasis on cosmetics, clothes, painted curtains, and carpentered contrivance, and feel the burden of the court's expectation that the designer would continue to call for pomp and put Ben's poetry to Inigo's service. It got so a ruffle would overtake a rhyme, a simulated storm quite drown a stanza, and special effects receive the applause the poet's lines had already bowed too low for.

Jonson's anger with Jones may have contained some anger at himself, for from the start of their collaboration, the poet had called for spectacle, and he had gotten spectacle. Then spectacle itself had spanked his pride. I shall paraphrase a few of his stage directions taken from the middle of *The Masque of Beautie,* one of his better and earlier confections. The curtain was to be drawn upon an island floating on calm water. In the middle of this island should sit the Throne of Beauty. It was to be divided into eight squares. Into each square a couple of maskers were to be placed, sixteen in all, and in the center of the throne should stand a translucent pillar, aglow with lights of several colors. Arches were to sustain the roof of the throne, which was also to be decked with lights and garlands. Jonson also called for "little cupids in flying posture" and at the cornice more wreaths and more lights. Ladies representing the eight elements of Beauty—some of them with breasts exposed—were to be represented in sumptuous garments: Splendor, Brightness, Springtime, Gladness, Proportion, Loveliness, Dignity, and Perfection. At the top of the throne, Jonson wanted a statue honoring Harmony to preside. And we are only beginning his instructions, which I have simplified and severely shortened. Except that the bared bosoms were the idea of Inigo Jones, otherwise a fierce Puritan, in this moment overcome by frippery.

The ladies of the court, who vied for the honor of a part, rehearsed their steps for weeks, while professional singers practiced Jonson's songs. The court orchestra was available. It knew when to play loudly in order to smother the noise that Inigo Jones's machinery made when the sea roiled and the earth quaked. A hundred men went to work preparing the royal banquet hall for the coming performance. Its ceiling was freshly adorned with scudding clouds. Bleachers were built for the audience and an elevated seat for King James. Throngs came, lines were long, and many had to stand, as if packed in a modern commuter train, to catch a few words and a bit of music, even though they were well out of sight of the stage. The point, after all, was to be there so you could afterward say you had been. These galas occurred not once but at every Twelfth Night for many years, and the canvas cover of the hall grew heavy with prior paint and former clouds.

Jonson's first masque, to which *The Masque of Beautie* was a sequel, cost the empire three thousand pounds, a huge sum for those times, though not the average outlay for a grade-B movie now. When, a year later, the queen asked for yet a grander spectacle (for it is the need of spectacles to exceed themselves), one to be called *The Masque of Queens,* the machinery required to make special its effects—a clockwork of cogs and wheels—was so marvelously contrived that the queen held rehearsals for the operation of Jones's contraption itself, so that the sight of its intricate workings could be enjoyed. The budget for the entire affair had been set at a thousand pounds, but expenses overran that limit as immediately as Achilles would the tortoise, if he were released from Zeno's paradox. The bill for fabric not yet cut and sewn exceeded two thousand. What fanciful conceits, what clever rhymes, what melodious intonations could stand against such expenditures? Jonson was nearly up for it. He called for witches. Jones gave him Hell, out of whose smoking maw the crones emerged. Jeremy Herne, the dancing master, made the ladies whirl like dervishes while Jonson's meters managed to keep up. The second scene, in which the queen and her ladies descend in chariots upon whose bumpers the witches had been bound in order to show how knowledge and fair virtue have triumphed over igno-rance and evil, is even more outlandish than Hell's howls and holy smoke, to the point that the audience's natural wonder at what's been done is eclipsed by the question, How did they do that?

It was not long before Inigo Jones's costume sketches were being collected, his impact on fashion everywhere felt, and expectations concerning his next exploit with water, smoke, elaborate props, deli-cate scrims, and painted drops were everywhere intense and eager, especially about his heaving, shifting stage. Conflicts of opinion between the queen's architect and the king's poet became public. It was a characteristic of the period that these differences should turn, in effect, upon an interpretation of Horace, whose definition of poetry as *"ut pictura poesis"* was a commonplace of criticism. Jones and Jonson agreed that poetry was a speaking picture, but Jones's stress was upon *picture* and Jonson's upon *speaking*. Pictures were mute and needed poets to give them words that would elucidate their meaning. The visual and the verbal: They were combatants in a war that had gone on for a long time—Jones and Jonson were just another pair of champions—and just as the English court masque or Louis XIV's ballets at Versailles would fall like the monarchs out of favor, the spectacle and its allurements would survive and assume another guise with other enemies in other eras.

Throughout the medieval period, the Church had carefully con-fined intellectual study to authorized and holy texts, and even among those of the public who might be able to read, only a select few were allowed so much as a peek at the Word of God. Instruction in mat-ters of the faith was performed by pictures; consequently, painters—visual artists of all kinds—were commissioned to illuminate pages and adorn walls, to carve figures and design windows that would depict and applaud the Christian message. The masses were illiter-ate and spoke a vulgar tongue. Their culture was crude and had been created close to those sharp edges of want and necessity that were likely to sever the lines of life at any luckless moment. God's Word might beat in the heart of things, but ordinary language was no more than the body's bad breath. Kept chaste and forced into clerical service, thus from a surfeit of both denial and privilege, the Latin language died.

Vigorous local lingoes rushed from the marketplace to take over Latin's solemn academic duties; and great poets and philosophers were ready to give these native tongues eloquence, grace, wit, beauty, learning, weight, and earn them, therefore, honor and respect: Dante and Rabelais, Montaigne and Marlowe, Hobbes and Descartes, Shakespeare and Jonson. The triumph of the raw, rambunctious word was soon complete. But this did not mean that all of the medieval schoolmen's textual habits had been broken by one bull browsing in the china shop. Jonson's erudition, his reverence for classical authorities, his lists, his logic chopping were clear holdovers from the past, as was the importance of public ceremonies for kings similar to the dependency on costume, choir, and spectacle on the part of the Pope and his cardinals.

In Italy, for example, the theater's loyalty to Aristotle's unities of place and time had made it difficult for scene designers to strut their stuff. They found themselves obliged to dress actors for only one round of the clock and create settings for a play—long forest glade or drawing room, battlefield or busy square. Moreover, the philosopher's objections to the use of deus ex machina discouraged gods from dramatically descending from Olympus upon those clouds they customarily arrived on just in time to cut the plot's recalcitrant knot. Audiences, starved for action, had to be appeased; stage managers hungered for a challenge; for costumers, only nudity would have been worse; so between the play's scenically frozen acts, they staged elaborate intermezzi that featured apparatus rather than actors, spectacle instead of speech: moons rose, suns set, comets crossed starry skies, patrons opened their purses, and the customers cried happily for more. "No expense has been spared," as the circus posters used to boast, and for any would-be Midas in attendance, it was like watching gold pile up upon the stage.

Spectacles

In 1545, the architect Sebastiano Serlio said, "The more such things cost, the more they are esteemed, for they are things which stately and great persons doe, which are enemies to niggardlinesse." And Stephen Orgel, from whose wonderfully informative essay on "The Poetics of Spectacle" I have lifted this quote, goes on to say that "The means of drama, the age asserted, was spectacle, its end was wonder, and the whole was an expression of the glory of princes." (*The Authentic Shakespeare*, London: Routledge, 2002, p. 56.)

Every evening, the sun set, just as it does now; the moon rose, stars peeked out, even comets occasionally spiced up the night sky or there was a meteor shower to draw you to a place of unimpeded observation, but you didn't see gods step out of a cloud every day, nor, as Serlio points out, could you view a whole city in so small a space. Formerly, you would have had to imagine, as the prologue to Shakespeare's *Henry V* hopes, that "this cockpit hold / The vasty fields of France," and when he wonders whether we may "cram within this wooden O the very casques that did affright the air at Agincourt," his answer has to be as rhetorical as his question. He begged his audience to "piece out our imperfections with your thoughts . . . think, when we talk of horses, that you see them printing their proud hoofs i'the receiving earth," but the stagecraft that put on spectacles had horses, towns with their towers were rendered in realistic perspective, ponds were dug and boated, and gardens were planned in which outdoor extravaganzas could be organized. Barges, waterworks, fireworks, flames: Mountains erupted, Pompeii was destroyed time and time again, battles were enacted. Neither the audience for those Italian intermezzi, Jonson's masques, nor for our modern cinema need exercise any such lofty faculty as Samuel Coleridge's esemplastic power—the imagination. We have wide screen and surround sound. Warhorses run right at us, yet we hold our ground—well, we keep our seats and chew our corn before the stallions get it.

The moviemaker's passion for accuracy is not misplaced. Realism does not require imagination. A single block of wood in a child's hand can be the cornice of a building, a length of fortification, a truck, a train, a statue for the square. What can the replication of a fire truck in rubber, tin, or plastic be but a small big thing, whose ladders can fortunately be removed to scale castle walls or, laid at length, fence in cattle. The truck must be wished away. It goes only to fires. Beckett's empty stage, his primitive props, like his terseness, his silences, are arguments.

Realism without remorse was what was wanted—the ideal real. The Italian architects of these great scenes and the monstrous engines that racked them into life, Vitruvius and Serlio, were moral dreamers, for their townscapes were visualizations so fetching in their appearance and promise that citizens longed to live in cities like them, full of parks, paths, and pleasing prospects. Ben Jonson, too, elevated his already-lofty aims to include moral edification once he had Queen Anne's attention and could think of himself in earshot of the crown. Oxford and Cambridge subscribed to these spectacles with reluctance, judging them vulgar. Moreover, when the king paid one of his occasional visits, many adjustments had to be made to their theatrical spaces. Orgel notes that as the theater gradually became "a machine for controlling the visual experience of the spectator," it was natural for designers like Jones to assume that the spectacle was the thing that would catch the conscience of the king, not a droning playlet, for the stage and its facilities remained after the play performed with their assistance retired behind its final curtain.

What was this theater like? It began as a room, a big room, a banquet hall often, at one end of which a stage was built above the previous floor by perhaps six feet or more, and fronted with a proscenium arch whose decoration was another concern of the architect. It must be grand, but it must also be temporary—as removable as so many of the exhibition halls erected for a world's fair or a venue for the Olympic Games. The stage advanced a few feet forward of the arch and extended back through and beyond it, sometimes to another, smaller platform, elevated once more and against the building's outer wall, where distant attractions could be placed. But matters did not end here. From the thrust-out stage, stairs of various sorts would be extended to the floor of the hall, and in this area, carpeted to mark it off, the dances were performed and the audience was invited to leave their seats and join the festivities. Certainly, the conclusion of the masque was marked by a mingling of players and an often equally costumed audience. This, Ben Jonson thought essential, because it represented the democracy of the aristocracy, the unity of the crown and its people that the poet so often strived to recommend.

The irony, of course, was heavy and cruel, for this was the period that immediately preceded England's Civil War. After Cromwell's triumph, there would be no more masques, no more Catholic artistic enterprises, and, if he could help it, no more Baroque prose. Milton would be no help to him there.

However, before that conflict, there would be lesser ones. From Ben Jonson and his followers, traditional complaints begin to emerge; traditional because their philosophical forebearers go back as far as our documented human history does. The spectator's *judgment* should be appealed to, not just his emotions, the poets insisted. The leadership of the heart will imperil the state, they warned. From poets, this position may seem strange, since philosophers have accused poets of just this irrationality for centuries, with Plato at their head. But circumstances alter opinions with rapidity when self-interest defines the circumstances and approves the opinions. Was the theater to provide a visual or a verbal experience? And if you wanted to mugwump it (that is, have it both ways and sit on the fence with your mug on one side and your rump on the other), you would have your face punched and your ass kicked. I remember (in the eighties), when serving on the Literature Panel of our National Endowment for the Arts, how earnestly the playwrights endeavored to secede, asking for their own panel and, of course, their own funds. The theater is not literature, they argued, and, in sorrow, after a survey of the then-contemporary scene, we had to agree.

Irascible and combative by nature, Ben Jonson finally feels upstaged beyond endurance, and he attacks his collaborator by—

what else?—putting him in a play, where he is called Lanthorn Leatherhead; and by—what more?—leaving Jones's name off the title page of one of their just-published masques, and through—what further?—several epistolary poems that he circulates like bad news. I quote a few lines that clearly address our case:

> And I have mett with those,
> That doe cry up the Machine! & the Showes!
> The majesty of Juno, in the Clouds!
> And peering forth of Iris, in the Shrowdes!

> O Showes! Showes! Mighty Showes!
> The Eloquence of Masques! What need of prose,
> Or Verse, or sense, t'express Immortall you?
> You are the Spectacles of State! T'is true . . .

I chose this moment of what may seem an irrelevant past because all the players are at their best in this game, all are old pros, and they are consummately representative. With power and patronage the prize, art and politics, eye and mind, will fight round after round forever; since it is really a conflict between, at any moment, what is marginal and what is central; a war that's always on, although its heat may be set sometimes at high, sometimes at simmer: between castoffs and nobility, serf and tsar, ruler and ruled, while among the king's hopeful flatterers will be sophisticate and philistine—all of whom bow perfectly, but some offer brightly polished compliments, others dull and rudimentary ones. At its widest reach, the conflict is grimmest between advanced overweening nations and backward disgruntled ones, deepest between man and nature, most usual between thought and feeling, faith and reason, word and image, music and meaning; and, notoriously, between all that is thought to be sacred and all that is deemed to be secular. It is not the categories that change; it is the things categorized that do.

The Greek world, for example, though its culture was an oral one and only a few of its citizens were literate, was predominately verbal, and Greek plays were static by our standards. Men in masks spoke poetry while a chorus chanted wise and appropriately solemn lines. What mattered was what was said. Until Euripides, whose breaches of decorum caused riots, bloody acts were kept offstage so that great speeches could give an account of them. The medieval world, on the other hand, was visual, and for that it has been called "the Dark Ages." The story of Jesus is so brief and fragmentary in its verbal origins as to be scarcely there at all, but in fresco it is full and glorious; Mary's figure draws the prayerful to her halo; Christ dies and Christ rises in front of pious eyes at all hours, on every sainted day of the holy year. Life is measured in ritual moments.

Masques may have been peculiar to the Stuart court, but spectacles were the rage throughout Europe during the seventeenth century, and were a social device the nobility employed to curry favor with their monarch. One instance may prove instructive, since a film was made of this spectacle, and, as so many films are, was a spectacle in itself. Gérard Depardieu stars as Vatel, the Prince de Condé's master steward. He is depicted as an artist masterfully arranging fêtes, banquets, and other frolics for the amusement of his prince and his prince's guests. This Condé is a retired general of the French army who was rewarded for his services with a province that he has managed to bankrupt. He needs Louis XIV's assistance to pay his debts and save his estates. Louis, for his part, thinks the general may be usefully returned to duty for a campaign against the Dutch that he is contemplating. The year is 1671. The prince asks his king to pay (the operative word) . . . to pay him a visit; and when the king accepts, he turns the three-day festivities over to his steward, Vatel.

This movie prides itself on being true. It is a lavish production filmed in a grand château on a large estate with mazes of hedge, gracefully bridged moats, boating lagoons and reflecting pools, lawns and gardens, statuary, woods, lodges, stables, and hovels, too. Vatel's banquets with their accompanying dances and recitals, as well as his engines of wonderment, are to be held and operated outdoors. The court will not have to suffer Twelfth Night's raw English weather.

Hundreds of extras cook and clean and carpenter while the camera dallies with equal deftness over décolletage and heaps of succulent melons, confections, and carcasses. The spectacles are elaborately re-created and executed, but only a few minutes of film time is allotted to each effect, and each will cost much in money, time, planning, design, and labor, just as the festival has. The movie is willing to waste much in order to record the wasteful at banquet, in the boudoir, or in their cups. It plays serious peekaboo, as its characters do, innocent of the irony in its condemnation of the lovely trifles it parades past our eyes. These unworthy, frivolous, callous, inherently vulgar people, on whom Vatel's art is lavished, are no worse or better than those who drowsed through the speaking of Jonson's lines, awakening only for the flying cupids. Where are these audiences now, in our more democratic days? They are eating popcorn in the darkened theater, a stranger not to be molested on one side, but a silken knee next door. And maybe, when the boat in the shape of a whale starts swimming between the banquet tables, jaws will cease chewing. "Marvelous photography," I hear myself mutter. Oh yes, Vatel will suffer like Mr. Barnum. He will suffer annoyances galore and momentary setbacks like the uneven course of an illness: expensive glass mantels purchased to shield candles from the wind will be broken by poor packing and bouncing on bad roads; not enough beef has been ordered, and the fish has not yet arrived; the king suffers from kidney stones, and gout has hobbled Vatel's patron, putting all of them in humors they would love to dump on someone else.

The true artist endures: Ben Jonson through his Jones, Inigo Jones through his Jonson. Roland Joffé, the director of *Vatel,* has his crowd of French, English, Italians, and Americans, too—Ennio Morricone leaves his spaghetti Westerns to put a little of Handel's "Water Music" in his score, and Tom Stoppard has done the English version of the text. The Prince de Condé's physician extracts the hearts from Vatel's pet parrots in order to bleed them upon the general's gouty foot; the prince loses (as he wisely must) his steward to Louis in a game of cards. Vatel's spectaculars have pleased the king. Now he must perform his wonders at Versailles. Vatel is not a soccer player. He prefers the minor leagues. But now he knows he has been nothing but a lowly servant his whole life, a slave to be wagered at table like a Super Bowl ring. He runs a sword through himself—a chef's death.

The spectacles kill a workman, but the soprano in the flying boat sails safely through the sky, false walls rise from the garden terraces as if asked for by a magician, tree trunks burst from the earth, and branches that have been folded like umbrellas in those hollow trunks unfold with a flourish; jets of water shoot suddenly heavenward, later rockets will stream, sparklers sparkle, pinwheels whirl, and the night will be lit with the momentary brightness of materiel and money. Spectacles make Romans of us.

All this, we must remember, in someone's good cause. In 1644, the dramatist Richard Flecknoe observed:

> Now for the difference between our Theatres and those of former times, they were but plain and simple, with no other Scenes nor Decorations of the Stage, but onely old Tapestry, and the Stage strew'd with Rushes, with their Habits accordingly, whereas ours now for cost and ornament are arriv'd to the height of Magnificence; but that which makes our Stage the better makes our Playes the worse perhaps, they striving now to make them more for sight than hearing. (Quoted by Orgel, p.61.)

To make money from the masses: That is the present formula. The movie, *Vatel,* has a social aim—to condemn the callous and profligate ways of ancient aristocracy and to comment on the artists' eternal predicaments. A love affair is added to make a point about the treatment of women as well-coiffed courtesans or body servants. Moreover, it is a decent movie as movies go. Yet it is a victim of its own extravagance and its own success.

Professor Orgel defends the masque against Richard Flecknoe's implication that it was the new visual emphasis which weakened the Elizabethan theater by pointing out that in masques later than Jonson's the language of the texts is even more rhetorical than before. However, I think this observation works against him. Imagine trying to recite Thoreau while sandwiched between a pair of noisy, popular, loud-shout vocalists, each of whom is miked in front of an amplified band. When the poet finds himself competing with ostrich plumes, comets, and volcanic eruptions, he is inclined to ratchet up his rhetoric.

We marvel at expense. We marvel at amplitude. We marvel at ingenuity. Does it increase our sense of worth just to be there? Kings James and Louis certainly thought so. And we do, too; we save up our sense of wonder—for the World Cup, the Olympic Games, coronations, world's fairs, the Super Bowl, the British Open, a concert by the Grateful Dead, the Beatles, or the Rolling Stones—whenever our team wins, we feel fortunate, a success, buoyed by the general euphoria, and to prove it, when we lose, we lose our tempers with other drinkers, other drivers, and our wives and kids.

But perhaps it is Easter Mass at St. Paul's or St. Peter's, or while attending the Passion play put on during Holy Week at Oberammergau, when we feel the awe that kings and flags have often endeavored to steal for themselves: perhaps at Red Square on May Day, when the workers paraded, and soldiers marched, tanks rumbled, and planes, rockets, massive cannon were pulled along on flatbed trucks past a stand where stood solemn-faced the secularly sainted leader and his company of thugs; or for a rally at Nuremburg, where searchlights lined the path the Führer took, and there were banners cracking like whips, bands made of brass that blew in unison, half a mile of polished boots that stomped upon command, a rhythm in a roaring crowd, as though its lungs were drums, and, to keep order, more teams of thugs, of whom there always seems to be a plentiful supply.

As a sign of the times, it was recently reported that in a village in the backlands of Brazil called Nova Jerusalem, a family of eleven, who ran the local hotel, decided (they had sufficient numbers) to put on, during Holy Week, a Passion play in the street in front of their establishment. Although the German original has been famous for a long time and is as commercial as Lourdes, it is doubtful that any member of the Mendonca family had ever heard of it. It was more than fifty years ago that their nine kids in white sheets gathered at the roadside and Epaminondas Mendonca roped together the first cross. The *New York Times* reports:

> Now titled "The Passion of Christ in New Jerusalem," it has become the best-known religious entertainment in Brazil, the largest Roman Catholic country. The play, being performed nightly through Saturday, has grown into a lavish million-dollar spectacle that annually draws as many as 70,000 people to what is described as the biggest open-air theater in the world. It is so successful that it has even inspired a rival, dissident pageant. (April 13, 2003.)

It was not the founder who made this business prosper so, although he may have believed that the family reenactment might draw some useful attention; but, as is so often the case, it was a son-in-law, who saw the possibilities and was overcome by the requisite obsession. He wrote his own Passion play, dreamed of building a replica of Jerusalem for the show, and then supervised its construction over thirty years.

At first, family members assumed the roles, then townspeople, but eventually (in 1996) they were replaced by actors from the local television network. The play obtained other corporate sponsors, who paid $125,000 dollars for the privilege. There are nine stages at present, each huge, the sets nearly life-size, and those in the crowd, who pay a modest sum for their tickets, move with the pageant through the precincts of this theme park. The townspeople now supply the five hundred extras necessary, and, as if the spirit of Inigo Jones were being solicited instead of the church's deity, a "hidden system of pulleys and ladders" lifts Jesus and the thieves into place. Yes, there are lasers and fireworks displays. The tormented face of the Savior is spotlit.

Rivals, who claim to be purists, complain of inaccuracies and commercialism, and there are always the squeamish, who believe suffering and sacrifice are better grieved for than watched. The performance has become less and less locally Brazilian in late years, and this has provoked criticism. From the actors, for example, regional accents are discouraged. One academic described the production, in terms certainly fashionable, as "domestic colonialism." In the year 2000 (perhaps as a tribute to the new century), an orgy scene in front of Herod's palace featured full frontal nudity. More recently, there were only a pair of topless Nubian maidens. Inigo Jones always supplied at least that.

Film had nibbled at the edges of this ecclesiastical cookie, held back by squeamishness and fear of offense, but a bloody sado-masochistic movie featuring the crucifixion was a payday certainty. "Look what He did for us" has been replaced by "Look what they did to Him."

The Brazilian Passion play has carried one necessary characteristic of a proper spectacle to an extreme: movement. Empty extravagance must be filled with more extravagance. Picasso's *Guernica* or Michelangelo's ceiling cannot not be spectacles because they remain moment by moment the same, thereby inviting serious scrutiny, or the risk of feelings of boredom and surfeit from the unworthy. An actor reciting allegorical verse may now and then raise a fist to smite the sky, but such gestures do not match those of *The Tempest,* where demonstrations of Prospero's art are given to us in the form of a masque, or those of *A Midsummer Night's Dream* when Bottom is metapunned into an ass. Miracles dare not dillydally. Lazarus must get himself off the set before the medicos arrive. Ballet, theater, sporting events, and, above all, movies show the greatest promise in this regard. And the contemporary camera is jittery, never remaining still to watch people sleep, as in Warhol's movie, or lingering like the images of Marienbad, or following the walk of a fly cross a cheek in the manner of Sergio Leone. The feats of a magician must snap, crackle, and pop. Spectacles, in short, have a brief life, or, even when long, are made of brief lives. In Brazil, the audience also moves, rather freely, up the streets from one staging area to another, stopping at the stations of the cross as the devout are supposed to.

Spectacles are made of illusions. The U.S. war on Iraq was, therefore, not a perfect spectacle, although it was legitimized by lies. Buildings may crumble under our bombs, but every death except the dictator's is an unhappy accident. Large audiences are helpful, because groups are more easily swayed than individuals. Our poets may attract fifty souls at loose ends to their readings, but Soviet poets chanted in sports palaces to twenty thousand faithful, who infected one another with their enthusiasms. In movie theaters, before TV screens, individuals sit in relative isolation and responsive silence, but they speak of what they've seen at work, with friends, children, husbands, wives. This is contagion of the second degree, for the next game, the next showing of a sitcom, the next day of the war, these will be observed by eyes that are at the same time altered eyes: the eyes I was using yesterday, the eyes my wife seems to have been watching with, the eyes of the *New York Times* reviewer, the eyes of a dozen yelling yazoos at the sports bar as they cheer a direct hit on a hut.

Vulgarity, lust, and cruelty are constants in world history, but the dominion of spectacle has waxed and waned, perhaps according to a law that has something Hegelian about it. Elements of the theater that have been regarded as secondary or subordinate to the dramatic text, such as costumes, blocking, set design, lighting, props, the building itself, the director even, and, in the case of opera, the libretto, too (when voice is what is worshiped): These elements have at times crept toward the center of things, as we witnessed with the English masque. In illuminated manuscripts did not the empty margins frequently fill with dainty colored images and trilling lines even when the text was holy and untouchable? As the importance of the book has apparently been replaced by the computer and its opening onto the Internet, book arts have perversely drawn increasing interest. Experimental books of all kinds have been produced, with pop-ups, foldouts, loose leaves, sheets the size of rooms, volumes so small that they can dangle from ears. Illustrations, papers, typefaces, bindings, forms: Every feature has been an object of focus, every one, that is, but the nature of the text itself, which is often of poor quality and the sickly result of a slack imagination.

Lost in this shuffle of cards has been Hiram—was that his name?—Barnum . . . No, Humphrey. How can we get him front and center, turn his bowl breaking into a spectacle, or at least a sliver of one? The only promising part of his accident was the smashed glass. Of course. We shall insert his mischance into cinema. We shall need the kind of glass that shatters safely, the way those poker-table chairs break when they are busted over cowboy heads in saloon scenes. Movie bar stools are built of woods so light and joints so flimsy they fly to pieces on command, and mirrors break into harmless shards, although with a satisfyingly scary clatter. In our script, the bowl will be bigger and priceless, perhaps not a bowl of anything—okay to eat the grapefruit—but a statuette standing for supreme excellence in custom catering. Get rid of the circusy Barnum name. He's now Utah Smyth and he throws the priceless piece to the floor in disgust and distain, since he knows the evil plot that put him in his present fix: how enemies of the state connived to obtain the menu for a barbecue to be held at some Texas ranch by blackmailing one of the sous-chefs in his kitchen to use the facilities without washing his hands so as to contaminate the grapefruit slices in the salad—cough up the grapefruit; it's back in the script—while the boss was away being rewarded for his absence with this trophy. But why go on? You've been to the movies, after all.

As the masque concluded, the queen and her court, costumed and concealed in their roles as divinities, came down from the stage into the audience, and there danced and mingled, creating, Jonson hoped, a sense of unity among the participants. Present-day spectacles seek unity, too, as well as shock and awe, but now for an enormously larger public. But such sensations, when they are passively observed, and are otherwise without significant consequence, produce only titillation. Moreover, Jonson's aim, unfortunately some may feel, to enhance the power of the monarchy in all eyes, has been made less ambition now by expanding its target. It is we the audience who are to feel empowered, and even ennobled, when, as Superman, we save the nation, or, as Woods, sink the putt, or, as Stallone, put regiments to rout. For Jonson and Jones both, the proper emblems came from Greek and Roman mythology—religious ones were eyesores, and a civil war was in the offing—but for Americans, at least, there are two legs upon which our democracy stands: the gun and the motorcar. Both are equalizers. Both are used to intimidate competition, escape from harm, maim or kill people if necessary. Movies make the most of both. Entire films have been fashioned out of plate glass and gasoline. We love to watch cars that, while chasing other cars, carom off cars inconveniently parked or otherwise in the way, en route to their own rollover and explosion.

I am in my auto, lord of my speeding space; I am packing my attitude—my suspicions content and excuse me; and sometimes I stash my resentment in the glove compartment. We also like miracles, although some societies prefer them above all others. Ours are astonishments of the secular kind, for we have heroes who live through hails of bullets, crawl out of wrecked cars only slightly mussed, fly through the air, dispose of enemies by electrocution, immolation, defenestration, or by sucking them in airplane engines, beheading them with helicopter blades, feeding them to sharks, forcing them to swallow a poisonous snake, shooting them, but only in the balls, snapping their twiggy necks, impaling them on the picket of an iron fence, cutting off tongues and gouging out eyes, dropping them into vats of acid or pits of congealing concrete, or, with wild horses, pulling them apart like wishbones, and in other ways so luxuriously inventive that merely shooting them full of holes, stabbing them repeatedly, or hanging them from a nearby tree seems gauche.

Horse operas are very much out of fashion, and occult reasons are sought for this. I would suggest that western weapons don't do enough damage. Fanning the trigger, you might kill two or three, but machine guns can mow down scores. (The Gatling gun has been revived.) For sport, a single stalker with a serrated knife is okay but a chain saw is better. Where will it all end? We have traveled through time, gone to galaxies so far away, we reached boredom first. We have blown up whole cities, death stars, moons. Special effects are the leading actors, but spectacles that are everyday, taped and replayed as often as the impacted towers, spectacles commercialized with the zeal of athletic shoes, are beginning to lose their shock, their awe-inspiring powers.

There was a brief revival of the social spectacle when reality arrived in the form of a sideshow so we could watch greedy wanna-bes come to grief, families humiliate themselves, and lucky ducks win millions. We can be shocked afresh by the weirdos on talk shows, and, best of all, now we have fresh wars to watch, although they tend to potshot and stumble into hastily photographed car bombings and ambushes that the Palestinians and the Israelis have already made boring, so you can be sure that the new war coming soon to our living room will show improvements for better viewing. Since the purpose of most of what we call culture is to so stuff our heads with fantasy and illusion, there'll be no room for anything serious—almost any new idea is upsetting to the system—we can expect pop culture, with a technology drunk on simulation, to surpass itself. In order to avoid becoming a servant of the king, Vatel killed himself. Not just in the movie. That act was persuasive. Nowadays, blood is our argument.

EVIL

Is the motorcar evil? Of course not, because it can have no intentions, no interior life, nurse no resentments and harbor no malice. In daily life, it has become commoner than the cold. In the moral realm, the auto lacks pizzazz. It is merely an instrument of evil, crippling or killing thousands every year, consuming many of the resources of the earth, eviscerating cities as routinely as butchers their beef, poisoning the atmosphere, fostering illusions of equality and dominion, encouraging envy and macho competitions, facilitating adolescent fornication, and ravaging the countryside. Its horrid offspring are garages, interchanges, hamburger stands, and gas stations. Popular delusions, much destruction, its increasing casualties do not make the motorcar evil, because these consequences were never aimed at. The word in vogue for the damage it does is *collateral*. But the most considerable obstacle to calling the car "evil" is that its effects are easily explicable. Carbon monoxide is odorless, but that is the extent of its mystery. The price we pay for our automobiles seems more onerous to us than the cost of their use. Just add air bags and buckle up. Our callous indifference to ruinous truth may be less readily formulated.

Perhaps the cigarette is Evil. Because it has within it, like Old Nick in *nicotine,* habituating elements that mimic the resolutions of intention. Because it encourages cancer to attack the lips that lip it, the lungs that suck its smoke, the eyes its blown smoke stings. Suppose the hands that held a wheel too many hours too many miles so many gallons began to lose their fingers. Then how would we feel? That justice had been done? For there is something that's suitable about dying from your vices: playing the slots, wasting water, eating burgers. If sins only sickened the sinner, if cramp crippled the fingers of the forger, if every quarter fed to the toothy machine clogged the player's small intestine, there would be some satisfaction in this world. A few zealots—foolish optimists about a moral universe— believe that AIDS is God's punishment for buggery, and that just deserts are at last being generously served. What of such thoughts? Is it in their vicinity that evil really lies? What sort of heart beats at that rate?

How about vices that have their virtues (most do), or go simply unrecognized and are therefore without stigmata? Movies of the thirties, forties, and fifties were filmed through clouds of Chesterfield, Old Gold, Lucky, and Camel smoke. Cigarettes were the expressive heart of human gesture. Like lighting a lady's Lucky. Like settling the tobacco in its tube by tapping it on a fingernail. It provided important moments of delay—while thoughts were collected, composure was attained. The methods for mooching a fag were numerous and expressive, as was spelling a long, slow, lazy sigh in smoke. Such rituals were social essentials.

We have learned to mistrust appearances. Beauty was the showing forth of virtue during pagan days, when virtue meant "manly" (that is, strong and brave); that was back when ample breasts and generous hips signified plow-girl fitness and maternity skills. But the devil, we've been warned, puts on a saintly face. Or at least a salesman's pleasant smile—seductive yet friendly. Where is his profit in being scary? Gluttony and lust, both beguiling sirens, kill millions every year. Fricatrix and fornicators waste away, go mad, and die, while wives and mistresses, who must be fornicators, too, are shamed, abandoned, and enslaved by repeated pregnancies—if they survive the new life they carry; if their new life lives and they don't pull through just to bury another baby. So the cigarette's calming qualities were a wicked deception: "All is well," our inner crier cried to the soul's sleeping city; "Keeping your kool is what counts," our innkeeper counseled. Once aware . . . no; once convinced . . . no; finally scared by its consequences and their cost, we gave up smoking to become self-righteous. Alleging that we'd been fooled, we sued.

I have for some time insisted that every virtue has seven vices, and one day I intend to prove it. I have used neatness as a showcase because it cancels, hides, and opposes history. Miss Tidy believes that everything has its place and that everything should be there. To deny the parade happened, ticker tape and flagwave must be swept and furled; to pretend the party was never thrown, its empties need to be recycled, its tin horns packed away; to be able to say some war was ever foolishly waged, its wounds needlessly suffered, accounts must be scrubbed, documents shredded, evidence dug up, and history rewritten. This starchy daughter of the regiment loves roll call, frequent inspections, and the constancy of the pyramids. Moreover, one might argue, without being simply contrary, that chastity is a vice and adultery a virtue. Which one does the sonnet favor?

Nor is any virtue, in Kant's terms, unqualifiedly virtuous, for if we were to give our allegiance exclusively to one of them (by dreaming of a society without hunger, for instance), we should have to sacrifice too much else. So that no one might starve, we might give everyone a job. To do that (and the Soviet Union and China did do that), we find ourselves asking six men to dig a hole that two might easily shovel, and demand that women we've trained as nurses sweep the street instead. People will not look for or find congenial jobs, but labor when and where they are posted. Making work for others is one such assignment. Roads are repaired with forks and spoons when the aim is full employment, and slowdowns are de rigueur. Shop stewards take frequent breaks and the featherbedding is of swan's down. Hurry up and wait is the military solution. When standing in ranks or queues, life is as level as a desert and time is too heavy to handle.

As Milton inadvertently demonstrated, goodness is confining and limits God's sphere of action, turning him into a droning bore. Eve ate to break the monotony. Eve ate to enjoy the appetite it would give her. Without misbehavior and misfortune, there would be no news. Some philosophers like to argue that *good* and *evil* are co-relative terms, and, like *long* and *short,* are necessary to each other. To know the meaning of *evil,* you must understand the meaning of *good,* as Satan certainly does, since he is a fallen angel. I'm sure he wondered how perfection could survive change. Perfection is more immobile than a mountain. Or, if in motion, as continuous as a heavenly body or a looped tape. Nietzsche thought a grazing cow could be happy because it had no memory of the past or vision of the future, hence no regrets, no anxieties, no invidious comparisons—an eternal now was enough.

Without history, how would we remember the injuries done to us by the grandfathers of our enemies? There is no other way to hand down hate from one generation to another; prejudice is fed on the excrement from former days; the chronicle of previous misdeeds is read aloud every day in the marketplace; catechisms are recited in the presence of sacred books. Our unfortunate lapses, on the other hand . . . Maybe Miss Tidy was right. There was no last night.

In his brilliant novel *The Living End,* Stanley Elkin gave God the best possible reason for the mess and misery of His Creation: It makes a better story.

My father had a driving habit. Many do, I suspect. Such men simply like "to take a drive" the way some step outside now "to have a smoke." "What if everybody did?" is the question Immanuel Kant suggested we put to ourselves (though less crudely than I have done). One can understand why philosophers are morally inconvenient. Which is worse: sickening people the way power plants and factories do, or polluting streams by hosing hogs? In any case, repeating the offense seems essential to the elevation of the cause. And the cause, to achieve evil, must be elevated. LADIES AND GEN-

TLEMAN, NOW PERFORMING IN THE CENTER RING! RACIAL CLEANS-
ING AND THE CONFISCATORS! Evil cannot be a simple sideshow—the
momentary ogle of a bearded lady or a lewd peek at some hermaph-
rodite's minuscule appliances. Evil is a limelight hog and wouldn't
mind a little wash from the hose.

Aristotle thought moral virtue was a habit. Certainly vice is. Think
of rape and murder as a serial rather than a snapshot—six unrelated
killings in a week versus four in a month with the same MO. The
American soldier who mistakenly shot Anton Webern can say oops,
but not if he's done away with the entire Vienna Philharmonic. What
onetime act can be called "evil," reach that kind of high-pitched
crime? The crucifixion? There have been many. Christ's? Yes, but He
had to be crucified, He had to suffer: Our sins required their goat;
nor would we be in a position to be saved as He was without a death
for Him to rise from on a ladder of hallelujahs. The Resurrection was
a proof, a promise, and a preview. All rise; here comes the judge.
Had Pontius Pilate known the plot, perhaps we might admire him
now for handing down a sentence so hard on the shepherd, yet so
humanly necessary for his flock.

If repetition is at least sometimes a significant factor, numbers—
higher and higher totals—would seem to matter. A RECORD NUMBER
OF CHEVROLETS WERE WRECKED THIS LABOR DAY WEEKEND. I have
wondered how many Jews had to die before their deaths qualified as
a holocaust, in contrast, say, to just another pogrom. How many
Africans must starve before the UN is moved to make a motion?
Which fish was it that grew too mercurial? The straw that broke the
camel's back was number—what? How much does the breakage
depend on the camel? If the Iraqis kill one GI a day, how many days
will it be before we withdraw? What a surprise withdrawal will be,
because, every day, our casualties were light. So was the straw.

It is apparently worse if the crimes committed against large numbers are not only intentional but organized as if they were actually
one outcome. The Chevrolets were wrecked higgledy-piggledy,
Africans die of unexpected thirst and unplanned famine, but the
Armenians were the chosen targets of the Turks. The German solu-

tion to the Jewish question was a bureaucratic action: Offices were opened, agents hired, papers signed, file cabinets filled.

The ancient Greeks did not trouble themselves much about evil. The malfunctions of man and nature were—to a point—easily understood: There were many gods and no dogma. The gods lusted, quarreled, were jealous of their prerogatives, and possessive about their powers. Under cover of animals, they raped young ladies, or in a fume of frustration turned the recalcitrant into trees. During wars, they chose sides and constantly interfered with the fulfillment of human intentions—bent flights of arrows, slowed swings of swords. Sacrifices were expected. If the gods demanded the slaughter of daughters, this became inconvenient. It was nonetheless like paying tithes. Evil itself was not an issue.

Bad luck could follow a family the way original sin semened its way through the womb of humanity, but, by and large, quarrels were personal, you and the god of light or wine or wheat or war had your bones to pick the way Prometheus's innards were repeatedly vultured, though his crime—the theft of fire from the hearth of the gods—was so serious, his punishment required renewal and his liver grew back overnight like a weed. When Prometheus suffered, he suffered alone; perhaps his mother might be disturbed in her sleep, but not, certainly, the boy next door or the grocer across town or some Spartan and his young companion. If, at Creation, the work went awry, it did so because the real was to mirror the ideal and could not be replicated in lowly sensuous materials without compromising its purity and falsifying its nature. Is Liberty really a torch-bearing lady? This world, Plato said, is but reflection and shadow.

Evil, as something more than routine wickedness, appears when the pagan world is swept aside by the Judaic/Christian. In its place there is dogma, with heresy as its offspring; law, hence centralized authority and clerical bureaucracy; duty, thus an even fiercer patriarchy than there had been; overwhelming authority, and the dictatorship of a deity who has triumphed over other chiefs and other tribes, banishing their gods in order to rule alone. Although He (for it is a He in deed if not in anatomy) is given powers beyond dreaming, He must nevertheless assume family or saintly disguises in order to get done all He must do, and includes Himself in His creation (since it is now His) like a drawing done in the draftsman's blood. Consequently, pantheism's presence is assured, and polytheism is only faintly obscured, because there are acres of angels in heaven and will be scores of saints on the earth. One of those angels, fallen from favor, is henceforth blamed for everything, since he possesses weapons of mass destruction and has moles and other minions everywhere that the ferrets of the Inquisition find convenient to go.

The realm of death is where the Titans once ruled, too deeply underground to be responsible for crops, and there the Prince of Darkness was sent, like a child to his room, for disobedience. The sun, the source of light and therefore understanding, blazed from above. The Form of the Good was the sun of the spiritual world, Plato said. Even earlier than he, light (knowledge) was identified with excellence, and darkness (ignorance) with evil. That is, ethical and epistemological concepts were fundamentally intertwined. This is the organizing premise of Susan Neiman's splendid new history of modern philosophy, *Evil in Modern Thought* (Princeton University Press, 2002), though she gives a priority to the ethical chicken that I might reserve for the epistemological egg.

The Greeks were concerned with right and wrong, less so with law and obligation. Knowledge exercised its moral suasion from within, but when there is one God, and when, as always, that God has rules, disobedience is the source and substance of every sin. From the first, philosophers and theologians tended to differ about this, and do so to this day. With the optimism every tautology confers, Plato insisted that men would follow the Good if they knew what it was (and if they did not behave, it was because their information, like the CIA's, was faulty). In the Judaic/Christian tradition, the law was handed out, to my mind, like leftover cheese to a starving population. *What* it was, was not nearly as important as *that* it was. Survival depended on unity, unity on regulation. Nourishment of whatever kind was the necessity. That there was a rule of law was more important than what the law ruled.

There is a day in every year when the hours of light precisely equal the hours of darkness, and the position of the sun (on a sundial) graphically represents the advance and retreat of its shine. These facts become characters in a moral story and soon enjoy the untrammeled dance of metaphor. The struggle between good and evil in the roles of day and night was continuous throughout the world because neither could be destroyed, only temporarily diluted or delayed. The seasons similarly warred with one another, each victorious, each beaten or making a comeback, arriving like the marines or fleeing the scene. Manichaeanism is an attractive theory if you want to simplify the problem of evil by making sense of it.

There were two warring forces, Mani, the man from Baghdad, said. Christ, the glowing God, represented the spiritual and ethical realm, while Satan, a night rider, represented what in pop cult is called "the darkside." The tourney between them was eternal. Mani (who proclaimed his prophetic role in c. 240) borrowed from everybody, especially his Persian predecessor, Zoroaster, who had divided the region's deities into bright and dim, set them at odds, and reserved salvation for the faithful (though my language once more favors the identification of evil with ignorance). The pleasure you might take in your own good fortune was ambiguous because someone else was paying its price, while the pain of your misfortunes was ironic, for you rarely knew who was enjoying the helping of happiness that you were being denied.

The triumph of monotheisms (odd there should be so many Almighties and no one able to put the others out of business) put a considerable intellectual strain on their attendant apologists, who were constantly personifying the moral characteristics of human action and giving them to the deity: God was vengeful, angry, loving, grateful, and forgiving, as well as attentive and merciless. They let these reified forces run loose as hounds. ". . . there is almost nothing that has a name," Hobbes complained, "that has not been esteemed amongst the Gentiles, in one place or another, a God, or Divell . . ."

Evil

(*Leviathan,* part 1, chapter 12.) In an effort to restore purity to waters irretrievably contaminated, and order to thoughts irrecoverably muddled, they put polytheism back in action, as I have already suggested (God has a son and that son a surrogate mother, Saint Christopher fills in for Hermes, imps hide in closets, dybbukim take possession of the innocent, and witches fly through the skies).

Between a gloriously perfect God and the human soul, imprisoned in the dirt of life and its own body, intermediaries were deemed necessary, and countless numbers of them appeared immediately if not before the need was seen. No ideology can exist without them. They literally keep it alive. Call them Popes, prophets, Mahdis, saints, bishops, mahatmas, lamas, rabbis, mullahs, merely clerics: they were as human as you and I, and as hungry—therefore as greedy; as fearful as you and I—and soon as cruel; as agile and inventive, as lusty and carelessly knockabout as you and I. They murdered their enemies and were murdered in turn, urged righteous war on infidel nations, and occasionally preached peace as if they believed in it. They pursued the evil in others the way some sought the deer and the fox, and scoured their religious institutions till they were cleansed of heresy. Like nations, leagues, and alliances, these institutions needed evil, the enemies who harbored it, and those who threatened them. Evil rarely feels so confident that it will risk appearing naked and without the tailless, unhoofed look of the good. Never mind that the world was made better because some of its members were burned alive.

You don't need a theory to explain this. You need only history.

When Susan Neiman takes up the tale of woe that is our Western intellectual enterprise, it is 1755 and Lisbon has just been shaken by an earthquake, with much loss of life, property, and confidence. Moreover, the disaster has taken place on the Day of the Dead, November 1, a calendar moment that would nowadays, like 9/11, be subject to many fanciful interpretations. Intellectuals sent twitters of pity to the ruined city, but to the side of their injured views they brought palliating judgments and soothing rationalizations. The air had been sweet with the optimism of Alexander Pope, and a light breeze bore Leibniz's phase—"This is the best of all possible worlds"—to every attentive ear. Newton had banished chaos. "God said, let Newton be, and all was light." The argument for design had been triumphantly upheld. Every event served a noble purpose and revealed the hand of divine providence in all things. Indeed, the human hand was evidence enough. It was how cleverly it held its knife that was admired, not the thrust that lodged it in a victim's chest.

In response to the tragedy, Voltaire first wrote a poem, a copy of which he requested a friend pass on, along with another on natural law, to Jean d'Alembert, Denis Diderot, and Jean-Jacques Rousseau. Upon their receipt, Rousseau objected to the Lisbon poem because it appeared to be an attack on Providence and therefore upon God himself. He complained that by overemphasizing human wretchedness, Voltaire had caused us to be more conscious of that wretchedness. This presumably made us more miserable, instead of more informed. Then, like a schoolmaster, Rousseau summed the problem in a single sentence: "If God exists, he is perfect; if he is perfect, he is wise, powerful, and just; if he is wise and powerful, everything is for the best; if he is just and powerful my soul is immortal." This domino-arranged rhetoric made its fall-down easy for Voltaire. If the Lisbon earthquake was not for the best, then, according to Rousseau's reasoning, God did not exist. But, we might reply, as if philosophy were a game, that the quake was for the best after all. Didn't fires encourage cities to build in brick and stone? Plagues compel them to improve their sanitation systems? So who knew what good would come from a vigorous shaking up?

A poem was an insufficient response to twenty thousand deaths, so Voltaire, familiar with the satirical tradition of Erasmus, Montesquieu, and Swift, as well as the pessimistic Pope of the *Dunciad,* in the space of a few days, wrote *Candide*—a better idea. The absurd could only be answered with ridicule. A few important facts did not escape Voltaire. The problem of evil was as much an invention of the human mind (and the emotions that often drove it into nonsense and contradiction) as it was the result of human nature or its environment. It frequently took catastrophes to stir us into action. Superstitions fell as well as buildings; dogmas died when all those people did. Good and evil were seen to be significantly intertwined. Good intentions did sometimes pave the road to hell, but malicious emotions and wicked ambitions often produced profitable politics, greed useful inventions, and envy many masterpieces.

Indeed, the victims of such catastrophes were all remembered as loving helpmates, breadwinners, heroic rescuers, decent citizens, devoted parents, consumers you could count on. After all, among the victims of 9/11 were bankers and brokers. Business and its commerce suffered. It was an attack on affluent America and its secretaries.

The problem of evil comes in two ontological sizes. The first is factual: Does it exist as a part of the human condition, and if it does, what is its nature? What are its causes? And how may we rid the world of them? Agents of evil are often identified with evil itself, as the members of Al Qaeda were after 9/11, making evil easier to remove, as if punishing them would fumigate Enron or allow Serbs to walk upright. The second is philosophical: How shall we define evil? Is its character human, natural, or divine? What is its justification? And what does its presence indicate? (Ordinary things signify; evil "portends.") Evil seems to be something added to simple immorality the way we put bananas in pancakes . . . or is it the way we brown a roast? Rape and theft, for instance, appear to differ the way cats and dogs or species do, whereas evils are more unified, like shades of red: the rape [of one's mother (is evil)], the theft [of donor organs (is evil)]. There are numerous subsidiary questions, of course, but these are the main ones. Occasionally, an issue will wear out its welcome and, without further argument, dwindle away. Events like the Lisbon earthquake or the Holocaust may prompt intellectual inquiries, and their results, in turn, may influence how we choose to cope with evil in the world; but many cosmic moral problems are purely philosophical because they are the result of assumptions that have been embarrassed by facts or come to grief on the shoals of events. Following the Final Solution, God's apologists had a lot of explaining to do. Humanists were equally shamefaced. A few threw up their hands. Wasn't it futile to speak of morality after such a failure of morality? Nevertheless, a thousand thumbs were thrust into the dike. Excuses were released like birthday balloons. The majority of these rationalizations continue to be theological and are not regarded with much seriousness by professional philosophers.

The history of philosophy can be roughly described as a series of proposed solutions to specific intellectual puzzles, followed by evaluations and rejoinders that lead to new solutions and fresh mysteries. That is: A thinker finds himself in a fix, thinks he has found a way out, is told he has failed dismally, valiantly, narrowly, utterly, tries to fix his fix, only to have more faults found, and so on; meanwhile, the kibitzers adopt one version of the fix as their own and begin to tinker with it. In this game of serve and volley, God has been called upon to rescue many a system from disaster, a savior indeed for principles that have been threatened with their own kind of extinction.

God certainly existed, at least as an apparently viable hypothesis, at the time Susan Neiman begins her history with the Voltaire-Rousseau quarrel, and she immediately examines Immanuel Kant's reaction to Rousseau's belief that the impulses in man that have led to the establishment of corrupt and corrupting societies are not evil in themselves but could have been (and can be) used to create social relations that do not suffer from the mistakes that have been previously made. Rousseau suggests that if children were taught, by word and example, that life punished vice and rewarded virtue, they would be able to follow their basically good impulses with confidence instead of trepidation. As it is, the virtuous are victimized, being more than usually defenseless. But Rousseau's view of history has insufficient scope, for the good are not handicapped, surely, if it is the classical virtues they possess. Wisdom, courage, temperance, justice: These are not traits of the modest and humble, but of the

strong, assured, and forthright. Pagan virtues give their owners an
edge, allowing them honesty, for instance, because the truth takes
grit to give and guts to receive. In their lives, inordinate demands
have not been made on attitudes or emotions such as "sympathy"
and "love," nor has obedience become the center of their moral
interests.

If you are a Kantian, and believe that virtue should be sought for
its own sake (as Aristotle also did), then to wish, out of a sense of
fairness, for a world where goodwill and good character might be
rewarded rather than exploited would be a terrible mistake, because,
in such circumstances, no one could say whether virtue or its profit
had been pursued. Suppose there were a Providence and that no leaf
fell without its say-so; then, Kant argues, "all our morality would
break down. In his every action, man would represent God to himself as rewarder or avenger. This image would force itself on his soul,
and his hope for reward and fear of punishment would take the
place of moral motives." (Quoted in Susan Neiman, p. 68.) I think,
on this point, Kant underestimated our human capacity for self-
deception and forgetfulness. Many people believe in Providence and
its Overseer, but when a tornado blows away the trailer park they
lived in, they thank God for sparing them and congratulate themselves, neglecting to notice who the wolf was who sent the wind
their way and flindered everything they treasured. We know that
gambling is for losers, that unprotected sex is risky, as drinking and
then driving at high speeds is murderous, but we do these things all
the same, and even congratulate those who escape the consequences; so I'm sure we'd be happy to call ourselves virtuous for
investing in good deeds only because they paid prolific dividends.
We want our happiness to be crowned with laurel leaves, as if we
deserved our prosperity, our reputation, our suburban ease. At best,
we may have earned it.

As Kant points out, happiness is a legitimate human end, but it
is not virtue's medal. The virtuous can only hope to be *worthy* of
happiness—like Job, whose suffering instructs us how far from justice are its deserts.

People are fond of excusing the deity from theological difficulties by maintaining that we cannot know God or His intentions, but they don't really believe what they say, since they continue to attribute to Him all sorts of enterprises. Prayer similarly assumes too much. That God has intentions of any kind assumes too much. That God cares assumes too much. That God exists in any form, or does not exist in any guise, assumes too much. Most human worship is idolatrous: It is commercial, narcissistic, childish—"Watch me, Daddy, while I somersault on the lawn"—"Jesus is looking out for me"— "God made my first million, and for that reason I have given it to the church, the remaining forty mil are mine." Instead, "Whereof one cannot speak, one should keep trap shut."

Neiman follows these arguments (which I have described too tersely for their own good), as they weave like impatient drivers through her book, paying great attention to nuance and detail while employing a scholarship that's wide-ranging as well as thorough; yet she represents them in a prose that is both clear and supple, turning intellectual corners without tire screech, and keeping even her careful pace vigorous and unimpeded by jargon or faddish ideological pretensions. Readers need only be willing to think while they read, and they will have a wonderful tussle, for hers is a subject of the greatest importance, open to opinions of every kind, and she approaches it in a manner that allows you to agree with pleasure, and disagree without animosity or any loss of esteem, experiencing that kind of happiness that comes when the mind is stretched to its own benefit; because when philosophy is done well (the doing is rare and difficult), then the trip is as breathtaking on account of the turns in the tracks as in the view from the windows, and the traveler is at last reluctant to complete a journey whose purpose seemed at first defined by its destination.

God was cleared of evildoing by denying His existence. It was His only excuse, Stendhal remarked, though a good one. However, when Nature was discovered to be indifferent, not just to our fate or to the fate of salmon, buffalo, or redwood forests but to life of any kind, to

Nature's own reification even—indifferent to the indifference of its minerals, to the careless flow of its streams, to the fecundity of its own mothering nature—then man became the prime suspect. The old argument from design, whose candidates for the intelligent cause were God, Nature, and Man—the latter two plainly set up to be lopped off—was turned as topsy-turvy as a lotto basket; since it now had to be acknowledged that not only was Nature the origin of all those dismaying "acts of God" insurance companies don't have to pony up for but it had allowed human societies of every stripe and character, of peculiar practices and dubious moral ideals (such as human sacrifice, public executions, racial cleansing, clitoridectomies, slavery, inquisitions, professional wrestling, scarification, and so on) to flourish the way the Aztecs and the Mayans or the Greeks and Romans did, as well as Islam managed at one time, or China during certain dynasties, the British Empire most recently, and even the American ego. Yet when these high societies stumble, fall, or fade away, it pays no never mind. Hills and valleys do not weep for Adonais or for anybody else. Nature's built-in sanctions (men are mortal) inhibit no one, including the intellectuals, who invent new immortalities to combat the death rate, because there is always a brisk market for solace and the honey of future rewards. Maybe it is the manufacture of myth and the promotion of superstition that is evil. I rather like that idea.

Neiman follows the argument like a sleuth, and indeed her book is a kind of thriller: What is it that menaces us? Will we find what evil is, and how may we escape it? She is a superb teacher, giving each side its due, accompanying the arguments with explanations that clarify, instruct, and surprise. The path leads from a God found absent past a Nature that's indifferent till it fetches up at the house of man himself: a castle made of rock, on a rugged mountain's top, its walls surrounded by a moat and defended by crenellated towers. For man to exist in harmony with nature had come to mean that he had to eat his meat raw, behave with indifference to everyone but his buddies, be wholesomely rude and free of customary social restraints. *Spontaneous* and *instinctive* were momentarily admirable words. A popular physical culture movement aped Greek and Roman statuary. The Reich liked hikers. Gauguin said he spat when he heard the word *civilization* (I bet he didn't), and others said they drew their pistols (I bet they did).

However, by this time, love of a "native" life was hopelessly reactionary. Perhaps, perversely, evil wrapped itself in glorious animality—D. H. Lawrence's Nature Boy, Adolf Hitler's blue-eyed blond ones—now that heaven was empty and the earth cruelly unconcerned. As the poet Rainer Maria Rilke wrote, "We're not in tune. Not like migratory birds. Outmoded, late, in haste, we force ourselves on winds which let us down upon indifferent ponds." ("Fourth Elegy," *Duino Elegies*) Without other devices, man surrounded himself with man. But was that a help? What, after all, were the moat and walls and towers for, the readied molten oil, the axes and the arrows? Not the bumblebee. Safe inside, we died of damp, infected by our own wastes, impoverished by the expense and loneliness of self-defense. Safe inside, we dozed while Judas opened the gate. When we woke to realize we were no longer safe inside, we murdered one another with a zeal that could only be described as sacerdotal. Our own bodies flung our own bodies to the dogs. We had not been created in God's image, but in that other guy's.

In the heyday of our reign, lies about man were as prevalent as those about God had been. We wore our hubris like a festival hat. The entire universe had been made for us. That's why the earth was the center of the solar system. Among the creatures of that earth, we were its hilly aim, the fairest of them all. Man was the measure. Wasn't that the ancient claim? So every human being was of intrinsic worth, equal with every other, and worthy of protection and praise; although we didn't really believe a word of the "worth and equality" cliché, since we were so callous about the welfare of our own species as to shock every other creature into kindness. But not for long were we the glory and the center. As Freud pointed out, the earth has been demoted, our kind tossed among the others like a dirty rag. Perhaps we had a rank. Perhaps we were stationed ahead of the giant lizards that might return when we melted the polar ice, but we certainly were listed behind cockroaches, which had already lived longer than we and had better prospects; nor were we even masters of our fate, but prey to drives as remorseless—and desires as insatiable—as wharf rats.

Human beings have rarely given their own lives good grades. Schopenhauer, for instance, was amply prefigured by the ancients. Only persistent thoughts of death, which most men have hated even more than life itself, made them hang around. Neiman quotes Goethe. "In all times and all countries things have been miserable. Men have always been in fear and trouble, they have pained and tortured each other; what little life they had, they made sour one to the other. . . . Thus life is; thus it always was; thus it will remain. That is the lot of man." (Neiman, pp. 209–210.)

What has emerged for me from this wrestle of the human mind with its own inhumanity, as Neiman opens her final chapter by returning to Lisbon's quake and the fascinating doctrinal wars it stimulated, is that while the ground of evil is mere immorality, the cause of evil is evil itself. We know that white bigotry produces black bigotry, and black bigotry confirms white. I drive by to shoot your aunt; you drive by and shoot my uncle. I drive by to do in your papa; you drive by to do in my mama—merrily merrily, life becomes obscene. This tit-for-tat forms a circle rightly named "vicious." But its beginnings lie in a muddle of ordinary misunderstanding and commonplace misfortune, in fatherly tyranny and motherly meanness. To steal Hannah Arendt's adjective, beginnings are usually banal: job losses here, status losses there, humiliations here, foreclosures there, new people moving in, ethnic irritations, chagrin, lifetime disappointment. There is nothing anyone does wrong exactly, but living habits grate, values clash, competitions occur that do not make for harmony and happiness, but, rather, encourage slander and acrimony. Put-upon, people tend to club together, and *club* is the right word. Their enemies, the agents of their economic woes, and the authors of intolerable blows to their pride, belong to another club, driven together by present prejudice and past subjugations of their own. Clubs, gangs, tribes, sects, cults, parties, movements, blocs: collections of people who have given their loyalty (hearts and minds, as it's often put) to a group whose reason for being is complaint and whose aim is redress and vengeance. Resentment is pursued like a hobby. The weak lie in wait for their opportunity to achieve justice through the infliction of reciprocal pain. They wait to be empowered.

Injustices (and fancied ones are soon added to the real) are cataloged and kept fresh for future use by politicians who lie, bureaucrats who organize, preachers who rant, historians who colorize, and schoolteachers who read and repeat every calumny they can collect, preparing their children to carry on crime. We are the pure, the chosen, the faithful, the saved, they brag—the state, the church, the schools, and finally the nation brays—while *they* are the beshat; *they* are the damned, the sinners, idolaters, and agents of evil. Soon every citizen has been trained in fear and blame and hatred like soldiers for battle. We call this being a good patriot.

The sandhog wishes to hold his jackhammer, the computer geek his keyboard. Surely that is reasonable. Everyone takes their local miseries to the schools for instruction, to court for justice, church for benediction, history for justification of their historical blames and claims, to the military for reassurance and saber rattle, the state for presumption, pride, and swagger; and there they receive indoctrination, bias, mythmaking, fabrication, bluster, and braggadocio. Evil, it seems to me, is a mosaic made of petty little pieces placed in malignant positions mostly by circumstance in company with the mediocrity of the bureaucratic mind, and empowered, of course, by a gunslinger's technology.

Auschwitz, as Neiman suggests, was our Lisbon, although we have had a number of powerful before-and-after shocks: Passchendaele, the Soviet gulags, Hiroshima, Cambodia, Kosovo, Rwanda . . . a list too long for 9/11 to obscure, crimes greater than our monuments can justify. However, we are ingenious, and we try: (1) the Holocaust was a display of God's wrath at Europe's left-wing, atheist, assimilating Jews—an excuse as old as Eden. (2) The human race advances by means of suffering and catastrophe the way we learn to fix bridges that fall down or prevent spaceships from exploding—but historical progress, even painful, is now impossible to carry a torch for. (3) Oh dear, God does work in mysterious ways, but this "event" was unique in its mystery and horror, so much so it falls out of history altogether, and has no real forerunners, as it will have no progeny, hence only its survivors are competent to comment on it; otherwise, silence and awe is all that's appropriate (Neiman slights this one, my favorite). (4) It was the largest and best organized pogrom in a long history of anti-Semitic persecutions, so, apart from size, there is no surprise; the Germans are demonically gifted, and this ritual of purification was German through and through; more-over, for most Germans, the killing was done at a distance and never became news; therefore, it was as easy to ignore as the mass mur-derer next door—a move that gets the human race off the hook at the expense of only one nation. (5) The evil that was Auschwitz is not like next year's SUV, simply bigger and more dangerous, or even a vehicle that runs on brand-new fuel, but an evil as novel as a new species, unique as number 3 claims, and therefore naturally mind-boggling—here, the theory of emergent evolution is applied to dastardliness, keeping the Holocaust historical. (6) Since God is gone and nature excused, evil is simply a moral matter, and the ques-tion now is: Just how much human behavior is so "natural" that nothing can be done about it except, as against earthquakes, to build better? We are what we are and that's all we are, said Popeye the Sailor. And Michel Foucault agrees with Popeye because he argues that the haves are permanently at war with the have-nots. Get used to it, he sternly tells us. It is no longer a matter of Manichean good versus evil, but a contest between those who have it and those who don't, until those who don't do, and those who do don't, whereupon the combatants switch ends of the field and go at it again.

Certainly, human horrors are old hat. It is history's major burden, our principal trait. In these recent cases, the surprise is the size of the crimes, not just the sum of the victims but also the zeal and numbers of those committing them. Still, it is business as usual down at the old abattoir and carnage yard. It's simply that business is now done at the global conglomerate level. In the near future, we shall drone our enemies to death between rounds of gamblers' golf or cowboy cookouts by the corral.

Neiman leads the reader through a careful analysis of the relation of intention, act, and consequence to kinds of useful knowledge and degrees of awareness. I give my son the keys to the car, knowing he has a tendency to drive too fast, but I don't want him to drink, to speed, to hit another car, injure his girl, raise my insurance rates, bill me for repairs, contaminate the atmosphere, violate his curfew, or make his mother mad, though I know some of these things will happen and that others are likely. "Intention" as a concept is as slippery as an icy street. Moreover, degrees of awareness are mostly issued by poor schools: If I stick a finger in hot grease, I know I will be burned immediately; if I fail to visit the dentist in six months, maybe I shall pay for it, but later (on a payment plan the British call "the never-never"). How many consequences am I responsible for when I loan the car or when, obedient to orders given me, I sign a writ of execution? How far should I see through eyes my superiors will shade and vector for me?

If Nature is morally indifferent (though not neutral exactly), and mankind is a species contained within Nature, then men can be indifferent, too. Or favor their own species, their own language, their own tribe, as Nature allows peonies their love of ants, or crows the flocks they fly in or the roadkill they flock to pick over, or we, for that matter, the meat we eat, leaves we chew, or friends we make. We can call good what our pecking orders suggest, and each of us support what supports our survival. Or not: Everything that happens, including the "unnatural," is natural. Tautology tells us so.

But Nature, even from the moral point of view, is not a homogeneous entity. Actually, the word is a wastebasket and probably should never be used for anything other than collecting its ambiguities. There are profound differences between rocks and trees (as the

Greeks already knew), between trees and birds, and birds and men, who are ultimately conscious creatures. As conscious creatures, we are aware of what it means to be neutral or indifferent or callous or uncaring or cruel and malevolent. Consciousness may seem transcendent to some, an impotent epiphenomenon to others, and a mistake to a few; but it is with that consciousness that we give meaning to a world that we should be grateful is as meaningless as an earth's shake, because otherwise its purposes would have to be deemed whimsical and malicious. It is consciousness that allows us to devise our works of art and discover Nature's laws, but it is also consciousness where we harbor hate, and allow our reason to be crowded into a servant's corner, our perceptions to be few and skewed, our sympathies buckled about us like a belt, our beliefs burdened to breaking by superstition.

A great portion of the human race is literally homeless; mass migration is one of the darkest marks of our age, with the hunger, disease, and suffering that attend such displacements. But all of us—even in the comforts of Palm Springs or Beacon Hill—are metaphysically homeless anyway. Consciousness, as Nietzsche observed, although our fundamental means of connection with the world, has cut us off from it because we cannot live in the moment like an animal, but rather dwell in anger at the past and anguish over our future. Home is supposed to spell ease, identity, love, and that wonderful Victorian invention, comfort. Which it can do and sometimes actually does—if one can afford it. Above all, it is our refuge from the world, where we seek protection from its heartless pains. But what a dreary illusion that is. Home is also where we commit murder, mayhem, and suicide, where we shake a crying child loose from its life, where we quarrel like squirrels toward eventual divorce, where we grow accustomed to tyranny and the utility of lies, where we cultivate ignorance and pass on bigotry like a chronic cough, where children get to disobey and disappoint their parents and parents to abandon them, where we find to what lengths "ought" has gone to escape "is," and where the tribe that we have allowed to define us claims its prize.

Evil is as man-made as the motorcar. I suspect that, like the motor-car, evil as a prevalent state of things suits a lot of people. If nature is uneven, we can try to even it, but it is we who have made a habit of injustice, and we who must design the institutions that will discourage resentment, malice, ill will, and ignorance while fostering justice, intelligence, learning, and respect. The question is whether it is better to die of a good life or from a bad one. If we fail (and I wouldn't bet on our success), there will be one satisfaction: We shall probably be eaten by our own greed, and live on only in our ruins, middens, and the fossil record.

A Note on the Type

This book was set in Fairfield, a typeface designed by the distinguished American artist and engraver Rudolph Ruzicka (1883–1978). In its structure Fairfield displays the sober and sane qualities of the master craftsman whose talents were dedicated to clarity. Ruzicka was born in Bohemia and came to America in 1894. He designed and illustrated many books, and was the creator of a considerable list of individual prints in a variety of techniques.

Composed by Creative Graphics
Allentown, Pennsylvania

Printed and bound by R. R. Donnelley & Sons
Harrisonburg, Virginia

808
GAS

Gass, William H.,
1924-

A temple of texts.

$26.95